The Biblical Seminar
48

THE BIBLE AND COLONIALISM

THE BIBLE AND COLONIALISM

A MORAL CRITIQUE

Michael Prior, CM

Sheffield Academic Press

Copyright © 1997 Sheffield Academic Press

Published by Sheffield Academic Press Ltd
Mansion House
19 Kingfield Road
Sheffield S11 9AS
England

Printed on acid-free paper in Great Britain
by The Cromwell Press
Melksham, Wiltshire

British Library Cataloguing in Publication Data

A catalogue record for this book is available
from the British Library

ISBN 1-85075-815-8

CONTENTS

ACKNOWLEDGMENTS

Much of the research for this study was done at considerable remove from the effects of colonial exploitation. My colleague at St Mary's University College, Dr Alan Lester, read an earlier draft of the chapter on South Africa, and offered many fundamental insights on the revisionist trends within more recent Afrikaner historiography. David McDowall made very valuable suggestions for the material on Zionism. I am grateful to St Mary's for granting me a sabbatical year which enabled me to complete the work.

The final revision was undertaken during my tenure as Visiting Professor at Bethlehem University and Scholar-in-Residence at Tantur Ecumenical Institute for Theology in Jerusalem. Movement between Tantur and the University was interrupted daily by the checkpoint preventing Bethlehemites entering Jerusalem. My context was a persistent reminder of the humiliation, degradation and oppression which colonizing enterprises invariably inflict on their indigenes. Working against a background of bullet fire and in the shadow of tanks added a certain intensity to my research. A former student of Bethlehem University was among those killed in the disturbances of 25 and 26 September 1996. Despite the difficulties, I was able to deliver a public lecture in Jerusalem on 'Does the God of the Bible sanction ethnic cleansing?' At the beginning of term, the staff of the University speculated whether the academic year would proceed without too much interruption to the teaching schedule. In all, we lost about a month's work. I am very grateful to my colleagues at the University, and to the De la Salle Brothers for the warmth of their hospitality. I am deeply indebted to the Vice-Chancellor, Br Ronald Gallagher FSC for getting me to Bethlehem University, and to the Superior of the Community, Br Cyril Litecky FSC for his daily kindnesses.

Professor Thomas L. Thompson of Copenhagen read a draft of Chapters 6 and 7, and offered many suggestions. Tantur postgraduate student, Fr René Otzoy, SDB of Guatemala read the chapter on Latin

America, and many others read different sections. Tantur scholars Dr Bengt Holmberg of Lund University, and Dr Marlin Jeschke of Goshen College read the entire manuscript, and offered very helpful suggestions. The staff and post-graduate students at Tantur provided a most pleasant and exciting context for my sabbatical study.

Almost at the end of the revision of the book, I developed one 'total closure' and one 'partial closure' in the arteries of my heart, as if mirroring the externals of my day at the Tantur checkpoint. Instructions I had left for its completion in the event of God surprising me with death proved to be redundant, thanks to the medical expertise of Dr Hisham Nassar and the staff of St Joseph's and the Hadassah hospitals in Jerusalem, to whom, under God, I am indebted for the opportunity of completing what I began several years ago. I was fully supported while I was ill by the concern of family, my Vincentian Community, and by friends and colleagues.

In the course of preparing the manuscript for publication I was greatly encouraged and helped by Dr John Jarick, and enthusiastically supported by Mrs Jean Allen of Sheffield Academic Press. I am very grateful to Steve Barganski, Malcolm Ward and Robert Knight for the care with which the book was produced. The anonymous reader of the draft manuscript offered many helpful suggestions.

> I can say that I know of only one people which felt able to assert that it actually had a divine command to exterminate whole populations among those it conquered; namely Israel. Nowadays Christians, as well as Jews, seldom care to dwell on the merciless ferocity of Jahweh, as revealed not by hostile sources but by the very literature they themselves regard as sacred. Indeed they continue as a rule to forget the very existence of this incriminating material (G.E.M. de Ste Croix, in Said 1988: 166).

The subject of this study is the biblical narrative of the promise of the land of Canaan to Abraham and his posterity, the reiteration of that promise to Moses and his fellow escapees from Egypt, and the account of the conquest of the land as reflected in Joshua and Judges. It also investigates how the biblical account has been used to justify the conquest of land in different regions and at different periods, focusing on the Spanish and Portuguese colonization and settlement of Latin America, the white settlement in southern Africa, and the Zionist conquest and settlement in Palestine. The subject matter demands that the discussion engage with the distinctive discourses of several disciplines.

The proliferation of academic disciplines and sub-disciplines has ensured that few deal with any subject in a way which respects its complexity. The discourse on colonialism is a good case in point. International law discusses titles to sovereignty. International conventions discuss human rights. Sociology and anthropology discuss questions concerning the diverse cultural, political and religious identity of the inhabitants. And there are religious and theological perspectives also. One of the disappointing features of such a diversified discourse is that each element functions in isolation from the others. Theological reflection has nothing to say about international law. International jurisprudence is silent on questions of human rights. Human rights' advocates steer clear of principles other than those universally agreed. Geographers and sociologists describe what is happening, and tend not to make value judgments. And yet each of these elements (and many more) reflects only an element of the fuller picture.

The specialization of scholarship in every branch of learning in our generation has been such that non-experts retire from the debate out of fear. Specialist knowledge intimidates outsiders, and even the most versatile scholars scarcely ever move beyond the limits of their own discipline. There is a general tendency to escape into specialization and evade the responsibility of engagement with the wider world, with the excuse that even critical moral questions must be left to the specialists. Every relevant discipline which deals with the question of the land of Canaan in the Bible falls victim to the affliction of specialization. Biblical scholars, in their concentration on questions of historical and literary criticism, pay virtually no attention to the ethical dimensions of the discussion. In general terms, scholars of human rights eschew any reference to the God question, while acknowledging perfunctorily the link between God and the land, and political scientists discuss the issue purely in terms of political power and interests.

What results is a series of truncated discourses, each peddling its own grasp of wisdom, with none respecting the complexity of the total question. Even within the biblical portion of the discourse, it would be a very brave person who would pontificate on more than one aspect. No specialist would be bold enough to risk a sortie into another area which is replete with expert comment: the patriarchal narratives, the archaeology, the history, the literary questions of genre and composition, the periods of exile and the attitudes to land reflected in the New Testament, etc. When a book attempts to deal with the question from the biblical outlook alone, invariably a team of scholars is invited to engage in the task (e.g. the nineteen scholars in Prudký 1995). A corresponding situation obtains in the other relevant discourses. The task is too large for any one person. And yet moral choice rests with the individual.

The particular perspective of this study is the moral question which arises on consideration of the impact which conquest and settlement have had on the indigenous populations. What are the appropriate criteria by which to evaluate enterprises of conquest and settlement? What is the role of the Bible? Is one to be guided by the criteria of human decency which are enshrined in conventions of human rights and international law? It is novel to subject traditions of the Bible, which is customarily viewed as a yardstick of moral excellence and as 'the soul of Theology', to an ethical evaluation which derives from general ethical principles. This study argues that such an enterprise is not only legitimate, but necessary. When a people is dispossessed, dispersed and humiliated by others, one's moral sensitivities are enlivened. When such activities are carried out, not only with alleged divine support, but at the alleged express command of God, one's moral self recoils in horror. Any association of God with the destruction of people must be subjected to an ethical analysis. The obvious contradiction between what some claim to be God's will and ordinary civilized, decent behaviour poses the question as to whether God is a chauvinistic, nationalistic and militaristic xenophobe.

However, in general, theological reflection has evaded such considerations. And yet, the discourse deriving from the perspectives of human rights and international law proceeds without serious interaction with religion and theology. My purpose here is to promote an examination of a text which is almost so familiar as to resist further enquiry. All study of the Bible of necessity involves 'an archaeological retrospective' (Foucault). What could have served in the past as solid foundations has become an open site, requiring the clearing away of the new site, inviting further investigation and opening up new questions. The focus of attention here is the role of the Bible in influencing human behaviour at a communal or national level. We know, of course, that no society was ever driven by one ideological factor alone, be that economic, nationalistic or religious. 'For any reasonably significant historical development, monocausal explanation is *ipso facto* wrong' (Lonsdale 1981: 140). In practice, systems advance through the interplay of a number of components.

In devising an appropriate methodology for the investigation of a situation which has multiple elements, perhaps we have something to learn from two of the principles of Quantum Theory, Complementarity and Uncertainty. Bohr's Principle of Complementarity argues that the classical definition of states in terms of space and time is unsatisfactory, and that it is only by combining these two complementary aspects that a true and complete picture of even the physical world can be obtained. At more complicated levels, different and even opposing elements complement each other in helping to describe a complex mechanism. On the other hand, Heisenberg's Principle of Uncertainty reveals that at any one time, only one of the elements in a system can be subjected to analysis: it is not possible to ascertain both the position and momentum of a particle. There is the dilemma that even the act of observation itself can distort the system, and does so, at least at the atomic level.

I propose to investigate the deployment of the Bible in a selection of instances in a way which attempts to respect the complexity of the social and political conditions in each case. The scope of the study is wide. It includes discussion of the Bible and modern biblical hermeneutics, post-biblical Jewish and Christian cultures, the colonization by Europeans of Latin America, South Africa and the Middle East, the history and development of Zionism, the international law of war and of occupation, and human rights. If the task of dealing competently with virtually every aspect of the problem is so formidable as to intimidate even the most versatile and gifted academic, the concerned individual person nevertheless is left with the moral imperative of deciding on the matter. While a committee of competent and versatile scholars is likely to do better than one individual, it does not have a unified conscience. Responsibility for moral judgment and action rests with the individual and cannot be exercised vicariously. Moral responsibility may not be shifted even to others more gifted, learned and morally upright than oneself.

I contend that theology should concern itself with the real conditions of people's lives, and not satisfy itself with comfortable survival in an academic or ecclesial ghetto. This book probes some of the theological and biblical hermeneutical issues involved in the impact of colonialist ideology and practice in different regions and from different periods. It examines the use of the Bible as a legitimization for the implementation of an ideological, political programme, the consequences of which have been, and continue to be, the irreversible suffering of entire communities and, in some cases, their virtual annihilation as a people. The recognition of the suffering caused by colonialism requires one to re-examine the biblical, theological and moral dimensions of the question. I understand theology to be a discourse which promotes a moral ideal and a better future for all people, oppressed and oppressors alike. This study is intended for those directly involved in biblical and theological discourse. It addresses aspects of biblical hermeneutics which have been neglected. It intends also to inform a wider public on issues which have implications for human well-being as well as for allegiance to God. While such a venture might be regarded as an instructive academic contribution by any competent scholar, to assume responsibility for doing so is for me of the order of a moral imperative.

Part I

THE MORAL PROBLEM OF THE BIBLICAL LAND TRADITIONS

Chapter 1

The Biblical Traditions on Land

The Biblical Traditions on Land, at Face Value

In this chapter I concentrate on the biblical texts that deal with the theme of land, especially Genesis–Joshua. To facilitate a straight-forward reading of the text critical comment is deferred to Chapters 6 and 7. However, some preliminary observations are in order. The Bible, like all libraries, reflects a range of different literary forms and contents. Moreover, neither its content nor its authority is identical for all interested parties. The New Testament has a special place of significance for Christians. They refer to the Hebrew Scriptures as the Old Testament, while Jews use the term *Tanakh*.[1] All 39 books are recognized as Sacred Scriptures by the Christian Church, and also by the Jewish community, although they enjoy distinct levels of authority in the different traditions.[2]

Even from biblical times, the *Torah* was considered to have a certain unity. There is a sense in which the two other divisions of the Hebrew Bible derive from it. The *Nebi'im* (former and latter Prophets) deal in the main with calling the people back to the vision outlined in the *Torah*, while the *Kethubim* (Writings) deal with living out the *Torah* on a day-to-day basis. The writings of the Prophets gradually took their place beside the *Torah* as a second category of 'sacred Scriptures', and some degree of canonical authority was transferred to

---

1. 'For the Jew, the books of the Bible are…Torah, a divine instruction, commandment and revelation addressed to Israel' (Schürer 1979: 321). Although the *Torah* strictly consists of only the first five books of the Bible, the term is used more loosely also to cover all the Hebrew Scriptures.

2. For example, in the Jewish community the *Torah* has a much greater prominence than the *Prophets*, which are so beloved of Christians.

them also (Schürer 1979: 316).[3] At a still later stage, the corpus of Writings also was elevated to the category of Scripture. While the origin of the collections of the Prophets and the Writings is not known, the earliest attestation to their association with the *Torah* is in the Prologue to the second-century BC book of Jesus ben Sira. The *Torah* has always occupied the highest place: 'In it is set down, in writing and in full, the original revelation given to Israel. The Prophets and the Writings merely hand down the message still further. For this reason they are described as "tradition"...and cited as such' (Schürer 1979: 319). It is legitimate, therefore, to concentrate on the *Torah* in our discussion of the land of Canaan.

There is no single, coherent view of 'the land' in the Bible, but rather a variety of perspectives from periods when 'the land' was evaluated variously. A unified, comprehensive treatment of the subject is impossible. The way in which the children of Israel settled in the land of Canaan is a matter of considerable scholastic interest, and of great relevance in both the past and the present. It has implications for our understanding of God, and his relation to the people of Israel, to non-Israelites such as the Canaanites, and, by extension, to all other peoples. A number of interrelated questions arises: how is one to read the Bible? and, what significance is attached to the uncovering of 'the meaning of the text'? Is it to be read as an integrated and coherent whole, as if it were the work of one author of one period? or is one obliged to take account of the long process of composition? What is the stance of the reader with respect to the text? and with what authority does one invest it and its interpretation? Does the reader consider it to be 'the Word of God', with the authority one associates with its allegedly divine provenance? I deal with these matters in Chapter 7. I focus here on some features of 'the land' in the Bible without attending to the mode of composition, that is, dealing mainly with the text *at face value*. I consider later the implications that a sensitivity to the mode of composition suggests (Chapter 6).

3. In several places in the New Testament we find the two-part formula, the Law and the Prophets (*ho nomos kai hoi prophetai*—e.g. Mt. 5.17; Lk. 24.27; Jn 1.46; Acts 13.15; Rom. 3.21). In Lk. 24.44 alone we have the trilogy, the Law of Moses, the Prophets and the Psalms.

The Land in the Torah

The Book of Genesis

Genesis 1–11 presents its perspective on the origins of the universe, the world, its animals and human beings, while Gen. 11.27–50.26 deals with the origins of the Israelite people, through its ancestors, Abra(ha)m and Sarah, down to the death of Jacob and Joseph in Egypt. I shall focus here on the place of land in the relationship between God and the people. There is much support in the Hebrew Scriptures for the belief that the land of Canaan was promised by God to Abraham and his descendants, and that their possession of it was in conformity with his will:

> Abram passed through the land to the place at Schechem, to the oak of Moreh. At that time the Canaanites were in the land. Then Yahweh appeared to Abram, and said, 'To your descendants I will give this land' (Gen. 12.6-7).

Abram left the land because of a famine and sojourned in Egypt. After he and his wife were deported (Gen. 12.20), they returned to the region of Bethel. Since the land could not support both Abram and Lot, tensions arose (Gen. 13.5-6). The writer adds, 'At that time the Canaanites and the Perizzites dwelt in the land' (Gen. 13.7). Notwithstanding, Abram and Lot divided the land between them, Lot choosing all the Jordan Valley, and Abram choosing to dwell in the land of Canaan. After this 'land-for-peace' settlement, Yahweh said to Abram,

> 'Raise your eyes now, and look from the place where you are, northward and southward and eastward and westward; for all the land that you see I will give to you and to your offspring forever. I will make your offspring like the dust of the earth; so that if one can count the dust of the earth, your offspring also can be counted. Rise up, walk through the length and the breadth of the land, for I will give it to you' (Gen. 13.14-17).

And so, with divine approval, Abram moved his tent and came to dwell by the oaks of Mamre at Hebron, where he built an altar to Yahweh (Gen. 13.18).

Yahweh made a covenant with Abram/Abraham, saying,

> 'To your descendants I give this land, from the river of Egypt to the great river, the river Euphrates, the land of the Kenites, the Kenizzites, the Kadmonites, the Hittites, the Perizzites, the Rephaim, the Amorites, the Canaanites, the Girgashites, and the Jebusites' (Gen. 15.18-21)...'No longer shall your name be Abram, but your name shall be Abraham; for I

have made you the ancestor of a multitude of nations. I will make you exceedingly fruitful; and I will make nations of you, and kings shall come from you. I will establish my covenant between me and you, and your offspring after you throughout their generations, for an everlasting covenant, to be God to you and to your offspring after you. And I will give to you, and to your offspring after you, the land where you are now an alien, all the land of Canaan, for a perpetual holding; and I will be their God' (Gen. 17. 5-8).

Subsequently, the promise is made to Isaac also (Gen. 26.3-4), and, to guarantee the inheritance, Isaac prayed that the promise to Abraham would be fulfilled in Jacob (Gen. 28.4). While Jacob was asleep near Haran, he heard the similar promise (Gen. 28.13-15). When God appeared to Jacob a second time, he changed his name to Israel, and promised the land again (Gen. 35.12). In the final verses of the book, Joseph said to his brothers,

'I am about to die; but God will surely come to you, and bring you up out of this land to the land that he swore to Abraham, to Isaac, and to Jacob' (Gen. 50.24).

The Book of Exodus
As the title suggests, the main theme is the exodus from Egypt (Exod. 1.1–15.21). But what transpires between that event and the settlement in Canaan is critical. There is the unique encounter between Yahweh and Moses on Mount Sinai (Exod. 19.1–40.38), where the people remain while Yahweh speaks to Moses (Exod. 19.2–Num. 10.10). Yahweh gives them all that an ancient people in transition require, a leader, an identity and a promise of a future resting place. Yahweh confirms Moses as the leader of the people, gives them the promises and the law, lays down the design of the portable shrine of his dwelling and speeds the people on their way to the possession of the land of Canaan. The contents of the book have had a vital influence on later biblical writers, and the significance of the story has been critical in both Jewish and Christian circles. It symbolizes the community of Yahweh, rescued by him from servitude in an alien land and led to the land of promise.

Moses signalled his intentions when he called his son Gershom, for he said, 'I have been a sojourner in a foreign land' (Exod. 2.22). When the people of Israel groaned under their bondage, Yahweh heard it, remembered his covenant (Exod. 2.24), and would rescue the people from the Land of Egypt:

> 'I have come down to deliver them from the Egyptians, and to bring them
> up out of that land to a good and broad land, a land flowing with milk and
> honey, to the country of the Canaanites, the Hittites, the Amorites, the
> Perizzites, the Hivites, and the Jebusites' (Exod. 3.8).

Moses is commanded to carry this message of liberation to the people
(Exod. 3.17), and Yahweh reaffirmed his covenant with the people
through Moses, saying,

> 'I am Yahweh. I appeared to Abraham, Isaac, and Jacob as El Shaddai,
> but by my name Yahweh I did not make myself known to them. I also
> established my covenant with them, to give them the land of Canaan, the
> land in which they resided as aliens' (Exod. 6. 2-4).

Moses is to assure the people that Yahweh would free them from the
burdens of the Egyptians, take them as his people, be their God and
bring them into the land that he swore to give to Abraham, Isaac and
Jacob (Exod. 6.6-8). In their dealings with Pharaoh, Moses and Aaron
stressed the 'Let my people go' petition, without any reference to
where they were to go, except to sacrifice to, or serve Yahweh (Exod.
7.14; 8.1, 8, 20; 9.13; 10.3). The land of promise appears again in the
instruction on the memorial of the Passover (Exod. 12.24-25).

Having been in Egypt for 430 years the Israelites journeyed from
Rameses to Succoth, about 600,000 men on foot, besides children
(Exod. 12.37-40). The instructions on celebrating the Passover later
include reference to being settled in the land (Exod. 12.8):

> 'When Yahweh brings you into the land of the Canaanites, the Hittites,
> the Amorites, the Hivites, and the Jebusites, which he swore to your
> ancestors to give you, a land flowing with milk and honey, you shall keep
> this observance in this month. Seven days you shall eat unleavened bread,
> and on the seventh day there shall be a festival to Yahweh' (Exod. 13.5-6).

The gift of the land is reiterated (Exod. 13.11-12).

The journey begins. Moses' Song of Victory after the crossing of
the Red Sea included reference to the consternation that the destruction of the Egyptians brought on the inhabitants of Philistia, the chiefs
of Edom, the leaders of Moab and all the inhabitants of Canaan (Exod.
15.1-16). Already the Israelites are virtually settled (Exod. 15.17-19).
While wandering in the wilderness they ate manna for 40 years, until
they came to the border of the land of Canaan (Exod. 16.35). But first
there was trouble with Amalek, whom Joshua and his people defeated
with the sword at Rephidim (Exod. 17.8-16). Yahweh promised at
Sinai that if they obeyed his commandments, the people would be his

treasured possession (Exod. 19.3-8). Exodus 20 deals with the words Yahweh spoke to Moses, and chs. 21–23 detail the ordinances, including those befitting a settled people, including,

> 'When my angel goes in front of you, and brings you to the Amorites, the Hittites, the Perizzites, the Canaanites, the Hivites, and the Jebusites, and I blot them out, you shall not bow down to their gods, or worship them, or follow their practices, but you shall utterly demolish them and break their pillars in pieces' (Exod. 23.23-24).

Their warrior god surely will be with them:

> I will send my terror in front of you...and I will make all your enemies turn their backs to you. And I will send the pestilence in front of you, which shall drive out the Hivites, the Canaanites, and the Hittites from before you. I will not drive them out from before you in one year...Little by little I will drive them out from before you, until you have increased and possess the land. I will set your borders from the Red Sea to the sea of the Philistines, and from the wilderness to the Euphrates; for I will hand over to you the inhabitants of the land, and you shall drive them out before you. You shall make no covenant with them and their gods. They shall not live in your land, or they will make you sin against me; for if you worship their gods, it will surely be a snare to you (Exod. 23.27-33).

Nevertheless, despite the widespread slaughter of the indigenes, we find the command not to oppress a resident alien (Exod. 22.21; 23.9). While Moses was delaying on the mountain the people sacrificed to the golden calf. Such was his anger that he broke the tablets and destroyed the golden calf (Exod. 32.19-21). He then commanded the sons of Levi to prove their loyalty and guarantee their ordination by slaughtering about 3000 of their kinspeople (Exod. 32.26-30). It was time to move on:

> Yahweh said to Moses, 'Go, leave this place, you and the people whom you have brought up out of the land of Egypt, and go to the land of which I swore to Abraham, Isaac, and Jacob, saying, "To your descendants I will give it." I will send an angel before you, and I will drive out the Canaanites, the Amorites, the Hittites, the Perizzites, the Hivites, and the Jebusites. Go up to a land flowing with milk and honey; but I will not go up among you, or I would consume you on the way, for you are a stiff-necked people' (Exod. 33.1-3).

The broken tablets would be replaced by Yahweh (Exod. 34.1-5). After the appearance of God Moses asked pardon on behalf of the people (Exod. 34.8-9). Yahweh promised to perform marvels for the people, and demanded uncompromising loyalty and separation:

> 'See, I will drive out before you the Amorites, the Canaanites, the
> Hittites, the Perizzites, the Hivites, and the Jebusites. Take care not to
> make a covenant with the inhabitants of the land to which you are going,
> or it will become a snare among you. You shall tear down their altars,
> break their pillars, and cut down their sacred poles (for you shall worship
> no other god, because Yahweh, whose name is Jealous, is a jealous
> God). You shall not make a covenant with the inhabitants of the land, for
> when they prostitute themselves to their gods and sacrifice to their gods,
> someone among them will invite you, and you will eat of the sacrifice'
> (Exod. 34.11-15).

The Israelites are warned against taking 'foreign' wives and making
cast idols, and are enjoined to keep the festivals (Exod. 34.16-23). The
divine benevolence is reiterated: 'For I will cast out nations before
you, and enlarge your borders; no one shall covet your land when you
go up to appear before Yahweh your God three times in the year'
(Exod. 34.24). Moses was commanded to 'write these words...I have
made a covenant with you and with Israel' (Exod. 34.27-28). After he
came down, Moses gave them 'in commandment all that Yahweh had
spoken with him on Mount Sinai' (Exod. 34.32). The book of Exodus
ends with chs. 35–40 describing the carrying out of the command to
construct the Dwelling of Yahweh.

The Book of Leviticus
The book is a liturgical handbook of the levitical priesthood composed
to ensure the holiness of every aspect of life. It follows on from
Exodus 25–40, and the general theme continues in the book of
Numbers. Lev. 1–7 legislates for the different kinds of sacrifices, and
Lev. 8–10 treats of the anointing (*ordination*) of Aaron and his sons.
Yahweh mandated Aaron to distinguish between the holy and the
common, the unclean and the clean, and to teach the children of Israel
all the statutes (Lev. 10.8-11). This is followed by a collection of the
laws of purity and climaxes in the purification of the Day of Atone-
ment (chs. 11–16—*Yom Kippurim* in Lev. 23.28). The Holiness Code
deals with the sacredness of blood, of sex, and various rules of conduct and penalties (Lev. 17–20), which is followed by matters of
priestly sanctity, rules on sacrifice (Lev. 21–22) and the festivals of
the liturgical year (Lev. 23). There is legislation for the Sabbatical
year and Jubilee year (Lev. 25). Sanctions are outlined (Lev. 26), and,
finally, ch. 27, which, as an appendix to the Holiness Code, deals with
gifts for the sanctuary.

The gift of the land of Canaan is reiterated (Lev. 14.34), and Yahweh insists on the observance of his statutes, rather than of those of Egypt or Canaan (Lev. 18.1-5). Adherence to the laws of purity is required to ensure residence in the land (Lev. 18). Specified prohibitions include giving any offspring for sacrifice to Molech (v. 21), lying with a male as with a woman (v. 22) and having sexual relations with any animal (v. 23). For such abuses the inhabitants of Canaan would be vomited out. The Israelites will be vomited out also should they commit such abominations, rather than keep Yahweh's statutes (Lev. 18.24-30).

Again, the persecution of resident aliens is forbidden (Lev. 19.33-34). The penalty of death by stoning is required for those who give any of their offspring to Molech (Lev. 20.2), and for other violations (Lev. 20.9-21). The conditions for continuing to reside in the land, and for the separateness of the people are reiterated (Lev. 20.22-27). After the legislation for the festivals, the entry into the land is brought to the fore (Lev. 25.2-3): the sabbatical year of rest for the land and the Jubilee Year are to be observed. Chapter 26 outlines the blessings which will befall the people if they carry out what Yahweh requires: fertility of the soil, peace, victory over enemies, abundant offspring and the assurance of Yahweh's presence (26.3-13). Disobedience will be rewarded by sevenfold punishment: disease, destruction of crops, lack of rain, the return of wild beasts, enemy, disease and famine, and one-tenth of the normal supply of bread, cannibalism, destruction of cities and sanctuaries (Lev. 26.11-39). Dispersion and exile will follow:

> 'I will devastate the land...and you I will scatter among the nations, and I will unsheathe the sword against you; your land shall be a desolation, and your cities a waste...You shall perish among the nations, and the land of your enemies shall devour you. And those of you who survive shall languish in the land of your enemies because of their iniquities; also they shall languish because of the iniquities of their ancestors' (Lev. 26.32-39).

However, if the people confess their iniquity and that of their ancestors, 'then will I remember my covenant with Jacob...and I will remember the land' (Lev. 26.40-42). But even in the land of exile, Yahweh will not spurn them nor break his covenant (Lev. 26.44-46). The book ends with an appendix detailing how one redeemed a votive offering (ch. 27).

The Book of Numbers
The Hebrew title, *b^emidbar* ('in the wilderness') reflects its contents. The book is organized around three phases of the wandering in the wilderness: the organization of the community before its departure from Sinai (Num. 1.1–10.10); the march through the desert from Sinai to the Plains of Moab (Num. 10.11–21.35); and the preparation for entry into the Promised Land from the Plains of Moab (Num. 22.1–36.13). No less than 603,550 males from 20 years old and upward (Num. 1.45-46), and 8580 Levites would set out (Num. 4.48). After ensuring the purity of the camp and the community (chs. 5–6), and performing the rites for the departure (Num. 7.1–10.10), they march through the desert in stages, as in a liturgical procession, punctuated by moaning and nostalgia for life in Egypt, from Sinai to the Desert of Paran (Num. 10.11–12.16), to the threshold of the Promised Land (Num. 13.1–15.41). The scouts who were sent out reported that the people who lived in the land were strong, and the towns were fortified and very large:

> 'The Amalekites live in the land of the Negeb; the Hittites, the Jebusites, and the Amorites live in the hill country; and the Canaanites live by the sea, and along the Jordan' (Num. 13.27-29).

After complaints from the congregation, and proposals to reverse the exodus, Joshua and Caleb besought the people not to rebel against Yahweh: 'Yahweh is with us; do not fear them' (Num. 14.7-9). After much entreaty and threat, the people set out (Num. 14.25). At Meribah, by striking the rock twice in search of water, Moses was deprived of leading the people into the Promised Land (Num. 20.12). Aaron's fate for his lack of trust was more severe, and issued in his death (Num. 20.22-29). Then things took a more violent turn, with the king of Arad capturing some of the Israelites:

> Then Israel made a vow to Yahweh and said, 'If you will indeed give this people into our hands, then we will utterly destroy their towns.' Yahweh listened to the voice of Israel, and handed over the Canaanites; and they utterly destroyed them and their towns; so the place was called Hormah (Num. 21.1-3).

After King Sihon of the Amorites refused free passage, Israel put his troops to the sword and took his land (Num. 21.21-24). King Og of Bashan met a similar fate (Num. 21.34-35). Fearing the people of Israel, the king of Moab summoned Balaam to curse the Israelites, but instead he blessed them (Num. 22-24). However, the people began to have sexual relations with the women of Moab, and to yoke themselves to the Baal of Peor. Yahweh's anger was kindled against Israel (Num. 25.1-3), but Phinehas assuaged it by killing two idolaters, an Israelite man and a Midianite woman, for which he was rewarded with Yahweh's 'covenant of peace' (Num. 25.12). Yahweh commanded Moses to harass the Midianites and defeat them (Num. 25.16-17).

Moses was to be given another gaze at the land he would never enter, and Yahweh appointed Joshua to succeed him (ch. 27). Chapter 31 brings us back to the war against the Midianites. Having killed every male, the Israelites killed the five kings of Midian, in addition to others, and also killed Balaam. They captured the women of Midian and their little ones, took all their cattle, burned all their towns and encampments, retaining all the booty, both people and animals. Moses was particularly aggrieved that they allowed the women to live—they had made the Israelites act treacherously against Yahweh in the affair of Peor (Num. 31.8-16). He ordered the killing of every male child and every woman who had slept with a man. The young girls who had not slept with a man they were to keep alive for themselves (Num. 31.18). Then they were to return to the more serious matters of religion, purifying themselves and their garments (Num. 31.19-20). The booty was divided and due offerings made to Yahweh.

Chapter 32 recounts how the Reubenites and the Gadites wished to occupy Transjordan rather than cross the Jordan, but Moses petitioned them to take up arms and cross the Jordan before Yahweh, until he has driven out his enemies from before him and the land is subdued. Then they could cross back and occupy Transjordan (Num. 32.6-23). They agreed. Moses gave them the kingdom of King Sihon of the Amorites and the kingdom of King Og of Bashan.

In the plains of Moab by the Jordan at Jericho, Yahweh spoke to Moses, saying,

> 'Speak to the Israelites, and say to them: "When you cross over the Jordan into the land of Canaan, you shall drive out all the inhabitants of the land from before you, destroy all their figured stones, destroy all their cast images, and demolish all their high places. You shall take possession of the land and settle in it, for I have given you the land to possess... But if you do not drive out the inhabitants of the land from before you, then those whom you let remain shall be as barbs in your eyes and thorns in your sides; they shall trouble you in the land where you are settling. And I will do to you as I thought to do to them"' (Num. 33.50-56).

Chapters 34–35 deal with the apportioning of the land, and the provision for the Levites. The final verse of the book recapitulates, 'These are the commandments and the ordinances that Yahweh commanded through Moses to the Israelites in the plains of Moab by the Jordan at Jericho' (Num. 36.13).

The Book of Deuteronomy
This is primarily a law book, adapting the legal tradition to new conditions. One of its distinctive emphases is the connection between people and land. Moses addresses the people (Deut. 1.1–4.49) and gives an homiletic introduction to the Law Book (Deut. 5.1–11.32). The Law Book (12.1–26.15) and the concluding account of the giving of the Law follow (Deut. 26.16–28.68). The third address (Deut. 29.1–30.20), the Last Will, Testament and death of Moses (Deut. 31.1–34.12) complete the work. Although it is hailed as the most theological book of the Old Testament, and advocates an utopian society in which the disadvantaged (the widows, orphans and aliens) are dealt with justly (Lohfink 1996), its treatment of the land and its indigenous inhabitants poses a moral problematic.

The book continues the theme of the promise of the land to Abraham, to Isaac and to Jacob and their descendants. Speaking in Moab, Moses reminded the people of Yahweh's instructions at Horeb: go to the hill country of the Amorites and the Arabah, the Negeb, the land of the Canaanites, and Lebanon, as far as the river Euphrates (Deut. 1.6-8). The people were not to be intimidated by the fortified cities, because, 'Yahweh your God who goes before you will himself fight for you, just as he did in Egypt...' (Deut. 1.30-31).

After Sihon, the Amorite king of Heshbon, refused passage to the Israelites, Yahweh gave him over to them. They captured and utterly destroyed all the cities, killing all the men, women and children (Deut. 2.33-34). The fate of Og, king of Bashan, was no better (Deut. 3.3). Joshua was not to fear the battles ahead, for Yahweh fights for him (Deut. 3.22). Moses would have to be satisfied with a mere view of the land across the Jordan, which Joshua would occupy (Deut. 3.27-29). Entry into the land was conditional upon keeping the statutes and ordinances of the Lord (Deut. 4.1-8). Should the new settlers abandon them they would be scattered among the nations (Deut. 4.26-27). Moses repeated the Decalogue of Yahweh (Deut. 5.6-21). The centrality of observing the Law is again emphasized. After the *Shema* we read,

> And when the Lord your God brings you into the land which he swore to your fathers, to Abraham, to Isaac, and to Jacob, to give you, with great and goodly cities, which you did not build, and houses full of all good things, which you did not fill, and cisterns hewn out, which you did not hew, and vineyards and olive trees, which you did not plant, and when you eat and are full, then take heed lest you forget the Lord, who brought you out of the land of Egypt, out of the house of bondage. You shall fear the Lord your God…lest the anger of the Lord your God be kindled against you, and he destroy you from off the face of the earth (Deut. 6.10-15; cf. 6.18-19).

Yahweh's role in the conquest would be vital:

> When Yahweh your God brings you into the land that you are about to enter and occupy, and he clears away many nations before you—the Hittites, the Girgashites, the Amorites, the Canaanites, the Perizzites, the Hivites, and the Jebusites, seven nations mightier and more numerous than you—and when Yahweh your God gives them over to you and you defeat them, then you must utterly destroy them. Make no covenant with them and show them no mercy. Do not intermarry with them…for that would turn away your children from following me, to serve other gods. Then the anger of Yahweh would be kindled against you, and he would destroy you quickly… Break down their altars, smash their pillars, hew down their sacred poles, and burn their idols with fire. For you are a people holy to Yahweh your God; Yahweh your God has chosen you out of all the peoples on earth to be his people, his treasured possession… It was because Yahweh loved you…that Yahweh has brought you out with a mighty hand, and redeemed you from the house of slavery, from the hand of Pharaoh king of Egypt… Therefore, observe diligently the commandment—the statutes, and the ordinances—that I am commanding you today (Deut. 7.1-11).

As they prepare to enter the land, Moses gives more instructions:

> 'Hear, O Israel! You are about to cross the Jordan today, to go in and dispossess nations larger and mightier than you… Know then today that Yahweh your God is the one who crosses over before you as a devouring fire; he will defeat them and subdue them before you, so that you may dispossess and destroy them quickly… When Yahweh your God thrusts them out before you, do not say to yourself, "It is because of my righteousness that Yahweh has brought me in to occupy this land"; it is rather because of the wickedness of these nations that Yahweh is dispossessing them before you…in order to fulfil the promise that Yahweh made on oath to your ancestors, to Abraham, to Isaac, and to Jacob' (Deut. 9.1-5).

He reminds the people of the apostasy at Horeb (Deut. 9.8-29), and invites them to keep the entire commandment, so that they may have strength to occupy the land and live long in it (Deut. 11.8-9; cf. 11.31-32). If they do so, Yahweh will drive out all the nations, whom they will dispossess (Deut. 11.23). The territory shall extend from the wilderness to the Lebanon, and from the Euphrates to the Western Sea (Deut. 11.24). Deut. 12.1–26.12 gives the details of the Law by which they are to live. They must demolish the shrines of the indigenous people, break down their altars, hew down the idols of their gods and thus blot out their name from their places (Deut. 12.2-3). They shall bring everything that Yahweh commanded to the place he would choose as a dwelling for his name (Deut. 12.11). Imitation or syncretism is ruled out (Deut. 12.29-30), and their promoters are to be stoned (Deut. 13.10). Distortion is to be avoided: 'Justice, and only justice, you shall pursue, so that you may live and occupy the land that Yahweh your God is giving you' (Deut. 16.20).

In the rules for the conduct of war (Deut. 20.1–21.14), the priest makes it clear that it is Yahweh who gives the victory (Deut. 20.4). When a besieged town surrenders, all its inhabitants shall serve at forced labour; if not, they shall kill all its males and take as booty the women, the children, the livestock and everything else in the town (Deut. 20.11-14).

> 'But as for the towns of these peoples that Yahweh your God is giving you as an inheritance, you must not let anything that breathes remain alive. You shall annihilate them—the Hittites and the Amorites, the Canaanites and the Perizzites, the Hivites and the Jebusites—just as Yahweh your God has commanded, so that they may not teach you to do all the abhorrent things that they do for their gods, and you thus sin against Yahweh your God' (Deut. 20.16-18).

The fruit-bearing trees, however, are to be spared, as is a captive 'beautiful woman whom you desire and want to marry' (Deut. 21.11).

Miscellaneous laws follow (Deut. 21.15–23.1), and then humanitarian and cultic laws (Deut. 23.2–25.19). The first fruits are to be offered, to the accompaniment of the 'cultic credo' (Deut. 26.6-10). Reiteration of keeping the law follows (Deut. 27.1-26), and blessings and curses (Deut. 28.1-69). Moses makes the covenant and warns the people that uprooting from the land would befall apostasy (Deut. 29.13-29). But if the exiled people remember the blessings and the curses and return to Yahweh, he would restore their fortunes and gather in the exiles from the ends of the world (Deut. 30.3-5). The two ways are put clearly before the people: if they obey the commandments of Yahweh they shall thrive in the land; if not, they shall not live long in the land (Deut. 30.15-20).

The remainder of the book deals with the Last Will and Testament of Moses, and his commissioning of Joshua, who would lead the people across the Jordan (Deut. 31.3-6). Moses reiterated the message to Joshua, and was given a premonition of his death and of the apostasy of the people (Deut. 31.16-21). Then he recited the words of a song, which alternated between the praise of God for his benevolence and the litany of the infidelities of the people, adding the customary warning against future disobedience (Deut. 32.1-43). Remaining in the land was conditional on observance of 'all the words of this law' (Deut. 32.46-47). Before he was to die, Moses ascended Mount Nebo at Yahweh's command to be given a view of the land from a distance (Deut. 32.52). Chapter 33 gives Moses' deathbed poem, detailing the favours of Yahweh (vv. 27-29).

The book ends with Moses' sight of the Promised Land: Gilead as far as Dan, all Naphtali, the land of Ephraim and Manasseh, all the land of Judah as far as the Western Sea, the Negeb, and the valley of Jericho, the city of palm trees—as far as Zoar (Deut. 34.1-3). Then Moses died and 'was buried in a valley in the land of Moab, opposite Beth-peor, but no one knows his burial place to this day' (v. 6). He was 120 years old when he died. Joshua was full of the spirit of wisdom, because Moses had laid his hands on him. Although Moses was unequalled in his deeds, he left a worthy successor (Deut. 34.4-12).

The Land in the Book of Joshua

The book presents its hero, Joshua, as the divinely chosen and worthy successor of Moses (Josh. 1), who, in many respects, is a carbon copy of him. He is destined to complete the work of Moses by leading the people into the land, wherein they will observe the commands as a condition of remaining there. The first major part (2.1–12.24) describes in epic style the conquest of the land, concentrating on the capture of a few key cities and their treatment in accordance with the laws of the Holy War. Then we have the division of the land (13.1–21.45), followed by an appendix (22.1–24.33).

After the death of Moses, Yahweh spoke to Joshua assuring him that he had given him as he promised to Moses: from the wilderness and the Lebanon as far as the Euphrates, all the land of the Hittites, to the

Great Sea in the west (Josh. 1.1-4). The spies Joshua sent to Jericho
reported back that all the inhabitants of the land melted in fear before
them (Josh. 1.24). The crossing of the Jordan is described in Josh.
3.1–5.1, followed by the ceremonies at Gilgal (Josh. 5.2-12) and the
destruction of Jericho (Josh. 5.13–6.27). After the seventh (ritual)
procession of the Ark around the walls of the city on the seventh day,
the wall fell down flat at the sound of the trumpets and the great shout
(Josh. 6.20). The city and all that was in it, with the exception of
Rahab and her house, would be devoted to Yahweh for destruction
(*herem*) (Josh. 6.17). The slaughter of all the men and women, oxen,
sheep and donkeys, and the burning of the city followed, sparing only
the silver and gold, etc. for the treasury of the house of Yahweh, and
Rahab's family. Joshua pronounced a curse on anyone who tries to
rebuild Jericho (Josh. 6.21-27). In the first show of Israelite infidelity,
Achan took some of the devoted things.

The first attack on Ai was repulsed, because of Israel's (Achan's) sin
(Josh. 7.11). The culprit was stoned to death and the confiscated booty
burned (Josh. 7.25-26). The marauding party moved on to Ai at
Yahweh's command to do to it what was done to Jericho: no one of
the 12,000 inhabitants survived or escaped, and Joshua burned it and
made it forever a heap of ruins, as it is to this day (Josh. 8.2, 19-29).
The liturgical *Te Deum* and reading of the Law followed in style,
with one choir on Mount Gerizim and the other on Mount Ebal (Josh.
8.30-35).

The ravaging troops of Joshua and Israel were to be met with a
concerted defence of the Hittites, the Amorites, the Canaanites, the
Perizzites, the Hivites and the Jebusites (Josh. 9.1-2). But the inhabitants of Gibeon, due to their cunning and deceit, were, in virtue of a
treaty, to be spared the conditions of the ban (*herem*). They were destined to become 'hewers of wood and drawers of water for all the
congregation' (Josh. 9.21, 23, 27). The elders complained at this lapse
in fidelity to the mandate to destroy all the inhabitants of the land
(Josh. 9.24).

The next two chapters give details of the shift in the theatre of
marauding. Chapter 10 describes the campaign in the south, and
ch. 11 that in the north, in each case, assuring the rigorous enforce-
ment of the ban. Chapter 10 describes how King Adoni-zedek of
Jerusalem, with King Hoham of Hebron, King Piram of Jarmuth,
King Japhia of Lachish and King Debir of Eglon made war against

Gibeon. The Gibeonites appealed to Joshua, who inflicted a great slaughter on the kings' forces at Gibeon. Those who escaped were killed by huge stones from heaven, hurled by the divine stone-thrower. Joshua commanded the sun to stand still at Gibeon, and the moon in the valley of Aijalon (Josh. 10.12-13). Later, Joshua struck down the five kings, who had been hiding in the cave at Makkedah, and put them to death. In conformity with the rules of the Holy War, Joshua took Makkedah and utterly destroyed every person in it (Josh. 10.28). A similar fate befell Libnah, Lachish, Eglon, Hebron and Debir (Josh. 10. 29-39). The author summarizes Joshua's destruction of everything that breathed, from Kadesh-barnea to Gaza and so forth as Yahweh commanded (Josh. 10. 40-43).

Chapter 11 describes the northern campaign, with the literary account showing signs of a conscious parallel with ch. 10. There was a coalition between King Jabin of Hazor, King Jobab of Madon, the king of Shimron, the king of Achshaph, and the kings who were in the northern hill country and the Arabah south of Chinneroth, and in the lowland, and in Naphoth-dor on the west, the Canaanites in the east and the west, the Amorites, the Hittites, the Perizzites, and the Jebusites in the hill country and the Hivites under Hermon in the land of Mizpah (Josh. 11.1-3). However, they were no match for Joshua, with Yahweh on his side. Israel struck them down until they had left no one remaining (Josh. 11.7-9). To complete matters, Joshua turned back and took Hazor, and killed its king and all who were in it, and burned Hazor with fire (v. 11). The reader is given a résumé of the military campaign. Joshua took all that land (the Negeb, all the land of Goshen, etc.), utterly destroying their inhabitants (Josh. 11.16-23).

Chapter 12 gives a full list of the kings defeated and the lands conquered, first under Moses on the east side of the Jordan (Josh. 12.1-6), and then on the west (Josh. 12.7-24). Chapters 13–21 give an account of the division of the land, which, although allegedly all conquered in the account of chs. 1–12, gives most attention to the territory of the later kingdom of Judah. The incompleteness of the conquest is reflected in the opening verses: 'Now Joshua was old and advanced in years; and Yahweh said to him, "You are old and advanced in years, and very much of the land still remains to be possessed. This is the land that still remains…"' (Josh. 13.1). The whole achievement is summed up in that Yahweh gave to Israel all the land that he swore to their ancestors that he would give them (Josh. 21.43-45). The appendices complete the picture of the ideal Israel under the leadership of Joshua (Josh. 22.1–24.33). The arrangements with the Reubenites, the Gadites and the half-tribe of Manasseh are honoured, and the legitimate place of worship (anticipating Shechem of ch. 24) is determined (Josh. 22.1-34). There follows Joshua's farewell speech (Josh. 23), the covenant at Shechem (Josh. 24.1-8) and the notes of the death and burial of Joshua, Joseph and Eleazar (Josh. 24.29-33).

The Land in Other Books of the Bible

The book of Judges deals with the transition from the period of Joshua to that of Saul. With the death of Joshua, the period of Moses comes to a close, and with the advent of Saul we are prepared for the advent of the age of David and the monarchy. The picture in the book of Judges is considerably different from that recorded in the book of Joshua. Whereas the book of Joshua gives details of the conquest in a series of 'punctiliar', efficient military activities, the book of Judges sees it as a more complex and gradual phenomenon, punctuated by partial success and failure. Apart from the references to them in Sir. 46.11-12 (and in the New Testament, Heb. 11.32-34) there is little reference to the Judges outside the Former Prophets.

The theme of land recurs in several other traditions within the Bible. However, the evidence that these traditions were in circulation before the exilic period is meagre. In the eighth-century Judean prophets, Isaiah and Micah, we read only of the Midian story (Isa. 10.26). In the northern kingdom, we have a reference to the Amorites in Amos 2.10, and a possible reference to the outrage at Gibeah in Hosea 9.9. With respect to the celebration of the occupation of the land within the cultic life of the community, there is little that one would have to put earlier than the exile. While Ps. 65.9-13 lauds Yahweh for his benevolence towards the land in general, Ps. 78.54-55 does so for his specific care of the Israelites:

> And he brought them to his holy hill, to the mountain that his right hand had won. He drove out nations before them; he apportioned them for a possession and settled the tribes of Israel in their tents.

This theme is reiterated in other psalms:

> So he brought his people out with joy, his chosen ones with singing. He gave them the lands of the nations, and they took possession of the wealth of the peoples (Ps. 105.43-44),

You brought a vine out of Egypt; you drove out the nations and planted it
(Ps. 80.8),

However, the details of the conquest are inconsiderable. Psalm 114 does refer to the stopping of the flow of the Jordan, and Pss. 78.54-66 and 81.11-12 refer to the disobedience of Israel. However, there is no reason to insist that these compositions pre-date the exile, or that they were not derived from the books of Joshua and Judges.

There is a notable lack of evidence, therefore, for predicating a popularity for the conquest and settlement traditions prior to the period of the exile. In the exilic period, they assume an importance in both Jeremiah and Ezekiel. However, neither in Jeremiah nor Ezekiel is there specific reference to the land having been conquered by Joshua and the Judges.[4] Moreover, there are no clear allusions to the conquest and settlement traditions in Isaiah 40–55 or in the post-exilic prophets. It is remarkable that, with the exception of their importance within the deuteronomistic traditions, the conquest and settlement traditions occupy such an insignificant place within the Bible (see Bartlett 1990: 55).[5] Let us consider now how the biblical texts at face value have been exploited in favour of colonial enterprises.

Exploitation of the Biblical Traditions on Land

The Bible enjoys unique authority within both Synagogue and Church. The *Torah* emanates from heaven.[6] Since it contains the demands

---

4. The land was given to Israel's ancestors (Jer. 7.7) as a possession (Jer. 32.22), or inheritance (Jer. 3.18). It was a land flowing with milk and honey (Jer. 11.5; 32.22-23; Ezek. 20.6, 15) that Israel defiled (Jer. 2.7) through disobedience (Jer. 32.23).

5. In the New Testament, Joshua's feat in driving out the nations is referred to in Stephen's speech (Acts 7.45), and his achievement in Heb. 4.8. In the Patristic period, Pseudo-Barnabas saw Moses' prayer with extended hands, interceding for the victory of Joshua over the Amalekites as a 'typos' of the Cross and the Crucified (12.2-3), and considered Joshua to be a figure of Christ (12.8-10). For Justin, Joshua was a type of Christ: just as he led the people into the land of Canaan, so Christ leads Christians into the true promised land (*Dial.* 113). Cyril of Alexandria also interpreted the Pentateuch in a christological way, from Cain and Abel to Joshua. Hilary too attached christological significance to Joshua (see Simonetti 1994: 14, 20, 33 n. 14, 79, 89).

6. At the heart of the differences in British Jewry between the United Synagogue and the Masorti movement is the appropriate understanding of the

which God made on his people, a punctilious observance of its laws is
the supreme religious duty. Israelite piety was primarily directed
towards zealously and lovingly obeying the *Torah* in all its details
(Schürer 1979: 314). The *Torah*, in such an interpretation, must be
accepted in its totality, and in all its parts. The Bible enjoys a corresponding authority in the Church as the Word of God (see Chapter 7).
However, the Bible poses a fundamental moral problem for anyone
who takes it at face value.

In the biblical narrative, the Hebrew slaves who left Egypt invaded
a land already occupied. The occupation of another people's land
invariably involves systematic pillage and killing. What distinguishes
the biblical accounts of this activity, whether through the *Blitzkrieg*
mode represented in the book of Joshua, or through the more gradual
one reflected in the book of Judges, is that it is presented as having not
only divine approval, but as being mandated by the divinity. In the
book of Joshua, in particular, the Israelites killed in conformity with
the directives of God. This presentation of God as requiring the destruction of others poses problems for anyone who presumes that the conduct of an ethical God will not fall lower than decent, secular behaviour.

The commandment that, 'You shall devour all the peoples that
Yahweh your God is giving over to you, showing them no pity' (Deut.
7.16) is seen in a new light, when one recalls how such texts were
used in support of colonialism in several regions and periods, in
which the native peoples were the counterparts of the Hittites, the
Girgashites, and others. Were it not for their religious provenance,
such biblical sentiments would be regarded as incitements to racial
hatred. *Prima facie*, judged by the standards of ethics and human
rights to which our society has become accustomed, the first six books
of the Hebrew Bible reflect some ethnocentric, racist and xenophobic
sentiments that appear to receive the highest possible legitimacy in the
form of divine approval. On moral grounds, one is forced to question
whether the *Torah* continues to provide divine legitimacy for the
occupation of other people's land and the virtual annihilation of the
indigenes.

Hebrew Bible, especially the Pentateuch. Chief Rabbi Jonathan Sacks claims, 'An
individual who does not believe in *Torah min haShamayim* (i.e. that the Torah is
from heaven) has severed his links with the faith of his ancestors.' The Masorti
movement, on the other hand, takes seriously the results of critical biblical
scholarship.

The Crusades provide a striking example of the link between religion and political power, and exemplify how the Bible has been employed as an agent of oppression (see Prior 1995b). It is sufficient here to indicate the kind of religious and theological thinking that was presented as justifying such behaviour. The papal justification for violence can be traced back to the views of St Augustine, who appealed to the Old Testament to show that God could directly command it. War waged in the name of God was a just war *par excellence*. To deny the morality of divinely approved war was tantamount to denying divine providence itself. Moreover, God would help those who fought divinely approved wars, just as he had helped the Israelites to conquer the Amorites. While Augustine's views were scattered throughout his many writings, collections were compiled just before the First Crusade (c. 1083 by St Anselm of Lucca; c. 1094 by Ivo of Chartres).

When Pope Urban II proclaimed the First Crusade at the Council of Clermont on 27 November 1095, he called out soldiers for Christ's war, guaranteeing them the remission of all their sins (Hagenmeyer 1901, in Riley-Smith 1981: 38). The four extant accounts of his sermon reflect the combination of Christian piety, xenophobia and imperialistic arrogance that characterizes many colonial ventures (see Riley-Smith 1981: 43-44). The liberation of 'Jerusalem' from 'unclean races', who, by their 'unclean practices treated dishonourably and polluted irreverently the Holy Places', justified aggression from those who were armed with both Testaments in one hand, a sword in the other, and the cross on their front or breast, in compliance with the Gospel exhortation, 'Whosoever does not carry his cross and come after me is not worthy of me.'

But the link between the sword and the Cross was even more overt in the establishment of military religious orders, 'monks of war'. Hugues de Payens arrived in Syria in 1115, and by 1118 had become a self-appointed protector of pilgrims (Seward 1995: 30). Together with seven other knights, he made a solemn vow to protect pilgrims and observe poverty, chastity and obedience. In 1126, he went back to France and sought the support of Bernard of Clairvaux, who promised to compose a rule for him and find recruits. For Bernard, the Templars were military Cistercians:

> There were two main meals, both eaten in silence with sacred reading
> from a French translation of the Bible, special emphasis being placed on
> the Books of Joshua and the Maccabees. All found inspiration in the

> ferocious exploits of Judas, his brothers and their war-bands in recon-
> quering the Holy Land from cruel infidels (Seward 1995: 32).

The knights saw no inconsistency between the two aspects of their
ideals, to fight for Christ and to pray. They followed St Bernard's
judgment that 'killing for Christ' was *malecide*, that is, the extermination of injustice, and not *homicide*, the extermination of the unjust.
Indeed, to kill a pagan was to win glory, since it gave glory to Christ.
Other orders, for example, the Hospitallers, placed more emphasis on
the service of the sick, but it has been said of even them that 'when
they had received the Body of the Lord they fought like devils'
(Seward 1995: 40). Death in battle was martyrdom, and it is estimated
that some 20,000 achieved that desired status in their various military
activities for Christ over the next two centuries (Seward 1995: 35).

The Bible and 'Catechesis': A Case Study
What effect does the biblical text have in contributing to the formation
of values and ethical principles? Eager to estimate the influence of
ethnic and religious prejudice on moral judgment, the Israeli socio-
psychologist Georges R. Tamarin investigated the effect of chauvinism
on moral judgment. He surveyed the presence of prejudices in the
ideology of Israeli youth and the effect of an uncritical teaching of the
Bible on the propensity for forming prejudices (1963). He was particularly anxious to evaluate the degree to which uncritical teaching of
notions of the 'chosen people', the superiority of monotheistic religion, and the study of acts of genocide carried out by biblical heroes
contributed to the development of prejudice.

Tamarin chose the book of Joshua because of its special position in
the Israeli educational system, both as national history and as one of
the cornerstones of Israel's national mythology. He divided his sample
into two groups, the main group, and a second, control group. He
asked the main group to comment: 'You are well acquainted with the
following passages of the Book of Joshua':

> So the people shouted, and the trumpets were blown. As soon as the
> people heard the sound of the trumpets, they raised a great shout, and the
> wall fell down flat; so the people charged straight ahead into the city and
> captured it. Then they devoted to destruction by the edge of the sword all
> in the city, both men and women, young and old, oxen, sheep, and
> donkeys (Josh. 6.20-21).
>
> Joshua took Makkedah on that day, and struck it and its king with the
> edge of the sword; he utterly destroyed every person in it; he left no one

remaining. And he did to the king of Makkedah as he had done to the king of Jericho. Then Joshua passed on from Makkedah, and all Israel with him, to Libnah, and fought against Libnah. Yahweh gave it also and its king into the hand of Israel; and he struck it with the edge of the sword, and every person in it; he left no one remaining in it; and he did to its king as he had done to the king of Jericho. Next Joshua passed on from Libnah, and all Israel with him, to Lachish, and laid siege to it, and assaulted it. Yahweh gave Lachish into the hand of Israel, and he took it on the second day, and struck it with the edge of the sword, and every person in it, as he had done to Libnah (Josh. 10.28-32).

He surveyed nine groups of pupils, ranging from 8.5 to 14 years of age, covering a wide spectrum (schools in cities, villages, a *Moshav*, two *Kibbutzim*, a religious school, a youth centre and an heterogeneous group from different schools). He asked:

Q 1   Do you think Joshua and the Israelites acted rightly or not? Explain why you think as you do.

Q 2   Suppose that the Israeli army conquers an Arab village in battle. Do you think it would be good or bad to act towards the inhabitants as Joshua did towards the people of Jericho and Makkedah? Explain why.

In calculating the responses, Tamarin distinguished between total approval of the genocide, partial approval and total disapproval.[7] The result can be presented as follows:

Attitudes towards Joshua and the Israeli Army

	% total approval	*% partial approval*	*% total disapproval*
Q.1. Attitudes to Joshua	66	8	26
Q.2. Attitudes to Israeli army and Arab village	30	8	62

7.   The small number of confused or irrelevant responses were not included in the computation. Tamarin draws attention to three answers in the 'total disapproval' category, which, nevertheless, betrayed discriminatory attitudes. One criticized Joshua's act, stating that 'the Sons of Israel learned many bad things from the Goyim.' Another rejected it, on the basis that the Bible says, 'Don't kill', yet approved of the action in the second question, stating, 'I think it would be good, as we want our enemies to fall into our hands, enlarge our frontiers, and kill the Arabs as Joshua did.' A third, a ten-year-old girl disapproved of Joshua's action, stating, 'I think it is not good, since the Arabs are impure and if one enters an impure land one will also become impure and share the curse' (Tamarin 1973: 187).

Tamarin concluded that this showed the existence of a highly preju-
diced attitude among a considerable number of the respondents, justifying discriminatory tendencies (religious, racial-nationalist, strategic
justification of the extermination, etc.). He divided the control group
into two sub-groups. The first received the text from Joshua, and was
asked to answer only Question 1. The second sub-group was given the
following 'Chinese version' of the book of Joshua:

> General Lin, who founded the Chinese Kingdom 3000 years ago, went to
> war with his army to conquer a land. They came to some great cities with
> high walls and strong fortresses. The Chinese War-God appeared to
> General Lin in his dream and promised him victory, ordering him to kill
> all living souls in the cities, because those people belonged to other reli-
> gions. General Lin and his soldiers took the towns and utterly destroyed
> all that was therein, both man and woman, young and old, and ox, and
> sheep, and ass, with the edge of the sword. After destroying the cities,
> they continued on their way, conquering many countries.

He asked this sub-group, 'Do you think that General Lin and his soldiers acted rightly or not? Explain why.'

The result of the control sub-groups can be presented as follows:

Attitudes towards the genocide

	% total approval	% partial approval	% total disapproval
By Joshua	60	20	20
By General Lin	7	18	75

Tamarin interpreted this result as proving unequivocally the influence
of chauvinism and nationalist-religious prejudices on moral judgment
(1973: 187-88).

Tamarin's analysis of the answers revealed that, among others,

> The uncritical teaching of the Bible—to students too young—even if not
> taught explicitly as a sacred text, but as national history or in a quasi-
> neutral atmosphere concerning the real or mythological character of its
> content, no doubt profoundly affects the genesis of prejudices...even
> among non-religious students, in accentuating the negative-hostile char-
> acter of the strangers...The overestimation of statehood as a supreme
> value and the idea that assimilation is the greatest evil, and the influences
> of militaristic values in ideological education, are further sources of dis-
> criminatory tendencies (1973: 189).

Tamarin concluded that the findings were a severe indictment of the
Israeli educational system, and an invitation to those responsible to

learn from them. His research brought him unsought and unexpected notoriety—the matter being called the *Tamarin Affair*—and led to his losing his professorship in Tel Aviv University. In a letter to the senate of the university he wrote that he had never dreamt that he would become the last victim of Joshua's conquest of Jericho (1973: 190).

The Bible, Peace and Colonialism
Discussion among biblical scholars and theologians on the subject of the settlement of the children of Israel in Canaan in antiquity, and of Jews in Palestine in modern times, is distinguished by its neglect of consideration for the inhabitants of the region prior to those occupations. The discourse in each case deals with such topics as *the land as God's gift*, or, *the possession of the land as the fulfilment of God's contractual agreement with the people of Israel.* And yet, as Arnold Toynbee notes, it was the same 'biblically recorded conviction of the Israelites that God had instigated them to exterminate the Canaanites' that sanctioned the British conquest of North America, Ireland and Australia, the Dutch conquest of South Africa, the Prussian conquest of Poland and the Zionist conquest of Palestine (1954: 310). The absence of concern for 'the natives' reflects the deeply ingrained Eurocentric, colonialist prejudice which characterizes virtually all historiography, as well as the discipline of biblical studies (see Whitelam 1996 *passim*).

Nevertheless, liberation theologians from virtually every region (Latin America, South Africa, South Korea, the Philippines, etc.) have appropriated the Exodus story in their long and tortuous struggle against colonialism, imperialism and dictatorship. Readers of the biblical narrative are easily impressed and consoled by that story's capacity to lift the spirits of the oppressed. However, one's perspective on the Exodus story takes on a different complexion when read with the eyes of the 'Canaanites', that is, of any of several different cultures, which have been victims of a colonialism fired by religious imperialism, whether of the Indians in North or Latin America, the Maoris in New Zealand, the Aborigines in Australia, the Khoikhoi and San in southern Africa or the Palestinians in Palestine.

The Palestinian liberation theologian, Canon Naim Ateek, poses the problematic in a striking fashion, since in his region, above all others, the applicability of the Exodus paradigm appears most natural.[8]

8. I discuss further the Exodus paradigm in Chapter 7.

> Before the creation of the State [of Israel], the Old Testament was consid-
> ered to be an essential part of Christian Scripture, pointing and witnessing
> to Jesus. Since the creation of the State, some Jewish and Christian inter-
> preters have read the Old Testament largely as a Zionist text to such an
> extent that it has become almost repugnant to Palestinian Christians... The
> fundamental question of many Christians, whether uttered or not, is:
> 'How can the Old Testament be the Word of God in the light of the
> Palestinian Christians' experience with its use to support Zionism?'
> (Ateek 1991: 283).

The Chinese theologian, Kwok Pui-lan, confesses to having no answer
to this question, and poses two further questions, 'Where is the promised land now?... Can I believe in a God who killed the Canaanites
and who seems not to have listened to the cry of the Palestinians now
for some forty years?' (Kwok 1995: 99). She cautions that one must
be careful not to identify the promised land with one's homeland, and
even more so with somebody else's homeland.

The Bible, commonly looked to as the supreme source-book of liberation, has functioned as a charter for oppression, both in the past
and the present. Understandably, the symbiotic relationship between
the political and religious discourses is most focused in the case of
Zionism and Palestine. If other peoples can apply the biblical paradigm of conquest and plunder by recourse to claims to analogous
'rights', the rights of Jews are accorded canonical and unique status
and are warmly supported in the West. The religious-political link
was illustrated dramatically on 13 September 1993, when President
Clinton introduced Prime Minister Rabin and President Arafat on the
White House lawn. He announced to the world that both people
pledged themselves to a shared future 'shaped by the values of the
Torah, the Koran, and the Bible'. According to a report in the
Washington Post, the President, fearing that his speech required more
work, had not been able to sleep on the night before the signing. He
woke at 3.00 a.m. and reread the entire book of Joshua and portions
of the New Testament (Prior 1994c: 20). His mode of address later in
the day was a mixture of Bible-based exhortation in the Baptist tradition and shrewd political manoeuvring. The late Premier Rabin's
speech also referred to the Bible. However, in the light of history one
must question whether *the values of the Torah, the Koran and the
Bible* can be relied upon to promote justice and peace, and underpin
the imperatives of human rights.

Another President of the USA had to deal with the conflict between the dictates of human rights and the imperatives of the biblical paradigm. When President Carter shocked American Christian evangelical fundamentalists and charismatics with his concern for human rights, and used the words 'Palestinian homeland' in a speech in March 1977, full-page advertisements, signed by prominent evangelicals, appeared throughout the USA, for example,

> The time has come for evangelicals to affirm their belief in biblical prophecy and Israel's divine right to the Holy Land ('Evangelicals' Concern for Israel', Paid Advertisement, the *Christian Science Monitor*, 3 November 1977).

With the USA Protestant churches beginning to champion third world countries and supporting the Palestine Liberation Organization (PLO), the pro-Israeli lobby targeted the 50–60 million American evangelicals. Televangelist Pat Robertson later interpreted the 1982 Israeli invasion of Lebanon according to the end-time fulfilment of biblical prophecy. Israel's attack was a modern Joshua event. He urged American viewers to phone President Reagan offering encouragement to Israel's war (O'Neill and Wagner 1993: 84). Meanwhile, in Lebanon, Rabbi Schlomo Riskin, who followed the army to study the Talmud with the troops, was deeply impressed by the fact that the soldiers, when resting from battle, spent long hours discussing whether it would be right to pick Lebanese cherries (see Bermant 1994).

While the biblical paradigm is unacceptable in our time as a justification for murder, it does enjoy the support of a strong body of opinion within religious circles in Israel. When Dr Baruch Goldstein, a graduate of the most prestigious yeshiva in the USA, massacred 29 worshippers in the Ibrahimi Mosque in Hebron (25 February 1994), there was widespread revulsion. Even advocates of the *Torah-from-Heaven* expressed shock at the unspeakably evil act of violence against those engaged in worship. Nevertheless, one asks what distinguishes this kind of behaviour from that presented as divinely mandated in some of the traditions of the *Torah*, and from the appropriation of those traditions by different forms of colonialism and imperialism? One wonders to what extent the book of Deuteronomy, the book of Joshua, and, in particular, the book of Esther, the prescribed reading for the feast of Purim, which occurred on that day, may have contributed to the world view of Dr Goldstein.[9] His actions were

9.   Robert Carroll reflects upon the possible effect on Mark Chapman, the

supported by some Zionists who lean heavily on a literalist reading of the biblical text (see Prior 1994c).

Sadly, Prime Minister Rabin left this particularly loathsome form of applied biblical hermeneutics unchecked. By a sad irony, Rabin himself was gunned down at a Tel Aviv peace rally on 4 November 1995. In the first hearing of his case, Yigal Amir explained that he derived his motivation from *halakhah*. Already on the eve of Yom Kippur just weeks before the assassination, a group of Jewish kabbalists stationed themselves before Premier Rabin's house, put on tefillin, lit black candles, blew the shofar, cursed him with the *pulsa denura* (lashes of fire) and intoned:

> And on him, Yitzhak, son of Rosa, known as Rabin, we have permission...to demand from the angels of destruction that they take a sword to this wicked man...to kill him...for handing over the Land of Israel to our enemies, the sons of Ishmael (*Jewish Chronicle*, 10 November 1995, p. 27).

British Chief Rabbi Sacks invited the Orthodox rabbinate to question whether they were really teaching Jewish values: the *Torah* was given 'not to wreak vengeance, but to create kindness, compassion and peace'. He went on to stress that it is 'people of religious conviction who must most forcibly defend the democratic process. We must absolutely—as a matter of Jewish principle—reject utterly the language of hate' (*Jewish Chronicle*, 10 November 1995, p. 56). Whether Rabbi Sacks owes more to the ideals of Enlightenment philosophy than to that particular form of Orthodox Judaism which reads the biblical text in a literalist way is not clear. Amir's five-month trial ended on 27 March 1996. On the day of his conviction and sentencing, he calmly assured the court, 'Everything I did, I did for the *Torah* of Israel, for the land of Israel'. His actions, he said, were guided by God and by the Jewish law. It was unforgivable for a Jew to give up part of the God-given land of Israel, he insisted. Asked if he had anything to say, Amir answered, 'I had no choice but to commit this act even though it ran against the grain of my personality, because the damage to the people of Israel is irreversible...I committed this act and I am willing to pay the price' (Derek Brown, *The Guardian*, 28 March

murderer of Beatle John Lennon, of reading about and meditating on Holden Caulfield: 'Some reading of *The Catcher in the Rye*! Books can kill—no, *readers* of books do the killing; books can inspire people to kill other people' (1991: 115).

1996). The judge tried to cut Amir short several times in the course of his five-minute speech, which he, looking at the judge, concluded with, 'May God help you'.

With respect to biblical hermeneutics, Goldstein and Amir are merely the tip of the iceberg of literalism, which justifies outrages on the basis of an alleged divine mandate. Constant exposure to a literalist interpretation of the *Torah*, whether in the curriculum of Israeli schools, or through some of the many schools of biblical and talmudic learning, avoids with difficulty descent into attitudes of racism, xenophobia and militarism (see Newman 1985). Moreover, there is abundant evidence, especially in traditions of imperialist colonialism emanating from so-called Christian countries, for appeal to sacred writings to justify inhumane behaviour.[10]

Reading the Bible with the Eyes of Canaanites
Contemporary liberation theologies look to the Bible for their underpinning. It is not difficult to discern a range of themes which fit the concept of liberation very comfortably (for example, liberation from oppression in Egypt, Babylon, etc.). However, does not a consistent reading of the biblical text require the liberating God of the Exodus to become the oppressive God of the occupation of Canaan? The problem is held in sharp relief in the comment of a North American Indian: 'The obvious characters for Native Americans to identify with are the Canaanites, the people who already lived in the promised land... I read the Exodus stories with Canaanite eyes' (Warrior 1991: 289).

Literary sources reflecting the experience of those displaced in antiquity are not available. We do not have the laments of the supplanted peoples, nor have we independent accounts of whatever disruption was entailed. In surveying the role of the Bible and theology in the furtherance of colonial and imperialistic enterprises one is aware of examples from so many regions and diverse periods of history which would illustrate the process. I have chosen to focus on three regions, from different periods, in which each colonialist ideology gained the support of a distinctive religious ideology. I choose the invasion of Latin America in the fifteenth century, the Afrikaner incursion into the Cape Colony of southern Africa in 1652 and its

---

10. My academic competence requires me to leave to others the urgent task of discussing the morality of the atrocities which are presented as deriving from a literalist exegesis of the sacred texts of other religions.

sequel in the nineteenth and twentieth centuries, and Zionist settler-colonialism of Palestine in this century. I leave it to others to deal with any other selection of a veritable panoply of examples from the range of imperialist enterprises.

In each region, the effects of the foundational injustice perdure: of the European incursion into Latin America, Aiban Wagua concludes, 'They set fire to the trunk, and the tree is still painfully burning' (1990: 48).

The legacy of *apartheid* includes the fact that South Africa has the greatest recorded inequality of any country of the world, with two-thirds of the black population surviving below a defined minimum level, and 9 million people completely destitute. The black people of South Africa recognize the central position which the Bible occupied in their colonization, national oppression and exploitation. Paradoxically, as converts to Christianity, the religion of their conquerors, they embraced the Bible, the textbook of their exploitation. However, accordingly as they encounter the Bible being used in support of unjust causes, they realize that the book itself is a serious problem for people in search of freedom. Many young South African blacks consider the Bible to be an oppressive document by its very nature and its very core, and even call for its displacement.

Religious and theological comment on contemporary developments in Palestine is substantial, but that reflecting a moral sensitivity to the underside of the establishment of the Jewish State of Israel, namely the disruption of the indigenous Arab population of Palestine is modest. Biblically- and theologically-based discussion concerning this region is singularly deficient in its interest in those issues with which human rights and humanitarian bodies concern themselves. This is not only surprising but alarming, since biblical scholars and theologians in virtually every other arena inform their discussions with a sensitivity to the victims of oppression. What is celebrated by Israeli Jews as the *War of Independence* of 1948, and by many Jews and some Christians as the fulfilment of biblical prophecy, is for Palestinians *Al-Nakba* (*The Catastrophe*), which involved the expulsion of the majority of the Palestinian population in creating the State of Israel. Restoration of the Israelite 'divinely ordained right', and 'fulfilment of biblical prophecy' was followed by great suffering in the region, including further wars in 1956, 1967, 1973 and 1982, and substantial military aggression in Lebanon in 1993 and 1996.

Until recently both Jewish and Christian scholars of the Bible have neglected the theme of the land. While we may never account for the relative academic silence in the past, the reasons for the recent interest are not difficult to discover. However, when one engages in a moral consideration of modern events in Palestine one trespasses on a virtual academic no-go area. The view that the Bible provides the title deed for the establishment of the modern state of Israel and for its policies since 1948 is so pervasive, not only in both Christian Zionist and Jewish Zionist circles but even within mainstream Christian theology and university biblical studies, that the very attempt to discuss the issue is sure to encounter opposition. On the other hand, there is an extensive library of 'secular' documentation on Israel and the Occupied Territories, but this discourse is conducted against a background of international law and the various principles and directives concerning human rights, with virtually no reference to overtly religious or theological concerns. This state of affairs is partly understandable, given that academic practitioners of international law and human rights discourse could not reasonably be expected to be secure also in biblical and theological learning. However, since virtually all students of the Middle East acknowledge, if only by way of perfunctory rhetoric, the significance of the religious or theological involvement in the region, such an academic lacuna is unacceptable.

I shall discuss the religious element in the ideology which propelled the European colonization of Latin America. I shall investigate how the biblical paradigm served the interests of an evolving Afrikaner nationalism, as it sought to advance its policies of 'separate development'. Finally, I shall investigate the religious motivation which was peripheral to, but residual in Zionism, and which became critical after the 1967 War. As I examine each of the three regions in turn I shall pay particular attention to the role of theology and biblical interpretation in supporting the social and political transformation in each place.

Many theologians sensitive to issues of human rights, especially those whose traditions depend heavily on the Bible, face a dilemma. While they revere the sacred text, they see how it has been used as an instrument of oppression. They seek refuge in the view that it is the misuse of the Bible rather than the text of the Bible itself which is the problem. The blame is shifted from the non-problematic biblical text to the perverse predispositions of the biblical interpreter. This 'solution' evades the problem. Examples from the past and the present indicate the pervasiveness, the persistence and the moral seriousness of the question. The ones I shall examine are from different periods of history, different regions, and different traditions of biblical hermeneutics, and highlight some of the moral problems at the heart of the Bible itself. It will be seen that several traditions within the Bible lend themselves to oppressive interpretations and applications precisely because of their inherently oppressive nature.

Part II

COLONIAL APPROPRIATIONS OF THE LAND TRADITIONS

Chapter 2

COLONIALISM AND LATIN AMERICA

To let their flower live
they damaged and swallowed up our flower.

That is how a Mayan poet assessed the European 'discovery' of
America (in Beozzo 1990: 88). Faced with the inevitable quincenten-
nial celebration of the 'discovery', Aiban Wagua, a Kuna Indian from
Panama and a Catholic priest, reminds readers that there are two
names, Abia Yala and America, and two histories, *kuna* history (that
of the indigenous peoples, who continue the struggle for survival) and
uaga history (that written by foreigners). And what have the indigenous people to celebrate?

> For indigenous history it is a question of whether it is possible or not to
> celebrate the marginalization, the violence, the genocide or ethnocide per-
> petrated against our indigenous communities of Abia Yala. We indigenous
> people know that we can only celebrate our resistance, our indomitable
> will to go on living in spite of the darkness around us (Wagua 1990: 49).

Let us recall first the events as seen from Europe.

12 October 1492: The 'Discovery'[1] of America and its Cost

Immediately after their defeat of the Muslims in Grenada in 1492,
Ferdinand of Aragon and Isabella of Castile pledged their support for
Christopher Columbus, who with 3 ships and 90 men sighted an island

---

1.   Already by 1535, Columbus's 'discovery' was being treated by G. Fernández
de Oviedo, Emperor Charles's official 'Chronicler of the Indies', not as the discovery of new lands, but as the recovery of Hesperides, the ancient kingdom of the
legendary Hispanic king Hésperos (*Historia general y natural de las Indias*, bk II,
ch. 3). The new lands, then, were not conquered, captured, or invaded, but justly
redeemed from lapse into forgetfulness (Kadir 1992: 132).

in the chain we call the Bahamas on 12 October 1492. He landed on what we call El Salvador. Further exploration revealed Hispaniola and Cuba. Columbus found gold and a docile Arawak population on Hispaniola, and, believing he had arrived in Asia, he dubbed the Arawaks 'Indians'. After the *Santa María* struck a reef and was wrecked, 39 of the sailors stayed behind, while the *Niña* and the *Pinta* returned to Spain in early 1493.

Columbus's achievement created great excitement in Europe, and the gold he procured in Hispaniola was enough to ensure a warm reception when he met Isabella in Barcelona in 1493. In line with mediaeval custom, and following on the precedent set by the Portuguese, they petitioned Pope Alexander VI for title to the newly-discovered lands. The Pope acceded in a bull of 3 May 1493. Later that year, in order to prevent disputes between Spain and Portugal, the Pope drew an imaginary north–south Line of Demarcation, some 563 kilometres west of the Azores and Cape Verde Islands. East of that line belonged to Portugal, and west to Castile. In the Treaty of Tordesillas (1494), these two countries agreed on a more equitable distribution which moved the north-south line some 2084 kilometres west. Portugal took possession of its area, Brazil, in 1500, with the arrival of Pedro Álvares Cabral on the east coast. Columbus made a number of expeditions to the region (1492–93, 1493–96, 1498–1500, 1502–1504), and other expeditions followed his discovery. The settlements in Hispaniola and the other islands of the Greater Antilles in the period 1492–1519 prepared the colonists for the advance to the mainland.

The Cost of the 'Discovery'
The original inhabitants of the region came to North America from Asia between 40,000 and 25,000 BC, crossing the land bridge now called the Bering Strait, which separates Alaska from Siberia. Archaeological evidence suggests that from about 10,000 BC human societies were present in the central highlands of Mexico, Central America and the high valleys of the Andes, while some areas of the Caribbean Basin and the plains of South America were occupied less than two thousand years before the arrival of Columbus. The regions contain evidence of the dawn of agriculture and the emergence of sophisticated civilizations. By 1492 the indigenous population is estimated to have been between 35 and 45 million, in a mosaic of tribal

groups, including the Aztecs, Incas, Araucasians, Arawaks, Caribs, Chibchas, and others (Burkholder and Johnson 1994: 3). The indigenous population developed highly sophisticated cultures (Olmec, Maya, Toltec, Aztec, Inca, etc.). The conquest of the Indians followed soon after the European discovery of the region.

Columbus returned in late 1493, this time with 1500 men, including seamen, officials and religious with clear settlement intentions. The settlers began to enslave the natives and demand tribute. The Spaniards devised the *encomienda* system, whereby colonists were granted vast tracts of land and the possession of the Indians living on them, which became a major instrument of colonization on the mainland. In return, the colonists were charged to protect the Indians and convert them to Catholicism, and teach them the rudiments of faith and the superior virtues of European civilization (see Harrison 1993: 106). The *encomienda* Indians on Hispaniola were forcibly moved to the gold fields, and were subjected to outrageous demands for food, labour and, in the case of women, sexual favours. Various forms of compulsory labour, including slavery, were employed, and when the stock of Indian slaves dried up, they were replaced by Africans. The Arawaks, weakened by harsh working conditions, an altered diet and the onset of disease (particularly smallpox, which reached the island in 1519), began to decline in number, with the result that the approximately one million inhabitants had virtually disappeared by the mid-sixteenth century (Burkholder and Johnson 1994: 28).

By 1509 the gold reserves of Hispaniola were running out, and new sources were sought elsewhere. Moreover, the decline in the native population reduced the numbers available for forced labour, and the Spanish population of some 10,000 sought slaves elsewhere. By 1519 they had devastated the Caribbean and much of Tierra Firme, but had established the basis for colonial exploitation. The island phase of colonization was over and the conquest of the mainland was at hand (Burkholder and Johnson 1994: 32-33). By the mid-1500s the Spanish adventurers (the *conquistadores*), with the advantage of horses and guns, had conquered the great Indian civilizations and given Spain firm control of Latin America. Spanish and Portuguese settlers began to pour into Latin America even before the conquest was completed. They came in search of wealth, status and power. Not for the first time, victorious Christians considered God to have supported their cause, and they brought this assurance with them as they embarked on the conquest of the Americas (Burkholder and Johnson 1994: 16-17).

The *conquistadores* came in noble style to live off the labour of others. Naked pillage was their first strategy, whereby they stole the entire wealth of the great empires of the Aztecs, the Incas, the Chibchas, and others, after which they turned their attention to more long-term goals, mining silver and gold and carving out for themselves great estates from the best Indian land. A continuous supply of cheap and docile labour was essential. The most telling device was to concentrate the Indian populations into *congregaciones*, or in Brazil into *aldeias* or villages. Ostensibly, this was to facilitate the work of evangelization, but in reality it was aimed at ensuring that the whites could have their land.[2] Harrison traces present day inequality to the primordial injustice of the European invasion (1993: 108).

Millions of Indians died in warfare, and of disease and overwork, so that the colonists were obliged to bring slaves from Africa to make up for the shortfall of labour. While there was some debate about the morality of making Indians slaves, there was no debate, legal or theological, about the propriety of doing so for black Africans. It is estimated that, over four centuries, in excess of 11 million slaves were imported to the Americas from Africa.[3] The African slave trade provided the labour power that developed the plantation economies of Brazil, Venezuela and the Caribbean. In other parts of Latin America it was an important supplement to Indian labour. Manifestly, the institution of slavery enjoyed the combined support of church, state, the nobility and public opinion.

Over the years Spain's economy became more and more dependent on Latin America. Colonial rule lasted some 300 years, after which time discontent grew in the colonies, influenced by the ideals of the French Revolution and the Revolutionary War in America (1775–83), leading ultimately to wars of independence. Mexico achieved independence in 1821, followed by Central America in 1822, but the united provinces of Central America began to dissolve in 1838, leading to the independence of Guatemala, El Salvador, Honduras, Nicaragua and Costa Rica by 1841. By 1824 the Spanish colonies in South America

2.   As we shall see, corresponding patterns were applied in South Africa (*Bantustans*) and Palestine (the areas under the Palestine National Authority, which constitute only some 4 per cent of the land of the West Bank).

3.   Some estimates are as high as 15 million (see Hurbon 1990: 91-93), and even 20 million (Richard 1990a: 59-60).

had wrested independence from Spain, and in 1822 Brazil declared itself independent of Portugal.[4]

Theological Underpinning: Mediaeval Christian Theology

European Christianity in the modern period shared the wider society's prevailing attitude of domination, not only the domination of nature but of alien races and cultures. The history of later European colonization has its roots here, and the history of Europe's engagement with Latin America also involved the culture of domination, with no place for the recognition of the value of the Other. Religion and politics have been closely intertwined in Latin America since the Conquest, providing ideological, material and institutional support and legitimation to one another (Levine 1981: 3). From its first appearance in the New World, the Catholic Church was an integral part of the colonizing venture. It was one of its functions to oversee and report on the conduct of the civil power (see Lockhart and Otte 1976: 203-207). The Mendicant Orders, especially the Franciscans, were prominent in the whole colonizing enterprise with their establishment of monasteries as centres of evangelization.

Moreover, there was no shortage of theological and biblical support to provide ideological underpinning. Mediaeval Christian theologians shared a common conception with Israelite theologians, involving a radical sacralization of the state and all its institutions, including its land. Both claimed that land was the gift of God, for the Israelites in their time, and later for the Spanish and Portuguese in the New World (see Padrón 1975: 42). God's possession of the land included his political sovereignty over all the territories of the earth (Lamadrid 1981: 329).

As in the Old Testament period, religion invaded every facet of life in the Middle Ages. The majority of theologians and jurists considered the Pope, as the vicar of Christ, to be sovereign of all the earth. The papal bulls are to be viewed in the context of the theocratic conception of the Middle Ages: the Pope was the Lord of the Earth, to whom Christ confided all power, in heaven and on earth (*Papa dominus orbis*). The bull *Aeterni Regis* of 1455 divided the New World, apportioning newly discovered lands to Portugal. The *Tractado de Alcoçoba*

---

4.   As in the USA, colonies wanted independence and freedom from slavery to another country, but remained indifferent to enslavement within its own borders.

(1479) ceded to Portugal all the discovered territories in Africa, and Pope Alexander VI's bull *Inter cetera divina* (1493) apportioned colonies to Spain. The Catholic kings were authorized to engage in a holy war which would implant the true faith in the regions of the infidel (Lamadrid 1981: 337).

Columbus reflected the religious component of his motivation in the dedicatory opening of his diary of the first voyage (Friday, 3 August 1492):

> Your highnesses, as Catholics, Christians and Princes who love the Christian faith and long to see it increase, and as enemies of the sect of Mahomet and of all idolatries and heresies, have seen fit to send me, Christopher Colombus, to the said parts of the Indies to see...what way there may be to convert them to our holy faith... (from the original in Las Casas 1989–94: XIV, 41).

Columbus began his diary, *In nomine Domini nostri Jesu Christi*. In this perspective, the religious motivation of the evangelization of the Indians became the justification for the whole enterprise of the conquest.[5] Introducing Columbus, Bartolomé de Las Casas, writing c. 1527, said that his motivation was to settle Spanish colonizers who would constitute a new, strong Christian Church and a happy republic, widespread and illustrious (from the original in Las Casas 1989–94: III, 359). Columbus saw in his discoveries the fulfilment of Scripture, especially, 'For I am about to create new heavens and a new earth' (Isa. 65.17), which he cites repeatedly; 'their voice goes out through all the earth, and their words to the end of the world' (Ps. 19.4), which he invokes five times in his *Libro de las profecías*; and, 'Then I saw a new heaven and a new earth' (Rev. 21.1). Moreover, in general, Columbus's figurative language, his sense of history and his cosmology are distinctly scriptural, intertestamental and prophetic, as reflected dramatically in his account of a hypnagogic swoon in Jamaica, 7 July 1503 (see Kadir 1992: 156-59).

Indeed, as his *Libro de las profecías* shows, Columbus interpreted his mission within the broad picture of a climactic end and a millennial beginning, incorporating the recovery of Mount Zion (for the accomplishment of which he hoped to finance 10,000 horsemen and 100,000 foot soldiers [see Kadir 1992: 202-203]), the geographical

---

5. This is a significant deviation from the biblical paradigm of the Israelite conquest, which never attempted to convert the Canaanites.

incorporation of all parts of the earth, and the conversion of all humanity to the light of the true faith, thereby constituting the Universal Church of one flock and one shepherd. At that point, the World Emperor (Ferdinand of Aragon) would defeat the Antichrist on Mount Zion, and an Angelic Pope of a renovated church would lead the faithful flock into a blissful millennium before the Last Judgment. And who better to initiate this process than Christopher, the 'bearer of Christ' (*Christoferens*) (see Kadir 1992: 30-32)?

And so, the evangelization practised by the Church underpinned the rapacious power of the state and gave it a control over the indigenous culture. God was identified with the European invaders and Satan with the barbarous infidels. Evangelization provided the ideological basis for subjugation, just as gunpowder and horse provided the military one, both in the service of the real goal of the conquest, the economic subjugation of the region. The major justification for holy war of the *Decreto de Graciano* derived from the Old Testament (Joshua, the Judges, Saul, David, *et al.*), reflecting the divine mandate to wage a holy war to conquer and consolidate their hold on the promised land. Doubts about belligerent aggression were assuaged by Augustine's claim that, without a doubt, a war ordained by God is just, since there can be no evil in God.

Juan Mair's *Libro II de las Sentencia*s, published in Paris in 1510, was the first to tackle theologically the problem of the conquest of the land of the infidels. Although he treated the subject in general terms, he referred to the Spanish conquest of the American Indians by way of example. The first justification for confiscating land already inhabited and subjugating the indigenous population was missionary: Christians may take to arms with the aim of preaching the Gospel. Moreover, since, in line with the theory of Aristotle, barbarians are slaves to naturalism, subjecting them to the rule of Christian principles was justifiable. Indeed, such was the general acceptance of those ideas that from 1513 Spaniards were required to read the *Requerimiento* to the native Indians before battle, often without the benefit of translation (see Todorov 1984: 148), urging them to

> ...recognize the Church as mistress and superior of the universe and the Holy Pontiff called Pope, in his own right, and the king and queen our lords, in his stead, as lords and masters and kings of these islands and mainland, by virtue of the said donation...Should you do so, you will do well...Should you not...I assure you that with God's help I shall attack you forcefully and make war against you everywhere and every way I

can...I shall capture you and your women and children and I shall enslave
you...and I protest that the deaths and calamaties that should ensue from
this will be due to your own fault, and not His Highness's, or mine, or
these gentlemen's who came with me (Kadir 1992: 86-87).

The theology of Genessi Sepulvedae (Juan Ginés de Sepúlveda) is
representative of the argument justifying war against the Indians as a
prerequisite for their future evangelization. Sepúlveda was born in
Spain c. 1490 and finished his treatise in 1545, but was forbidden to
publish it. His theology is significant for many reasons, but principally
because of the manner in which he managed to subordinate the
imperatives of the Christian Gospel to the political and ideological
actuality of the conquest. He discusses the conditions for a just war,
first, in general terms and then with respect to the American context.
There were three general conditions for waging a just war. The principle of self-defence justified the need to repel force with force. The
protection of one's own rights permitted the recovery of things which
had been unjustly taken. Thirdly, it was permissible to punish the
evildoers. And he added a fourth: the right to force the submission, if
necessary by force of arms, of those who, by their natural condition,
should obey others but refuse their authority. The greatest philoso-
phers, he claimed, justify such a war.

In applying the general conditions for a just war to the American
context, the fourth condition became the foremost. Because it is natural that prudent, honest and humane men should rule over those who
are not, it follows that Spaniards have the perfect right to rule over
the barbarians of the New World, who, in prudence, intellect, virtue
and humanity, are as much inferior to the Spaniards as children are to
adults and women are to men, applying the Aristotelian distinction
between those born masters and those born slaves (*Politics* 1254b—a
work which Sepúlveda had translated into Latin). Indeed, in his view,
the barbarian races were wild and cruel, as compared with the Spanish
who were a race of the greatest clemency. For Sepúlveda, the indigenous people were *barbarians*, and even *hombrecillos* (midgets). It was
all the more reason, then, that they should accept the dominion of
their superiors, which dominion would bring them great benefits. The
civilized Spaniards would bring the most salutary benefits to the barbarians, who hardly deserved the name of human being, converting
them from being slothful and libidinous to being honest and honourable. He added that they would be rescued from being irreligious

and enslaved to demons to become Christians and worshippers of the
true God. Oviedo, Emperor Charles's official chronicler went further:
'Who can deny that the use of gunpowder against pagans is the burning of incense to Our Lord' (in Todorov 1984: 151).

Sepúlveda's arguments justifying colonial domination follow from
attitudes that are racist, patriarchal and sexist. Moreover, they derive
from what he calls *the natural order*, rather than from the more elevated values of an enlightened moral theology. Far from it being the
case that the Church would employ the Gospel as an agent to liberate
the indigenous people, some of its theologians were justifying the
domination and massacre of others in the name of bringing them to
the higher values of the Gospel. Evangelization, then, was becoming
an ideological underpinning of colonial conquest.

While one recoils from his attitudes and arguments, one realizes
that it would not have been difficult for Sepúlveda to find in the more
ethnocentric traditions of the Bible further justification for his attitudes. He cited the many familiar passages from Deuteronomy and
Leviticus, detailing the ideal of the violent expulsion of the Canaanites
from their land, and their replacement by Israelites, at the behest of
God. He held that the preaching of the Gospel would not be possible
before the people were subjected politically to the Christians, and that,
in any case, the pagan barbarism of the Indians was such as to make
them fit to be no more than slaves. What was coming in the name of
Christianity, then, was in fact much more an expression of western
colonial Christendom, fresh from its victory over the Moors: Christianity received the highest form of secular recognition, and in its turn
supplied religious legitimation to the secular power.

However, in practice, the role of religion was no crude, unadulter-
ated exploitation of the natives. It proceeded along widely accepted
lines of teaching the Christian faith, supported by education and works
of mercy, as attested by Fray Pedro de Gant, a Franciscan lay brother,
who wrote to the Emperor in 1532 (see Lockhart and Otte 1976: 213-
14). Writing to his family in Spain in 1574, Fray Juan de Mora, an
Augustinian friar and professor of Holy Scripture, betrays a combination of shrewd business acumen and professional piety in advising that
any one of his nephews wishing to come from Spain should invest in
some Bibles, recently printed in Salamanca. He assures them that such
an investment would be doubly repaid in the New World (see
Lockhart and Otte 1976: 213-14).

It was the arrival of members of religious orders which hastened the work of evangelization. Cortés repeatedly besought Charles I to send friars, and twelve Franciscans arrived in May 1524, being the first contingent of the order that was most prominent in the 'spiritual conquest'. They were soon joined by the Dominicans, who were already active in the Caribbean colonies, and Augustinians. The God of the Christian evangelizers was a jealous god who tolerated no rivals, and hence the destruction of the native religions was systematic and continuous. By 1559 in Mexico there were some 800 friars, who approached the task of evangelization by seeking the conversion of the native chieftains and nobles, in the hope that they would bring their people with them to the Christian faith. The friars used the native languages as media of evangelization, especially the Aztec language, Nahuatl in New Spain, Kekchi in Central America and Quechua and Aymara in Peru. They were happy to keep the natives separated from the Europeans, whom they feared would corrupt them. The friars founded villages to bring the Indians together, and thereby oversaw the political and economic as well as the religious activities of the Indians. Many Indians accepted Christianity enthusiastically. Soon the Church became a powerful and wealthy institution which permeated the new colonial order and became a bastion of European culture and civilization throughout the colonial era.

Dissenting Voices

There were, of course, dissenting voices within the Church (see Dussel 1979). In particular, Fray Antón de Montesinos of Hispaniola, in his celebrated Advent sermon (1511) on the text *Vox clamantis in deserto*, said:

> This voice declares that you are all in mortal sin, and live and die in it, because of the cruelty and tyranny you practise among the innocent people. Say with what right and justice you keep these Indians in such cruel and horrible slavery. By what authority have you waged such detestable wars on these peoples, who were living on their own lands, inoffensively and peacefully, and exterminated such vast numbers of them with deaths and slaughter the like of which was never known? How can you keep them so oppressed and weary, without giving them food or relieving them in their sicknesses, from which, because of the excessive labours you force on them, they fall sick and die or, better, you kill them, so that you can seize and acquire gold every day (from Bartolomé de Las Casas' account in *Historia de las Indias*, bk III, ch. 4).

Montesinos goes on to criticize the audience for not attending to the spiritual welfare of the Indians (the responsibility of the *encomendero* in the *encomienda* system), and asks, 'Are these not men? Do they not have rational souls?' Las Casas recalls how the townspeople made every effort to have Fray Antón retract, and returned to the church on the following Sunday, expecting to hear it. However, this time choosing Elihu's words in Job 36.2-4, Montesinos repeated the charge that the Indian slaves were dealt with unjustly and tyrannically. He assured the audience that God does not keep the wicked alive, but gives the afflicted their right. That he declares the transgressions of kings, when they behave arrogantly (Job 36.10-12).

Bartolomé de Las Casas (1474–1566) has provided the most thorough theological reflection on the cruel exploitation of the Amerindians (edited 1989–94). The changes that took place in his evaluation of things reflect the power of experience to influence one's values. His predictable European's attitude to the conquest underwent a fundamental change. Las Casas's father and brothers were part of Columbus's second voyage, and he himself came to Hispaniola in 1502. He was ordained a priest in Hispaniola in 1512, the first ordained priest in the New World. In 1513 he accompanied Panfilo de Narváez as a chaplain in the Spanish conquest of Cuba. By spring 1514 he became convinced of the injustice of the Spanish conquest, and although he himself had held Indian slaves, underwent a conversion, strongly influenced by his reading from the book of Sirach 34.21-27 (see *Historia de las Indias*, bk III, chs. 79–80).

He gave up his *encomienda* and resolved to defend the Indians. In December 1515 he protested at the Spanish court against the mistreatment of the Indians (see *Historia de las Indias*, bk III, chs. 84–85). In 1516 Las Casas was appointed 'Protector of the Indians'. In December 1522 he entered the Dominican Order in Hispaniola, and in 1527 he founded a Dominican monastery in Puerto de Plata and began his *Historia de las Indias*. In 1544 he was consecrated Bishop of Chiapa in Mexico, but in 1547 he returned to Spain, where he took up permanent residency. From July to September of 1550 he debated before a royal commission the justification of the Spanish conquest with Sepúlveda, who had finished his treatise in 1545, justifying the Latin American colonial war. Las Casas died in a Dominican monastery in Madrid on 18 July 1566.

According to Las Casas, the main motive of the conquerors was,

> Their insatiable greed and ambition, the greatest ever seen in the world. And also, those lands are so rich and felicitous, the native peoples so meek and patient...that our Spaniards have no more consideration for them than beasts... But I should not say 'than beasts', for, thanks be to God, they have treated beasts with some respect; I should say instead like excrement on the public squares (1974: 41-42, in Dussel 1990: 41).

While Las Casas initially supported the importation of black slaves in the hope that their arrival would affect the release of the Indians, he later repented of his decision (Beozzo 1990: 87). He insisted that the Indians were better off as living pagans than as dead Christians, and that they rather ought to be won over by the saving power of the Gospel than by the force of arms (Berryman 1987: 10).

Although Francisco de Vitoria, theologian, jurist and one of the pinnacles of Spanish humanism in the sixteenth century, demolished the conventional justifications for the Spanish destruction of the Indians, and is widely lauded as the first internationalist who challenged the theocratic imperialism of the mediaeval period, some of his arguments defending 'just wars' ideologically underpin the subjugation of the Indians. If the Indians offered resistance to the rights of the Spanish to do commerce etc., one could wage justifiable war (Vitoria 1538–39: 702). Fundamentally, the Indians were not far from being mad, and were incapable of governing themselves. Hence intervention by superior guardians was permissible (see Todorov 1984: 149-50).

In general, for Christian theologians in the mediaeval period, the Indians' unbelief, abominations and crimes against nature justified the occupation of their lands. Justification for violence was based on the conquest of Canaan by the Israelites. The majority of the mediaeval theologians, in espousing theocratic imperialism and supporting the notion of holy war, bypassed the higher tendencies reflected in much of the Hebrew prophetic tradition, and the altogether non-violence tendencies within the New Testament. They settled for a regression to those traditions within the Old Testament which glorify war as an instrument of divine justice, thereby doing a serious injustice to the spirit of the Gospel in ignoring its detachment from the concept of territoriality so prominent in the *Torah*.

The prophetic opposition to Spanish colonialism grew out of communities of lay people, priests, religious and bishops, who used the language of the prophets to describe their plight. They were 'in Babylon' rather than in the realm of the King of Spain. They were preaching 'in Nineveh', or announcing God's judgment on their people. On the feast of Pentecost in Cuba in 1514, Las Casas realized that an offering made to God without the practice of justice was stained with the blood of the poor (Sir. 34.18-22). The Christian Quecha prophet, Felipe Guamán Poma de Ayala (1534–1616) noted that 'where the poor are, there is Jesus Christ himself'. Of course these prophets of justice endured the fate of all prophets. Las Casas earned the opprobrium of both Church and state. The Audience of Santo Domingo ordered him to retire to a monastery, and in 1548 Charles V ordered the withdrawal of his confessional. Sepúlveda branded him 'rash, scandalous and a heretic', and after his death, Philip II approved the measures to confiscate his works (in Salinas 1990: 102-103).

The clash between the polarities of evangelization is manifest in the stringent criticism of Las Casas by Fray Toribio de Motolinia who dispatched to the Emperor on 2 January 1555 a detailed riposte to Las Casas's denunciation of the conquest: 'His confusion appears great, his humility small. He thinks that all err and he alone is right.' Fray Toribio marvelled at the long-suffering patience of the Emperor and his council for having borne 'for so long with a man so vexatious, unquiet, importunate, argumentative and litigious, in a friar's habit, so restless, so poorly bred, insulting, prejudicial and trouble making', and so on. Fray Toribio assured the Emperor that Las Casas was motivated by an impassioned animosity towards the Spaniards and a love of the Indians which was little more than theoretical. 'He never sought to know the good, only the bad, and he never settled down here in New Spain.' In a word, 'Your majesty ought to order him to be shut up in a monastery so that he could not cause greater evils' (in Lockhart and Otte 1976: 224-29). Fray Toribio made an impassioned plea for the Emperor's support on behalf of the extension to the infidels of the fifth kingdom, that of Jesus Christ, of which the Emperor was leader and captain. As for Las Casas, 15 or 20 years confessing 10 or 12 sick, ailing Indians daily would remedy him (in Lockhart and Otte 1976: 232).

To make matters worse, in the course of writing his long report to the Emperor, Fray Toribio received and studied another of Las Casas's tracts, which added to his self-righteous anger. Contrary to the claims of Las Casas, the great diminishment in the numbers of the indigenous Indian population was not the bad treatment of the

Spaniards, but diseases and plagues, or, using the biblical paradigm, the idolatries of the natives:

> Whether or not the great sins and idolatries that took place in this land cause it, I do not know; nevertheless I see that those seven idolatrous generations that possessed the promised land were destroyed by Joshua and then the children of Israel populated it (in Lockhart and Otte 1976: 239).

According to Fray Toribio, in their pre-Christian phase, the Indians 'went about everywhere making war and assaulting people in order to sacrifice them, offering their hearts and human blood to the demons, in which many innocents suffered' (in Lockhart and Otte: 241). The improvement brought to the region by Christianity was plain to see.

The followers of Las Casas, called the *lascasianos*, faced similar problems. Bishop Juan del Valle of Popayán (1548–60) protested that he would continue to speak out against the abuses of the *conquistadores* 'even if they stone me'. He tried to bring the plight of the Indians to the Council of Trent, but he died on the way. Several bishops were martyred. Antonio de Validivieso, bishop of Nicaragua (1544–50) was stabbed to death. These prophetic voices witnessed to the greatest genocide in human history, and the end of the indigenous world order. No less than the survival of the indigenous population was at stake. Fray Pedro de Córdoba, vice-provincial of the Dominicans on Hispaniola, wrote to Charles V on 28 May 1517:

> I do not read or find any nation, even among the infidel, has perpetrated so many evils and cruelties on their enemies in the style and manner in which Christians have done on these sad people who have been their friends and helpers in their own land... Not even Pharaoh and the Egyptians inflicted such cruelty on the people of Israel (in Salinas 1990: 105-106).

Later (1597), in a similar vein, Fray Luis López de Solis, bishop of Quito wrote:

> The cries of these natives, because of the many and great hardships they experience at the hands of the Spaniards, reach the ears of God (in Salinas 1990: 101-102).

The plight of the Indians evoked like sentiments from the Franciscan, Fray Diego de Humanzoro, bishop of Santiago de Chile in 1666, who wrote to the Holy See:

> The cries of the Indians are so great and insistent that they reach the heavens. And unless we go to the aid of these wretches or our ardent tears

dry up their tears, I shall be called before the court of the same most just
Judge...And those who oppress and insult the poor to increase their
wealth will be condemned by the Lord (in Salinas 1990: 102).

Pleading before Queen Mariana of Austria in 1699, Fray Diego de
Humanzoro bewailed:

In four hundred years of captivity...the Hebrews increased in numbers
and did not die. But our Indians in their own land, ever since the
Spaniards entered in, have been wasted away in hundreds of millions by
the harassment and tyranny they suffer, and by the severity of the personal service which is greater and more terrible than that exacted by the
Pharaohs of Egypt (in Salinas 1990: 107).

The voices dissenting from theological support for European colonization compared the situation of the Indians with that of the suffering Israelites in exile, whether in Egypt or Babylon, or of the early
Church in its persecution by the Roman Empire. Nothing in the Bible
compared with the destruction of Indian culture and life; the dissenters, of course, were reading the Bible with Israelite, rather than
Canaanite eyes. Moreover, they used those portions of the Scriptures
which supported their own stance, for example, Jon. 1.2 and Sir.
34.23-26. The dissenters saw themselves like John the Baptist crying
in the wilderness, prepared to pay the ultimate sacrifice for their
prophetic protest (Mk 6.17-20). If 'they' persecuted Jesus, 'they'
would persecute his followers (Jn 15.20). In their association with
the sufferings of the victims, they saw themselves also as victims
(Mk 13.12-13).

   In the eyes of these prophetic dissidents, those who purported to be
bringing the civilization of the Gospel to the Indians were in reality
demons. As Francisco Nuñez de Pineda y Bascuñan (1608–80) put it,
the Europeans in words sought to appear ministers of Christ, but by
their evil deeds they showed themselves to be ambassadors and servants of Satan (in Salinas 1990: 108). They merited the censure of
Jesus as recorded in Mt. 23.15-38: 'Woe to you, scribes and Pharisees,
hypocrites! For you cross sea and land to make a single convert, and
you make the new convert twice as much a child of hell as
yourselves...'

Modern Theological Reflection and the Bible

The 1970s witnessed an unprecedented rise in ethnic militancy among
Indians. They reclaimed the right to speak for themselves, and to

present their own cultural heritage. This was not an uniquely Latin American phenomenon, but one shared by almost all indigenous peoples who were questioning their position of being dominated by others. Over the past several decades the Churches of Latin America have developed from being unquestioned allies of the established order to becoming its most vigorous critics, thereby bringing them into conflict with many of the regimes of the region, especially those governed by the military. In fact, the Churches have done more than any other institution to highlight the disparities of wealth within the societies of Latin America (see Levine 1979). Priests, religious and laity have taken a strong moral stance in support of the Indian peoples, and the Latin American Church has been at the forefront of a world-wide movement to recover the liberating vocation of theology (see Hennelly 1995). To some extent this can be attributed to the guilt which invariably arises when a moral person analyzes the social conditions of the oppressed. Las Casas serves as an outstanding example of such criticism, and is a hero of Latin American liberation theology, as witnessed by the encomium of his great admirer and imitator, the Peruvian Indian priest Gustavo Gutiérrez (1993). Anthropologists, too, have added their voices to the chorus of support for the voiceless oppressed (see Arizpe 1988: 153).

In coming to terms with the imperialist past of European Christendom the survivors of the indigenous culture must rise above the neurosis of unrelieved lament, while the descendants of the European invaders must avoid a 'neurotically arrogant cult of self-accusation'. However, the reality of the cries of the poor, those long dead, and those who cling on to life must be heard loud and clear, and must enter the *logos* of theological discourse (Metz 1990: 118).

Ignacio Ellacuría, one of the Jesuits murdered in El Salvador, wrote of the *crucified people* of Latin America (1989), whom Jon Sobrino insists must be brought down from the cross (1990: 125). In Latin American liberation theology perspectives, 12 October 1492 marks the beginning of a long and bloody Good Friday in Latin America and the Caribbean, which continues to this day, with little sign of Easter Day (Boff and Elizondo 1990: vii). The original sin of colonial exploitation is summed up as follows: 'In 1492 death came to this continent: the deaths of human beings, the death of the environment, death of the spirit, of indigenous religion and culture' (Richard 1990a: 59).

Nothing in the history of humanity compares with the demographic disaster (or genocide, if one wishes to apportion blame) of the indigenous population south of the Rio Grande (Latin America and the Caribbean). While there is no consensus about the estimated populations of the region, it is generally agreed that the Iberian settlement caused a massive fall in the native population. Some modern studies estimate that in 1492 there were as many as 100 million indigenous people, which in less than a century (in 1570) had plummeted to no more than 10–12 million.[6] Meanwhile, the small numbers of settlers from the Iberian peninsula grew steadily and rapidly.

The most extensive demographic research has focused on Central Mexico. Woodrow W. Borah estimates a fall in population from 25.2 million in 1518 to 0.75 million in 1622 (1983: 26). The fall in population varied throughout the continent, but, by any reckoning it was of disastrous proportions. The arrival of plague and smallpox devastated about one-third of the population of Central America. Peru's population fell from some 9.0 million in 1520 to only 1.3 million in 1570, and drops of between 80 and 50 per cent were registered in Colombia, Venezuela and Ecuador (Burkholder and Johnson 1994: 100).

Cruel wars contributed to the destruction of whole indigenous communities, and other factors included disease, ill-treatment and forced labour, and the wholesale destruction of families. Indigenous women were particularly badly treated, mostly as instruments of animal satisfaction, a practice which continues today (Esquivel 1990). The reasons for the plummeting of the population are many and interrelated:

> The devastation and disruption that accompanied military conflict, the mistreatment of the Indians through overwork and abuse, their starvation and malnutrition as a result of altered subsistence systems and natural disasters that destroyed entire crops, and the psychological trauma that weakened the Indians' will to live and reproduce all helped to reduce the population. Among other things, these conditions facilitated the horrific effects of epidemic diseases introduced by the Europeans and Africans. More than any other single reason, these new diseases to which the native populations had no immunity led to astronomical mortality rates (Burkholder and Johnson 1994: 101).

6.   Overall estimates range from 8 million to 100 million. See the discussion in Burkholder and Johnson 1994: 98-124; they opt for an overall population for the Americas of between 35 and 45 million (p. 99).

Smallpox and measles were the main killers. There was a general recovery by the eighteenth century due to the increased immunity of the natives to the diseases that accompanied the Iberian conquest and settlement.

Moreover, some 10 million black slaves were brought from Africa to Latin America and the Caribbeans, beginning with 3 million to Spanish America in the colonial period and 4 million to Brazil up to 1850, and some 3 million to the English and French Caribbean. Some estimate the number of black slaves to have been 20 million (Richard 1990a: 59-60).

The demographic changes in Latin America are summarized as follows:

> Throughout the Hispanic world the Indian population declined by 90 per cent or more from its precontact numbers, before beginning, in the fortunate cases, a modest recovery at the end of the sixteenth century. Nowhere was the indigenous population as large in 1808 as it had been before the Europeans reached the New World. The white population grew because of high levels of reproduction and, at least until the mid-seventeenth century, immigration. In the Caribbean islands and adjacent lowlands and in the lowlands of the Pacific slope, African slaves largely replaced semisedentary native populations devastated by disease. Finally, the racially mixed population was expanding rapidly by the late sixteenth century and continued to increase its proportion of the total population of Latin America as the colonial era progressed (Burkholder and Johnson 1994: 107-108).

The following Mayan testimony, from the prophecy of the book of the Linajes, is a typical lament of the destruction as seen from the perspective of the victims:

> It was only because of the mad time, the mad priests, that sadness came among us, that Christianity came among us; for the great Christians came here with the true God; but that was the beginning of our distress,
> the beginning of the tribute, the beginning of the alms, which made the hidden discord disappear,
> the beginning of the fighting with firearms,
> the beginning of the outrages,
> the beginning of being stripped of everything,
> the beginning of slavery for debts,
> the beginning of the debts bound to the shoulders,
> the beginning of the constant quarrelling,
> the beginning of the suffering.
> It was the beginning of the work of the Spaniards and the priests,

the beginning of the manipulation of chiefs, schoolmasters and officials...
The poor people did not protest against what they felt a slavery,
the Antichrist on earth, tiger of the peoples,
wildcat of the peoples, sucking the Indian people dry.
But the day will come when the tears of their eyes
reach God and God's justice
comes down and strikes the world (in Richard 1990a: 60).

This genocide could not have been done without an appropriate theology. For every genocide, there was a theological violence (Mires 1986). As in other cases of colonial exploitation, the natives of Latin America are never considered to be within the community of communication. But from the point of view of the indigenous Outsiders, the *discovery* and *conquest* were invasions which excluded them in so many different ways, beginning their suffering, which has continued to this day

The Situation Today

Faced with the prospect of a celebration of the quincentenary (1492–1992) of the 'discovery', leaders of 15 different indigenous nations met at an ecumenical consultation in Quito, Ecuador, and declared that

There was no such discovery or genuine evangelization as has been claimed, but an invasion with the following consequences:

(a) Genocide through the war of occupation, infection with European diseases, death from excessive exploitation and the separation of parents from children, causing the extermination of over seventy-five million of our brothers and sisters.
(b) Violent usurpation of our territories.
(c) The fragmentation of our socio-political and cultural organizations.
(d) Ideological and religious subjection, to the detriment of the internal logic of our religious beliefs (in Beozzo 1990: 79).

Beozzo catalogues the political humiliation, the humiliation of women and of native languages and religion, and the ongoing humiliation of such peoples as the Yanomami today, of whom he writes:

A people turned into strangers in their own land, stripped of their territory, of their history, of their memory, devastated by disease and death, the survivors treated like animals (Beozzo 1990: 82).

Today in Latin America and the Caribbean there are about 70 million indigenous people. In Guatemala and Bolivia they make up the majority of the population, while in Equador, Peru and Mexico they are the base of the rural population and of the migrants on the edges of the big cities. In Brazil, Chile, Argentina, El Salvador and Costa Rica they have been reduced to hard-pressed minorities (Beozzo 1990: 78). The indigenous people are persecuted in various ways in virtually all the countries. They are confined to indigenous reserves, discriminated against in education, health and housing, and exploited in all ways possible. The marginalization extends to practices within the Church also. Richard makes an impassioned plea for the Church to accept its part in the genocide of the indigenous people and to strive to help them live with respect (1990a: 64-65).

The economic situation is Latin America is gruesome. It is estimated that by the end of the century some 170 million Latin Americans will be living in dire poverty, and another 170 million in poverty critical to life (Sobrino 1990: 120). The majority of Latin Americans live on the edge of economic catastrophe. However, to attribute the poor economic and social conditions of today to the original European invasion would be facile. The prevailing conditions reflect the enormous rise in population from some 61 million in 1900 to some 390 million in the 1980s, which swamped gains in productivity and spawned the social evils of unemployment and the estimated 40 million abandoned children. However, the unique degree of inequality, exploitation and injustice that characterizes Latin America today (which has been called a 'pigmentocracy') can be traced back to its colonial past.

Nor can one ignore the influence of the authoritarian militarism of many of the countries, which up to recently could depend on the support of the clergy. But no less trite is the utopian expectation of the 1960s that all that was needed was the right mix of mystical Marxism, dependency analysis and an apocalyptic world view which reflects millennial aspirations. Liberation theologies rest on an assumption that history can be transcended through the creation of a new human type, which is the product of a new consciousness raised to a higher power. This higher consciousness is considered to be able to overcome the imperfections of the material life, which, for their part, are the product of the false consciousness of earlier generations (see Pike 1993: 463).

Sobrino insists that confronting contemporary reality helps one to assess the original and originating sin of the fifteenth century invasion. What happened in history is best described by the metaphor of crucified

peoples. Such language avoids a cover-up. Crucifixion implies not
only death but having been put to death. The Latin American cross has
been inflicted on the people by various empires. These peoples represent the Crucified Lord of History, and constitute the historical continuation of the Lord's servant, whom the sin of the world continues
to deprive of any human decency, and from whom the powerful of
this world continue to rob everything, especially life itself (Ellacuría,
in Sobrino 1990: 122). Sobrino invites a meditation on Isaiah's
Servant Songs, keeping one's eyes on the crucified people. It remains
to be seen whether the mythology of the Suffering Servant will be
more influential in contributing to a new order than the sacralization
of a new business culture.

The Role of the Bible
We have seen that the Amerindians were subjected to the worst
excesses of colonialist imperialism at the hands of European settlers,
whose authority derived from that combination of secular power and
religious legitimation which characterized mediaeval Christendom. In
a theocratic society religious arguments have a compelling power. For
some Christian theologians at least (e.g. Sepulvedae), the Indians'
unbelief, abominations and crimes against nature justified the occupation of their lands, and the Israelites' conquest of Canaan legitimated
the use of arms against them (cf. Deut. 9.5; 18.9-14; Lev. 18.24-25).
We have seen that, in addition to the support which the Bible and
Christian theologians gave to the European invasion, there were
notable voices of dissent. What is at stake in considering the theological reflection on the exploitation of Latin America is whether God is
on the side of the poor, exploited Indians, whom the Peruvian Indian,
Guamán Poma called 'the poor of Jesus Christ' (Beozzo 1990: 85), or
whether he aligns himself with the powerful and ravenous exploiters.
For his part, Poma had no doubt that all the Spaniards would go to
hell for their ill-treatment of the Indians (in Beozzo 1990: 87).

  In our own day, when Pope John-Paul II visited Peru, he received
an open letter from various indigenous movements:

> John-Paul II, we, Andean and American Indians, have decided to take
> advantage of your visit to return to you your Bible, since in five centuries
> it has not given us love, peace or justice.
>
>   Please take back your Bible and give it back to our oppressors, because
> they need its moral teachings more than we do. Ever since the arrival of
> Christopher Columbus a culture, a language, religion and values which

belong to Europe have been imposed on Latin America by force.

The Bible came to us as part of the imposed colonial transformation. It was the ideological weapon of this colonialist assault. The Spanish sword which attacked and murdered the bodies of Indians by day and night became the cross which attacked the Indian soul (Richard 1990a: 64-65).

Richard judges that 'The problem is not the Bible itself, but the way it has been interpreted' (1990a: 66). The task of the indigenous peoples, in such a view, is to construct a new hermeneutic which decolonizes the interpretation of the Bible and takes possession of it from an indigenous perspective. Such a hermeneutic, reflecting the consciousness-raising (*conscientização* in Portuguese, *conscientización* in Spanish) of the Brazilian educator, Paolo Freire, must acknowledge the primacy of experience. History, the cosmos, the lives and the cultures of the indigenous peoples are God's *first* book, and the Bible is God's *second* book, given to believers in order to help in 'reading' the first. Secondly, the indigenous peoples must be the *authors* of biblical interpretation. Such a programme is already in place within the Christian base communities through the method of people's reading of the Bible, as described in the monograph *Lectura Popular de la Bíblia en América Latina: Una Hermenéutica de la Liberación*, in the review, *Revista de Interpretación Bíblica Latinoamericana* (San José: Costa Rica, 1988, no. 1).

Similarly, Leif Vaage (1991) discusses developments at the interface between biblical reflection and social struggle in Latin America, also against a background of the use of the Bible as an instrument of oppression in that region. The Centre for the Study of the Bible in Brazil operates on the basis of three crucial commitments: to begin with reality as perceived; to read the Bible in community; and to engage in socio-political transformation through Bible reading. In this so-called Contextual Bible Study process, biblical scholars become servants who are invited to participate as the people choose. The scholars must be committed to biblical studies from the perspective of the poor and oppressed.

Paradoxically, defenders of the rights of the Amerindians used some of the prophetic traditions of the Bible and the teaching of Jesus as agents of liberation, even though the warring traditions of the same Old Testament were a major instrument of oppression in the hands of the *conquistadores*. In contemporary theological reflection, every effort is made to appeal to the liberating themes of the Bible. The emphasis in a liberation hermeneutics is to reread the Bible from the basis of the poor and their liberation, with an emphasis on application rather than on merely dragging out 'the meaning-in-itself'. In a *praxis*-perspective, the important thing is to interpret life according to the scriptures, rather than merely to interpret the text of the scriptures (Boff and Boff 1987: 33-34). However, the Bible is an ambivalent document for promoting liberation. We shall see that in respecting the combination of the *exodus* from Egypt and the *eisodus* into the land of the Canaanites etc., the biblical paradigm justifies the behaviour of the *conquistadores*, rather than serves as a liberating charter for the oppressed (see Chapter 7).

Meanwhile we change location and move on in time to examine how the Bible and Christian theology underpinned the evolution of Afrikaner nationalism in southern Africa. We shall see a development in the use of the biblical paradigm. Whereas the Bible was used as a justification for, and, paradoxically, as a condemnation of Spanish and Portuguese colonialism as that enterprise was in process of development, in the case of Afrikaner colonialism and nationalism, we shall see how the Exodus-settlement paradigm was appealed to only *post factum* as a justifying device for colonialism, but as an ever-present support for *separate development*. And no less paradoxically than in the case of Latin America, the rejection of oppression as an acceptable ideology was greatly assisted by appeal to the Bible.

Chapter 3

COLONIALISM AND SOUTH AFRICA

We shall see that the Bible and Christian theology played a significant part also in the development of Afrikaner colonialism and nationalism, and that theological and biblical justification for it was retrojected into the past, and presented as having provided the motivation for earlier developments. The majority of South African Dutch Reformed theologians in the period 1930–60, during which the policy of *apartheid* was invented, formulated and defended, underpinned it by recourse to the Bible, especially the book of Deuteronomy (Deist 1994). Of course, biblical interpretation was not the only, or the most important factor in underpinning *apartheid*, since societal transformation reflects a matrix of social, political and religious factors. In sketching the major developments in Afrikaner history, we shall see how certain elements of this historical framework were transposed later into constitutive components of a fabricated myth of origins, some of which were underpinned by theological and biblical factors, and were adapted to fit the evolution of Afrikaner political ideology. Finally, I shall discuss the validity of retaining a myth of origins in the face of the findings of historical and scientific research and theological reassessment, and in virtue of moral considerations.

Sketching Boer History

Since theological and biblical issues always find their place within a complex matrix of many political and social components, it is instructive to review the broader picture from the beginning. We shall see later that theological and biblical factors assumed importance only in the modern period when Afrikaner nationalism was being fabricated. It would not be difficult to make a case for the centrality of the biblical and theological aspects in the overall discourse. However, while

theological commentators give the impression that the religious
element was at the core at every stage, the vast bibliography on *apartheid* does not bear out such a claim (for example, see the modest
number of references to theological factors in Kalley 1987). A history
of ideas approach, emphasizing the biblical and theological components without respect for the wider social discourse, would be facile.
What follows is a summary of relevant events, rather than an artificial
construct composed on the basis of a later 'myth of origins'.[1]

In 1652 officials of the Dutch East India Company established a
small settlement on the Cape of Good Hope to provide refreshment
for the company's ships on their way to the Far East, and were joined
in 1688 by some 200 Huguenots fleeing religious persecution in
France. Initially relations with the indigenous peoples, Khoikhoi (called
Hottentots by the settlers) and San (called Bushmen), were amicable,
but as the settlers became more dominant relations became strained.
After some fighting in 1659–60 and 1673–77, the whites subdued the
pastoral Khoikhoi quite easily, but bands of San defended their territory well into the nineteenth century. A British force took the Cape
in 1795, and although it was returned to the Dutch in 1803, the British
repossessed it in 1806.

By 1800 most of the Khoikhoi in the interior were landless and
almost entirely dependent on white farmers. In the course of the nineteenth century a 'white space' had been created, which black Africans
could enter only with the white man's permission. Although the Dutch
settlers shared a common language, religion, interests and colour consciousness, there was no sense of a national consciousness. They were
more a community of settlers in a relatively hostile colonial environment than a nation in the making (Lester 1996: ch. 1). By the end of
the nineteenth century, white ownership of the land was secured by
occupation, while the indigenous people had been dispossessed and
displaced.

Lord Somerset, governor of the Cape from 1814 to 1826, instituted
an Anglicization policy. The European settlers shared many of the
ethnocentric attitudes of most European colonizers of the New World.
Slavery was finally abolished in 1834, and later historians claimed that
the British failure to compensate the slave-owners rather than the

1.   I am indebted to my colleague, Dr Alan Lester, for making available the
manuscript of his major study (1996), which I use extensively here.

abolition itself, was a major source of Boer discontent.

In 1836 some 15,000 Boers left the colony and moved north and east to embark on their own enterprise away from British control.[2] Later historians attribute this so-called 'Great Trek' of 1836 to mal-treatment under the British: 'It was not so much love for the native that underlay the apparent negrophilistic policy [of the British] as hatred and contempt of the Boer' (Reitz 1900: 92, in Moodie 1975: 3). After much struggle, the Boers settled peacefully in Natal and estab-lished a republic there. But when the British annexed Natal, some Boers left and settled in the already established Republic of the Orange Free State and the Transvaal Republic.

The Making of Afrikaner Nationalism
By the 1870s the subcontinent was divided into a large number of dis-tinct political entities, and when in 1877 the British annexed the Transvaal Republic also, the Boers turned to force, which led to the first of two Anglo-Boer Wars (1881–82). The people came together at Paardekraal on 16 December 1880 to renew the covenant with the Lord (du Plessis n.d.: 96, in Moodie 1975: 7-8). Britain's growing interest in the area was due in large measure to the discovery of sub-stantial amounts of diamond and gold in 1886–87, which yielded enor-mous profits to mainly English-speaking whites. Racial segregation and discrimination were the hallmarks of the industry (L. Thompson 1995: 121).

From about 1870 to the end of the century, the combination of British regiments, colonial militia and Afrikaner commandos com-pleted the conquest of the black Africans. The whites, British and Boers alike, had a sense of superiority *vis-à-vis* the African, in virtue of belonging to a civilized race and a noble religion. This justified the

2. Terminology has played a part in the assessment of this emigration move-ment. Before the 1870s the Boers who left the Cape Colony in the 1830s and 1840s were usually referred to as *emigrante* (emigrants), and sometimes as *verhuisers* (migrants), or *uitgewekeners* (refugees), or *weggetrokkeners* (leavers), though some used *voortrekkers* (pioneers) to describe those who arrived in a given locality. During the late 1860s a few individuals applied the term *voortrekkers* to all the Boers who trekked from the Cape Colony between 1836 and 1854, and by the end of the century virtually all Afrikaners used the term in that sense. By that time also, the movement was treated as a great central saga in South African history, and Afrikaners and some English-speaking South Africans were calling it the Great Trek (L. Thompson 1985: 173).

expropriation of native land, the control of native labour and the subordination of the indigenes. Serious rivalries between the two white groups were put aside in the task of conquering the Africans.

However, the British-inspired drive to control southern Africa and create a confederation subject to the crown was resisted by the Boer republics, culminating in the second Anglo-Boer War (1899–1902). By June 1900, both the Orange Free State and the Transvaal had been declared British territory. Thousands of Boer deaths, including those of 26,370 women and children in British concentration camps, coupled with the hopelessness of their chances, forced the Boers to surrender. The Treaty of Vereeniging in 1902 marked the surrender of the Boer republics and their incorporation into the British Empire. However, despite the defeat, the growing sense of unity against a powerful enemy fuelled Afrikaner nationalism.

Mining had transformed patterns of black employment, so that by 1899 some 100,000 Africans were working in the gold mines, with blacks living in segregated compounds. Increasingly, white urban-dwellers objected to the influx of blacks, who threatened the demise of 'white civilization', and patterns of segregation developed. By 1910 and the Act of Union, whereby the Cape Colony, Natal, the Transvaal and the Orange Free State joined to form the Union of South Africa—a white-controlled, self-governing British dominion—racial segregation was already part of the official discourse, and had the support of both the British administrators and Afrikaner leaders. Under the 1913 Land Act, black Africans were forbidden to be on the land of a European, except as a hired servant.

In 1914 General Hertzog established the first Afrikaner National Party, which institutionalized the two-stream model for the future united South Africa. The Afrikaner Broederbond was formed in 1918 to fight for the Afrikanerization of South Africa, and was at the vanguard in transforming Afrikaner society—the thesis of Bloomberg's study (1990). Its members were Protestants who were pledged to the ideal of the eternal existence of a separate Afrikaner nation, which had been called into being by God and was to stand firm upon the Christian historical tradition and the Holy Law of God (Moodie 1975: 103-104).

In 1934, Dr Daniel F. Malan established the breakaway ('purified') National Party, which embraced the ideal that the destiny of South Africa was to be a republic, independent of the British crown. It formally embraced Christian Nationalism, against the trend in Europe: 'The Enlightenment dethroned God; but Afrikanerdom crowned Him as the sovereign of their Republic' (Bloomberg 1990: xxviii). From then on there existed a national party which stood unequivocally for Christian National ideals, separate mother-tongue education, strict segregation between white and black and a republic. Malan, an ex-pastor, was to become the first nationalist Prime Minister (1948–54).

The groundwork for a policy of *apartheid* was already laid in the period 1910–48. By the beginning of the twentieth century, under the influence of a crude Darwinian scientific racism, the superiority of the white race was presumed. Moreover, segregation was viewed as being the best protection against the possible mobilization of the African workers. Separating them into 'reserves' was a mode of social control: the Natives (Urban Areas) Act was passed in 1923, and several other acts followed, enabling the cities to function with black workers, but without their presence in numbers sufficient to disturb white domination.

The growth in Afrikaner nationalism in the 1930s is attributed variously to the material plight of white urban workers experiencing discrimination under British-dominated capitalism (a Marxist perspective), or to the growth of Afrikaner identity and culture, which reflected the differences in language, religion and historical experience between the Afrikaner and the Englishman (a liberal perspective). Specifically biblical and theological factors, as we shall see, also played their part. In practice, of course, significant cultural change was effected by a combination of ideological and material factors, and, as Lester insists, by a spatial factor also. This included the disorientation brought about by commercialization, industrialization and the concomitant drift to the cities (Lester 1996: ch. 3).

The full-blown *apartheid* legislation introduced after the accession of the National Party to government in 1948 was a pragmatic and tortuous process to underpin the ideology of the Afrikaner nationalist movement. Its rationale involved a number of factors: the drive to maintain a segregated society in keeping with the Afrikaner politico-religious precepts; obsession with racial purity and eugenics; and the securing of white political supremacy and economic privilege against the threat of African urbanization and social advancement. Another goal of the National Party was for the Afrikaners to gain equality with, or even dominance over the English-speaking population (Lester 1996: 107).

Ideological justification for *apartheid* was provided partially through the anthropological work of W.W.M. Eiselen, who propounded the view that race separation offered the only solution, provided that it was undertaken in an honest and constructive spirit (1948). However, recognizing that the racist elements of a crude social Darwinism would not be acceptable in the 1950s, Eiselen and his students had recourse to the primacy of distinctive culture, rather than superiority of race, as the basis for separate development. *Apartheid* was designed to preserve the cherished cultural identity of each group: all distinct ethnic units must be allowed to survive, each with its own language, religion and traditions.

The major Dutch Reformed Church was well-situated to play its part in elevating *apartheid* into a moral crusade, and the Church's annual congress of 1950 adopted a policy of eventual total separation of white and black. However, as a blatantly racist ideology, *apartheid* was appearing increasingly anachronistic. While it received widespread Afrikaner support, it ran in the face of the international movement against racial oppression and the African opposition, spearheaded by the African National Congress (ANC, founded in 1912). Tensions within the ANC led to a split and the formation of the more radical Pan-Africanist Congress (PAC).

The Bantu Education Act of 1953 forced the closure of most of the church schools. The Department of Native Affairs devised syllabi which would support *apartheid*, but such was the disjuncture between the White Man's History and the Truth as experienced by others, that by the 1950s coloured teachers were dictating two sets of notes, one 'For Examination Purposes Only' and the other headed 'The Truth' (L. Thompson 1985: 67-68). The history syllabus focused on the revelation of God's choice of separate nations of people, reflecting the core values of Christian Nationalism.

The second phase of *apartheid* was pushed through under the influence of H.F. Verwoerd, Prime Minister from 1958 to 1966, who made a strong alliance with the Broederbond. The 1960s saw the launch of an ambitious and ruthless programme of social engineering which stripped the majority of Africans of South African citizenship and forcibly removed over $3\frac{1}{2}$ million blacks from allegedly 'white' areas to putative ethnic 'homelands' (Posel 1991: 1). Ironically, just as racial supremacy was being institutionalized in South Africa, decolonization was the order of the day throughout much of the rest of the continent. The development of the homelands could be presented as a kind of internal decolonization and a recognition of autonomous African nationhood (Lester 1996: 126). However, the homelands would always be too poor and too dominated by the South African government to be regarded as national states by any credible government other than South Africa (see Lester 1996: 129). The real intention of the Afrikaners was to corral the blacks into areas outside the conurbations and bus them in only as required.

Verwoerd's policy reached explosive proportions with the Sharpeville slaughter of 69 Africans engaged in the anti-pass campaign of 1960. The shootings and the banning of opposition precipitated a crisis on the international front, which led to withdrawal from the Commonwealth and the declaration of South Africa as a republic in 1961. After the UN condemnation of *apartheid* in 1963, an arms embargo was applied that contributed to the economy's relative isolation.

Opposition to the social effects of segregation was being expressed among leading Afrikaner churchmen, as exemplified by the Cottesloe Consultation of December 1960. Nevertheless, the Broederbond took upon itself the evangelization of the republic into an acceptance of the ideal of separate development. All cabinet members, all university principals, half the school principals and inspectors, and some 40 per cent of Dutch Reformed Church ministers were members of the Bond, and all members of the Bond supported the ideals of Christian Nationalism.

However, by the late 1970s, the *apartheid* system was showing fatal cracks. On his accession to the premiership in 1978, P.W. Botha hoped that it would be possible to rescue the system by reforming it. However, black opposition threatened widespread insurrection and rendered the townships ungovernable. Theological support for *apartheid* took a dramatic turn with the publication of the *Kairos Document* on 13 September 1985, a joint effort of 50 theologians in and around Soweto. Like the Liberation Theology of Latin America, the starting-point of its theological reflection was the experience of the poor blacks.

After Botha's heart attack in 1989, F.W. De Klerk assumed the presidential office on a reformist ticket, leading to the unbanning of the ANC, the PAC and the South African Communist Party, and the freeing of prisoners, including Walter Sisulu and Nelson Mandela in February 1990. In June 1991, a series of Acts was repealed ending statutory *apartheid*. Negotiations with the black parties followed, and the historic elections of 1994 changed the face of South African politics. Nelson Mandela was elected President and F.W. De Klerk became one of two Vice-Presidents, with Chief Mangosuthu Buthelezi becoming regional Premier in KwaZulu/Natal and Minister for Home Affairs.

However, the legacy of *apartheid* left South Africa with the greatest recorded inequality of any country of the world, with two-thirds of its black population surviving below a defined minimum level and 9 million people completely destitute: currently, 60 per cent of the population lives below the breadline, 55 per cent are illiterate and over 40 per cent are unemployed (Lester 1996: 240). The cost to the African blacks of the realization of the Afrikaner dream holds in relief the words of Dr D.F. Malan: 'The history of the Afrikaner reveals a will and a determination which makes one feel that Afrikanerdom is not the work of men but the creation of God' (quoted in Moodie 1975: 1).

Fabricating the Myth of Early Afrikaner Nationalism

A distinctive Afrikaner identity and nationalism began to develop towards the end of the nineteenth century and the early part of this century. In general, national communities and nation states reclaim, or fabricate their 'past' in order to justify their present condition and aspirations. Typically, where the real past is either inadequately known, or contains realities unhelpful to nationalist identity, 'facts' about the past are fabricated to support the ideology and 'myths of origins' are created. Afrikaners also appropriated the past as part of the politics of the present, and in their reconstruction of history, the group and nationalist identity which had begun to develop only towards the end of the nineteenth century was ascribed to the earlier decades also.

The emerging Afrikaner nationalist identity had to contend with the double threat from British imperialism and domination of commercial life, and from the unenviable Afrikaner status of being a minority within a predominantly black African population. Its ideologues, politicians, writers and clergy countered these two threats by creating an effective mobilizing mythology. One element of this asserted that when the Dutch arrived in the Cape in 1652 they found only some recently arrived black nomads, giving the Dutch as much right to the land as the blacks. Indeed, they had more, since the blacks had refused the gift of western Christian civilization.

The Dutch Reformed Church minister, S.J. du Toit (1847–1911), created the nucleus of an exclusive ethnic mythology. His distinctively Afrikaner history, *Die Geskiedenis van ons Land in die Taal van ons Volk* (The history of our country in the language of our people) was the first book published in Afrikaans (1877). According to du Toit, Afrikaners constituted a distinct people occupying a distinct father-land, charged by God with the mandate to rule South Africa and civi-lize its heathen inhabitants. He was the first Afrikaner intellectual to adopt the concept of the Afrikaners as a chosen people. Although du Toit's pan-Afrikaner nationalist ideology did win out ultimately in the general election of 1948, it did not dominate Afrikaner political insti-tutions in the nineteenth century, where it was opposed by Presidents Brand and Kruger, who were intent on preserving the separate identi-ties of their states (L. Thompson 1995: 135).

The message of a distinctive Afrikaner identity and desire for inde-pendence was promulgated very widely through private Dutch Reformed schools and preaching in the Afrikaner Calvinist tradition, and through the multifarious activities of the Broederbond (Moodie 1975: 110-11). The early decades of the century saw an orchestrated effort to create an Afrikaans literature which fabricated appropriate myths of origin. The passionate nationalism of the intellectuals was quickly translated into textbooks, so that the whole nation was engaged in creating its mythological nationalist past (see L. Thompson 1985: 35-68). This depended on a number of ideological constructions of the past, including the myths of Slagtersnek and the Great Trek and the Vow, myths which were easily adaptable to changing circumstances, and the myth of racial superiority.

The Political Myth of Slagtersnek
The hanging of Afrikaner rebels at Vanaardtspos, 12 miles from Slagtersnek on the eastern frontier of the Cape Colony in 1815, is a foundational myth of Afrikaner nationalism (see L. Thompson 1985: 105-43). Although not treated as a prominent event in the formation

of Afrikaner society before the 1870s, from that time on it provided in microcosm verification of the two great threats to Afrikaner survival, English and black, and the fabricated account became a significant element in the emerging mythology of Afrikaner nationalism.

'Freek' Bezuidenhout was found guilty of holding back the pay of a Khoikhoi labourer and refusing to allow him to leave his employment on the expiry of his contract. He was sentenced *in absentia* to imprisonment, and when he refused to surrender on 10 October 1815, the officer in command ordered his arrest. Seeing him standing with a gun at his shoulder, the coloured sergeant shot him dead. Bezuidenhout's brother, Hans, swore vengeance and began to organize a conspiracy whose aim was to oust the British regime and the hated Cape Regiment.

On 18 November, about 60 of Hans's supporters were at Slagtersnek when a loyalist force of Boers and British dragoons caught up with them. Hans and his family and others fled northward into Xhosa country. On 29 October, nearly 50 miles north-east of Slagtersnek, Bezuidenhout and his wife and son resisted the combined forces of Boers and members of the Cape Regiment, and as a result of his wounds Hans died. Soon afterwards, 47 conspirators were tried at Uitenhage, and on 22 January 1816 the judges gave their verdict that 6 were to be hanged. The hangings were carried out at Vanaardtspos, 12 miles south of Slagtersnek, on 9 March 1816. The event marked the coming of law and order to a previously anarchic frontier zone and was a turning point in the history of the Cape Colony: white colonists had been tried, convicted of high treason, and executed.

From Vanaardtspos to Slagtersnek
There was no widespread reaction to the events at the time, and they faded into oblivion in the works published before the 1870s. However, the testimony of Henry Cloete in the 1850s, 'We can never forget Slachters Nek' was to play a major part in fabricating the myth. His is the first record of the confusion between the place of the hanging, Vanaardtspos, which was 12 miles away from the emotive name Slagtersnek (Butchers' Neck), a place where butchers' agents from Cape Town bought cattle from the Boers. The application of the term *slagter* to 'the place of the hangings' conjured up visions of a slaughter.

When in the 1870s and 1880s British imperialist interests were threatening the autonomy of the Boer republics, attitudes to the British were retrojected into the earlier period also. The Slagtersnek myth became firmly established in the mythology of Afrikaner nationalism by 1877, when S.J. du Toit produced his history. For him, the issue in 1815–16 was not law and order but 'tyranny'. The 'Uprising of Bezuidenhout' was against the British government, the great 'oppressor'. The Boers who collaborated were 'traitors' and the rebels 'heroes'. The uprising and its suppression, he claimed, were a major cause of the Great Trek, and the two together constituted the foundation of the Afrikaner national spirit (see his lament, in Moodie 1974: 4). Other Afrikaner histories embellished the hagiographic portrayal of the rebels (for example, J.D. Kestell, and also under the pseudonym Leinad). Around this time, too, the Afrikaners were being identified with the Israelites: 'Just as the old Israel was planted in Canaan and was protected, so our people, through God's providence, are planted in Africa from Holland, France and Germany, according to Psalm 80.9-16 and Isaiah 27.1-3' (C.P. Bezuidenhout in 1883: ii, in L. Thompson 1985: 268 n. 55).

Although by the end of the century the myth was firmly established in the struggle against British imperialism, the need for white solidarity ensured that the treatment of it did not exacerbate inner-white tension (L. Thompson 1985: 132-37). On 9 March 1916, a thousand people gathered at Vanaardtspos for the unveiling of a monument to the rebels. Good wishes were sent by the founder of the Afrikaner National Party, General J.B.M. Hertzog, and the main speaker was Dr D.F. Malan, who would lead the National Party to victory in 1948. Since historians have exposed the factual inaccuracies of the myth it has undergone a certain transformation in the Afrikaner identity. But, in any case, it was not of the same order as the myth of the Great Trek.

The Political Myth of the Great Trek
The 'Great Trek' of Boers from the Cape Colony to the Orange Free State and Transvaal (1835–40) became foundational for the South African nationalist myth of origins. The myth claims that the Bible served as the source of Boer identity, and that as they trekked, the Boers considered themselves to be the chosen people, rescued from Egypt (British oppression), on their way to the promised land. The

indigenous black people were the 'Canaanites' who served foreign gods, whom 'Israel' should not marry (see A. Du Toit 1984: 55). President M.W. Pretorius is reported to have addressed a large gathering in 1871 after the following fashion:

> His Excellency then addressed himself to the original Voortrekkers, calling them Fathers of Israel, and depicting and likening them to the chosen of the Lord, who even as the Israelites had trekked from Egypt to escape Pharaoh's yoke, had themselves withdrawn from the yoke of the detestable English Government to found their own government and administration (see A. Du Toit 1984: 64-65).

However, as Du Toit (1984) shows, a critical study of the source material presents a different picture. There is little to suggest that the emigrants considered themselves in that light, and much to reinforce the interpretation that their self-perception had an altogether different provenance. Some of the emigrants used biblical imagery, for example, describing Natal as a 'land overflowing with milk and honey', and their trek as a 'wandering in the desert', but that is hardly sufficient to prove that they considered themselves to enjoy the divine mandate corresponding to the Israelite conquest of Canaan. Indeed, a year before the trek, the Cape Synod of the Dutch Reformed Church criticized the venture in terms of 'those who have left their hearths and altars, without a Moses or Aaron, to trek into the wilderness to seek out a land of Canaan for themselves without promises or guidance' (quoted in A. Du Toit 1984: 69). Du Toit has shown that before the 1850s the Boers made no claim to be a chosen people (1983):

> We must conclude…that despite the claims about the abundance of evidence in support of the contention that the trekkers identified themselves with Israel and the Chosen People of the Lord…[there is not] a single convincing and clear statement of these ideas from a primary source in the period before the 1870s (A. Du Toit 1984: 70, 73).

Nevertheless, by 1880 several Transvaal clergy were asserting that the emigrants ('trekkers') did consider themselves to be a chosen people (A. Du Toit 1983: 939-47).

In fact, the emigrants expressed their motivation for escaping in terms of the changed conditions brought about by the British freeing of slaves, which exacerbated a labour shortage, the more efficient collection of rents, the land shortage and frequent raids from the Xhosa rather than of the biblical Exodus–settlement narrative (see Lester 1996: 64). Their leader, Piet Retief, summed up the reasons for the Boer emigration of 1838, talking of 'the severe losses which we have been forced to sustain by the emancipation of slaves', and so on (see also the two reasons given by Retief's niece:[3] the continual depredations by the 'Kafirs' and the failure of the government to honour its promises, in L. Thompson 1985: 149).

Afrikaner nationalist historians from the 1870s onwards, however, reinterpreted the trek in biblical terms, as Afrikaners faced the pressures of British imperialism, which culminated in the Anglo-Boer War of 1899–1902, and the conditions of the 1930s. The fabricated nationalist history read as follows. After 20 years of British oppression, the Boers set out from the Cape Colony and sought 'shelter in the unknown wilderness of the North'. It was a 'pilgrimage of martyrdom' of 'our people', who were pursued by the British army (after the fashion of Pharaoh), and everywhere they were beset by the unbelieving black 'Canaanites'. But because God's people acted according to his will, he delivered them out of the hands of their enemies and gave them freedom in the promised land (Moodie 1975: 5; Reitz 1900: 92-93). Savage barbarians descended on the vanguard and murdered men, women and children. The survivors, trusting in God, drove them off (du Plessis n.d.: 94, in Moodie 1975: 6). The emigrants then turned east and sent Piet Retief and others to purchase land from the Zulu chief, Dingane. Later, the Zulus treacherously murdered Retief and the deputation and routed the other emigrants: 'The earth swarmed with thousands of enemies. No human help was possible and even tiny children cried to the Lord and the voice of the people came up to God' (du Plessis n.d.: 104, in Moodie 1975: 6; see also the heroic version of Preller 1909: 152-53, in Moodie 1975: 6). Those who survived sent for reinforcements from their brothers in the Colony and Free State:

> Andreis Pretorius arrived with his brave band to unite with them and punish the enemy and subjugate him. There followed the memorable battle of Blood River on December 16, 1838, where the solemn oath was sworn to celebrate that day each year to the glory of the Lord if He would grant

3.   Anna Steenkamp wrote of the emancipation of the slaves: 'It is not so much their freedom that drove us to such lengths, as their being placed on a equal footing with Christians, contrary to the laws of God and the natural distinction of race and religion, so that it was intolerable for any decent Christian to bow down beneath such a yoke; wherefore we rather withdrew in order thus to preserve our doctrines in purity' (in L. Thompson 1995: 88).

them victory. And God gave them victory over thousands of enemies (du
Plessis n.d.: 94, in Moodie 1975: 6-7).

The Boers then settled down peacefully in Natal and established a
republic: 'The territory had been purchased with our money and bap-
tized with our blood' (Reitz 1900: 13, in Moodie 1975: 7).

While the sense of suffering in the Anglo-Boer War was the genera-
tive stimulus to an emerging Afrikaner nationalism, by the 1920s it
was being traced back to the epic of the Great Trek, due to the
influence of J.D. du Toit (Totius), Langenhoven, D.F. Malherbe and
others. Indeed the foundation of the Voortrekker Monument was not
laid until December 1938, and it was not officially opened until 1949.
On 16 December (*Geloftedag*, the Day of the Covenant) each year
until recently, Afrikaners gathered in cities, towns and villages to
renew their covenant with God, and, after speeches from clergy, academics and politicians, sang psalms, notably Psalms 38, 46, 118, 130
and 146, and civil-religious hymns (especially 'Die Stem van Suid-
Afrika', later the national anthem). By 1938 most Afrikaners believed
that they belonged to an elect people, and that sooner rather than later
God would give them another republic (Moodie 1975: 21).

The Centenary of the Great Trek
Henning Klopper, one of the founders of the Broederbond, prepared a
mass centenary re-enactment of the Great Trek and the Blood River
vow (for details see Moodie 1975: 175-87). On 8 August 1938, at the
foot of van Riebeeck's statue in Cape Town, he addressed the large
crowd gathered to see off the first two wagons. His speech alluded to
'the covenant vow of Sarel Cilliers', allegedly made by the *voortrekkers*, and ended his speech by 'dedicating these wagons to our
People and our God' (Moodie 1975: 179).

The re-enactment created spontaneous paraliturgies and evoked a
vocabulary replete with biblical resonances. An old man recited the
Canticle of Simeon (the *Nunc Dimittis* of Lk. 2.29-32), the 'Golgotha
of Dingane' was commemorated and an altar built. 'The national grain
of wheat had first to die before it could bear fruit,' Klopper insisted at
Vegkop. Dr J.F.J. van Rensburg sketched the *Via Dolorosa* of the
voortrekkers and pointed to the guidepost of their faith: 'Even death
could not check them, and rightly so, because without graves there is
no resurrection.' At the graveside of Sarel Cilliers, Klopper said that
Cilliers erected the beacon of the first covenant between God and the

People, and that the covenant altar was sealed at Blood River. God had kept his part of the covenant, but Afrikanerdom had failed to keep its part. His message was,

> Return to the God who will honour us…The continued existence of our People is a miracle. Our People is like the thornbush at Horeb—it burns and burns but is never consumed. Our People were frequently in deep grief and divided, but always became united again (Klopper, quoted in Moodie 1975: 181).

This 'oxwagon unity' constituted a potent political force during the next decade and advanced the goal of republicanism. The popular media, for example, Preller's hagiographic biography of Piet Retief and his script for the 1916 film *Die Voortrekkers*, played a vital role through disseminating a shared vision of Afrikaner identity and nationalism (see Lester 1996: ch. 3). The growing number of hagiographical biographies and histories percolated into the schools, largely due to Theal's multivolume *History*, which was reprinted several times after his death in 1919, wherein we read that the *voortrekkers* 'came to regard themselves as God's peculiar people', a view which reached its highest point of development with those who grew up in the wandering (in L. Thompson 1985: 182).

The Political Myth of the Vow
On 16 December every year up to recent times, when the ceremony recalls the suffering of the conquest rather than the victory over the Zulu King Dingane, South Africans commemorated the events of 16 December 1838 when 468 Afrikaners, with their Coloured and African servants and about 60 African allies, repulsed repeated attacks by some 10,000 Zulu warriors. The Zulus retreated with some 3000 dead, while not a single emigrant was killed. The Boers named it the Battle of Blood River, from the staining of the adjacent stream with Zulu blood. The name of the celebration has changed from Dingane's Day to the Day of the Covenant (from 1952) to the Day of the Vow (from 1980). The occasion has been used by prominent politicians to further their brand of Afrikaner nationalism. Until recently, it was taboo to question the origin and tradition of the celebration.

According to the reports of the leader, Andreis Pretorius, and his amanuensis, Bantjes, the Victory Commando was inspired by profound religious fervour. The crucial religious meeting occurred on Sunday, 9 December. Bantjes writes that Pretorius told the men who would conduct the services in the different tents to suggest that all should pray to God for his help. He wanted to make a vow that 'should the Lord give us the victory, we would raise a house to the memory of his Great Name, wherever it shall please Him'. He invited them to invoke the assistance of God to enable them to fulfil the vow, and to note the day of the victory in a book and make it known and celebrated to the honour of God, 'even to our latest posterity'. Sarel Cilliers, who was a church elder, conducted the service in Pretorius's tent with the singing of Ps. 38.12-16, a prayer, a sermon on Judg. 6.1-24, followed by prayer in which the vow was made. Psalm 38.12, 21 was sung, and the service ended with the singing of Ps. 134. After his description of the battle Bantje wrote, 'Prayers and thanksgiving were offered to God, and after divine service...the chief commandant again sent a strong party to pursue the Zulus' (in L. Thompson 1985: 152-53).

Subsequently the principal encampment was named Pietermaritz-burg, in honour of Piet Retief and Gert Maritz, and made the capital of the Republic of Natal.

There are reasons to question the historicity of the vow. The early Afrikaner historians did not mention it, and, while Pretorius erected a modest barn-like church in 1841, there is no surviving record that it was considered to be in fulfilment of the vow. It ceased to be used for services in 1861, after which it was used for a variety of commercial purposes until in 1908 it was converted into the Voortrekkers' Museum. Moreover, the annual celebration of the battle was widely ignored for a quarter of a century.

However, in 1864, P. Huet and F. Lion Cachet, two Dutch Reformed clergy, persuaded the general assembly of the Dutch Reformed Church in Natal that 16 December should be celebrated religiously as a day of thanks, but when in 1867 Cachet organized a celebration at the Blood River *laager*, there was no special focus on the vow. Nevertheless, H.J. Hofstede published the first history of the Orange Free State in 1876, which included a deathbed journal of Sarel Cilliers (1871), which Hofstede and others put together. It focused on the piety of Pretorius and on Cilliers's own role. Seeing the superiority of the Zulu numbers, he and Pretorius decided that, as with the Jews of the Old Testament, 'we, too, were bound to make a promise to the Lord, that if He gave us the victory over our enemy, we would consecrate that day, and keep it holy as a Sabbath in each year'.

Cilliers's version differs from that of Bantjes, in that he made the vow before all the congregation in the open, rather than, as in Bantjes's version, in Pretorius's tent. Secondly, there is no mention of building a memorial church (see L. Thompson 1985: 167). Moreover, there was no mention of a vow when in 1865 the Transvaal government proclaimed 16 December to be a public holiday.

However, when Afrikaners rebelled in 1880, after Theophilus Shepstone proclaimed the Transvaal to be a British colony in 1877, they 'renewed' the covenant at Paardekraal by piling a cairn of stones, symbolizing past deliverance from black domination and future striving for independence from the British. Thereafter, in 1881 and every fifth year, the government organized patriotic festivals on Dingane's Day. There was no mention of the original vow in the 1881 celebration, but Cilliers's version of events was printed in the programme in the celebration of 1891. A monument was erected over the historic heap of stones and President Kruger spoke about the Battle of Blood River.

In December 1895, Transvaal clergy and officials organized a ceremony near Weenen in Natal. They collected the bones of Retief and the other victims of the 1838 massacre and buried them in a casket in the foundation of what was to be a memorial monument. Moreover, towards the end of the century there was a mushrooming of publications dealing with the trek, and much of it emphasized the religious intensity of the participants. Theal observed that the commando resembled an itinerant prayer meeting rather than a modern army (L. Thompson 1985: 172-77). Some drew attention to the vow, but others ignored it completely.[4]

In the last quarter of the nineteenth century, then, clergy, politicians and intellectuals in the Transvaal and Orange Free State resurrected, embellished, codified and celebrated a version of the events of 16 December 1838, with a view to promoting pride in Afrikaner identity in the face of British aggression. However, with the waning of British imperialism in this century, their successors modified the interpretation of the alleged events and presented them as supporting Afrikaner identity in the face of the threat posed by black African nationalism. This is a striking example of the classical political myth: partial

---

4.   Leonard Thompson suggests that Cilliers's vow was merely one of loyalty to the leadership, for which there were precedents in Boer society (1985: 162-63).

concordance with the historical reality; delayed codification and rapid development; fervent deployment for political purposes; and ability to be changed to suit circumstances. Its major difference from the Myth of Slagtersnek is its religious overtones and the degree to which it has been at the centre of Afrikaner identity.

The Political Myth of Racial Superiority
The political mythology of Afrikaner nationalism rested upon the assumption that humanity was divided according to race, however inadequately defined, and that races were divinely ordained to preserve their distinctiveness. Separation (*apartheid*), therefore, was a necessary condition for living. In line with the attitudes of European colonizers, from the beginning of the Boer settlement in 1652 we have stereotypical descriptions of the blacks as an idolatrous, licentious, thieving, lying, lazy, dirty, cannibalistic and beast-like people.[5] A commission of the British colonial government of Natal in 1852 reveals the widespread Afrikaner estimation of the black man as one who had to be flogged to get him to work, and who did not know even his own true interests. These Afrikaners spoke in secular, pragmatic terms rather than in theological, philosophical or historical ones (L. Thompson 1985: 83-84).

The theory of the Great Chain of Being, according to which humans could be placed in strict hierarchy, beginning with the most perfect (European) and reaching to the orang-outang, could not be applied simply to the black African, since their skulls were no different from those of Europeans. But there was no doubt that human races were distinct populations, each with specific and enduring cultural as well as physical characteristics, and that each was at a given place on a scale of civilization between 'civilized men' (that is, Europeans, preferably Englishmen) and 'savages' (L. Thompson 1985: 90-93). Depending on how much 'white blood' they had managed to accumulate in north Africa, occasional individuals might be capable of rising to the high standard of European culture. Moreover, it was considered that the intelligence of a black child stopped developing at puberty.

Nearly all white South Africans in the first half of the twentieth century subscribed to the view that they belonged to a race which was

---

5.   In the *Oxford English Dictionary* (1983) the term 'Hottentot' is applied to 'a person of inferior culture'.

superior to all other races in Africa, and that their superiority was reflected in their religion, technology, politics and arts, and in their power and wealth. 'Scientific' underpinning of these racist attitudes relied upon views which derived from craniology, eugenics and hereditarian theories of intelligence quotient, all of which have been shown to be products of inadequate methodology, false logic and, in one case at least, of concoction (Gould 1981). Nevertheless, this racial superiority validated the conquest of the native population and the theft of their land in a way analogous to the white colonialist imperialism of the rest of Africa, Asia and the Caribbean, and the whites' exploitation of Afro-Americans. They also justified white political supremacy and exploitation of 'coloured' labour.

The Biblical-Theological Core of Afrikaner Nationalism

Woven into the fabric of South African society are distinctive threads which are so intertwined as virtually to lose their separate identity. One such thread is the theological factors which have influenced developments within the society. The evidence for the influence of theological and biblical factors is abundant. Sir John Robinson, Prime Minister of Natal, wrote of 'those Predikants whose influence over the minds and hearts of their flocks has contributed so greatly to present events' (in L. Thompson 1985: 172). Several political leaders, for example, Paul Kruger, President of the South African Republic from 1881 to 1902, leaned heavily on Calvin's teaching on God's revelation to, and covenant with the people (*Institutes* III, 24:8), which applied not only in the Old Testament but in Kruger's own time.

According to Kruger, God chose his *Volk* in the Cape Colony and brought them out into the wilderness, and, having chastened them, made a covenant with them, and 'the enemies were defeated and the trekkers inhabited the land which God had given them in this rightful manner'. God had visited his *Volk* with British imperialism because they had not fulfilled their covenantal obligations in celebrating the renewal of the covenant for over 30 years. At Paardekraal in 1880, he recognized that the people of the Transvaal Republic were 'a People of God in the external calling', and 'God's People' (du Plessis n.d.: 103, 89, in Moodie 1975: 26-27). However, the choice of the *Volk* demanded total loyalty and fidelity. The miraculous outcome of the war of 1881 was more than final proof of God's election of the

Transvaal people. His theology reflected the cycle of transgression, retribution and reconciliation mirrored in his favourite psalm, Ps. 89.31-34.

For Kruger, black Africans were not among God's people, and were destined to be kept in perpetual subjugation to their white masters. The British onslaught on the republics was an attack of the devil against the Church of the Lord. Although the British might have thousands in the field and the Boers only hundreds, the Boers had Jesus Christ, the supreme commander of heaven and earth. As early as 1900, Kruger related the sufferings of his people to Christ's passion, and spoke of the necessity of undergoing Gethsemane and Golgotha before the daybreak of their liberation (Moodie 1975: 32-36). Kruger urged General Smuts to read the book of Joel, wherein surely the devastation (Joel 1.6-10) and restoration (Joel 1.15-2.1; 3.1-21) motif would comfort him.

The Christian Nationalism of Abraham Kuyper

Running parallel with other elements within emerging Afrikaner nationalism was the ideal of establishing a Christian National state based on the Christian nationalism of Calvin, which was at the heart of the Broederbond ideology. This stressed that all authority came from God, and all government was to be guided by Calvinist Christianity as interpreted and updated by the inspirational Dutch Reformed theologian Abraham Kuyper (1837–1920), who popularized the term 'Christian-National'. Kuyper believed that Calvinists formed the 'core of the nation', whose mission was to bring the whole of life under the canopy of God. In South Africa, his theological position was determinative within the Nederduitse Gereformeerde Kerk, and the Gereformeerde Kerk. Despite the defeat of the Boers, Kuyper was confident that they would ultimately triumph, provided they never abandoned the Reformed faith of their fathers. In his view, God created a diversity of races, colours and cultures which should be acknowledged as givens.

Bloomberg traces the core ideas of Afrikaner Nationalists back to Kuyper's influence: the national principle must always be under the guidance of the Christian principle; Calvinism is 'totalist' or 'universal', with all human affairs falling within its domain; and Calvinism is a 'this-worldly' and 'open' creed which could align itself with nationalism (Bloomberg 1990: 10). The destiny of the Afrikaners was to be custodians of a Christian nation, with the Bible as the primary source for all political life. However, Kuyperian theology had to struggle with the more secular nationalism in the Broederbond, with the return in the 1930s from Germany of such academics as H.F. Verwoerd (later Prime Minister) and Dr Nicholaas Diederichs (who was to become Minister of Finance and then President of the Republic of South Africa), who brought with them a sense of the people bound together by a common culture and history. Although this tendency gave precedence to the nation in terms of language, culture and national experience, it found common cause with the more religious sentiment among the Afrikaners who were a *Volk* of God's choosing. Man is called to belong to a *national* community: 'Only in the nation as the most total, most inclusive human community can man realize himself to the full' (Diederichs, in Moodie 1975: 156-58), and so Protestant-Christian and Cultural-National were to be the principles of the nation. Diederichs was opposed to any doctrine of human equality. The very diversity of nations was determined by God, and, more importantly, each nation was created by God to execute his will (in Moodie 1975: 159). For Diederichs, then, service to the nation was service to God, a view which took him close to deifying the nation.

Boer Nationalism and the Bible
The place of the Bible in the Afrikaner psyche is seminal (see e.g. Loubser 1987), and biblical language infused political discourse. C.J. Langenhoven spoke of the trekker martyrs as 'an Afrikaner nation, worthy to bear the crown won upon the Way of the Cross by the fathers who died'. This *Via Dolorosa* of South Africa did not 'run dead' on 'Dingane's Golgotha' but passed over and beyond it into God's future, which held a republican resurrection (in Moodie 1975: 14). But the period 1920–50 saw the rapid urbanization of the Afrikaans' section of South Africa. This urbanization was reflected in several social changes, including the great increase in the number of urban Dutch Reformed congregations. The readers of the Bible in this period were Afrikaners who, from having been independent farmers and land owners with a culture of their own, suddenly became urban day labourers in a foreign culture, and at the bottom of the social ladder (see details in Deist 1994: 14-15). The Afrikaans Churches were not ready for these changes. Moreover, the influx of black people into the cities, competing for unskilled, low-cost jobs exacerbated the

problem for the Afrikaans-speaking people, who began to insist that the principle of *geen gelykstelling* (no equalization) between blacks and whites be applied (see Deist 1986).

The Boer Exodus

Although there is no evidence that the emigrants in the Great Trek considered themselves to be the chosen people on the way to the promised land, the biblical paradigm was employed widely in the service of the South African nationalist myth of origins, as the spontaneous naive identification with early Israel shows (see Deist 1994):

Israel	*Afrikaners*
Went from Palestine to Egypt	Went from Europe to Africa
Suffered under foreign rulers	Suffered under British rule
Escaped from Egypt to Canaan	Escaped from the Cape Colony to the north
Considered the nations as numerous and strong	Considered black people as numerous and strong
Miraculously received a new land	Miraculously received a new land
Made a covenant with God	Made a covenant with God
Erected memorial stones	Erected the Cilliers memorial church
Fathers recounted their history to posterity.	Fathers recounted their history to posterity.

The theologically informed Afrikaans intelligentsia in the 1930s, who bemoaned the lack of religious feeling in, and the increasing secularization of the urban 'poor white' Afrikaners, found a spiritual home in Kuyper's Free University of Amsterdam, and developed their own 'Boer Calvinism', which was based on the plain sense of the Bible (Deist 1994: 18-19). It invoked a naive-realist reading of Deuteronomy and played a significant role in the establishment of the policy of *apartheid*. Sermons and official publications of the Dutch Reformed Church kept reminding their Bible readers of the *kairos*, the moment when, like Moses, they were on the verge of a new creation, a white South Africa for their children. But the Afrikaners saw their situation as vulnerable, corresponding to that of the Israelites (see Stuhlman 1990: 626). Like Moses, the Church leadership saw that survival lay in strictly keeping to God's commandments, in particular Deuteronomy's divinely instituted division of nations (see Deut. 4.37-38; 7.7-8; 10.14-15). If God had divided the nations, no one had the right to unite them. Deuteronomy promoted the unity of the Afrikaners, on the one hand, and their separation from the black peoples, on the other. J.D. du Toit (Totius) wrote concerning Deut. 22.9-11:

Firstly, what God united, no one may divide. This is the basis of our plea for unity among Afrikaners…Secondly, we may not unite what God has divided. The council of God is realized in pluriformity…Consequently we do not want any equalization or bastardization (in Deist 1994: 23).

P.J. Loots wrote,

From this reformed principle of separate, independent groups within the kingdom (of God) flows our policy of *apartheid* in church and state. This is a universal principle which was, according to Scripture and Nature, instituted by the great Creator and which the Afrikaner people and the Church of the Boers have to defend to the utmost, especially against modern liberalism's policy of equalization (in Deist 1994: 23).

Clearly, scriptural pluriformity is preferable to humanly fabricated equality. The separation of peoples is based on Scripture, equality of the races is a human construct. Deuteronomy's prohibition of mixing with the indigenous people (7.3-4—see Cohen 1983; Dion 1985; O'Connell 1992) provided the scriptural basis for the South African immorality act prohibiting mixed marriages, so that Afrikaners would be kept pure. Just as the Israelites were a minority, who, through the help of God, acquired possession of the land, so too the South African Calvinists regarded their possession of the land as divinely ordained. Like the authors of Deuteronomy, the South African Calvinists were insensitive to the fact that the land had already been inhabited. The occupation of the land was to be celebrated, rather than questioned along ordinary historical lines.

At the Blood River centennial celebrations on 16 December 1938, Dr Malan developed the theme of the *Second Great Trek*: as the Afrikaners prevailed over the blacks at Blood River in 1838, now they were on a second trek, to the cities, where the new battlefield was the labour market:

Here at Blood River you stand on holy ground. Here was made the great decision about the future of South Africa, about Christian civilization in our land, and about the continued existence and responsible power of the White race…You stand here upon the boundary of two centuries. Behind you, you rest your eyes upon the year 1838…Before you, upon the yet untrodden Path of South Africa, lies the year 2038…Behind you lie the traces of the Voortrekker wagons…Your Blood River lies in the city…[The new trek] is not away from the centres of civilization…but a trek back—back from the country to the city…Today Black and White jostle together in the same labour market…Their [i.e. the *voortrekkers'*] freedom was…above all, the freedom to preserve themselves as a White

race. As you could never otherwise have realized, you realize today their
task to make South Africa a White man's land is ten times more your task
(in Moodie 1975: 198-200).

Theological and biblical factors, then, played a significant part in
underpinning Afrikaner nationalist ideology, as it developed and
adapted itself to changing circumstances. Of course the dominant
theological-biblical support did not go unchallenged within the Dutch
Reformed Churches. Indeed, the policy of *apartheid* was criticized
strongly, and later branded a heresy by theologians and *predikants*
operating from within different theological and biblical perspectives.

Myth, History, Science and Morality

At the heart of the Afrikaner history of South Africa is the unquestioned assurance of the superiority of *white civilization*. General
Hertzog insisted that in South Africa, '"European" is synonymous
with civilization; and the extinction of the White man must inevitably
be the extinction of civilization' (in Moodie 1975: 261). Compared
with the mature white men, the black man is as an eight-year-old, a
child in religion and moral conviction, without art or science, and
with only the most elementary knowledge. However, South Africa was
pursuing its policy of racial *apartheid* when the majority of the rest of
the world was moving in the opposite direction, and by the 1980s it
was a unique phenomenon, 'a pigmentocratic industrialized state'
(L. Thompson 1985: 191).

In order to underpin the *apartheid* system in a world where racial
mixing was becoming the norm, it was necessary to reiterate its ideological base, fabricate its history, and reinterpret its mythology. The
inherent distinction between races was emphasized, inevitably with the
self-confident whites assumed to be millennia in advance of the blacks,
as a consequence of which separation was an imperative. With respect
to origins, the blacks had no more claims to the land than the whites,
since they had come down from the north at around the same time as
the whites had landed in the south, and, in any case, their lives were
semi-nomadic (see the government-sponsored information newsletter
in L. Thompson 1985: 199-200). In addition, recourse was had to the
'historical' components of the nationalist mythology (Slagtersnek, the
Great Trek, the Vow, etc.), and biblical and theological elements also
were woven into the fabric of the Afrikaner *apologia*.

Challenging the Core Myths

However, after the Second World War, historians, anthropologists and theologians began to subject every facet of the nationalist fabrication of South African history to investigation, and many began to reject it. This led to the demolition of the Slagtersnek myth, the dilution of the strength of the Covenant myth and the breakdown of the myth of the vacant land.

Richard Elphick showed that all the people whom the Dutch had encountered in the western Cape were members of the same basic genetic population, which had lived in the region for millennia (1977). The application of carbon-14 dating to the archaeological finds, revealing 'early Iron Age' pottery (in Transvaal, c. 300 AD), exploded the myth of the empty land. The ancestors of the Bantu-speaking people of South Africa had lived in the region for at least 1400 years before the Dutch arrived. Human communities had hunted, fished and collected edible plants for many thousands of years. By 1000 AD there were farmers in Natal, the Cape Province, the Transvaal, Swaziland, eastern Botswana and the north-eastern Orange Free State.[6]

The political myth of Slagtersnek, which had developed as an Anglophobic legend, began to wane when the English- and Afrikaans-speaking peoples had common cause against the threat posed by the majority black population. From the mid-1950s, it virtually disappeared from the South African school textbooks, and by the 1980s historical investigation continued to undermine it. It was no great loss, since its Anglophobic origins were counterproductive, and, since it was a secular myth, the Afrikaner Churches never promoted it as much as other elements of nationalist mythology.

The Battle of Blood River and the Covenant (1838) continued to be the prime symbol of Afrikaner Christian identity. But in March 1979 the University of South Africa convened a conference whose main speaker, Professor Floris van Jaarsveld, it was known beforehand, would treat the Covenant in secular terms and question some of its elements. As soon as he went to the podium a gang of men tarred and feathered him. Eugene Terreblanche seized the microphone and protested: 'On what grounds can Professor van Jaarsveld question

---

6. See L. Thompson 1995: ch. 1, and the summary of the evidence and sources in Marks 1980.

Sarel Cilliers' vow that the Day of the Covenant would always remain a day of reverence?' (*Sunday Times*, 8 April 1979, in L. Thompson 1985: 280). Van Jaarsveld's paper argued that there was no way of knowing the exact wording of the Vow, that it was not observed before 1864, and that Afrikaners were not the only people to claim that God was on their side.

Theological Rethinking

Meanwhile, there was growing discontent concerning *apartheid* within the Christian Churches, both at home and abroad. South Africa was one of the most 'Christian' countries in the world, with some 83.9 per cent of its inhabitants and 93.8 per cent of its whites being members of a Christian Church, and some 35 of its 40 government ministers belonging to one of the three Dutch Reformed Churches. Some 49 per cent of the white population was affiliated to these Churches (40.1 per cent to the Nederduitse Gereformeerde Kerk [NGK], 6 per cent to the Nederduitse Hervormde Kerk [NHK], and 2.9 per cent to the Gereformeerde Kerk van Suid Afrika [GKSA]), with Anglicans (10.76 per cent of whites), Methodists (9.6 per cent), Roman Catholics (8.2 per cent), Presbyterians (3.1 per cent), etc. constituting the remaining 45 per cent of white Christians—some 3 per cent of whites were Jews. But Christianity was also the major religion of the oppressed, with 69 per cent of the 18 million black Africans, and some 91 per cent of coloureds belonging to a Christian Church (of which 28.5 per cent belonged to the Nederduitse Gereformeerde Sending Kerk [NGSK], the Dutch Reformed Mission Church for Coloureds established in 1881 for coloured members of the NGK [see Goguel and Buis n.d.: 6-8 for figures for 1970 and 1977]). The General Synod of the NGK, meeting every four years, had supported the policy of separate development. The more conservative Transvaal NHK was strongly supportive also, and the growing dissent came from within the GKSA, the smallest of the three (De Gruchy 1979, 1991; De Gruchy and Villa-Vicencio 1983;[7] Moodie 1975; Hope and Young 1981).

---

7.   This is a collection of essays by theologians of different denominations and cultural backgrounds (Boesak, Tutu, *et al*.), compiled with the intention of enabling South Africans to interrogate themselves in the light of the decision of the World Alliance of Churches to declare *apartheid* a heresy.

As early as 1948 most of the other Christian Churches in South Africa had issued separate statements condemning the proposed *apartheid* legislation. The Rosettenville Conference of 1949, the first ecumenical gathering since the National Party had come to power, with, however, only one fraternal delegate of the NGK, affirmed the unity of all God's people and declared that, 'The real need of South Africa is not *"Apartheid"* but *"Eendrag"* [unity through teamwork]' (De Gruchy 1979: 54-56). The meeting convened by the Federal Missionary Council of the NGK in Pretoria in November 1953, which invited Church leaders from other denominations, acknowledged a threefold division among the representatives that was reflected also in the wider society: those who believed in the biblical righteousness of racial separation; those who did not share that view but practised some form for pragmatic reasons; and those who were convinced that separation in the Church was wrong and stood condemned according to Scripture (De Gruchy 1979: 57-58).

There was some criticism of *apartheid* within the NGK throughout the 1950s, during which the legislation was implemented at full speed. Two leading theologians, Professors Ben Marais and B.B. Keet undermined the theological and biblical base of *apartheid*. In his reflections of the impact of *apartheid* in Sophiatown, the Anglican missionary, Father Trevor Huddleston, charged that the acts and motives of *apartheid* were fundamentally evil and un-Christian. *Apartheid* was inspired by 'The desire to dominate in order to preserve a position of racial superiority, and in the process of domination to destroy personal relationships, the foundation of love itself. That is anti-Christ' (Huddleston 1956: 182).

The Sharpeville massacre of 21 March 1960 precipitated a major crisis for *apartheid*, both at home and abroad, and revealed the cleavage between the NGK and the other Christian Churches, with a call by the controversial Anglican Archbishop of Cape Town, Joost de Blank, to expel the NGK from the WCC. Instead the WCC agreed to help arrange a consultation on Christian race relations and social problems in South Africa.

The Cottesloe Consultation (1960) consisted of ten delegates from each of the South African member Churches of the WCC, including eighteen black participants, and five representatives of the WCC. This representative body issued a concluding statement rejecting all unjust discrimination, proclaiming the common dignity of all people, the

equal rights of all racial groups in South Africa and the appropriateness of common worship of all believers. While the 'English-speaking'
Churches—a loose term to describe the autonomous Anglican,
Presbyterian, Methodist and Congregational Churches—might have
wished the resolutions to go further, the NHK delegates rejected them.
The real question, however, was how the NGK synods would react.
After strong criticism from conservative groups within the Church,
the Cape and Transvaal Synods rejected the resolutions and the NGK
withdrew from the WCC.

On the international front, the Christian Church had been coming to
terms with the challenge which racism posed for the Christian faith.
The WCC and member Churches issued a steady stream of ecumenical
resolutions, statements and actions on racism from as early as 1937
(see the WCC Programme to Combat Racism 1986 publication [WCC
1986]). The Fourth Assembly of the WCC (Uppsala, 1968) condemned racism, especially the *white racism* of persons of European
ancestry, which entitles all white peoples to a position of dominance
and privilege while professing the innate inferiority of all darker
peoples, especially those of African ancestry, which justifies their subordination and exploitation (in WCC 1986: 35). The Fifth Assembly
of the WCC (Nairobi 1975) condemned racism as

> A sin against God and against fellow human beings. It is contrary to the
> justice and the love of God revealed in Jesus Christ. It destroys the human
> dignity of both the racist and the victim. When practised by Christians it
> denies the very faith we profess and undoes the credibility of the Church
> in its witness to Jesus Christ. Therefore, we condemn racism in all its
> forms both inside and outside the Church (WCC 1986: 53).

The Assembly went on to confess the Church's conscious and unconscious complicity in racism, and its failure to eradicate it even from
its own house.

In 1976 the Central Committee of the WCC reiterated the WCC's
opposition to *apartheid* and racism as being 'contrary to the Gospel
and incompatible with the nature of the Church of Christ and violating
basic human rights', and condemned the deceptive manoeuvre of the
South African government to perpetuate and consolidate *apartheid* by
the creation of 'independent' Transkei. It called on member Churches
to expose the evil of the Bantustan policy (in WCC 1986: 59). In the
following year, the Central Committee denounced as blasphemous the
grave and blatant injustices being perpetrated in the name of

'Christian civilization' by governments and powerful oppressors in southern Africa (in WCC 1986: 64). The 1980 International Consultation of 'The Churches' Response to Racism in the 1980s' designated racism as a sin which must be openly fought against by all those on Christ's side, and again, the Church regretted and repented for coming to this realization so late (in WCC 1986: 74).

The Sixth Assembly of the WCC (Vancouver, 1983) dealt *inter alia* with the institutionalized racism in South Africa. It reiterated the WCC's opposition to *apartheid* and called on all Christians to oppose it:

> *Apartheid* raises barriers and denies the fullness of life in Christ. Christians and the Churches are called to obedience to Jesus Christ the life of the world, and to maintain the integrity of the Church, to oppose *apartheid* in all its forms, to support those who struggle against this sinful system of injustice, and to denounce any theological justification of *apartheid* as a heretical perversion of the Gospel (par. 2 of the Preamble to the Statement on Southern Africa, in WCC 1986: 85).

It acknowledged that against a background of state repression the Church could not avoid confrontation with the government (par. 5 in WCC 1986: 85). In its Recommendations, the WCC Assembly '(a) *reiterates* its conviction that *apartheid* stands condemned by the Gospel of Jesus Christ the life of the world, and that any theology which supports or condones it is heretical' (in WCC 1986: 87), and calls for the dismantlement of *apartheid* (Resolution [h], in WCC 1986: 88).

Meanwhile, at home, the NGK had issued two synodical documents, *Human Relations in South Africa* (1966) and *Human Relations and the South African Scene in the Light of Scripture* (1974). Without offering any justification for the claim, the latter document, like all NGK statements, assumed the authority of the Bible as containing normative principles for the guidance of all areas of life. The text, at one and the same time, emphasized that humankind was essentially one and fundamentally equal and that ethnic diversity in its very origin was in conformity with the will of God: 'A political system based on the autogenous or separate development of various population groups can be justified from the Bible' (par. 49.6). The NGK then rejected racial injustice and discrimination in principle but affirmed the policy of separate development. In such a hermeneutic, the Bible becomes a kind of oracle book of proof texts, a selective use of which can substantiate a particular political policy—in this case about 50 texts, with particular dependence on the following favourites selected in support of *apartheid*: Gen. 1.28; 11.1-9; Deut. 32.8-9; Acts 2.5-11; 17.26 (Vorster 1983: 96-99). Bax shows how unconvincing these appeals are (1983: 114-32), and how the report passes over or ignores other biblical passages which promote the unity and integrity of God's people (1983: 133-40).

Throughout the 1960s and 1970s individual NGK theologians and *predikants* took bold stands against government policy. Opposition to *apartheid* was coming also from other Reformed sources, especially in Holland, leading to a break in relations in 1978 between the NGK and the Gereformeerde Kerken in that country. Already in 1968 the South African Council of Churches (SACC) had published a statement maintaining that *apartheid* and separate development were contrary to the Christian gospel. One detects around that time, also, the beginnings of a South African black theology, influenced by James Cone's ideas. In its South African context, black theology aimed at conscientizing blacks with a sense of their own black identity and dignity. Looking to the Bible, this theology fixed on the Exodus paradigm, or at least on the first half of it, and the message of Jesus which presents a God on the side of the oppressed. While one notes the caution in the survey of Ukpong (1984), black theology became an important factor in the change of perspectives through the writings of Allan Boesak (1976, 1984), Takatso Mofokeng (1983) and others, and particularly the charismatic leadership of Archbishop Desmond Tutu.

In the 1980s the SACC intensified its opposition to *apartheid* under its general secretary, the then Bishop Tutu; 1982 was a crisis year for the Church. While the NGK had withdrawn from the WCC in 1960, it had kept its membership of the World Alliance of Reformed Churches (WARC), but when that body, in its forthright statement *Racism and South Africa* (Ottawa, 1982), declared *apartheid* to be a heresy and accused the Afrikaner Churches of 'theological heresy', WARC suspended the membership of the NGK and the NHK and elected as its president Allan Boesak, a member of the NGSK. Later in the year Boesak's Church joined the South African Council of Churches.

The NGSK drafted a *status confessionis* in 1982 which declared that *apartheid* was idolatry and its theological justification a heresy, and published it in 1986, challenging the *apartheid* theology of the NGK. However, conservative forces retained control of the NGK at the General Synod of October 1982. But all the while opposition to racial discrimination was mounting from the 'English-speaking' Churches, the Roman Catholic Church and the Lutheran Church, as well as from significant segments within the NGK (see e.g. De Gruchy 1979; Hope and Young 1981; Regehr 1979).

The publication of *The Kairos Document* on 25 September 1985, and its revised second edition one year later, signalled the climax of indigenous theological comment on a political situation that was becoming increasingly uncontrollable. It provided a critique of the prevailing theological models of the Churches ('Church Theology'), and proposed an alternative biblical and theological one which the authors hoped would make a real difference to the future of South Africa. It criticized the 'State Theology' of the *apartheid* state for its misuse of theological concepts and biblical texts for its own purposes (Chapter 2). It charged that Church Theology's guarded and cautious critique of *apartheid* was superficial and counterproductive, since it employed the stock ideas of reconciliation, justice and non-violence without engaging in an in-depth analysis of the signs of the times. It insisted that there could be no peace without justice, and that some conflicts were between a fully armed and violent oppressor and a defenceless oppressed:

> Nowhere in the Bible or in Christian tradition has it ever been suggested that we ought to try to reconcile good and evil, God and the devil. We are supposed to do away with evil, injustice, oppression and sin—not come to terms with it. We are supposed to oppose, confront and reject the devil and not try to sup with the devil (*The Kairos Document* 3.1).

To require blacks to engage in reconciliation without justice was to demand that they be accomplices in their own oppression. The peace the world offered was merely 'a unity that compromises the truth, covers over injustice and oppression and is totally motivated by self-ishness'. It pleaded:

> To be truly biblical our Church leaders must adopt a...biblical theology of direct confrontation with the forces of evil rather than a theology of rec-onciliation with sin and the devil (*The Kairos Document* 3.1).

It compared state oppression, injustice and domination with the vio-lence of the rapist, and acts of common resistance and self-defence with the physical force used by a woman to resist the rapist, accepting the defensive use of force as the lesser of two guilts. It criticized the premise of the Church leadership that the *apartheid* regime was a

legitimate authority, and charged that its neutrality gave tacit support
to the oppressor (3.3). 'Church Theology' should have an adequate
understanding of politics and political strategy, and should extend its
concept of salvation to the here and now (3.4).

The starting point of a Prophetic Theology must be the experience
of oppression and tyranny. While Prophetic Theology of its nature is
always confrontational, it must hold out hope. It must name the sin of
apartheid as 'an offence against God', but also announce the hopeful
good news of future liberation (4.1). The South African crisis was one
of tyranny, with the tyrannical regime being hostile to the common
good (*hostis boni communis*) in principle, and permanently, know-
ingly or unknowingly representing a sinful cause and unjust interests
(4.3). A tyrannical regime, albeit the *de facto* government, had no
moral legitimacy. *Apartheid* represented a regime of tyranny which
was the enemy not only of the people but of God, and as such had to
be removed (4.4). Nevertheless, the message of hope must be sustained, and the oppressors must be made aware of the diabolical evils
of the system and be called to repentance (4.6).

While the majority of the Church was among the oppressed already,
those still on the side of the oppressor must cross over and participate
in the struggle for a just society. Moreover, the Church should not
collaborate with a tyrannical regime, nor do anything that confers
legitimacy on a morally illegitimate administration. It must be prepared to disobey the state in order to obey God. The Church should
challenge, inspire and motivate people with the example of the cross,
rather than be a bastion of caution and moderation (5.5-6).

The *Document* had a powerful impact in the townships. Its method
of doing theology, with ordinary people reflecting on their oppression, had a profound effect not only at home but abroad (see e.g.
McAfee Brown, 1990). In conformity with the dictates of the
Reformed tradition, its appeal to the Scriptures was fundamental but
characteristically selective. For example, in appealing to an historical-
critical reading of Rom. 13.1-7 and the critique of Ezek. 13.10-14, it
avoids any engagement with those traditions in the pentateuchal narratives which mandate the destruction of the indigenous population, and
in the book of Joshua which detail their implementation (Chapter 2).
Instead it finds refuge in a selective reading of the prophetic and
wisdom literature (especially psalms). In its reference to biblical violence it appeals only to that of Israel's enemies (Chapter 3). In dealing

with suffering and oppression in the Old Testament, it confines itself to that inflicted on the Israelites by the Egyptians, the various Canaanite kings and so forth (Chapter 4).

In dealing with the biblical themes of liberation and hope, the authors choose those passages which present oppression as sinful and wicked (for example, the state of servitude of the Israelites in the Exodus legend [Exod. 3.7], and in several verses from the Psalms [Pss. 74.14; 9.4; 10.18; 103.6]) but omit any reference to the divinely mandated conquest of the promised land and the treatment to be meted out to the Canaanites and others. There is appeal to the preaching of Jesus (Lk. 4.18-19) and to his invitation to the rich to repent. It stresses that, despite the presence of evil, the message of Jesus is one of transforming hopeless and evil situations to good, so that God's Kingdom may come. Goodness, justice and love will triumph in the end, when all tears will be wiped away (Rev. 7.14) and the lamb will lie down with the lion (Isa. 11.16). True peace and hope are not only desirable but are guaranteed (4.5). Nevertheless, for all its liberation rhetoric, the biblical hermeneutic of *The Kairos Document* is a form of proof-texting, with an emphasis on those traditions which support the case of the Israelite poor. It does not rise to the challenge of reading the Scriptures with Canaanite eyes.

Conclusion

The Afrikaner nationalist political mythology which had been created at the turn of the century was crumbling. We have seen how Afrikaner nationalism created, sustained and modified political mythologies to further its goals, and how each constituent element of the nationalist myth did not stand up to the test of historical and anthropological investigation. The myth of a vacant land for a landless people was dislodged by the evidence for a black African population in the region since early in the Christian era. The Boers who had taken up arms against the Cape colonial government in 1815 were deviants rather than heroes. The uncertain circumstances of the vow of 1838 made its historical reliability suspect. Moreover, virtually all historians working on the nineteenth century now reject the still commonly held view that the Afrikaners who embarked on the Great Trek considered themselves to be sanctioned to dispossess the indigenous black population, after the fashion of the Israelites whom the biblical accounts present as having been mandated by the divinity to cleanse Canaan of its population.[8] Moreover, the biological basis for racism and crude theories of racial differentiation were discarded, and both imperialism and discrimination based solely on ethnic difference were widely rejected internationally, making the practice of racism virtually unique to South Africa.

In South African society, in which there was a coalition between religion and the state, religion provided a transcendent referent for the exercise of political sovereignty. However, while the prevailing Dutch Reformed theology underpinned *apartheid*, the theological and biblical assault against it also undermined its viability for much longer. In effect, the whole racist paradigm was under terminal strain in many quarters, not least among the whites, including Afrikaners. Thus, all the elements of the nationalist mythology had to face the challenge of new information from archaeology, historical study, scientific discovery and theological and biblical rethinking. Afrikaner nationalism was increasingly less secure, intellectually as well as morally.

When historical and other kinds of investigation invalidate the claims of harmful myths, there is a responsibility to discredit them and to ensure that false fabrications of the past are not employed in a deleterious fashion. Biblical scholars accept such responsibility with some hesitation. Deist, for example, concludes his study:

> Perhaps Deuteronomy *does* contain dangerous ideologies and therefore might very well *be* a dangerous book. But the greater danger lies in its (uncritical) *readers*. In so far as the tragic history of South Africa and the still threatening national disaster have been the result of Biblical interpretation, this tragedy is the consequence not so much of wrong or dangerous exegetical *methods*...but the result of a lack of critical self-awareness on the part of the *exegetes*. The South African experience points to the critical importance of a heavy emphasis on reader oriented hermeneutical approaches and the creation of a critical consciousness of the historicity of any piece of literature and any form of interpretation, and therefore on the ethics of interpretation (1994: 28-29, my italics).

While Deist points up the problem which the biblical text presents to a reader, he is reluctant to concede that the book of Deuteronomy in itself is a dangerous book since it predicates racist, xenophobic and

---

8.   The myth finds popular expression in De Klerk 1975, Villet 1982, and others, and in James Michener's novel *The Covenant* (1980).

militaristic tendencies as deriving from the will of God. He deals with the problem by exonerating the biblical authors and by ascribing to the reader alone any morally dubious predispositions.

Reflecting the black experience, however, Mofokeng goes to the heart of the matter. Black people of South Africa point to three dialectically related realities:

> They show the central position which the Bible occupied in the ongoing process of colonization, national oppression and exploitation. They also confess the incomprehensible paradox of being colonised by a Christian people and yet being converted to their religion and accepting the Bible, their ideological instrument of colonization, oppression and exploitation. Thirdly, they express a historic commitment that is accepted solemnly by one generation and passed onto another—a commitment to terminate exploitation of humans by other humans (Mofokeng 1988: 34).

He goes on:

> When Black christians see all these conservative and reactionary efforts and hear the Bible being quoted in support of reactionary causes they realize that the Bible itself is a serious problem to people who want to be free (1988: 37).

Mofokeng contends that there are numerous traditions in the Bible which lend themselves only to oppressive interpretations and oppressive uses precisely because of their inherently oppressive nature. He goes on to say that any attempt to 'save' or 'co-opt' these oppressive texts for the oppressed only serves the interests of the oppressors. Young blacks, he adds, have identified the Bible as an oppressive document by its very nature and its very core, and call for its displacement (Mofokeng 1988: 38).[9]

---

9.   On the positive side, West and Draper report on the activities of the recently founded South African Institute for the Study of the Bible, which attempts to develop an interface between biblical studies and ordinary readers of the Bible (1991: 369-70). They draw attention to the very impressive work being done by the collaboration of a great number of institutions in the land.

Chapter 4

COLONIALISM AND PALESTINE

The matrix of elements within the broad ideology of Zionism[1] is no less complex than in Afrikaner nationalism, and while the ideologies share much in common, they represent different social contexts. It is of interest to enquire into whether Zionist historians fabricated Jewish history in a manner analogous to what we have seen in the case of Afrikaner ideologues. In the case of Zionism, the role of the Bible will be of particular interest, since whatever justification the European settlers in South America and South Africa had for deploying it as a legitimating charter for their settler colonization, Jews appear to require less defence. However, overt appeal to the Bible in under-pinning Zionist nationalism was not prominent from the beginning until the wake of the 1967 War. My investigation will suggest that the concept of the fabrication of national myths of origin helps to understand the nature of the biblical text itself. Although this study is a moral critique of the Bible and colonialism, it is necessary to establish the social context in which the discussion takes place. Therefore, as in the other examples, it is instructive to review the developments from the birth of Zionism to the present day.

The Early Phase of Zionism (1896–1917)

While Theodor Herzl (1860–1904) was not the first to lay down plans for the migration of Jews from Europe to Palestine, nor the first to suggest the establishment of a state for Jews, he was the one who most systematically planned the elevation into practice of his vision, and nobody matches him in his attention to its practical implementation. It

1. The term *Zionism* in its modern sense was used for the first time by Nathan Birnbaum in 1890 (Bein 1961: 33).

is appropriate, therefore, to examine both his utopian dream and his strategy to realize it.

Herzl interested himself in the Jewish Question as early as 1881 or 1882 (Herzl 1960, 1: 4),[2] and while in Vienna he had considered mass Jewish conversion to Catholicism as a solution to the problem of being a Jew in European society (Herzl 1960, 1: 7). By 1895 he judged the efforts to combat anti-Semitism to be futile (Herzl 1960, 1: 6). He composed the first draft of *Der Judenstaat* between June and July 1895, and on 17 November explained his ideas to Dr Max Nordau in Paris, who reacted enthusiastically.[3] The public degradation of Captain Dreyfus, an Alsatian Jew on the French general staff, wrongly convicted of selling military secrets to the Germans (5 January 1896), signalled for Herzl the end of the enterprise to assimilate Jews into European society and confirmed him as a Zionist. On 17 January 1896 the *Jewish Chronicle* published his article 'A "Solution of the Jewish Question"'. The editorial was sceptical: 'We hardly anticipate a great future for a scheme which is the outcome of despair.' In February, Herzl published the full statement of his programme.

The Vision and its Underpinning

Herzl argued that the solution to the Jewish question could be achieved only through 'the restoration of the Jewish State' (1988: 69).[4] He insisted that Jews constituted one people (pp. 76, 79), and spoke of *the distinctive nationality of Jews* (p. 79). Wherever they were, they were destined to be persecuted (pp. 75-78). Anti-Semitism for Herzl was a national question, more than a social, civil rights or religious issue, and

2.   Herzl began his diaries in (Pentecost) 1895 and continued until shortly before his death. All seven volumes of the letters and diaries have been published, the first three edited by Johannes Wachten *et al.* (1983–85), and the remaining four by Barbara Schäfer (1990–96). The most complete English translation is in the five volumes edited by Raphael Patai. In general, I quote from Patai's edition (rendered Herzl 1960), which I have checked against the original in Wachten and Schäfer. Where I judge it to be important, I give the original German etc. from the latter (rendered Herzl 1983–96). I indicate the volume number of the English translation by 1, 2, etc., and the German ones by I, II, etc.

3.   Invariably, the items of Herzl's affairs I note are described fully in his *Diaries*, at the appropriate date, for example, in this case in the complete German edition, vol. II, 277-78.

4.   Quotes in what follows are from the *The Jewish State* (New York: Dover, 1988).

could be solved only by making it a political world-question (p. 76).

While Herzl's appeal to religious motivation was sparse, he did have recourse to the phrase, *Next year in Jerusalem* (p. 82). The heart of his plan was that 'sovereignty be granted us over a portion of the globe large enough to satisfy the rightful requirements of a nation' (p. 92). Jews could rely on the governments of all countries scourged by anti-Semitism to assist them obtain that sovereignty (p. 93). He looked to the Powers to admit Jewish sovereignty over a neutral piece of land. Jews could bring the present possessors of the land enormous advantages, and the creation of a Jewish state would be beneficial to adjacent countries also (p. 95). In discussing whether the state should be established in Argentina or Palestine, he said, 'Palestine is our ever-memorable historic home. The very name Palestine would attract our people with a force of marvellous potency' (p. 96).

The Jewish state would be 'a portion of the rampart of Europe against Asia, an outpost of civilization opposed to barbarism' (p. 96). Herzl adds, 'The Temple will be visible from long distances, for it is only our ancient faith that has kept us together' (p. 102). He appealed for the support of the rabbis, and foresaw that getting Jews to emigrate would be difficult (p. 129). He asserted, 'Our community of race is peculiar and unique, for we are bound together only by the faith of our fathers' (p. 146). But the Jewish state would not be a theocracy: 'We shall keep our priests within the confines of their temples in the same way as we keep our professional army within the confines of their barracks' (p. 146).[5] Herzl's final words were:

> I believe that a wondrous generation of Jews will spring into existence. The Maccabeans will rise again... The Jews who wish for a State will have it. We shall live at last as free men on our own soil, and die peacefully in our own homes. The world will be freed by our liberty, enriched by our wealth, magnified by our greatness. And whatever we attempt there to accomplish for our own welfare, will react powerfully and beneficially for the good of humanity (pp. 156-57).

Herzl's proposal met with considerable opposition, not least from Chief Rabbi Moritz Güdemann of Vienna, who maintained that the

5. On 8 May 1896, the hassid Ahron Marcus informed him that it was likely that 3 million hassidic Poles would support the venture. Herzl replied that the support of the Orthodox would be very welcome, but that a theocracy would not be created: 'Die Mitwirkung der Orthodoxen noch willkommen ist—aber Theokratie wird nicht gemacht' (II, 340).

Jews were not a nation, and that Zionism was incompatible with the teachings of Judaism.[6] On the Zionist side, his critics found little specifically Jewish about the state he envisaged. Herzl's tactics would combine mobilizing the Jews with negotiating with the imperial powers, and colonization. Intensive diplomatic negotiations at the highest level, and propaganda on the largest scale would be necessary (11 May 1896, Herzl 1983–96: II, 340-41). He obtained audiences with the Sultan, the Kaiser, the Pope, King Victor Emmanuel, Chamberlain, prominent Tsarists and with many other key figures.

Herzl acknowledged that the notions of *chosen people* and *return* to the *promised land* would be potent factors in mobilizing Jewish opinion, despite the fact that the leading Zionists were either non-religious, atheists or agnostics. On 6 March 1897 the *Zionsverein* decided upon a Zionist Congress in Munich for August, but the Munich Jews refused to host it. The rabbis, representing all shades of opinion, denounced Zionism as a fanaticism, and contrary to the Jewish scriptures, and affirmed their loyalty to Germany. Moreover, the executive committee of the German Rabbinical Council 'formally and publicly condemned the "efforts of the so-called Zionists to create a Jewish national state in Palestine" as contrary to Holy Writ' (Vital 1975: 336).

Herzl convened the First Zionist Congress (29–31 August 1897) in Basle. On the day before the Congress, though non-religious, Herzl attended a synagogue service, having been prepared for the reading of the Law (Vital 1975: 355). The purpose of the Congress, he declared in his speech, was to lay the foundation stone of the house to shelter the Jewish nation, and advance the interests of civilization:[7]

> It is more and more to the interest of the civilized nations and of civilization in general that a cultural station be established on the shortest road to Asia. Palestine is this station and we Jews are the bearers of culture who are ready to give our property and our lives to bring about its creation... Zionism seeks to secure for the Jewish people a publicly recognized, legally secured [*öffentlich-rechtlich*] home in Palestine for the Jewish people.

6.   *Nationaljudentum* (Leipzig and Vienna, 1897), p. 42, quoted in Laqueur 1972: 96.

7.   Herzl's own words are: 'In drei Tagen haben wir viel Wichtiges zu besorgen. Wir wollen den Grundstein legen zu dem Haus, das dereinst die jüdische Nation behebergen wird (*Protokoll des I. Zionistenkongresses in Basel vom 29. bis 31. August 1897*. Prag 1911. Selbstverlag—Druck von Richard Brandeis in Prag, p. 15).

The Congress also formed the World Zionist Organization, and on the final day adopted the motion in principle to establish a fund to acquire Jewish territory which 'shall be inalienable and cannot be sold even to individual Jews; it can only be leased for periods of forty-nine years maximum' (in Lehn 1988: 18), the 49 years reflecting the divine provenance of land possession (Leviticus 25).[8]

Herzl envisaged that the European powers would endorse Zionism for imperialist self-interest, to rid themselves of Jews and anti-Semitism and to use organized Jewish influence to combat revolutionary movements. After the Congress, Herzl wrote in his diary (3 September),

> If I were to sum up the congress in a word—which I shall guard against pronouncing publicly—it would be this: At Basle I founded the Jewish state. If I said this out loudly today, I would be greeted by universal laughter. Perhaps in five years, and certainly in fifty, everyone will know it (Herzl 1960, 2: 581).

Herzl and his party landed at Jaffa on 26 October 1898 and toured the Jewish settlements of Palestine. Jerusalem made a terrible impression on him, with its musty deposits of 2000 years of inhumanity, intolerance and uncleanness lying in the foul-smelling little streets (31 October, 1983–96: II, 680).

On 2 November 1898, Herzl was received at his headquarters outside Jerusalem by the German emperor, Wilhelm II, after which he realized that the Zionist goal would not be achieved under German protection. In May 1901 he had an audience with Sultan Abdul Hamid and promised that Jews would help him pay his foreign debt and promote the country's industrialization. The Sultan promised lasting protection if the Jews would seek refuge in Turkey as citizens. Further meetings with the Sultan followed in February and July 1902. However, Herzl was not able to raise a fraction of the money involved, and he decided to open negotiations with Britain.

Because of its interests in neighbouring Arab countries and in securing the overland route to India, Britain would avail of Herzl's proposal for a joint Anglo-Zionist partnership involving colonial concessions for Jews in Cyprus, El Arish and the Sinai Peninsula. Herzl

---

8.   The Fifth Zionist Congress in Basle (29–31 December 1901) established the Jewish National Fund (JNF). From the beginning the JNF was an instrument for the realization of a Jewish state.

met Joseph Chamberlain, the Colonial Secretary, on 22 October 1902, and explained that in patronizing the Zionist endeavour the British Empire would have ten million agents for her greatness and her influence all over the world, bringing political and economic benefits (1983–96: III, 469). In this *quid pro quo*, England would undertake to protect the Jewish state and world Jewry would advance British interests, with the Jewish settler state becoming its client. On the following day (24 October), Herzl wrote that yesterday was a great day in Jewish history.

In August 1903, Herzl discussed with the Tsarist government the speeding up of the emigration of Russian Jews. He argued that the European powers would support Jewish colonization in Palestine not only because of the historic right guaranteed in the Bible, but because of the European inclination to let Jews go. Earlier, Chamberlain had raised the option of Jews settling in Uganda, which was discussed at length at the Sixth Zionist Congress at Basle (22–28 August 1903). Herzl and Nordau emphasized that Uganda would only be a staging post to the ultimate goal of Palestine, but, fearing that the issue might split the Zionist movement, Herzl reiterated the Zionist programme by lifting his right hand and saying, 'Im Yeshkakhekh Yerushalayim...' (If I forget you, O Jerusalem, may my right hand wither), quoting Ps. 137.5 (Laqueur 1972: 129). The Seventh Congress, at which Herzl was not present, officially buried the Uganda scheme.

With failing health, Herzl visited Rome on 23 January 1904 and met King Victor Emanuel III and Pius X. To his request for a Jewish state in Tripoli, the king replied, 'Ma è ancora casa di altri' (But it is already the home of other people) (Herzl 1983–96: III, 653). Neither Pope Pius X nor the Secretary of State, Cardinal Merri del Val, considered it proper to support the Zionist intentions in any way (Herzl 1960, 4: 1602-603), opposing it on religious grounds (Kreutz 1990: 33). Herzl made the last entry in his diaries on 16 May 1904. He died in Edlach on 3 July. On the day of his burial Zangwill compared him with Moses, who had been vouchsafed only a sight of the promised land. But, like Moses, Herzl 'has laid his hands upon the head of more than one Joshua, and filled them with the spirit of his wisdom to carry on his work' (Zangwill 1937: 131-32).

Critique of Herzl

Herzl provided the inspiration, the leadership and the organization of the Zionist movement, reflected in Ben-Gurion's proclamation of the State of Israel (14 May 1948) under his portrait and the transfer of his remains to Jerusalem in 1949. His genius lay not in his analysis of the plight of the Jews, nor in the clarity of his vision for a solution, but in his elevation of the plan into action, through his remarkable organizational and diplomatic skills. He was very much a man of action, a 'Tatmensch', as Martin Buber put it. At various times people referred to him as the Messiah, or King of Israel, and as the fulfilment of the prophecies of the Jewish Scriptures. His diaries and letters reflect his indefatigable zeal in searching out all possible ways of winning support to his cause. To have met the Kaiser, the Sultan, a king, and the Pope, and have dealt with them as though he were the leader of a state was no mean achievement. His early death ensured that he could be embraced by all factions within the broad Zionist and Israeli camp.

Herzl's motivation was not dictated by a religious longing for the ancient homeland, nor by appeal to biblical injunctions, for example, to go to the Promised Land in order to carry out the *mitzvot*. His Zionism had much in common with the notion of Pan-Germanism, with its emphasis on *das Volk*: all persons of German race, blood or descent, wherever they lived, and under whatever political system, owed their primary loyalty to Germany, the *Heimat*. For Herzl, Jews, wherever they lived, constituted a distinct nation, whose success could be advanced only by establishing a Jewish nation state. The Renaissance and Reformation had helped to create new societies and states which challenged the mediaeval idea of world empire. However, while the basic assumption of eighteenth- and nineteenth-century European nationalisms was the indigenous nature of a specific community and its desire for independence from the imperial power, Zionists had no such context. The Jewish claim to construct a separate state like every other nation amounted to special pleading.

The rights of the indigenous people never featured in Herzl's plans. The discourse proceeded as if Palestine were a *terra nullius* at the free disposal of the Powers. Notwithstanding, he knew what was needed to establish a state for Jews in a land already inhabited. Among the items of his diary entry for 12 June 1895 we find,

> When we occupy the land, we shall bring immediate benefits to the state
> that receives us. We must expropriate gently the private property on the

estates assigned to us. We shall try to spirit the penniless population
across the border by procuring employment for it in the transit countries
while denying it any employment in our own country.[9] The property
owners will come to our side. Both the process of expropriation and the
removal of the poor must be carried out discreetly and circumspectly
(Herzl 1960, 1: 87-88).

Before spiriting them away, however, he envisaged that the Zionists
would be forced to use native labour, especially when fever attacked
the workers, a fate from which he wished to protect the Zionists.

The Background to Herzl's Vision and Plan
While a certain longing for Zion was present at virtually all periods
of Jewish history, as reflected in the prayer book exclamation, *Next
Year in Jerusalem*, a pious longing for Jerusalem and its lamented
Temple is not to be confused with the desire to establish a nation state
for Jews in Palestine. The Zionist aspiration was prompted by a host
of nationalist movements within the turbulent politics of Europe since
the French Revolution, and was a retort to the hope that civic emancipation would solve the Jewish problem.[10] Although there were substantial differences between it and other European nationalist and
imperialist movements, Zionism was a product of both of them.
Several factors acted as catalysts for some Jews to promote the ideal
of settlement in Palestine after so many centuries of passivity: the lure
of assimilation, the rise of anti-Semitism, the appearance of racist theories in Germany, the pogroms in Russia in 1881–82, etc. However,
these alone do not account for the movement to Zion, since even in the
face of persecution in different places, Jews had emigrated to other
countries, but not to Palestine. It is estimated that while almost three
million Jews emigrated from Russia between 1882 and 1914 as a
result of the Russian pogroms and the anti-Semitic policies of the
Tsarist government, only about one per cent went to Palestine
(Avineri 1981: 5).

Throughout their history Jews displayed a remarkable unity which

9.   'Die arme Bevölkerung trachten wir unbemerkt über die Grenze zu schaffen,
indem wir in den Durchzugsländern Arbeit verschaffen aber in unserem eigenem
Lande jederlei Arbeit verweigern' (1983–96: II, 117-18).

10. About 90 per cent of the world's 2.5 million Jews lived in Europe at the
beginning of the nineteenth century. There was a significant increase in the world
Jewish population from the fifteenth century until 1939.

derived from a strong attachment to shared religious values. But the scientific spirit promoted by Descartes, Locke and Newton in the seventeenth century which issued in the Enlightenment fundamentally challenged Jewish identity. Its *Wissenschaft* was characterized by autonomous, critical, historical enquiry, which pursued truth through reason, observation and experiment unhindered by dogma, tradition or a hierarchy higher than autonomous reason. The movement, in general, was suspicious of, and often hostile to the claims of religion.

Discrimination was a problem in several regions and expressed itself in intermittent persecution. But since the French National Assembly voted for the recognition of Jews as citizens and the removal of existing restrictions (28 September 1791), their lot changed for the better. By 1860, the equality of Jews was generally accepted in Europe (Halpern 1969: 4). Indeed, the nineteenth century was the best century they had experienced, collectively and individually, since the destruction of the Temple: from being a marginal community in the early part of the century, Jews had become the great beneficiaries of the Enlightenment, Emancipation and the Industrial Revolution within a hundred years (Avineri 1981: 5-6).

The danger, however, was that European Jews would be *assimilated*, a term with overtones of xenophobia and superiority. The Enlightenment and Emancipation provided a climate in which some Jews discarded some of the practices which were the 'mortar keeping the building together'. Western Jews insisted that they were not a separate nation, but a religious body, which denied any intention to 'return to Zion' (Halpern 1969: 10). Wilhelm Marr, the first to use the term *antisemitism*,[11] complained that Jewish influence had already penetrated too far into European economic life (Laqueur 1972: 28-29). While the 1850s and 1860s were a happy period for Jews in

---

11. In popular usage the disparaging epithet *anti-Semitic* is applied with little discrimination to a perpetrator of any form of perceived anti-Jewishness, covering the spectrum from Hitler's *Final Solution* to a human rights' critique of the behaviour of the State of Israel. The term is imprecise and problematic. The eighteenth-century division of peoples into racial categories reflected patterns of similarity between languages. Because similarities between one group of languages were detected, they were clustered within a category of *Semitic* languages. On that basis, a specific people (race?), *Semites*, was designated, introducing the terms *Semitic* and *anti-Semitic*. The terms *Judaeophobia* or *Jew-hatred* are more apposite. The Nazi hatred for Jews is more appropriately conveyed by the German terms, *Judenhass*, or *Judenfeindschaft*.

Germany, hostility increased by the 1870s. The mood in Russia was assimilationist in the 1860s and 1870s, and Jewish pride in Russia was very strong, but the pogroms of the 1880s dealt a severe blow to the hopes for total assimilation.

Although Herzl does not appear to have been influenced by his ideological predecessors, the surfacing of Zionist ideas in several places in the nineteenth century made the reception of his programme less forbidding. The growth in acceptance of a 'Jewish Return' to Palestine was facilitated by Byron's *Hebrew Melodies*, Disraeli's *Tancred* and George Eliot's *Daniel Deronda* (1876).[12] In Germany in 1840, an anonymous pamphlet accepted the idea of a Jewish state but rejected Palestine for practical reasons. The author proposed Arkansas or Oregon, in which $10 million would buy a territory the size of France, where Jews could show their full potential.[13] Another anonymous piece, in *Orient*, 27 June 1840, argued that the best solution to the plight of Jews in Europe was an early return to Palestine, where the Sultan and Mehmet Ali could be persuaded to protect them.

One detects a development of ideas for which the establishment of a nation state could be the logical outcome. Heinrich Graetz (1817–91) contributed more than most to the view of Jews as a nation (Avineri 1981: 35). He insisted that Judaism required concrete and manifest expression, and that its interwoven religious and political nature would require territorial manifestation.[14] If the Law was the spirit of Judaism, and the Jewish people its historical subject, the Holy Land was its material foundation, giving the triad

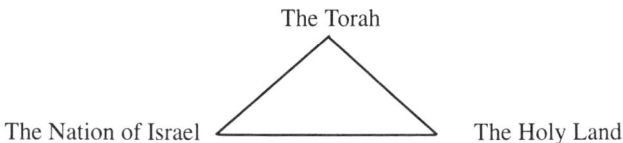

---

12. On 7 June 1895 Herzl determined to read it: 'Daniel Deronda lesen. Teweles spricht davon. Ich kenn's noch nicht' (I, 71). Zangwill claimed that it was Eliot who invented Zionism (1920: 78).

13. *Neujudäa: Entwurf zum Wiederaufbau eines Selbständigen jüdischen Staates von C.L.K.*

14. Between 1853 and 1876 Graetz published his eleven-volume *Geschichte der Juden von den ältesten Zeiten bis auf die Gegenwart*, which was translated into several European languages.

He regarded these three elements as standing in a mystical relationship to each other, inseparably united by an invisible bond. Without corporate, national life in the land, Judaism, he asserted, could never be more than a shadow of its reality (see Avineri 1981: 28-29).

The growth of chauvinistic nationalism in nineteenth-century Europe provided a catalyst for Jewish nationalism. Inspired by Giuseppe Mazzini's Rome and the rise of Italian nationalism, the *Rom und Jerusalem: Die letzte Nationalitätenfrage* (1862) of Moses Hess (1812–75) predicted the liberation of the Eternal City on Mount Moriah, after the fashion of the liberation of the Eternal City on the Tiber (Avineri 1981: 39-42).[15] In Hess's judgment, Jews were not simply a religious group, but were a separate nation, a special race which should avoid assimilation and reassert its uniqueness by reconstituting a national centre as a Jewish, model socialist commonwealth in Palestine. While Hess's views were unknown to either Pinsker or Herzl, their aspirations reappear in Jewish nationalist-socialist tendencies later.

While the Orthodox religious establishment retained its traditional approach to the notion of redemption and its messianic ambience, two Orthodox rabbis suggested a more active role for Jews in bringing redemption forward. In his *Minhat Yehuda* (1845), Rabbi Judah Alkalai of Bosnia (1788–1878) gave a territorial dimension to traditional messianic redemption. While retaining traditional teleology, that final, supernatural redemption would be brought about by the Messiah, he argued that the physical return of the Jews to Zion must precede the Redeemer's advent. Alkalai supported his proposals with biblical and talmudic texts, thereby deflecting the charge that he was 'Forcing the End of Days' (*Dehikat ha-Ketz*). He proposed the revival of *spoken* Hebrew, the establishment of a Perpetual Fund (*Keren Kayemet*) and a representative assembly of Jews (Avineri 1981: 50-51). In 1857 he called for the establishment of a Jewish state, and was, perhaps the first to do so. In old age he emigrated to Jerusalem.

As early as 1832, Rabbi Zwi Hirsch Kalischer of Posen (1795–1874) also declared that the redemption of Zion would have to begin with action on the part of the Jewish people, and that the messianic

---

15. The earlier Hess had judged that Jews had a future only if as individuals they broke from their group identity and became citizens of the world. His 'New Jerusalem', based on nationalism rather than religion, would be built in the heart of Europe, not in Palestine.

miracle would then follow. In the same year as Hess's pamphlet (1862), he published *Derishat Zion* (Seeking Zion), which had much in common with the views of Alkalai, but while reaching the same broad conclusions as Hess, had a very different ideological frame-work. His starting point was the Bible, the Mishnah and the Talmud.

> The Redemption of Israel, for which we long, is not to be imagined as a sudden miracle. The Almighty, blessed be His Name, will not suddenly descend from on high and command His people to go forth. Neither will he send the Messiah in a twinkling of an eye, to sound the great trumpet for the scattered of Israel and gather them into Jerusalem...The Redemption of Israel will come by slow degree and the ray of deliverance will shine forth gradually (Kalischer, in Avineri 1981: 53).

Settlement of Jews in the land of Israel would hasten the Day of Redemption. It should take the form of self-supporting agricultural communities, which would make it possible to observe the religious commandments related to working the land (*mitzvot ha-teluyot ba-aretz*): 'As we bring redemption to the land in this-worldly way, the ray of heavenly deliverance will gradually appear' (in Avineri 1981: 54).

Kalischer and Alkalai showed how it was possible to unite the nationalist and emancipationist spirit of the age with the traditions of rabbinic Judaism. Each subjected the doctrine of passive messianism to the influence of the vibrant aspirations for cultural and national iden-tity with which their immediate culture was surrounded. The task of Jews was to take the first steps, and speed the coming of the Messiah's redemption.[16] Although Alkalai and Kalischer were lone voices in the Orthodox rabbinate in the nineteenth century, they showed how it was possible to reinterpret Jewish identity and aspirations in a world which was changing drastically around them. Their stress on collec-tive Jewish cultural and religious identity coincided with the aspira-tions of Zionists later in the century, whose cultural roots were within the secularized, nationalist traditions of nineteenth-century Europe, more than within traditional religious ones.

Leo Pinsker (1821–91), one of the leading exponents of assimila-tion, had his confidence in the future of Jews in Russia dented by the

---

16. A corresponding tension was manifest within Christian theology about the role of Christians who awaited the Second Coming of Christ. See, for example, the contrasting views of Albrecht Ritschl (1822–89) and that of his son-in-law, Johannes Weiss (1843–1914).

Odessa riots of 1871, and destroyed by the pogroms of 1881. Unaware of the work of Hess, he published a pamphlet anonymously, arguing that anti-Semitism was an hereditary psychosis, which was incurable (1882).[17] Being at home nowhere, Jews were strangers *par excellence*. Many Jews did not aspire to independent national existence in the same way as sick people have no desire for food. Russian Jews would have to emigrate to escape their parasitical condition and settle in a home of their own. The time was ripe for the organized societies of Jews to convene a national congress with a view to purchasing a territory for the settlement of millions of Jews, for which the support of the Powers would be necessary to guarantee stability. Since the Holy Land could not be the target, *a land of our own* could be any-where, whether in North America or Asiatic Turkey.

Several Jews openly canvassed the idea of settling in Palestine and reviving Hebrew as a living language. Already in 1877, the poet Yehuda Leib Gordon anonymously wrote a pamphlet proposing the establishment of a Jewish state in Palestine under British suzerainty.[18] Eliezer Perlman (*Ben Yehuda*) called for the revival of Hebrew as the spoken language, which could take place only in Palestine. Judging that Jews would always be aliens, Moshe Leib Lilienblum (1834–1910) declared, 'We need a corner of our own. We need Palestine,' and from 1881 he advocated the purchase of land in Palestine.

Already in 1878–79, there had been an attempt by a group of Orthodox Jews from Jerusalem to establish an agricultural settlement, Petah Tiqvah, on 3000 dunums (a dunum being 1000 square metres, that is, about one-quarter of an acre), north-east of Jaffa. Although the attempt failed, the move inspired some from Russia, who turned out to be no more skilled in agriculture (Lehn 1988: 9). After the Russian pogroms of 1881, Russian and Romanian Jewish immigration to Palestine increased, with the first settlement of fourteen families in August 1882 on 3200 dunums south-east of Jaffa, at Rishon le-Tsiyyon. In the same year, about 200 Romanian emigrants established Zikhron Ya'aqov near the coast, south of Haifa, and 50 Romanian families established Rosh Pinnah east of Safed. These were followed by other settlers, so that by the end of 1884 there were eight new Jewish villages with a total population in 1890 of 2415. In all, the

17. *Autoemanzipation, ein Mahnruf an seine Stammesgenossen, von einem russischen Juden.*
   18. *Die jüdische Frage in der orientalischen Frage.*

immigration to Palestine in the First Aliya of 1882–1903 represented just under 3 per cent of the full emigration of Jews from Europe (Vital 1975: 93, 99-100).

An offshoot of the Lovers of Zion in Russia, the so-called *Biluim* (the plural of an acronym of the opening words of Isa. 2.5, *bylw*, 'O house of Jacob, come, let us walk in the light of Yahweh!'), came to the conclusion that the only solution to the discrimination against Jews in Russia was national renaissance through the establishment of a Jewish state in Palestine. Although only 14 Biluim immigrated in July 1882, and reached at most 20 by the end of 1884, they achieved an importance out of proportion to their numbers. Their programme involved the establishment of self-sustaining, exclusively Hebrew-speaking Jewish colonies, employing no non-Jewish worker.

Of course, it would be even easier to identify a pantheon of anti-Zionist champions than it has been to construct one of Zionist heroes in the nineteenth century, and to fashion a catena of relevant proof texts to support one's case. However, unless one can demonstrate a cause-and-effect relationship between the elements of each list, one may not legitimately regard an earlier argument as a development towards its inevitable consummation in a particular form of Jewish living. We return to the conclusion that what distinguished Herzl from his predecessors was his ability to chart out the stages of his utopian vision and his remarkable determination to see that they would be carried through.

Zionism and European Imperialism
The early Zionists realized the necessity of winning the support of at least one of the major Europeans powers, whose own agenda might favour the creation of a Jewish state in Palestine. Throughout the Ottoman period, international politics entered into the controversies surrounding Jerusalem and the Holy Places (O'Mahony 1994: 13). Britain stationed a consular agent in Jerusalem in 1838, and on the religious front a Protestant (Anglican) bishopric in Jerusalem was established in 1841 (El-Assal 1994: 131-32). Britain's interest increased as a result of her acquisition of territories in India, and the need to ensure safe and speedy overland communication. Moreover, she wished to protect her trade with the Persian Gulf region, as well as to keep Mohammad 'Ali of Egypt in his place.[19] Throughout the second

19. 'The Jewish *people*, if *returning* under the sanction and protection and at the

half of the century, the expansion in Church institutions in the Holy Land reflected renewed international interest.

Britain occupied Egypt in 1882, and in the years before the outbreak of the Great War, had set its sights on Iraq. Meanwhile, in anticipation of the break-up of the Ottoman Empire, the French invested heavily in Syria. This was part of the wider colonial context in which Zionism was emerging, a context in which the European powers presumed on their superiority over others and their right to exploit natives. Chaim Weizmann, the Zionist leader and later first President of Israel put his case as follows:

> We can reasonably say that should Palestine fall within the British sphere of influence, and should Britain encourage Jewish settlement there, as a British dependency, we could have in twenty to thirty years a million Jews out there, perhaps more; they would develop the country, bring back civilization to it and form a very effective guard for the Suez Canal (Letter to *Manchester Guardian,* November 1914, in Weizmann 1949: 149).

Weizmann realized that Britain had much to gain from supporting Zionism. He considered it self-evident that England needed Palestine for the safeguarding of the approaches to Egypt, and that if Palestine were thrown open for the settlement of Jews, 'England would have an effective barrier, and we would have a country' (letter to Zangwill on 10 October 1914, in Stein 1961: 14-15).

The First World War
The entry of the Ottoman Empire into the war in October 1914 had a profound impact on future developments in the Middle East. When Turkey became an enemy, the British Government, fearing a hostile Pan-Islamic opposition led by the Ottoman Sultan-Caliph, favoured a Muslim centre relatively independent of Istanbul, preferably under British influence, and looked to the Sharif of Mecca, Husayn ibn 'Ali to advance its interests. The Sharif agreed, on condition that when the Turks were defeated, the British would support Arab independence in the whole of the Arabian Peninsula (with the exception of Aden), Syria, Lebanon, Palestine, Trans-Jordan and Iraq (Ingrams 1972: 1-2). Sir Henry McMahon, the British High Commissioner in Egypt, with

invitation of the Sultan, would be a check upon any future evil designs of Mohammed Ali or his successor' (my italics; Viscount Palmerston to Viscount Ponsonby, 2 August 1840, Foreign Office 79/390 [No. 134], Public Record Office).

certain important reservations, agreed on 24 October 1915 'to recognise and support the independence of the Arabs within the territories included in the limits and boundaries proposed by the Sharif of Mecca', that is, from Cilicia in the north to the Indian Ocean in the south, and from the Mediterranean to Iran (Letter to the Sharif, in Yapp 1987: 279).

Nevertheless, in the Sykes–Picot Agreement between France and Britain (3 January 1916) France was given *carte blanche* in Cilicia, coastal Syria and Lebanon, and Britain given Basra and Baghdad, and the southern region of the Middle East. Britain would also acquire Haifa and Acre, with the rest of Palestine being placed under an undefined international administration. Among the differences between the terms of the Sykes–Picot Agreement and the letter from McMahon to Husayn were the status of Iraq, the degree of independence of the Arab state(s), the position of Haifa and the status of Palestine. The absence of reference to Palestine in the McMahon letter suggests that it would presumably fall within the Arab state(s), whereas in the Sykes–Picot Agreement it was to be internationalized. However, whether or not Britain intended to exclude Palestine from the Arab area, the McMahon to Husayn letter was more a statement of intent than a formal agreement. More to the point, promises and declarations of intent made in the heat of war were only to be honoured if they still seemed profitable at the end of hostilities. Meanwhile, the new British Prime Minister, Lloyd George, decided on an advance into Palestine. British forces captured Jerusalem on 9 December 1917 under General Allenby, and had penetrated into Aleppo by September 1918. Since the Ottoman armies began to wane in 1917, and Russian efforts began to diminish, Britain was on the way to becoming the dominant Entente power in the region.

Meanwhile, the Zionists had made little progress in winning international support for the creation of a Jewish state in Palestine, or in settling large numbers of Jews there before the outbreak of the war. Estimates of the number of Jews in Palestine at the outbreak of the war vary from 38,000 to 85,000 Jews, constituting some 5–10 per cent of the total population,[20] of whom only about half were political

20. There are no exact figures for the number of Jews in Palestine before World War I. Justin McCarthy's analysis of the demographic situation (1990) concluded that in 1880 Palestine's population was c. 450,000, of which some 15,000 (less than 5 per cent) were Jews, and by 1914, after the first and second aliyahs, it was

Zionists. Since the Sykes–Picot Agreement deprived France of exercising influence over Palestine, Britain considered the area to be vital to its strategic interests, being a buffer against Egypt and a means of protecting the Suez Canal as its route to India, and a link between its interests there and its hoped-for interests in Iraq. Towards the end of the war, then, there was a coincidence of interests between the Zionists and Britain. A Jewish Palestine would serve as a local garrison to defend British interests in the Suez Canal, and at the same time be a loyal political island for the British in a sea of newly-established independent Arab states. Realizing that Palestinian Arabs would not acquiesce in the Zionist dream, it was clear that British support would be necessary to ensure its realization.

The Second Phase of Zionism (1917–1948)

Britain's undertaking to honour both its guarantee of Arab independence at the end of the war and the terms of the Sykes–Picot Agreement would be matched by its no less incompatible determination both to support the goal of Zionism and to guarantee the rights of the indigenous Palestinians. I shall trace here only the most significant developments in political Zionism during the 30 years between the end of the war and the establishment of the state of Israel. These include the Balfour Declaration and its elevation into an internationally supported programme in the Mandate of the League of Nations, and the UN Partition Plan of 1947.

c. 710,000, of which some 38,000 (still only 5 per cent) were Jews. According to studies based on Zionist sources there may have been 80,000–85,000. However, as many as half of the immigrants may have departed again, while others retained their nationalities rather than become Ottoman subjects (see Khalidi 1988: 213, 231). Ingrams gives the figures for 1914 as 500,000 Muslims and 60,000 each of Jews and Christians (1972: 1). The Jewish National Fund, legally established in 1907, whose *primary object* was to acquire land for exclusive and inalienable Jewish settlement, purchased its first Arab-owned land in 1910 from absentee landlords. So difficult was it to purchase land from small holders that by 1919 it had obtained only 16,366 dunums (Lehn 1988: 30-39). The director of its Palestine office, Arthur Ruppin (1876-1943), promoted *economic segregation*, as signalled in the axioms of *self-help* or *self-labour*.

Balfour Declaration

Dr Chaim Weizmann (1874–1952), elected president of the English Zionist Federation on 11 February 1917, quickly influenced government policy, with a view to having a declaration of support for the Zionist goal from the British Government. Edwin S. Montague, the only Jewish member of the Cabinet, who regarded Zionism as a mischievous political creed untenable by any patriotic citizen of the United Kingdom (Mayhew 1975: 50, in Adams and Mayhew 1975), argued against such a declaration, and insisted that the project of creating a Jewish state would end by driving out the present inhabitants (minutes of War Cabinet meeting, 4 October 1917, in Ingrams 1972: 11). At that meeting, Lord Curzon wondered 'how was it proposed to get rid of the existing majority of Mussulman inhabitants and to introduce the Jews in their place?' He proposed securing equal rights for Jews already in Palestine as a better policy than repatriation on a large scale, which he regarded as 'sentimental idealism, which would never be realized' (Ingrams 1972: 12). The War Cabinet decided to hear the views of representative Zionist and non-Zionist Jews, and that a draft of a declaration be submitted confidentially to President Wilson, leaders of the Zionist Movement and representative persons in Anglo-Jewry opposed to Zionism (PRO.CAB.23–24, in Ingrams 1972: 13). Apparently, there was no need to canvas Arab opinion on the draft declaration. Lord Milner's draft was:

> His Majesty's Government views with favour the establishment in Palestine of a National Home for the Jewish Race, and will use its best endeavours to facilitate the achievement of this object; it being clearly understood that nothing shall be done which may prejudice the civil and religious rights of the non-Jewish communities in Palestine, or the rights and political status enjoyed in any other country by such Jews who are fully contented with their existing nationality and citizenship (Ingrams 1972: 12-13).

Chief Rabbi J.H. Herz had 'feelings of the profoundest gratification' on hearing that His Majesty's Government was to lend its powerful support to the re-establishment of a national home in Palestine for Jews. He welcomed the reference to the civil and religious rights of the existing non-Jewish communities in Palestine, which, he assured the Cabinet, was 'but a translation of the basic principle of the Mosaic legislation: "If a stranger sojourn with thee in your land, ye shall not vex [oppress] him. But the stranger that dwelleth with you shall be

unto you as one born among you, and thou shalt love him as thyself'"
(Lev. 19.33, 34) (in Ingrams 1972: 13). Lord Rothschild considered
the proviso a slur on Zionism, as it presupposed the possibility of a
danger to non-Zionists. There would be no encroachment on the
rights of the other inhabitants of the country (in Ingrams 1972: 13).
Weizmann requested 'one or two alterations' and suggested three,
including that 're-establishment' replace 'establishment', so that 'the
historical connection with the ancient tradition would be indicated',
and that 'Jewish people' be substituted for 'Jewish race' (in Ingrams
1972: 14). Nahum Sokolov assured the Government that 'The safe-
guards mentioned...always have been regarded by Zionists as a matter
of course' (in Ingrams 1972: 15).

Other prominent Jews replied, opposing the Zionist programme. Sir
Philip Magnus MP insisted that 'the great bond that unites Israel is not
one of race but the bond of a common religion', and that 'we have no
national aspirations apart from those of the country of our birth'. He
found the reference to 'a national home for the Jewish race' both
undesirable and inaccurate (in Ingrams 1972: 15). C.G. Montefiore,
President of the Anglo-Jewish Association, observed that the emancipation and liberty of the Jewish race in the countries of the world
were a thousand times more important than a 'home' (in Ingrams
1972: 15-16). L.L. Cohen, Chairman of the Jewish Board of
Guardians, stated that he denied that the Jews are a nation, and repudiated the implication that Jews are a separate entity unidentified with
the interests of the places where they live (in Ingrams 1972: 16).

The Secretary of State for Foreign Affairs, Arthur James Balfour,
assured the War Cabinet on 31 October that a declaration favourable
to Zionism, which would promote extremely useful propaganda in
Russia and America, be made without delay. An independent Jewish
state would follow only after some form of British, American or
other protectorate, as a 'gradual development in accordance with the
ordinary laws of political evolution' (in Ingrams 1972: 17). The
Cabinet authorized Balfour to take a suitable opportunity for making
the declaration, which he did in his letter to Lord Rothschild. The so-
called Balfour Declaration promised the longed-for imperial patron-
age which was required for a Jewish national home:

Foreign Office
November 2nd, 1917

Dear Lord Rothschild,

I have much pleasure in conveying to you, on behalf of His Majesty's Government, the following *Declaration* of sympathy with Jewish Zionist aspirations which has been submitted to, and approved by, the Cabinet.

> 'His Majesty's Government view with favour the establish-
> ment in Palestine of a national home for the Jewish people,
> and will use their best endeavours to facilitate the achieve-
> ment of this object, it being clearly understood that nothing
> shall be done which may prejudice the civil and religious
> rights of existing non-Jewish communities in Palestine, or
> the rights and political status enjoyed by Jews in any other
> country.'

I should be grateful if you would bring this *Declaration* to the knowledge of the Zionist Federation.

Yours
Arthur James Balfour

The Declaration mentioned neither the name nor the political rights of the Palestinian Arabs. Balfour acknowledged that at his request the first draft of the Declaration was drawn up by Rothschild and Weizmann (PRO FO371/3058, in Ingrams 1972: 9).

According to the Duke of Devonshire, Churchill's successor as Secretary of State for the Colonies, 'The Balfour Declaration was a war measure…designed to secure tangible benefits which it was hoped could contribute to the ultimate victory of the Allies,' by enlisting international Jewish support for the Allies and bringing forward the date of the US entry into the war (PRO.CAB.24/159, in Ingrams 1972: 173). The Arabs saw the Declaration as a betrayal, but a series of petitions protesting at the injustice of settling another people on the Arab homeland was brushed aside (Mayhew 1975: 40-41, in Adams and Mayhew 1975). To support the intention to establish a Jewish homeland (state), without the consent of the indigenous population, was an audacious undertaking: 'In this document [Balfour Declaration] one nation solemnly promised to a second nation the country of a third' (Koestler 1949: 4). The audacity of the project can be gauged from the fact that the Jews in Palestine in 1919 constituted no more than 9.7 per cent of the population and owned 2.04 per cent of the land (Khalidi 1992: 21).

Weizmann's letter to Balfour on 30 May 1918 reflected racialist and imperialist values likely to impress him. He wrote of the treacherous, and blackmailing nature of the Arab, whose Oriental mind was full of subtleties and subterfuges, compared with the enlightened and honest, fair and clean-minded English official. Moreover, while the *fellah* was at least four centuries behind the times, the *effendi* was dishonest, uneducated and greedy, and as unpatriotic as he was inefficient (Weizmann PRO FO.371/3395, quoted in Ingrams 1972: 31-32). Neither Balfour nor the Powers cared much for the indigenous population:

> In Palestine we do not propose even to go through the form of consulting the wishes of the present inhabitants of the country...The Four Great Powers are committed to Zionism. And Zionism, be it right or wrong, good or bad, is rooted in age-long traditions, in present needs, in future hopes, of far profounder import than the desires and prejudices of the 700,000 Arabs who now inhabit that ancient land. In my opinion that is right...I do not think that Zionism will hurt the Arab...Whatever deference should be paid to the views of those living there, the Powers in their selection of a mandatory do not propose...to consult them. In short, so far as Palestine is concerned, the powers have made no statement of fact which is not admittedly wrong, and no declaration of policy which, at least in the letter, they have not always intended to violate (Balfour memo to Lord Curzon, 11 August 1919, PRO.FO.371/4183, in Ingrams 1972: 73).

The Foreign Office set up a special branch for Jewish propaganda under the control of A. Hyamson. Propaganda materials were distributed to virtually every known Jewish community in the world. Leaflets were dropped over German and Austrian territory, and pamphlets in Yiddish were distributed to Jewish soldiers in Central European armies after the fall of Jerusalem with the message, 'The hour of Jewish redemption has arrived...Palestine must be the national home of the Jewish people once more...The Allies are giving the Land of Israel to the people of Israel', encouraging them to stop fighting the Allies (in Ingrams 1972: 19).

At the suggestion of its Middle East Committee, the War Cabinet dispatched a Zionist Commission to Palestine to further the intentions of His Majesty's Government. It was led by Weizmann, who assured Arabs that,

> ...it was his ambition to see Palestine governed by some stable government like that of Great Britain, that a Jewish government would be fatal to

> his plans and that it was simply his wish to provide a home for the Jews
> in the Holy Land where they could live their own national life, sharing
> equal rights with the other inhabitants (Memorandum of Major
> Cornwallis, 20 April, in Ingrams 1972: 29).

He assured Arabs and Jews in Jaffa that 'It is not our aim to get hold of the supreme power and administration in Palestine, nor to deprive any native of his possession' (in Ingrams 1972: 30).

Weizmann displayed his diplomatic versatility at the Foreign Office on 4 December 1918, assuring Balfour that 'A community of four to five million Jews in Palestine could radiate out into the near East and so contribute mightily to the reconstruction of countries which were once flourishing.' This would require a Jewish national home in Palestine, 'not mere facilities for colonization...so that we should be able to settle in Palestine about four to five million Jews within a generation, and so make Palestine a Jewish country' (PRO.FO.371/3385, in Ingrams 1972: 46). The attraction of such a proposal for British interests was considerable. A memorandum by the General Staff at the War Office, 'The Strategic Importance of Syria to the British Empire' (9 December 1918), reads, 'The creation of a buffer Jewish state in Palestine, though this state will be weak in itself, is strategically desirable for Great Britain' (PRO.FO.371/4178, in Kayyali 1979: 16-17). Already by 1917, the victory of the allies and the fragmentation of the Ottoman Empire seemed probable, securing Britain's controlling influence over Palestine.

On the meaning of Jewish national home, Lloyd George replied to Weizmann's question, 'We meant a Jewish state.' This was confirmed also in conversation with the Prime Minister, Balfour, Churchill and Weizmann: Lloyd George and Balfour always meant an eventual Jewish state. That the British used *homeland* rather than *state* merely as a tactic to deflect Arab opposition is clear from a memorandum of Herbert Young, a Foreign Office official in 1921, who wrote that the problem of coping with Palestinian opposition was 'one of tactics, not strategy, the general strategic idea...being the gradual immigration of Jews into Palestine until that country becomes a predominantly Jewish state... But it is questionable whether we are in a position to tell the Arabs what our policy really means' (cited in Lehn 1988: 326-27 n. 101).

It is clear that *homeland* was a mere circumlocution for *state*. While Herzl himself at the First Zionist Congress in 1897 had defined the

aim of Zionism to be the creation of a home for the Jewish people in
Palestine, he recorded in his diary of 3 September 1897: 'At Basle I
founded the Jewish state' (Herzl 1960, 2: 581). Reflecting the same
ambiguity, Nordau wrote in 1920:

> I did my best to persuade the claimants of the Jewish state in Palestine that
> we might find a circumlocution that would express all we meant, but
> would say it in a way so as to avoid provoking the Turkish rulers of the
> coveted land. I suggested *Heimstätte* as a synonym for state...It was
> equivocal, but we all understood what it meant. To us it signified
> *Judenstaat* then and it signifies the same now (Sykes 1953: 160 n. 1).

Zangwill in February 1919 also was in no doubt about the exclusivist
claims of Zionism: 'The Jews must possess Palestine as the Arabs are
to possess Arabia or the Poles Poland' (1937: 342). Weizmann's view
was similar: 'We, not less than Herzl, regarded it as the Jewish state in
the making' (1949: 68).

Britain's aid to the project immediately revolutionized it. It would
support the creation of a client Jewish settler state in Palestine, which
would prevent the growth of pan-Arab nationalism, serve the purposes of the sponsor national state and evade the problem of Jewish
immigration at home.[21] The creation of a Jewish state in Palestine
financed by Jews and supported by interested Western bodies would be
an ideal and inexpensive resolution to the designs of a European
power.[22]

21. Defending the Aliens Bill in 1905, Balfour, the then Prime Minister noted that
'it would not be to the advantage of the civilisation of this country that there should
be an immense body of persons, who, however patriotic...remained a people apart,
and not merely held a religion differing from the vast majority of their fellow-
countrymen, but only inter-married among themselves' (quoted in Khalidi 1992: 23).
22. 'I wish to be able to say that a great event is taking place here, a great event in
the world's destiny. It is taking place without injury to anyone; it is transforming
waste places into fertile...and the people of the country who are in a great majority,
are deriving great benefit in the general development and advancement...' (Winston
Churchill, in Palestine, March 1921, PRO.CO.733/2, in Ingrams 1972: 119-20). Sir
Ronald Storrs, Britain's military governor of Jerusalem and later of Palestine, said
that Zionism 'blessed him that gave as well as him that took by forming for England
"a little loyal Jewish Ulster" in a sea of potentially hostile Arabism' (*Memoirs* 1937:
364, in Quigley 1990: 8).

The League of Nations and the Mandate

Immediately after the end of World War I the victors embarked upon the division of the spoils. The San Remo Conference (April 1920) agreed that France would be mandatory for Syria and Britain for Palestine and Mesopotamia. Clearly, this was contrary to Article 22 of the League Covenant, which specified that 'the wishes of these communities [recognized as prospective "independent nations"] must be a principal consideration in the selection of the mandatory'. The League of Nations entrusted to Britain the responsibility for the establishment of the Jewish national home, and for safeguarding the civil and religious rights of all the inhabitants of Palestine, irrespective of race and religion (The Mandate for Palestine, Article 2, 24 July 1922). The Balfour Declaration was incorporated into the Mandate (the preamble; see also Articles 2, 4, 6, 7, 15, 22 and 23). The League of Nations' indifference to the indigenous population can be gauged from the fact that the designation *Arab* does not occur in the Mandate. The Eleventh Zionist Congress, held in London in July 1920, was devoted to the development of Palestine as *the* Jewish national home. The purchased land would be solely in Jewish hands, and, contrary to the claims of the Jewish National Fund (JNF), this required the displacement of the Arab peasants before the sale (Lehn 1988: 57).

Arab Opposition

After the serious rioting which broke out in Jerusalem in August 1929 and quickly spread, leaving some 240 Jews and Arabs dead, Britain appointed a commission which discovered that the underlying cause of the riots was Arab opposition to the policy of establishing a Jewish national home at their expense. A second commission in 1930 confirmed that Jewish colonization was causing Arab eviction from land bought from Arabs. The Passfield White Paper of the Labour Government (October 1930) reminded all concerned that Britain's support for Jewish immigration and the national home was conditional upon the guarantee in the Balfour Declaration that the rights of the indigenous community were to be safeguarded.

Between 1932 and 1937 some 144,093 Jews immigrated to Palestine, and Jewish ownership of land more than doubled, but was still only 5.7 per cent of the total in 1939. In all, between 1922 and 1939 the Jewish population rose from 10 per cent to 30 per cent of Palestine (450,000) (W. Khalidi 1992: 31-33). Arab alarm led to the establishment of the Arab Higher Committee in April 1936, which called for a general strike to last until Zionist immigration and land purchases were stopped and steps were taken to establish independence for Palestine. Sporadic but increasing violence followed, to which the British responded by sending a royal commission in November 1936. The Peel Commission reported in July 1937, acknowledging that the mandate was unworkable, since it involved two irreconcilables, a Jewish homeland and the independence of the Palestinian Arabs. It resorted to 'Solomonic wisdom' and recommended partition (Lehn 1988: 58).

The Palestinian Arabs saw the partition plan as the vivisection of their country, proposing to give Jews, who owned only 5.7 per cent of the land, some 40 per cent of Palestine. Moreover, the proposed Jewish state would embrace hundreds of Arab villages and the solid Arab bloc in Galilee. Moreover, if necessary, there would be a forcible transfer of Arabs from the Arab lands allotted to the Jewish state. Peel's plan rekindled the flames of Arab rebellion, and the British responded with massive repressive measures, leading to 5000 killed and 15,000 wounded Arab casualties for the rebellion of 1936–39 out of a population of 1 million Arabs (Khalidi 1992: 34). This was followed by systematic disarming of the Arab population and the breaking up of Arab political organization.

Ben-Gurion and Weizmann were jubilant, since the Peel partition plan was the first admission that the Jewish national home was to be a Jewish state. Moreover, it proposed some 40 per cent of Palestine at one stroke, which was seven times greater than the land already owned by Jews. But Jabotinsky, the leader of the Zionist opposition, regarded it as a betrayal of the vision of Greater Israel on both sides of the Jordan. Even though it had to be shelved, the partition plan elevated the Zionist aspiration to its partial fulfilment and became a benchmark against which to measure what could be achieved later. In November 1937, the Jewish Agency formed a special Population Transfer Committee. Britain, recognizing that partition would not work, outlined its intentions in the White Paper of 17 May 1939. Its new policy was 'the establishment within ten years of an independent Palestine state...in which Arabs and Jews share in government in such a way as to ensure that the essential interests of each community are safeguarded'. The White Paper required restrictions on land acquisition and Jewish immigration.

Yosef Weitz, the moving spirit of the Population Transfer Committee, and Director of the Land Department of the JNF, wrote in his diary on 20 December 1940:

> Among ourselves it must be clear that there is no room in the country for both peoples…If the Arabs leave it, the country will become wide and spacious for us…The only solution is the Land of Israel…without Arabs. There is no room here for compromises…There is no way but to transfer the Arabs from here to the neighbouring countries, to transfer all of them, save perhaps for [those] of Bethlehem, Nazareth, and old Jerusalem. Not one village must be left, not one [bedouin] tribe must be left. The transfer must be directed at Iraq, Syria and even Transjordan. For this goal funds will be found…And only after the transfer will the country be able to absorb millions of our brothers and the Jewish problem will cease to exist. There is no other solution (Weitz 1965: II, 181, quoted in Morris 1987: 27).

Realizing that British interests could conflict with Zionist ones, Ben-Gurion began to activate American Jewry and gain more US support, while Weizmann continued his diplomatic work in wartime London. The death of President Roosevelt in April 1945 brought Vice-President Harry Truman to the White House, and immediately he proved to be an ardent supporter of Zionist intentions. President Truman wrote to Churchill on 24 April 1945, calling for the removal of restrictions on immigration to Palestine of Jews who had been so cruelly uprooted by ruthless Nazi persecutions (Khalidi 1992: 48). One might have expected Truman to lead the way and receive, at America's own expense, some of the 300,000 survivors of the Nazi barbarism who were in various relief centres. But his tactic gave him a double victory: he won the support of the Zionists and allayed all fears that the US might bear the brunt of responsibility for Jewish immigration. In October 1945, he explained to Arab diplomats to the US: 'I am sorry, gentlemen, but I have to answer to hundreds of thousands who are anxious for the success of Zionism; I do not have hundreds of thousands of Arabs among my constituents' (Khalidi 1992: 50-51).

Although Truman's letter of 24 July 1945 was addressed to Churchill, by 26 July the British election had brought the Labour Party to power under Prime Minister Attlee. By that time, sympathy for Zionism was widespread in the party, which had its own solution: 'Let the Arabs be encouraged to move out, as the Jews move in' (1944 Annual General Conference Report, p. 9, in Mayhew 1975: 34, in Adams and Mayhew 1975).

The British made the disbanding of the Zionist military establishment a condition for the admission of 100,000 Jewish immigrants, as recommended by a joint Anglo-American Committee. Truman's endorsement (4 October 1946) of the Zionist UDI plan of August killed off the proposal of the Arab delegates to a conference in London (September 1946) that there be a unitary Palestinian state, wherein Palestinian citizenship would be acquired through ten years residence in the country and Jewish rights guaranteed. At the time Truman gave his support to the Zionist plan, Palestine was divided into 16 sub-districts, in only one of which (the Jaffa sub-district) was there a Jewish majority. Nevertheless, the Zionist map, sponsored by Truman on 4 October 1946 (*Yom Kippur*), envisaged the incorporation of 9 of the 16 sub-districts into the Jewish state, as well as the bulk of others. The Zionists envisaged a special status for Jerusalem. In terms of territory, the Truman-sponsored Zionist map would give 75 per cent of Palestine to the Jews, who owned less than 7 per cent of it. While only 10 Jewish settlements (2000 inhabitants) would come under Arab rule, about 450 Arab villages (700,000 inhabitants) would come under Zionist rule. Moreover, the Arabs would lose their richest lands and access to the sea, except for a corridor leading to Jaffa.

White House support for the Zionist plan was critical. The Attlee government was under considerable pressure from the USA, whose ambassador conveyed the President's request for Britain to admit 100,000 Jews into Palestine immediately. To the objections of Christopher Mayhew, the Under-Secretary at the Foreign Office, that that would be a prescription for war,

> The Ambassador replied, carefully and deliberately, that the President wished it to be known that if we could help him over this it would enable our friends in Washington to get our Marshall Aid appropriation through Congress. In other words, we must do as the Zionists wished—or starve. Bevin surrendered (Mayhew 1975: 18-19, in Adams and Mayhew 1975).

The United Nations Partition Plan, 1947

Because Britain failed to make any progress towards an agreed settlement in Palestine, His Majesty's Government declared (18 February 1947) that 'The only course now open to us is to submit the problem to the judgement of the UN.' In April 1947 the General Assembly met in special session at Britain's request and agreed to send a commission of inquiry, the United Nations Special Committee for Palestine

4. *Colonialism and Palestine*   133

(UNSCOP). After a tour of the region the Committee recommended partition along the lines of the Truman *Yom Kippur* map. Significantly, it conceded the Negev to the Jewish state, although some 100,000 bedouin cultivated a vast area of it, while only some 475 Jews lived in four Jewish settlements there.

In the UNSCOP recommendation, the Zionists stood to gain 57 per cent of the land, including most of the best arable land, which was already home to a substantial Arab population, against 43 per cent for a Palestinian Arab state, even though by 1948 Jews had still reached only 6.6 per cent of the total ownership of Palestine (see Gresh and Vidal, 1988: 29; Khoury 1985: 18; Lehn 1988: 70-80). Moreover Jews constituted only one-third of the population (some 500,000–600,000 Jews against some 1.4 million Palestinians), having risen from the 11 per cent (83,794 of 757,182) in the British census of 1922. On 29 November 1947 the UN General Assembly, by a vote of 33 to 13, with 10 members abstaining, endorsed the UNSCOP partition plan (with minor modifications) and recommended the partition of Palestine into independent Arab and Jewish states, with an internationalized Jerusalem.[23] The partition plan was unacceptable to the Arabs, whose delegates at the General Assembly tested opinion as to the UN's competence to enforce such a plan on an unwilling Arab population. Moreover, their draft resolution that the members of the UN, in proportion to their resources, take in 'the distressed European Jews' did not win sufficient support.

Following the partition resolution, and with inter-communal strife and anti-British activity increasing to a level approaching civil war, the British announced their intention to terminate the Mandate and leave hastily. Britain would cede its Mandate on 15 May 1948, after which date the UN would be free to supervise the interregnum leading to the partition arrangements. The failure of the UN to provide for an international force to supervise matters was an invitation to strife between the contending parties, which, given the superiority of Zionist

23. 'The city of Jerusalem shall be established as a *corpus separatum* under a special international regime and shall be administered by the United Nations...The City of Jerusalem shall include the present municipality of Jerusalem plus the surrounding villages and towns, the most eastern of which shall be Abu Dis; the most southern, Bethlehem; the most western, Ein Karim (including the built-up area of Motsa); and the most northern Shu'fat' (Official Records of the Second Session of the General Assembly, Resolutions, No. 181 (II), pp. 131-33).

resources, was bound to end in a Zionist victory. From that point on, the Zionists would evade the problem of purchasing Arab land.

Between the Partition Plan and the End of the Mandate
The six-month period between the UN Declaration and the expiry of the Mandate (29 November 1947–15 May 1948) would be critical for Zionist possession of its bounty. The Yishuv (the Jewish community in Palestine before and during 1948) was militarily and administratively vastly superior to the Palestinian Arabs (Morris 1988: 7). The Palestinian national movement lagged behind its Jewish counterpart in cohesion, organization, motivation and performance. It was too divided, too poorly organized and too politically inexperienced for the complexity of the challenge ahead (Mo'az 1992: 153). The Zionist military planners drew up two new operational plans, Plan Gimmel and Plan Dalet, the master plan for the takeover of as much Arab territory and the expulsion of as many Palestinians as possible, whose major architect was Yigael Yadin, the Haganah OC Operations. Plan Gimmel aimed at buying time for the mobilization of forces to carry out the comprehensive Plan Dalet. Places vacated by the British would have to be occupied. Throughout most of the period, Arab resistance was such that by mid-March 1948 the US State Department reconsidered its position and spoke of the need for a special session of the UN General Assembly to discuss the possibility of UN trusteeship over Palestine.

With only some weeks to go before the expiry of the Mandate, Plan Dalet would have to be executed without delay. The strategy was one of massive surprise attack against civilian populations softened by continuous mortar and rocket bombardment. On the psychological level, clandestine Haganah radio stations broadcast threats of dire punishment in Arabic and advised on modes of escape. These tactics were supplemented by carefully calculated acts of histrionic cruelty which were designed to speed up the exodus from both the towns and the countryside. Benny Morris puts the best possible face on the programme, suggesting that it was governed by military considerations and goals rather than ethnic ones (1987: 62-63).

In order to relieve the pressure on Jerusalem's Jews, Ben-Gurion and the Haganah General Staff decided on the night of 31 March–1 April that all Arab villages along the Khulda–Jerusalem axis were to be treated as enemy assembly or jump-off points. Within the terms of Plan Dalet villages which resisted could be destroyed and their inhabitants expelled. Villages fell in quick succession (Al Qastal, Qaluniya, Khulda, Saris, Biddu and Beit Suriq). Demolishing villages without having encountered resistance marked a deviation from the terms of Plan Dalet, but was in conformity with the Zionist dream. In Morris's vocabulary, in the face of a life and death struggle, the gloves of the Yishuv had to be, and were taken off (1987: 113).

A more sinister operation was enacted, with what Morris calls the reluctant, qualified consent of the Haganah commander in Jerusalem (1987: 113). On the night of 9 April 1948, the combined forces of approximately 132 members of the Irgun[24] and Stern[25] organizations, supported by Haganah mortars, began an attack on the Palestinian village of Deir Yassin, on the western outskirts of Jerusalem. By noon of the following day, 254 inhabitants, including more than 100 women and children, had been slaughtered. Their bodies were thrown into a well, doused with kerosene and set alight.[26] There were also cases of mutilation and rape. Morris opines that the troops did not intend committing a massacre, 'but lost their heads during the battle'. He does concede that their intention probably was to expel the village's inhabitants. In any event, the massacre at Deir Yassin promoted terror and dread in the surrounding Arab villages, whose inhabitants abandoned their homes immediately (Morris 1987: 115). The Zionist organizations responsible for the slaughter were headed by two future Prime Ministers of Israel: Menachem Begin was the leader of the Irgun from 1943 to 1948, and Yitzhak Shamir was a co-commander of the Stern organization.

The execution of Plan Dalet had devastating effect on the Palestinian population.[27] Hundreds of men, women and children from the coastal

24. The Irgun Zvai Leumi (National Military Organization) was a Jewish underground armed group formed in 1931 by revisionist Zionist leaders who were committed to the establishment of a state with a Jewish majority in the whole of Mandated Palestine, including Transjordan.

25. Lehi (Lohamei Herut Yisrael), better known at the Stern Gang, after its founder Avraham Stern broke away from the Irgun in June 1940. The organization called for the compulsory evacuation of the entire Arab population of Palestine, and advocated an exchange of Jews from Arab lands.

26. A former Stern Gang intelligence officer, a participant in the massacre wrote of some of the brutality involved (*Haaretz*, 25 April 1993). His testimony and that of a Mossad intelligence officer on the scene is summarized by Finkelstein (1995: 189 n. 16).

27. 'The Jewish policy as exemplified by Plan D is the principal explanation for

towns of Jaffa, Haifa and Acre were drowned in their efforts to scramble for any vessel that would take them to safety. Hundreds of thousands were driven over the borders by the victorious Jewish brigades. By 23 April Plan Dalet had achieved its purpose. President Truman sent a message to Weizmann that if a Jewish state were declared, the President would recognize it immediately. On 14 May, the last day of the Mandate, the Chief Secretary of the British administration called a press conference in his office in the King David Hotel in Jerusalem. To a journalist's question, 'And to whom do you intend to give the keys of your office?' the Chief Secretary replied, 'I shall put them under the mat' (Khalidi ed. 1992: 76). On the same day, the Yishuv declared the establishment of the State of Israel, and immediately Truman authorized its recognition by the USA.

The Third Phase of Zionism (The State of Israel, 1948–1967)

On 14 May 1948, David Ben-Gurion declared the establishment of the State of Israel. On the following day, units of the regular armies of the surrounding Arab states went into Palestine. They amounted to some 14,000 troops and were not likely to match the superior Zionist forces, which prevailed in the ensuing conflict and ultimately conquered 78 per cent of Palestine. At the end of the war, Israel controlled all of Mandatory Palestine, with the exception of the West Bank and Gaza. There is a number of ways in which the extent of the Palestinian catastrophe[28] can be measured.[29]

Flight of Palestinian Refugees[30] in 1948
The extent of the Palestinian catastrophe is gauged also by the creation of displaced persons, the great majority of whom fled or were expelled from the area of the newly-created state. With few exceptions, the

the departure of most of the Arabs of Palestine' (Pappé 1992: 93).

28. *Al-Nakba* (*The Disaster*) is the title of the six-volume history of 1948 by the Palestinian historian 'Arif al-'Arif (Beirut and Sidon: Al-Maktaba al-'Asriyya, 1956–60).

29. Some 13,000, mostly civilian Palestinians were killed (Khalidi ed. 1992: Appendix III, pp. 581-82), families were dispersed, surrounding countries were damaged and so on. Hadawi estimates the financial cost (1988: 183).

30. The UN Security Council's Resolution 242 refers to the displaced Palestinians as 'refugees'. The term 'refugee' is not satisfactory, since in international

major urban centres of Palestine, including substantially Arab towns, were emptied of their Palestinian residents, with their assets falling to the Zionists. Moreover, hundreds of Arab villages were depopulated and destroyed. Some 156,000 Palestinian Arabs remained in their towns and villages in the territory that became Israel. Others, some 25 per cent of the Arab population of Israel, were driven from their villages and settled elsewhere in Israel, becoming 'internal refugees' (or, in terms of rights to their property, 'present absentees'), and are not included in the figures for displaced persons. The total number of Palestinian Arab displaced persons in 1948 is conservatively estimated at 714,150 to 744,150.[31] This constituted 54 per cent of the total Palestinian population of Mandatory Palestine. Moreover, about 6 million dunums, some four times the total area of Palestine purchased by the Zionist movement in the previous 70 years, were summarily divided among the old and new Jewish colonies (Khalidi ed. 1992: xxxiii).

The Physical Destruction of the Villages
That the international community has paid little attention to the wilful destruction of hundreds of Palestinian villages by the Israelis is a tribute to the determination of the State of Israel to preserve one of its best-guarded secrets. Until recently no publication gave either the number or location of these villages, and the fact that they were completely destroyed helps perpetuate the claim that Palestine was virtually an empty country before the Jews entered and made the desert bloom.[32] The failure of the Palestinians to narrate the story of their

practice, and in the UN convention on refugees, it refers to one who seeks to reside in a foreign country because one does not want to reside in one's own country, for fear of persecution etc. Palestinian 'refugees', on the contrary, want only to reside in their own country, and should be referred to as 'displaced persons'. I owe this insight to John Quigley, Professor of Law and Political Science, Ohio State University.

31. Janet Abu Lughod puts the number at around 770,000–780,000 (1987: 161). Elia Zureik comprehensively surveys the estimates, showing that they fall within the range, 700–800,000 (1994: table 3, p. 11). According to the 1994 report of the United Nations Relief and Welfare Agency's Commissioner General, there were 504,070 'refugees' in the West Bank, 42 per cent of the population, and 643,000 in the Gaza Strip, 75.7 per cent of the population (see Sabella 1996: 193). The UNRWA 1995 Report estimated that there are now some 4,645,248 Palestinian displaced persons in camps throughout Syria, Lebanon, Jordan and beyond.

32. As late as September 1987 a document was distributed in Switzerland appealing for 6 million Swiss francs to plant a *Swiss Forest* in the region of Tiberias. The

loss indicates the level of their powerlessness, but also what Edward Said calls their 'collective incompetence', with the result that there been no substantial Palestinian narrative of 1948 and after to challenge the dominant Israeli one.

By the end of the 1948 war, hundreds of villages had been completely depopulated and their houses blown up or bulldozed. Only about 100 Palestinian villages in the area conquered by Israel were neither destroyed nor depopulated and survive to this day. However, over 80 per cent of the lands of those who never left their homes have been confiscated since 1948, and are at the exclusive disposal of the Jewish citizens of the state (Khalidi ed. 1992: xxxii; see Geraisy 1994: 50-1). Khalidi's exhaustive study give details of the destruction of each village, supplying statistical, topographical, historical, architectural, archaeological and economic material, as well as the circumstances of each village's occupation and depopulation, and a description of what remains (Khalidi ed. 1992: xviii-xix). All that remains is 'a kind of *in memoriam*...[It] is an acknowledgement of the suffering of hundreds of thousands of men, women and children. It is a gesture of homage to their collective memories and their sense of ancestral affiliation' (Khalidi ed. 1992: xvii, xxxiv).

Khalidi's figure of 418 destroyed villages is the most reliable one, and amounts to half the total number of Arab villages in Mandated Palestine.[33] Of the 418 villages, 293 (70 per cent) were totally destroyed and 90 (22 per cent) were largely destroyed. Seven survived, including 'Ayn Karim, but were taken by Israeli settlers. While an observant traveller can still see some evidence for these villages, in the main all that remains is 'a scattering of stones and rubble across a

JNF thanked its benefactors in anticipation, assuring them that their contributions would transform a desert into a green land. Forests frequently cover over the remaining traces of destroyed Palestinian villages (Aldeeb 1992: 8).

33. Benny Morris included a list of occupied towns and villages in his 1990 study. Israel Shahak also compiled lists of the destroyed villages (1975). The nearest the Israeli Government came to providing a list of destroyed villages is in the map, originally produced by the British Mandate and re-issued with Hebrew overprint in 1950, on which the destroyed villages are stamped with the word *harus*, Hebrew for *demolished*. The efforts to quantify the destroyed villages range from 290 (from the Israeli topographical maps) to 472.

forgotten landscape' (Khalidi ed. 1992: xv).[34] The profanation of sacred places is particularly offensive.[35]

The depopulation and destruction of the 418 Arab villages displaced some 383,150 inhabitants, plus some 6994 from the surrounding villages, giving a total of 390,144 rural displaced persons. The figure is probably an undercount (Khalidi ed. 1992: 581). The total population of urban displaced persons is estimated at 254,016, and again is probably an undercount. Moreover, it is estimated that the 1948 war created between 70,000 and 100,000 Bedouin displaced persons. Having surveyed the extent of the catastrophe, Khalidi concludes:

> Retrospective as this book is, it is not a call for the reversal of the tide of history, nor for the delegitimization of Zionism. But it is a call...for...a break into the chain of causation which has…created the dimensions of the tragedy of the Palestinian people…It is in this spirit that this volume has been compiled, as a reminder that in much of human endeavour, building for one's self is often accompanied by destruction for the other (Khalidi ed. 1992: xxxiv).

34. Khalidi's researchers visited all sites except 14, made comprehensive reports and took photographs, recording all the detail that remains (Khalidi ed. 1992: xix). The photographs include some village sites on which theme parks or recreation grounds have been constructed, for example, the sites of al-Tantura, Zirin and the cemetery of Salama (p. xxxix), as well as the remains of shrines, mosques and churches and cemeteries (pp. xliii-xliv).

35. See Geraisy 1994: 49. An Orthodox church in 'Ayn Karim was converted into public toilets, the mosque in Safed into an art gallery, and one in Caesarea and 'Ayn Hud into a restaurant and bar. The Hilton Hotel in Tel Aviv, the Plaza Hotel in Jerusalem and the adjacent parks, both called Independence Park, were constructed over Muslim cemeteries (U. Davis 1987: 24). The case of the Christian village of Biram is particularly poignant. Its inhabitants left their village in 1948, with the written guarantee that they would be allowed back in two weeks, which did not happen. In the closing months of 1950, the displaced elders were informed by the Israeli Supreme Court that they could return to their village and resume occupancy in their houses, but the commander of the army refused to comply with the judgment of the Supreme Court (Chacour 1985: 36-38, 71). In order to ensure that the former villagers would not return, Ben-Gurion ordered the destruction of the village on 16 September 1953. Later, in 1987, followers of Rabbi Meir Kahane, under police protection, erased the crosses and other symbols of the Christian religion which were sculpted into the stones of the ruined houses. In September, they defiled the tomb of the priest who had been interred in the ruined church eight months earlier (Aldeeb 1992: 9). The remains of Deir Yassin were converted into a mental hospital for Israelis.

Many still believe that the Palestinian displaced persons of the 1948 left voluntarily, despite abundant evidence that Jewish settlement required the expulsion of most of the indigenous population (Masalha 1992: *passim*). But, even if there were no evidence of expulsions and massacres to counter the propaganda, Israel's persistence in not allowing Palestinians to return to their homes is revealing.[36] Moreover, its refusal to allow the 1967 displaced persons also to return consolidates the judgment that Zionism in its essence required Jewish supplanting of the indigenous Palestinian population.

The Fourth Phase of Zionism (1967–)

Israel's pre-emptive strike against Egypt, under the pretext of the imminence of Arab aggression which 'threatened the very existence of the state', initiated the war of 5–11 June 1967. In fact, Israel was under no significant threat, let alone in mortal danger. The most likely explanation for Israel's action was its intent to reap the fruits of victory which the war certainly would bring. On the eve of the war, Cabinet Minister Yigal Allon, insisted that Israel must set as one of its central aims 'the territorial fulfilment of the Land of Israel' (see Finkelstein 1995: 132-43).

Israel's victory resulted in the capture of the West Bank (including East Jerusalem) from Jordan, the Golan Heights from Syria and Gaza and the Sinai from Egypt. Its long-term territorial intentions were signalled by its destruction of 135 Arab houses in the ancient Maghrebi Quarter to make way for a plaza in front of the Wailing Wall, and by the passing of a law extending the boundaries of East Jerusalem to include villages close to Bethlehem in the south and Ramallah in the north within days of the occupation. This was condemned by the UN and almost all states as illegal (see Playfair 1992: 1), but was confirmed by Israel in 1980, when the Knesset declared 'Jerusalem in its entirety' (i.e. West and East) to be the 'eternal capital' of Israel.

There was virtual unanimity in the Fifth Emergency Special Session of the General Assembly of the United Nations that there should be a withdrawal of forces to the borders obtaining on 4 June 1967. The

---

36. On 16 June 1948, the 13 members of the 'Provisional Government' agreed to bar the refugees' return. The decision was never published, and the statements of Ben-Gurion and Sharett had to undergo successive rewritings to conform to accepted international political norms (Morris 1995: 56).

Security Council passed Resolution 242 (22 November), emphasizing 'the inadmissibility of the acquisition of territory by war and the need to work for a just and lasting peace in which every State in the area can live in security', and called for the 'withdrawal of Israeli armed forces from territories occupied in the recent conflict'. All parties, other than Israel, understood the indefinite 'from territories occupied' (rather than 'from *the* territories occupied') to require Israel to withdraw from all the territory occupied, while allowing for the possibility of minor rationalizations of the pre-5 June 1967 borders (see Neff 1991: 17, for Lord Caradon, Dean Rusk, Presidents Carter, Reagan, and Bush).

An opportunity for a peaceful solution was lost in 1971, when both Egypt and Jordan independently assured Gunnar Jarring, the UN special envoy, that they would make a peace agreement with Israel, provided Israel conformed with the withdrawal required by Resolution 242. However, neither US pressure, nor the international consensus reflected in votes in the General Assembly in 1971 and 1972 could budge Israel to withdraw. At the Security Council, meeting in special session in July 1973, 13 votes were cast in favour, with no abstentions, strongly deploring Israel's continuing occupation of *the* territories, and expressing serious concern at its lack of co-operation with the Special Representative of the Secretary-General. However, the US delegate vetoed the resolution, thereby dashing the last hope for averting a war.

On 6 October 1973 (*Yom Kippur*), 200 Egyptian planes targeted Israeli airfields and army bases deep in the Sinai. At the same time the Syrian front attacked the Golan Heights. Initially the assault petrified the Israelis. However, the Egyptian drive toward the Sinai passes on 14 October was repulsed comprehensively. With an Israeli bridgehead established on the west of the Suez Canal and the Egyptian army surrounded, there was a cease-fire on 22 October and a cessation of hostilities on 24 October. After the war, which dented Israel's self-confidence and raised Arab morale, there was a return to the demands of Resolution 242, with Resolution 338 (22 October 1973) calling for the implementation of Resolution 242. The following year, at the Rabat Summit, the Arab states designated the Palestine Liberation Organization (PLO) as 'the sole legitimate representative of the Palestine people', and PLO Chairman Yasser Arafat made his first visit to the United Nations in November 1974.

The Judaization of the Occupied Territories
The systematic seizing of private and public (communal) Palestinian property followed the Israeli occupation of the West Bank and Gaza, and developments since suggest that the war was a further stage in the strategy of Zionist settlement of 'biblical Israel'. All Israeli governments since 1967 have pursued a policy of the acquisition of Arab land. During the period of the Labour-led governments of 1967–77, East Jerusalem and one-third of the West Bank were seized and controlled by the Jewish state.

Gush Emunim, the chief colonizing group founded in 1974, set about settling all of Eretz Israel. The process of Judaization accelerated with the advent of the Likud-led governments of 1977–84. The Gush Emunim aim in a modified form (the Drobless Plan) was adopted as government policy (Benvenisti and Khayat 1988: 64, 102). Its intention was to ensure through a process of comprehensive Jewish settlement that Arab control could not be re-established (see Aronson 1987; Benvenisti 1984; W. Harris 1980).

Israel in Lebanon
Ever since the reinforcements of Palestinian positions in Lebanon at the end of the 1960s, Israel had assumed the right to police the region. Some incursions were spectacular, such as the attack on Beirut airport in 1968 and the invasion of southern Lebanon with 20,000 troops in 1978. UN Security Council Resolution 425 (19 March 1978) calling upon Israel to cease immediately its military action and withdraw forthwith from all Lebanese territory was supported by President Carter. Israel did withdraw, but has retained a 'security zone' above the Israeli border in some 10 per cent of the territory of Lebanon. The Israel–Egyptian signing of the Camp David Accords, made over the heads of the Palestinian people in September 1978, added urgency to the settler policy.

After the 1981 bombardment of Lebanon, and, using the pretext of the attempt on the life of Schlomo Argov, the Israeli Ambassador to Britain (4 June 1982), Israeli jets and gunboats struck at Palestinian positions in southern Lebanon and East Beirut. The Security Council passed Resolution 508, demanding a cessation of Israeli hostilities. Israel's motivation was to exterminate Palestinian nationalism and to curb the power of the PLO (see MacBride 1983: 65; Shahak 1994: 18-19). The figures for the dead (17,825) and injured (30,203) are likely to be underestimates. Estimates of Palestinian and Lebanese displaced persons are between 500,000 and 800,000. The International Commission of Enquiry into Israel's conduct concluded that Israel violated the laws of war in several respects (MacBride 1983: 34-35, 38, 40-42, 99, 108, etc.).

'National Unity' Coalition Government, 1984–88
During the period of the 'National Unity' Coalition (Likud and Labour) Government (1984–88) there was an acceleration in the settlement programme. By 1988, land confiscation had resulted in Jewish control of over 52 per cent of the West Bank. In addition, over 40 per cent of the Gaza Strip was declared to be 'state land', and hence under exclusively Jewish control (Matar 1992: 444-48; for a complete analysis, see Halabi 1985). By early 1988, there were 117 Jewish colonies in the West Bank, with a population of over 67,000, built on seized land. This was in addition to the 8 large Jewish residential colonies, with a total population of 100,000, built in fortress style in annexed East Jerusalem. In the Gaza Strip there were 14 Jewish colonies, with a population of 2500. Up to that time polls showed that approximately a quarter of the Palestinian population of the West Bank and the Gaza Strip had been dispossessed of all or parts of their lands (Matar 1992: 448).

Since 1967, the water resource of the West Bank has been developed virtually exclusively for Jews, both in the Occupied Territories and in Israel itself. By 1987, the Jewish water company, Mekorot, had drilled more than 40 deep-bore wells and was pumping some 42 million cubic metres per year from West Bank underground water supplies, exclusively for Jewish colonies. By contrast, Palestinians pump only 20 million cubic metres from their pre-1967 shallow wells. In some cases, Mekorot drilled deep-bore wells in close proximity to springs used by Palestinian farmers, with the result that their springs and wells dried up. It is estimated that pre-1967 Israel pumps one-third of its annual needs of 1.8 billion cubic metres from underground West Bank basins. Hence, Israelis exploit the water, first, to provide water for Israel proper, and second, to provide water for the Jewish colonies in the Occupied Territories. Meanwhile, the Palestinians are prevented from developing their own water resources for their own welfare and economic survival (Matar 1992: 454).

The Intifada

The Israeli occupation prompted an inevitable explosion of resistance, bringing a new word to the international discourse. The *intifada* (from a root meaning 'to shake off, to recover, to recuperate, to jump to one's feet') denoted the Palestinian eruption to shake off the occupation, beginning on 8 December 1987. The Israeli efforts to restore the *status quo* shocked the international community and some Israelis. The *intifada* politicized the Christian Churches, both in the Holy Land and abroad (see Prior 1990, 1993, 1996), and gained widespread international sympathy for the Palestinians and condemnation of the Israeli occupation. The Palestine National Council made its declaration of the State of Palestine (15 November 1988), which was to exist side by side with the State of Israel. Chairman Arafat confirmed the PLO's acceptance of Israel, its renunciation of violence and its willingness to negotiate a peaceful settlement based on UN resolutions.

The Peace Process

The Palestinian euphoria in anticipation of the Madrid Conference in November 1991 yielded to depression, so that by August 1993 there was virtually no Palestinian hopeful of any improvement in the lot of the people. While I was in Jerusalem working on this study, the Israeli systematic and sustained bombardment of Lebanon, Operation Accountability (25–31 July 1993), forced some 400,000 displaced persons north, killed some 130, mostly civilians, and badly damaged at least 55 towns and villages. Israel's merciless bombardment had the effect of forging an unprecedented unity among the Lebanese people, divided since its civil war began in 1975.[37] In the end Israel had to settle for an American-brokered, unwritten 'understanding' that Hizbullah would cease firing Katyushas into northern Israel. During the week Hizbullah played a major part in caring for the displaced persons, with the result that, as the source of the only active resistance to Israel, its standing among the Lebanese grew.

After 22 months of frustration with the lack of any progress in the

---

37. Israel's behaviour in Operation Accountability violated the principles of the law of war, and those responsible for it, especially Premier and Minister of Defence Yitzhak Rabin, and Chief of Staff Ehud Barak could well have been charged with war crimes and crimes against humanity. Despite Israel's confession that its policy was to destroy the villages of southern Lebanon and create hundreds of thousands of refugees, newly-elected President Clinton did not condemn the operation.

Madrid Process, the Palestinian negotiators threatened to boycott the tenth round of talks scheduled for Washington in early September 1993. Arafat, aware of the progress of the secret Oslo track, prevailed upon them not to break off negotiations but to return for one more round. One of the negotiators assured me that he was disillusioned by the process but was ready at any time to leave for preparatory meetings in Amman, prior to going to Washington. At the end of August the secret contacts between the Israelis and the Palestinians in Oslo and other European cities suggested that there was going to be an historic compromise. Gaza and Jericho would be the first fruits, giving the Palestinians self-rule for the interim five-year period, after the third year of which discussions would begin on the permanent status, including the future of Jerusalem, the settlements and the fate of the displaced Palestinians.

The preamble to the Oslo Accord (Declaration of Principles [DOP]) stated the readiness of both parties 'to put an end to decades of confrontation and conflict, recognize their mutual legitimate and political rights, and strive to live in peaceful co-existence and mutual dignity and security and achieve a just, lasting and comprehensive peace settlement and historic reconciliation through the agreed political process'. The 13 September 1993 White House lawn handshake between Premier Rabin and Chairman Arafat promised a new beginning. Prime Minister Rabin's 12 November meeting with President Clinton yielded a cornucopia of economic, technological and military handouts, with the President renewing 'America's unshakeable pledge to maintain and enhance Israel's qualitative security edge'.

The failure to meet the Accord's deadline for Israeli withdrawal from Gaza–Jericho on 13 December caused some to wonder whether Israel was serious in its peace intentions. The massacre of 29 worshipping Muslims in Hebron (25 February 1994) appeared to be the last nail in the Oslo Accord's coffin. Matters were exacerbated in early April with attacks by Hamas's *Izz al-Din al-Qassam* guerrillas in Afula and Hadera. After months of protracted negotiations, 4 May saw the signing of the 450-page agreement on Palestinian self-rule in Gaza and Jericho. There was some rejoicing when Yasser Arafat crossed the Rafah terminal into Gaza on 1 July.

Religious opposition to the peace process was developing. Former Israeli Chief Rabbi Schlomo Goren called on soldiers to disobey any orders they might receive to dismantle settlements in the Occupied

Territories. Efrat Rabbi, Shlomo Riskin, was arrested with 100 other settlers, demanding a referendum on Oslo II (the second phase of the Oslo process, passed by the Knesset in October 1995 with a margin of one vote), and at an anti-Rabin rally outside the Israeli Embassy in London on 9 August 1995, the President of Jerusalem's Great Synagogue described Rabin as heading a 'Nazi Jewish government'.

By the Taba agreement of 24(–28) September 1995, Israel would deploy from six towns—amounting to 4 per cent of the West Bank area, inhabiting 250,000 Palestinians. The Palestinian Authority would have partial control of Hebron and responsibility for 'public order' in the 440 villages of the West Bank, inhabited by 68 per cent of the Palestinian population and occupying 23 per cent of West Bank territory. Israel would retain control of 73 per cent of the territory of the West Bank. Therefore, Oslo II gave the Palestinian Authority effective control over only 4 per cent of the land and limited administrative responsibility for 98 per cent of the Palestinian population of the West Bank.

The agreement, derided by Palestinian dissidents as 'catastrophic' and a 'negotiated surrender', reflected the asymmetry of the negotiating parties, with the PLO virtually politically impotent and financially bankrupt. It remains to be seen whether the functional autonomy which the agreement offers will inaugurate 'a true start for a new era in which the Palestinian people will live free and sovereign in their own country', as Arafat promised. Although modest, the Israeli restitution does amount to some dilution of the Zionist dream of a Greater Israel. Redeployment began from Jenin on 25 October. The assassination of Prime Minister Rabin by a nationalist, religious Jew on 4 November brought shock and grief to most Israelis and delight to others, especially settlers and various religious factions, some of whom danced in the street.[38] Shimon Peres assumed the leadership.

After the Israel army deployed from Tulkarm, Nablus, Qalqilya, Bethlehem and Ramallah in December 1995, President Arafat visited each town, promising that at the end of the peace 'tunnel' would stand 'the minarets, walls and churches of Jerusalem'. In Bethlehem, which

38. Former British Chief Rabbi Lord Jakobovits had written to Rabin as a gesture of support for his part in the peace process: 'As one of the very few Orthodox rabbis broadly supporting your peace efforts, I thought I might render some assistance in moderating the bitter hostility of the two principal opposition groups: the settlers and the various religious factions' (*Jewish Chronicle*, 18 August 1995, p. 17).

he described as the 'birthplace of the Palestinian, Jesus Christ', he was the guest of honour at the traditional Midnight Mass. Greek Orthodox Patriarch, Diodoros I compared Arafat to the seventh-century Caliph Omar ibn-Khatab, who had received the 'keys of Jerusalem' after pledging to protect the Christians of the city, a report which an editor of *al-Quds* relegated to page 8, which led to his being detained for six days by Arafat's police.

The long-awaited Palestinian elections were duly held on 20 January 1996, without the participation of the Palestinian rejectionist parties. Some 68 per cent of the electorate in the West Bank, including East Jerusalem, where, due to widespread Israeli intimidation, only 40 per cent voted, and 90 per cent in Gaza demonstrated the Palestinians' desire to engage in the democratic process. Arafat won 88 per cent in the presidential contest, while his Fatah party won 50 of the 88 seats on the Council. Another 16 Fatah members, who stood in protest against Arafat's official list, were also elected. The euphoria of the election yielded almost immediately to violence. Suicide bombings on a bus in central Jerusalem (which left 24 dead, including Palestinian passengers, 25 February) and elsewhere brought horrors which might derail the *peace process*. Israel imposed draconian collective punishment in the Occupied Territories, this time supported by the Palestinian police. The 'internal closure' of both Gaza and the towns and villages of the West Bank confirmed the fears of many that what Oslo II prefigured was merely a Zionist corralling of natives into what in South African were called *Bantustans*, and in Latin America *congregaciones* or *aldeias.*

Violence erupted in southern Lebanon and Israel's northern border, culminating on 11 April in Premier Peres's Operation Grapes of Wrath. The 16 days of merciless bombing from air, land and sea killed over 150 Lebanese civilians, created up to half a million displaced persons and wreaked havoc on the infrastructure of civilian life in southern Lebanon. The 'surgical strikes' at purely Hizbullah targets by 'smart bombs' yielded to savage assaults on civilians, most spectacularly the killing of more than 100 displaced civilians in the UN's Fijian battalion's headquarters at Qana (18 April), which seemed to go beyond what could be tolerated even by a generally forgiving, pro-Israeli West.[39] Israel's offensive against mainly civilian targets

39. Ironically, I was informed of this development at the reception for a London

violated the 1949 Geneva Convention, for which the perpetrators might be brought before tribunals for war crimes and crimes against humanity.[40] Rabbi Yehuda Amital, a member of Peres's cabinet, called the Qana killings a desecration of God's name (*chilul hashem*) (*Jewish Chronicle*, 3 May 1996, p. 1). However, the Nobel Peace Prize winner's murderous ruthlessness towards Lebanese civilians proved to be a monumental political miscalculation.

Grapes of Wrath welded the different factions of Lebanese society into an uncharacteristic unity of purpose against Israel, and precipitated the day when Israel will have to conform to UN Resolution 425 and withdraw from southern Lebanon. The uncritical support which Israel received from President Clinton and Secretary of State Christopher betrayed that administration's disregard for international law and civilized behaviour when its own foreign policy interests were at stake, and when a presidential election was on the horizon. The Lebanon incursion did not advance Premier Peres's case, and he was beaten narrowly by Binyamin Netanyahu in the 29 May elections. However, President Clinton was elected for a second term.

In the negotiations between Israel and the Palestinians, which are scheduled to deal with the substantive issues leading to a comprehensive peace settlement, the demands of justice and conformity with the requirements of international law and the conventions on human rights will have to yield to the reality of the political imbalance of power. The partners in the negotiations enjoy an asymmetric bargaining relationship. Israel is unlikely to conform to UN Resolutions and to respect the rights of the Palestinian people as enshrined in a range of human rights conventions. The foundational injustice done to the indigenous Palestinian people by the Zionist venture will not be righted, at least at this stage. A just solution to the problem would require a rolling back of the achievement of Zionism and the abandonment of its ideology, including that the Palestinian displaced persons be allowed return to their former homes, or be adequately

Conference marking the centenary of Herzl's *Der Judenstaat*.

40. During the period of Israel's incursion (15 April), Szymon Serafinowicz, an 85-year-old refugee was committed for Britain's first war crimes trial, charged with murdering 3 Jews during the winter of 1941–42. Sixteen witnesses came from as far afield as Israel, Siberia, Belarus, Cape Town and USA. The Chief Executive of the Board of Deputies of British Jews applauded the action in recognition of the fundamental principle that justice must be done, however much time may have elapsed.

compensated in accordance with international law. It is not likely that the State of Israel will acknowledge the injustice Zionism has perpetrated on the Palestinians, beg their forgiveness and make commensurate reparation. There can, of course, be a pragmatic solution based on compromise by the parties concerned. But justice will have to wait another day.

The Religious Dimension

The murder of 29 Muslim worshippers in the Ibrahimi Mosque in Hebron by a Jewish religious settler (25 February 1994),[41] and the assassination of Premier Rabin (4 November 1995) by a religious Jew, who protested that he was acting in God's name, focus on the religious dimension to Zionism. Yigal Amir, the son of an orthodox rabbi, was a student in the Institute for Advanced *Torah* Studies in Bar-Ilan University, founded by the National Religious Party (NRP). Among the books found in his room was one lauding Goldstein (*Jewish Chronicle*, 10 November 1995, p. 3). Prior to Rabin's assassination, Likud leader Binjamin Netanyahu had sat on platforms at opposition rallies at which Rabin was lampooned as a Hitler and demonstrators cried out *Rabin boged* (Rabin is a traitor). A number of rabbis, for example, Moshe Tendler of Monsey, New York, and Abraham Hecht of Brooklyn, stressed that not an inch of occupied land could be surrendered (sic!), and Hecht added that any Jewish leader who would give back land should be killed (Hertzberg 1996: 37). We shall see that such views derive from a particular interpretation of the land traditions of the Bible.

The promise of land to Abraham and his descendants, while a singular eruption into human history in the biblical narrative, is appropriated by every generation of Jews and is spelled out daily in the *Siddur*. However, in the diaspora, 'Zion' gradually became increasingly metaphysical, and 'portable': 'The Rabbis, undaunted even by the fall of

---

41. The burial-place of Baruch Goldstein, 'the upright, martyr', has the appearance of a garden of remembrance in Kahane Park in Kiryat Arba, and is fully equipped for prayer services for pilgrims to the shrine, with a bookcase and a suitable apparatus for burning memorial candles. Supporters kiss his tomb, and pray over his grave. Rabbi Dov Lior addressed Goldstein's son on the occasion of his *bar mitzvah*: 'Ya'akov Yair, follow in your father's footsteps. He was righteous and a great hero' (*Jerusalem Report*, 12 December 1996, p. 10).

their state, had discovered that Palestine was portable. And so, by a network of institutions, they contrived that Palestine should live in Israel, if not Israel in Palestine' (Zangwill 1937: 3-4).

In kabbalistic literature the land of Israel, the *Torah* and God are one. The spiritual unity of the people and the land made it natural to accept the people's physical separation from it until the end of time (see Schweid 1987: 539).

In the modern period, those Jews who opted for emancipation and regarded the place of their citizenship as their fatherland considered Zion to be the symbol of universal redemption, and rejected the re-establishment of Jewish sovereignty. The Orthodox minority, however, rejected emancipation but retained the view of the temporal nature of exile until the coming of the Messiah. The Zionists, for their part, aspired to equality and emancipation for Jews, but insisted that it would be achieved only within the framework of an independent Jewish state in Uganda, northern Sinai, Argentina, Biro Bidzhan (Laquer 1972: 157-58, 427-28) or, preferably, in Zion.

While there is no appeal in *Der Judenstaat* to the injunction to carry out the *mitzvot* in the Promised Land, the symbiotic relationship between the secular and the religious motivation is reflected in the Hebrew name for the Jewish National Fund (JNF). In the daily Morning Service of the *Siddur*, after preliminary prayers, the reading from Exodus 13.1-10 enlivens the memory of the deliverance from Egypt. The reading invites all readers and hearers to consider *themselves* to be on the journey from slavery to freedom (with *you* italicized here to indicate the stress on the contemporary reader):

> *Today*, in the month of Abib, *you* are going out. When Yahweh brings *you* into the land of the Canaanites, the Hittites, the Amorites, the Hivites, and the Jebusites, which he swore to *your* ancestors to give *you*...For with a strong hand Yahweh brought *you* out of Egypt (Exod. 13.4-9).

The reading continues:

> When Yahweh has brought *you* into the land of the Canaanites, as he swore to *you* and *your* ancestors, and has given it to *you*, *you* shall set apart to Yahweh all that first opens the womb...'By strength of hand Yahweh brought us out of Egypt, from the house of slavery...Therefore I sacrifice to Yahweh every male that first opens the womb'...It shall serve as a sign on *your* hand and as an emblem on *your* forehead that by strength of hand Yahweh brought us out of Egypt (Exod. 13.11-16).

The Blessings for the study of the *Torah* follow, and the Priestly Blessings (Num. 6.24-26). Then, in the second text from the Babylonian Talmud (*Šab.* 127a), we read,

> These are the precepts whose fruits a person enjoys in This World but whose principal [fruit] remains intact for him [*ha-keren kayemet lô*] in the World to Come. They are the honour due to father and mother, acts of kindness, early attendance at the house of study morning and evening, hospitality to guests, visiting the sick, providing for a bride, escorting the dead, absorption in prayer, bringing peace between man and his fellow—and the study of *Torah* is equivalent to them all.

The Hebrew name for the JNF, Keren Kayemet L'Yisrael, evoked the foundational legend of deliverance from Egypt and entrance into the Promised Land, already occupied by others. It appealed to the sacrificial spirit of Jews to make a generous offering as a gesture of thanksgiving, corresponding to the offering of 'the firstborn of *your* livestock'. While the liturgical offering was to Yahweh, the contemporary one would be to the JNF, as an act of sacrifice on a par with those other commandments, which, in addition to meriting returns in this life (through gathering interest), would be rewarded in the World to Come.

  In the early stages, Palestine was considered to be a free land, but difficulties surfaced in the first wave of immigration when it was realized that there was no free land and a population in excess of half a million already in the mid-nineteenth century (J. Abu-Lughod 1987: 140). Even though the implementation of the Ottoman Land Code of 1858, whereby all land was to be registered in the name of individual owners, led to the manipulation of the process by absentee landlords, the *fellahin* working the land had a developed sense of ownership, and in some cases realized the precariousness of their plight only when 'their land' was sold over their heads to Jews (see Khalidi 1988: 211-24). Moreover, the land was expensive, and more so with immigration. Even the arid land was in somebody's possession (e.g. the Sultan, or later the British Crown). Zangwill saw at once the problem and a Bible-based solution:

> There is, however, a difficulty from which the Zionist dares not avert his eyes, though he rarely likes to face it. Palestine proper has already its inhabitants...So we must be prepared either to drive out by the sword the tribes in possession as our forefathers did, or to grapple with the problem of a large alien population, mostly Mohammedan and accustomed for centuries to despise us (in April 1905, 1937: 201).

Since Jewish immigration coincided with the beginnings of political awareness among the Arabs there was bound to be a conflict of interests.

There was little debate within political Zionism on the right of Jews to go to an already inhabited Palestine. Whereas one might expect to find debates centring around such concepts as natural right, historical right, moral right, or religious right, the discourse was content to stake a claim by virtue of a perceived 'national' need, with a presumption that a need constituted a right.

Then there were some pressing questions of quality. Would the state be the home of a secular people, or a holy land in which the *mitzvot* would be carried out? Was it legitimate to anticipate the divine initiative and use secular tools to establish a national homeland? Within Jewish eschatology there has always been a certain tension between the aspiration to redemption through a divine initiative and that facilitated by human intervention. There was a danger that auto-redemption, being primarily a secular, political aspiration, would lead to total estrangement from the religious tradition. The secular–sacred tension is the subject of intense debate in Israel to this day.

Biblical Literalism and Political Hermeneutics
The role in the Zionist enterprise played by Jewish theology and appeal to the Bible is difficult to assess precisely. Political Zionism was not only not supported by the religious establishment in the beginning but was bitterly opposed. As we shall see, rather late in the day, Orthodox theology performed a *volte face* and made common cause with secular, political Zionism. In this new context, appeal to the traditions of the Bible and their interpretation in the Mishnah and Talmud and elsewhere within Jewish theology provided secular Zionism with a theological foundation which was able to root settlement in the land with traditions much older than those of European nationalism and colonialism.

The key figure in this fundamental re-interpretation of classical Orthodoxy was Rabbi Avraham Yitzhak Kook (HaRav, or, simply Rav, 1865–1935), who was to become the first Ashkenazi Chief Rabbi of Palestine. His task was formidable, since, with the exception of the earlier Rabbis Alkalai and Kalischer, and some later voices within the religious wing of the Hovevei Zion movement, for example, Shmuel Mohiliver, Yitzhak Reines and Yehiel Michal Pines (Avineri 1981: 187), virtually the whole of Orthodox and Reform Jewry was opposed

to Zionism. In particular the pietists who made up the old Jewish settlement in Palestine were bitterly opposed to the secularists who systematically violated the *Torah* while embarking on their secular
redemption of the Jewish people. For the newcomer Zionists, the
pietists were decadent parasites who were blind to the vision of Jewish
redemption. Rav Kook's tolerance of the secularists who mocked at
traditional sanctities brought abuse from many noted rabbis (Ben Zion
Bokser, in Kook 1979: 10). Putting the new wine of the activist secular political movement of Zionism into the old bottles of Orthodox
Judaism would be a precarious activity.

Rav Kook's writings and teachings provided the first systematic
attempt to integrate the traditional, passive religious longing for the
land with the modern, secular and aggressively active praxis of
Zionism, giving birth to a comprehensive religious-nationalist
Zionism.[42] Rav Kook displayed an exceptional ability to integrate the
many traditions of Judaism into a whole. He called for a renewal of
the old and a hallowing of the new. In line with his seeking 'the holy
sparks' in every Jewish ideology, he saw secular Zionism as an instrument of God to further the messianic redemption and restoration
(*tikun*) not only of Jews but of all humanity (*tikun olam*—humankind
was one body and one soul), a critical aspect of the Rav's teleology,
widely ignored by his disciples: 'It is impossible not to be filled with
love for every creature, for the flow of the light of God shines in
everything, and everything discloses the pleasantness of Yahweh. "The
mercy of Yahweh fills the earth" (Ps. 33.5)' ('The Moral Principles:
Love', Kook 1979: 135, par. 3). All human history was evolving
inexorably towards the divine perfection of the Kingdom of the
Almighty: even the secular had sparks of the sacred. Such was the
immediacy of God that everything was a crust with an inner essence, a
divine dimension.

However, his religious perspective was not received enthusiastically
when he set foot in Palestine in 1904. In the mind of the Zionist pioneers, the time of ghettoized Orthodox religion had passed, while in
the mind of the Orthodox establishment, secular Zionism was so riv-
eted to the soil that its eyes missed the skies: 'They refuse to mention
God. Their focus on power and glory obscures the all-pervasive

---

42. See Kook 1979: 390-92 for a note on his writings, many of which were published only after his death in 1935.

sacred and Divine' (in Yaron 1991: 216). For Rav Kook, however, the divine plan depended on the totality of the Jewish people and not on the Orthodox alone. In his day, the divine energy was at its strongest in the creative pioneers of the secular Zionist revolution. If their utopian secularism was heretical in the minds of the Orthodox establishment, for Kook it represented the source of renewal.

Rav Kook's Judaism was a synthesis of Orthodoxy, nationalist Zionism and the liberalism of the Enlightenment, although his advocacy of the values of the Enlightenment has not impressed itself on his followers. Orthodoxy had run dry, and nationalism alone would not satisfy the longings of the Jewish heart for long, since, like all parochialisms, it settles for a segment rather than the whole of life. Zionism was not a novel principle but was a means of realizing the ancient ideal of settlement in the land for the purpose of fulfilling the *mitzvot*, thus foreshortening the wait for divine redemption. Return to Zion was an immediate imperative for every Jew, and not a mere messianic postulate to be carried out in God's good time. It was the real, terrestrial Jerusalem and not just the celestial Jerusalem of prophetic visions that interested the Rav.

For Rav Kook the link between People and Land was of divine provenance: 'Our indelible inner nature, heart and soul, remain firmly committed to the Holy Land...*Eretz Israel* constitutes the indispensable basis for the fulfilment of the Jewish People's Divine vocation.' No genuine Jewish life could prosper outside Eretz Israel. Israel's divine genius will shine forth and illuminate the world once the entire nation is physically and spiritually reunited with the land. Israel's re-establishment in its homeland is a precondition of the corporate Jewish sanctity's consummation. The JNF's land acquisition from Gentiles implemented the divinely ordained 'Conquest of *Eretz Israel*' (in Yaron 1991: 208-12).

In conformity with his unique kabbalistic messianic view—more is hidden from the eye than is seen—Rav Kook claimed that God was bringing about his redemption through the 'Divinely inspired' Balfour Declaration that 'mirrored the Dawn of Salvation' (Yaron 1991: 226),[43] and the entire Zionist enterprise, even through people who

43. He wrote to Lord Rothschild after the Balfour Declaration, and at a London rally after the Declaration, he stated: 'I have not come to thank the British but to congratulate them for being privileged to be the source of this Declaration to the People of Israel' (Yaron 1991: 318 n. 12).

never suspected the deeper significance of their role. Practical activities were inseparable from spiritual aspirations, and social activity as well as mysticism had religious meaning: stirrings 'down below' were a necessary preamble to evoking messianic grace 'from above' (Hertzberg 1996: 39). Whereas religious Zionists, such as Ahad Ha'am, stressed the spiritual dimension of the return, and secular Zionists, such as Herzl, the political, Rav Kook sought a synthesis, holding that the political and metaphysical dimensions would be united in a state. Even self-professed atheists and proponents of a wholly secular Zionism reflect the divine, once imbued with the spirit of Israel (Yaron 1991: 203). Even if the secular Zionists were motivated by European nationalism and socialism, at the objective cosmic level the real meaning of their activity was suffused with the divine will, which their seemingly atheistic motivation clouded over. Even though they might deny the ultimate coming of the Messiah, their activities speed up his arrival. Without knowing it, they were instruments in the divine plan. Religious Jewry should penetrate beyond the shell of secular atheistic nationalism into the divine spark at the core of Zionism. The spirit of God and the spirit of Israel (Jewish nationalism) were identical.

Such a fusion of secularism and Orthodoxy evoked strong opposition, especially from those who could not concede that Zionist nationalism was an adequate expression of the Jewish nation's sense of being impregnated with the divine. Initially, some rabbis in Palestine ceremonially excommunicated the Zionist pioneers, especially those of the second aliyah, who were impregnated with the spirit of Russian socialist revolution. If it appeared to others that Zionism had abandoned its Jewish religious roots in seeking normality rather than the singularity and distinctiveness befitting a people saturated with the divine *Shekhinah*, Rav Kook's vision was able to penetrate through the secular clouds that overshadowed and the multiple veils that obscured the core religious values of the Jewish tradition.

As Chief Rabbi of Jerusalem and Palestine for 16 years until his death in 1935, Rav Kook had abundant opportunities to infuse his unique form of political mysticism into the discourse of Zionism. As we shall see, his prodigious writings, and perhaps especially his founding of Merkaz HaRav,[44] have proven to be critical in the renaissance

44. He founded Merkaz HaRav (the Rabbi's Centre) in 1921, as a Jerusalem

of religio-political Zionism up to the present. The excerpts of his writings available popularly do not deal with the reality that the renewal of the People of Israel would take place in a land wherein the Jews were a minority and in which there was already a well-established indigenous population. In the light of developments which took place 13 years after his death, one speculates whether Rav Kook's confidence in the divine will operating within secular Zionism, with history moving inexorably towards the Kingdom of the Heavens, would have been disturbed by the outrages attendant upon the partial realization of the secularist Zionist dream in 1948–49, and of the iniquities which have been perpetrated by his disciples up to the present, which, while emanating from religious fervour, shock decent people by their brutality. Perhaps, like Herzl, his death before the first beginnings of the messianic era in 1948 saved his reputation as a mystic, a philosopher and a saint from being terminally tainted.

The State of Israel
Israel's proclamation as a 'Jewish state' ensured that there would be close ties between religion and political life, and that ideologies based on religious principles would permeate the much wider political discourse. Appeal to the foundational significance of *Torah* has enjoyed widespread support, even from atheistic Jews.[45] However, religious values are not confined to the Israeli religious parties (which won 23 of the 120 seats in the Knesset in 1996), and on some fundamental questions, such as territoriality, agreement transcends party

---

Higher Yeshiva catering for the entire Jewish people, and providing a six-year programme, involving the study of the *Halakhah*, Biblical Studies, Jewish History, Eretz Israel Studies, Jewish Philosophy and Science, and Literary Style (Yaron 1991: 177-79).

45. Ben-Gurion regularly convened the 'Prime Minster's Bible Study Circle', which included Zalman Shazar, the then President of Israel. His lecture, 'The Bible and the Jewish People', delivered at Nahalal, 20 July 1964, makes abundant use of biblical texts, especially those dealing with the promise of restoration. While he alludes to the Hebrew prophets and their concern for justice, he does not deal with the injunctions to disinherit the Canaanites, the Joshua legend, nor with the traditions that reflect racist, ethnicist, xenophobic and militaristic tendencies. His sole, oblique reference to the indigenous Palestinians is that while the whole world regarded Israel with respect and admiration, 'Our Arab neighbours have as yet not made peace with our existence, and their leaders are declaring their desire to destroy us' (1972: 294). See also Moshe Dayan's *Living with the Bible* (1978).

boundaries, reflecting in some alignments the Kookist doctrine of the unity of the secular and sacred. Moreover, the extent to which the ideology of non-parliamentary groups can infiltrate the political discourse is one of the most distinctive features of the Israeli body politic.

Moreover, the Israeli electoral system guarantees minority ideologies a greater influence than their numerical support would enjoy in other democracies. With no electoral constituencies in Israel, any party or electoral list winning as little as 1.5 per cent (raised from 1 per cent) of the national vote gains representation in the Knesset in proportion to its percentage vote. This has led to a proliferation of parties, most of which obtain only a few, but critical seats in the 120 member Knesset. In the May 1996 election there were 20 lists, of which 11 won seats, with 5 winning no more than 5 seats. Moreover, since no political party has ever won an overall majority, all Israeli Prime Ministers have had to construct coalitions, all of which have involved religious parties. Some 90 per cent of the supporters of the religious parties voted for Binyamin Netanyahu, who was elected Prime Minister with the narrowest of margins. He was able to form of a coalition involving 19 MKs of the Sephardic Orthodox Shas and the National Religious parties, with the support of 4 United Torah Judaism MKs. In the newly-formed coalition government, Shas and the NRP members took control of the ministries of education and culture, labour and interior, and increased their numbers on several Knesset committees.[46] Religious parties, however, sacrifice some of

46. The 1996 election yielded 34 seats to Labour, 32 to the Likud/Gesher/ Tzomet list (with 5 seats surrendered to Gesher and 4 to Tzomet), 10 to Shas, 9 to the NRP, 9 to Meretz, 7 to Israel ba-Aliya, 5 to DFPE, 4 each to United Torah Judaism, Third Way, United Arab List and 2 to Moledet. The nine other parties/lists which contested the election won 3 per cent of the national vote between them but no seats. In order to obtain a working parliamentary majority, Netanyahu formed a government with Shas and the NRP, and with Israel ba-Aliya (newly-formed immigrants' party), the Third Way (a breakaway faction from Labour), as well as with the Gesher and the militantly nationalist Tzomet factions of his own list, giving a total of 62 seats, and the additional 4 supporting votes of United Torah Judaism. The three religious parties increased their combined Knesset representation from 16 to 23. Labour, Meretz (a left of centre alignment of Mapam, Shinui and Ratz, a civil rights movement), DFPE (Democratic Front for Peace and Equality, an alliance of the Communist Party, Rakkah and other leftist, Israeli-Arab groups), and the United Arab List formed the main body of opposition. Israeli-Arab representation reached a

their ideology in a compromise with more secular ideologies and pragmatic considerations. In the survey which follows, I review some of the ways in which *Torah* values penetrate Israeli society.

Far Right Zionism

The Far Right, or Radical Right in Israel refers to those groups which aspire to a Greater Israel, with borders extending well beyond the Green Line of the 1949 Armistice. For some that means annexing the Occupied Territories only, while others have their eyes fixed on the east bank of the Jordan also. Together with secular ultra-nationalist ideologies, religion and the *Torah* feature prominently in this ideology, which in most forms betrays a strongly xenophobic element, and in many cases advocates violence and fascist activities as a means to its politico-religious goal. The movements and parties whose principal objective is the creation of Greater Israel include Gush Emunim, Tehiya-Tzomet, Morasha, Moledet and the now illegal Kach.[47] Kach has been the most extreme in its advocacy of an overt, *Torah*-driven xenophobic policy, and Gush Emunim has proved to be by far the most influential group. One of the features of modern Israeli politics is the ascendancy of the nationalist-religious right wing since the 1980s, with the result that what were extreme nationalistic, ethnocentric, xenophobic and militaristic positions earlier have become respectable.

If the outline of a Jewish renaissance was laid down in the writings of the elder Rav Kook, it was left to his son, Rabbi Zvi Yehuda Kook, and his disciples in the Merkaz HaRav to carry it forward. While the elder Rav Kook's view that the messianic era had begun was not taken seriously in his own day, his son supported it later with a programme of messianic-political activism. Reflecting claims of pre-eminence (*segulah*) and group superiority, the younger Kook emphasized the unique and holy nature of the Jewish people, and of every Jew, even non- and indeed anti-religious Zionists, and saw in the rebirth of the Jewish state the first step towards the coming of the Messiah. All the institutions of the state were means to a messianic end: the government and the army were *Kadosh* (in Kook 1991: 353).

new high of 11 (4 DFPE, whose fifth MK is Jewish, 4 UAL, 2 Labour and 1 Meretz) (see Peretz and Doron 1996).

47. See further Lustick 1988 and Sprinzak 1991. Parties rise and disappear quickly in the turbulent world of Israeli right-wing politics.

On the eve of Independence Day (2 May) 1967, the younger Kook addressed a gathering of alumni of Merkaz HaRav. Rising to a crescendo, he bewailed the partition of historic Eretz Israel. The 1947 UN Partition Plan had cut Eretz Israel, 'the inheritance of our fore-fathers' into pieces, placing 'portions of our country in foreign hands', leaving him in 1947 desolate in his father's old room in Jerusalem's Jaffa Street, while Jews were dancing in the streets outside. Now in 1967, recalling that sad day, and reflecting on, 'They have divided my land' (Joel 3.2), and bewailing, he exclaimed,

> Where is our Hebron? Do we forget this? And where is our Shechem? Do we forget this? And where is our Jericho? Do we forget this too? And where is our other side of the Jordan? Where is each block of earth? Each part and parcel, and four cubits of *Hashem's* land. Is it in our hands to relinquish any millimetre of this?

and answered, 'G-d forbid' (Kook 1991: 338-39).

When, three weeks later, Jerusalem, Hebron, Shechem and Jericho 'miraculously fell into our hands' and Israel was in control of an enlarged state, with the Occupied Territories three times the size of Israel, his disciples were sure that a genuine spirit of prophecy had come over their rabbi on that day (Sprinzak 1985: 37-38). The war strengthened the sense of national solidarity among Jews in Israel and abroad, signalling the revival of 'territorial maximalism' (Sprinzak 1991: 35-69) and, for those religiously inclined, a religious-national awakening. The occupation of East Jerusalem and all the Holy Places within her walls was proof that there was a process of divine redemption, founded on the trinity of the Land of Israel, the People of Israel, and the *Torah* of Israel. The religious camp was ready to fill the vacuum of a Zionist idealism which had become a spent force. The days of the Messiah were at hand and his arrival could be speeded up by political action, including force when necessary. As one was to learn gradually, such views were not the preserve of the flamboyant Rabbi Meir Kahane, but were shared by some of the most important Orthodox figures of the twentieth century (Hertzberg 1996: 37).

For the late Rabbi Meir Kahane and his followers in Kach (Thus it is, the political party he founded in 1972) and Kahane Chai (Kahane lives), religion and the *Torah*, rather than democracy, were the basis of the state. Zionism and Western democracy were irreconcilable. The *Torah* alone distinguishes Jews from non-Jews: secular Judaism is just atheism wrapped in a prayer shawl. The *Torah* legitimizes the Jewish state, since God delivered the Jews from slavery in Egypt and gave them the Promised Land, and commanded Jews to live in Eretz Israel. The *Torah* provides the only reason to live in a country which is miserable and uninteresting, and an absolute disaster from a geographical as well as a material viewpoint (Kahane, in Mergui and Simonnot 1987: 38-40). Jews should leave the diaspora and settle in the land, at God's command. The Bible establishes the borders: '...minimally, from El Arish, northern Sinai, including Yamit, part of the east bank of the Jordan, part of Lebanon and certain parts of Syria, and part of Iraq, to the Tigris river' (Mergui and Simonnot 1987: 54-55).

It is God's desire that Jews live separately and have the least possible contact with what is foreign in order to create a pure Jewish culture based on the *Torah*. In line with 'Kookism', Kahane held that Zionism accelerated the coming of the Messiah, and that the creation of the State of Israel marked the beginning of the messianic era. These factors override any consideration for the indigenes. To avoid future problems, Arabs should be deported with as little force as necessary. They have no right to be in Jerusalem, and Kahane would applaud anyone who blew up the two mosques on Temple Mount (Mergui and Simonnot 1987: 43-48, 85-86). Kahane claimed that all the rabbis supported the expulsion of the Arabs just as clearly, but in private.

Having failed in 1977 and 1981, he was elected to the Knesset in July 1984 with 1.3 per cent of the national vote. Throughout the 1970s until his assassination on 5 November 1990, he was the most aggressive of the zealots for the implementation of the biblical paradigm for Jewish settlement of the land (see Friedman 1990; 1992; Sprinzak 1991). While Kahane's ideology was offensive to people who respect democracy, there was a clear consistency between his programme and the values of the *Torah*, interpreted in a literalist fashion. He cannot be faulted for seeking the implementation of the divine mandate of the *Torah*, which not only sanctions the expulsion of the indigenous population, but requires it as a commandment. Moreover, his association of the State of Israel with the events of the messianic eschaton resonated sympathetically with the increasingly popular teleology of the religious-ultra-nationalist camp.

Kahane's brazenly violent methods and offensive language confounded the political establishment, leading to the banning of his party from the elections in 1988 and the locating of Kach on what was then the 'lunatic' fringe of Israeli society. But there were more subtle and less embarrassing ways of arriving at a similar goal. The June War of 1967 provided the catalyst for a rejuvenated religious Zionism and brought to public prominence a whole culture of eschatological Zionism which up to then had been largely confined to a number of *yeshivot*. It led to the founding of Hatenua Lemaan Eretz Yisrael Hashlema (Movement for the Whole of Eretz Yisrael, or Land of Israel Movement) in September 1967, which proclaimed that the conquest of Arab territory was irreversible and that Israel could embark on the absorption of more immigrants and settlement (see Sprinzak 1991: 38-43).

Furthermore, the Yom Kippur War of 1973 (the *mechdal*, culpable blunder), interpreted by Rabbi Yehuda Amital as a reaffirmation of the messianic process of redemption, emphasized the need for decisive action to consolidate and enlarge the Jewish presence in the land of Israel. It was this urgency which led to the founding of Gush Emunim (Bloc of the Faithful) by former students of Merkaz HaRav. It was officially established in February 1974 as an extra-parliamentary movement, in preference to remaining as a pressure group within the NRP (Sprinzak 1991: 64-66). From the beginning, it has been a professional, influential and well-funded organization which has consistently refused to transform itself into a political party, or to support any one party. Its membership has come from the extreme Right, the Right, and even the Left.

The movement was guided by the teachings of the elder Kook and those of his son, Rabbi Zvi Yehuda Kook, the major spiritual leader of the Gush until his death in 1982. For the younger Kook and his disciples, the war of 1967 was a turning point in the tortuous process of messianic redemption. Since the dimensions of Erez Israel were those of Genesis 15, rather than of pre-1967 Israel, Jews were obliged to fulfil the 'commandment of conquest' by settling in the whole land and defending Jewish sovereignty over it. Only then would they be at home and in place for redemption. Hence, one could never abandon Judea and Samaria.

Concerning the Arab inhabitants of the region, the example of Joshua's divine mission was eternally true. The Arabs could stay, provided they accepted minority status and gave no trouble. After the Arabs have learned that the land is Jewish, friendly relations may obtain. Moreover, for Zvi Yehuda Kook, the Jews never expelled the Arabs in 1948–49: they ran away on their own, 'whether from cowardice or exaggerated fear'. Jewish claims to the land rest on parental inheritance, as witnessed in the Bible and history (1991: 196-98). Moreover, since the Holocaust symbolized the extent of the evil of the Gentiles and their deep hatred of Jews, it was all the more necessary for Jews to set up a state away from the Gentiles, reinforcing some of the more xenophobic and ethnocentric traditions of the biblical narrative (e.g. Ezra 6.21; 9.1; 10.11; Neh. 9.2; 10.28; 13.3).

While the Gush focused on settlement of Jews in the Occupied Territories, it saw itself as a more general renewal movement within Zionism. After the establishment of the state Zionism had settled for the creation of a materialistic society in which the individual's pleasure replaced the national goal and mission. The Gush determined to put into effect the process of national redemption as mandated by the *Torah* and highlighted by 'Kookism'. The settlement of Judea and Samaria was a critical element in the process of messianic redemption, in which every Jew was obliged to play a part. This contrasted sharply with the traditional concept of Jewish Messianism, which favoured a more passive and a-political attitude of awaiting patiently the miraculous coming of the Messiah. Moreover, the Gush injected a strong political, and violent element into religious Zionism.

From the beginning, the Gush was led by Rabbi Moshe Levinger. A product of the Merkaz HaRav, Levinger too sees the struggle for Jewish settlement as paving the way for the advent of the Messiah. The fulfilment of Greater Israel was as sacred a duty as respect for the Sabbath. The practical decisions to settle Judea and Samaria were a natural extension of the ideological foundation laid down in the teachings of Rav Kook. The dozens of *Torah* communities which began to appear on the hills of Judea and Samaria grew out of his insistence that the settlement of Hebron and Shechem, like that of Tel Aviv and Jerusalem, was a straightforward commandant of the *Torah*. The first settlements after the 1967 War (Kfar Etzion, Kiryat Arba and Hebron) were founded by young rabbis from the Merkaz HaRav. Settlement was a natural complement to *Torah*, just as Joshua's conquest was a continuation of what Moses taught in the wilderness. Each new settlement was a witness to God's choice of the People of Israel, to the truth of *Torah*, and to the word of *Hashem* and his prophets (see Ezek. 36.34-36; in Zvi Yehuda Kook 1991: 351-52). To this day, Levinger and his followers pursue their goal with distinctively knitted skullcaps, prayer books and machine-guns. Their appearance on TV with guns ablaze in Hebron witnessed to a kind of *Torah*-observance which conforms with the Joshua narrative. Levinger himself was jailed for ten weeks for the 'criminally negligent homicide' of a Hebron Palestinian in September 1988.

The policy of the Gush is to expand the settlements and settle a million Jews in the West Bank before the turn of the millennium, so that territorial compromise becomes impossible and eventual annexation of the territories becomes the obvious conclusion. Having failed to get much support initially for *aliyah* from abroad, the Gush turned to encouraging Jews living in the state of Israel to settle in the Golan, the West Bank and Gaza. According to Hanan Porat, its director of settlement activities, 'Working in a settlement is a spiritual uplift, an antidote to the materialism and permissiveness which have swept the country. This is why the leadership of this country has passed from the secular into the national-religious camp' (in Mergui and Simonnot 1987: 126-27).

Because of its independence of all political parties, the Gush has exercised great influence on all governments. While the first settlements were set up by the Labour-led government, the rise to power of the Likud-led government of Menachem Begin in 1977—an earthquake in Israeli politics, when the pariahs of Zionism had replaced the party that built the nation (Friedman 1992: 20)—gave the movement a legitimacy at the highest levels of state and brought an end to the cautious settlement policy of the Labour-led administration (Sprinzak 1991: 71-105). Levinger was able to utilize splits within the government to establish the settlement of Kiryat Arba. Furthermore, at three o'clock on a March morning 1979, his wife, Miriam, led the occupation of the property in the heart of Hebron which became the nucleus of the some 400 Jews now living in fortress-like conditions among some 150,000 Palestinians.

All Israeli governments have succumbed to Levinger's pressures. The group has pursued a policy of *fait accompli*. First it establishes settlements which are 'illegal', and afterwards it receives the government's blessing and financial support. The Gush cares little about the implications of the alleged divine plan for the indigenous population. The land belongs to the Jews by divine command, which has binding implications. The universal principle of self-determination does not hold in the case of Eretz Israel, and hence the demand by the

Palestinians for national self-determination is meaningless. The Palestinians are *gerim* (non-Jewish residents), who, according to the *Torah* are to be treated with tolerance and respect but not more (Sprinzak 1985: 31-32). Palestinians have three choices: to acknowledge the legitimacy of the Gush's version of Zionism and to receive full civil rights; or to obey the laws of the state without formal recognition of Zionism and be granted the full rights of resident aliens; or to be granted incentives to emigrate to other Arab countries.

Theologically, the Palestinians are no more than religiously illegitimate tenants, and a threat to the redemptive process. Their human rights are no match for the divine imperative. Armed with the inerrant certainty of the *Torah*, which not only justifies violence, but gives the divine mandate for it, and the glorious example of Joshua, the Gush pursues its policy of settling, in disregard for the indigenous population. The ideology of the Gush has strong roots in the national religious camp and 'is only the tip of an iceberg of a broader religious subculture, which started its meteoric development in the 1950's' (Sprinzak 1985: 27). The major reason for its success lies in its having been able to redefine some of the pioneering values of Zionism at a time when Zionism had lost most of its foundational vision.

The Tehiya ('Renaissance') Party was founded in 1979 by Professor Yuval Neeman and Geula Cohen, disillusioned ex-Likud supporters, following Premier Begin's *treason* at Camp David. They were joined soon by members of Gush Emunim and of the Land of Israel Movement, and Rav Zvi Yehuda Kook gave them his blessing. Although an atheist, Neeman believes that traditions are important for a revolutionary movement, and he strongly defends the spiritual heritage of the Jewish people, preaches a return to biblical sources, and is in constant dialogue with the ultra-nationalist-religious groupings. A renaissance of Zionism would halt the moral decline of Israeli youth. Tehiya saw itself as a bridge in the 'Kookist' spirit between religious and secular Jews (Sprinzak 1991: 169).

After extensive Jewish settlement, the Arabs would forget Judea and Samaria, as they have Galilee. Neeman predicted 20 seats in the 1981 elections but won only 3, and then 5 in 1984. The party agrees that Israel must not cede an inch, for to do so would be to engage in the dialectic of retreat and be a prelude to a Palestinian state. Its policy required the annexation of the Occupied Territories to be made irreversible by increasing the number of Jewish settlements. Tehiya's coalition of secular and religious Zionism is reflected in the participation of Raphael Eitan, who was the Israeli army chief of staff (1978–83) and Rabbi Eliezer Waldman. Having left the army, Eitan joined Tehiya with his Tzomet (Crossroads) group and announced his platform to annexe the Occupied Territories and deal firmly with recalcitrant Arabs, favouring collective punishment, and insisting that Arab parents should be punished for offences committed by their children. 'It is not for us to solve the Palestinian problem. There are 100 million Arabs; the Saudis have a $130 billion surplus; let them solve it' (quoted in Mergui and Simonnot 1987: 113). Eitan was elected to the Knesset in July 1984.

During this period an underground movement of Jewish radicals surfaced. This was a loose federation of activists from the settlement communities, some with former ties with Kach and other religious groups who share the 'Kookist' ideology, and others reflecting the pre-state ultra-nationalist undergrounds. Impatient with the 'subservience' of the Gush to the government and with the tactics of Kahane, they rejected compromises with the secular government, and in conformity with the dictates of the land traditions of the Bible considered war against the enemies as obligatory. They shared with Kahane the views that the Arabs must be expelled, that democracy must be rejected and that the Haram el-Sharif (the Temple Mount for them) must be wrested from the Muslims. Their orthodox purity and learned interpretation of Scriptures, and their inclusion of prominent rabbis, give them considerable weight among the Israeli right. Their home-grown advocacy of Jewish terrorism, unlike that imported by USA-born Kahane, shocked the Israeli establishment, which, overlooking its own noble tradition of terrorism in pre-state days and the many examples of state-sponsored terrorism, had come to denounce it as a peculiarly Arab barbarism. Sprinzak discusses the theological ideologies of the various underground groups and the support they received from prominent rabbis, which transferred Jewish terrorism from the margin to the centre of the debate about Jewish identity and destiny (1991: 252-88). Within 12 years, the movement which began with *Torah*-driven but illegal settlement in Judea and Samaria had become infected with elements which promoted not only illegality but even indiscriminate terrorism. However offensive to Western liberalism, such a transformation is in line with fidelity to a particular reading of the biblical land traditions.

Within the sphere of more conventional Israeli politics, Rabbi Eliezer Waldman was re-elected to the Knesset in July 1984. Also a disciple of Rabbi Zvi Yehuda Kook in Merkaz HaRav, he became the religious figurehead of the Tehiya movement. With Levinger, he created the settlement in Kiryat Arba, which became a hotbed of colonizing rabbis who spread their roots throughout the West Bank and the Golan Heights. He feared a polarization in Israeli society between religious and secular groupings, and justified belonging to Tehiya, a party which included the profane Neeman, Cohen and Eitan, by insisting on their devotion to Zionism, to the Jewish people, to the land of Israel, to its social ideals and its pioneer spirit (in Mergui and Simonnot 1987: 115). While Tehiya had to condemn Jewish terrorism, Waldman was ambivalent, and was charged with being an instigator of the attack on the Arab mayors in 1980, but was released for lack of evidence. For Waldman, it is a matter of divine law that not an inch of the Promised Land be ceded: 'In 1967, God gave us a unique opportunity. But the Israelis did not seize it. They did not colonize the newly conquered land...It's as if they had refused the offer of the Almighty while at the same time thanking him. Therefore God inflicted upon Israel the sufferings of the Yom Kippur War' (in Mergui and Simonnot 1987: 114).

However, Rafael Eitan split from Tehiya in 1987 and re-established Tzomet, which won two seats in the 1988 election. It won four seats in the 1996 election, after which Eitan was rewarded for his alignment with Likud by being made Minister of Agriculture and Environment Quality in the Netanyahu government.

Another indication of the movement to the right in the religious camp is provided by Rabbi Haim Drukman, a senior Gush activist and also a student of Rabbi Yehuda Kook, who was elevated to number two on the NRP list for the 1977 elections and elected to the Knesset. He became disillusioned with the party's attitudes towards Greater Israel, and in 1981 was re-elected under the banner of his own party, Matzad. On the eve of the 1984 elections Matzad joined with Poalei Agudat Israel (a religious, working-class party) to form Morasha (Tradition), which became a combination of the pioneering movements of early Israel and religious fundamentalism, and won two seats in the Knesset. For Drukman 'Zionism is part of the Torah. You cannot separate the two. Just as you can't say: "I believe in the Torah but not in the Sabbath"...If I believe in the Torah, I also believe in

Zionism' (Mergui and Simonnot 1987: 167). Drukman subsequently dissolved Morasha and rejoined the NRP, having ensured that it would allow Gush Enumim people into all echelons of the party.

Since 1985 another radical ultra-nationalist, Rehavam Ze'evi, proposed the negotiated 'transfer' of all the Arabs in the Occupied Territories to the neighbouring Arab countries. He founded Moledet (Homeland) and made 'transfer' the sole plank of its platform, and, together with his colleague Professor Yair Sprinzak, was elected to the Knesset in the 1988 election. While in 1984 even most of the radical right judged Kahane, whose Kach alone called for expulsion of the Arabs, to be a racist, the concept of 'transfer' was alive and well in the public debate of 1988, despite the damage the creation of yet another 'Arab refugee problem' would cause internationally. Ze'evi's slogan, 'We are here, they are there, and peace for Israel!' enjoyed tremendous appeal. His literature demonstrates the central role of 'transfer' in Zionist ideology and praxis and berates the hypocrisy of the centre-left establishment, which, from the high moral ground of their kibbutzim founded on former Arab soil, accused him of racism and Kahanism (see Sprinzak 1991: 173-74).

Orthodox Rabbis
Nearly all the religious parties, and the overwhelming majority of Orthodox rabbis in Israel, have denounced the so-called *peace process* between Israel, the Palestinians and its Arab neighbours. In the midst of the prolonged *halakhic* debates on whether one may or may not cede Jewish land (i.e. land taken from the Arabs) to non-Jews, considerations of the human rights of non-Jews is never brought into the picture. Some of the most vociferous and extreme opponents of *territorial compromise* come from the Orthodox religious camp.

Some Orthodox rabbis have issued statements from time to time reflecting their practical hermeneutic of the biblical traditions of land. Rabbi Schlomo Goren (1917–94), a former Israeli Chief Rabbi (1973–83) and Chief Military Rabbi, typified the fusion of Orthodox and political extremism that gave rise to Gush Emunim, and called on soldiers to disobey any orders they might receive to dismantle Jewish settlements in the Occupied Territories. He decried 'concessions' to the Palestinians, demanded that a synagogue be built on the Temple Mount in Jerusalem and wrote that Yasser Arafat deserved death (Landau 1994). Rabbi Goren distributed leaflets to synagogues throughout the Occupied Territories on 18 December 1993 reiterating that Jews had a God-given right to the biblical land of Israel. On the following day he rejected the view that he was inciting rebellion and argued that the supreme law in the land was the law of Moses: 'Any other orders contradictory to the orders of Moses [are] a rebellion against Moses, against the Torah, against Judaism. There does not exist any kind of rebellion if the refusal is based on obeying the laws of Moses' (from Derek Brown in Jerusalem, *The Guardian*, Monday, 20 December 1993).

Rabbi Ben Yosef, formerly Baruch Greene who came on *aliyah* from New York in 1976, was a candidate for mayor of Jerusalem in 1993. His *Torah*-observance demanded a totally Jewish Jerusalem:

> There should be no mosques nor churches in Jerusalem...No goyim should be allowed to live in Jerusalem at all...They can visit here, yes, but not live here. There should be no idol worship in the city at all... Jerusalem has no borders. It should be constantly expanding. The bigger the better, until Damascus (in S. Leibowitz 1993).

Dissenting Voices

Of course, the ideology and tactics of Gush Emunim and other broadly aligned groups have not progressed without opposition from within both the secular and the religious camps. In addition to the religious groups which do not attach significance to the notion of a nation state, and some which regard it as an apostasy,[48] the religious constituency has seen the rise of several human rights groups (Oz veShalom, Netivot Shalom, Rabbis for Human Rights, Clergy for

---

48. The ultra-Orthodox Haredim claim that the survival of the Jewish people rests above all on the keeping of *Torah*, and they stress that a *Torah* society comes before a specific territory. Their concern is to ensure the land is worth protecting. They adopt an attitude of indifference or hostility towards the state. The Orthodox Jews of Mea Shearim still hold that Israel was the work of Satan. The ultra-Orthodox NEturei Karta rejects the existence of the state, and maintains that the existence of Israel is a sacrilege, as Jews are to wait for the Messiah before their biblical homeland can be regained. The group wants Israel to be replaced by a Palestinian state and the members consider themselves 'Palestinian Jews'. Rabbi Hirsh, the head of the group, insists on Israel's destruction. The Satmar Chasidim, from Brooklyn, also are virulently anti-Zionist. They mount anti-Zionist demonstrations outside the Israeli consulate. Their late leader, Rabbi Joel Teitelbaum, intimated that he would rather see his movement disappear than accept a Jewish state not brought to life by the Messiah (Geoffrey Paul, *Jewish Chronicle*, 8 July 1994, p. 22).

Peace, etc.), which emphasize the supremacy of the moral values of Judaism over the territorial ones stressed by the Gush. In general, however, they bypass the foundational injustice associated with Zionism, and their critique relates only to the abuses of human rights in the Occupied Territories. Whether the fervour of their observance of the *Torah* has been infected by the values of the Enlightment or moderated by the more universalist of the Hebrew prophetic tradition is subject to speculation.

Lord Jakobovits accuses the Orthodox camp in Israel of having supported the politics of might and violence in exchange for financial favours. He bemoans the 'bankruptcy' of traditional spiritual leadership there, and accuses the Orthodox rabbis of 'maintaining a stance of complacent self-righteousness' which seems to have departed completely from the prophetic tradition. It was the religious Jews who kept the Israeli Government in power during the Lebanese invasion, 'leaving it to the secularists to articulate the Jewish conscience and salvage the Jewish honour. What a perverse reversal of our roles!' (*Jewish Chronicle*, 18 August 1995, p. 17). In September 1995, several rabbis from the nationalist wing of the Orthodox religious sector issued a document in support of the Action Committee for the Abolition of the Autonomy Plan. The recently deceased Yeshayahu Leibowitz, a strictly Orthodox Jew, and one of the foremost Jewish scholars of his day, regarded the entire religious establishment with contempt and the mix of religion and politics as poisonous. In the immediate aftermath of the Six Day War, when the entire country was in the grip of religious euphoria, he warned: 'This brilliant victory will be a historical and political disaster for the state of Israel.' He denounced the Western Wall as a disco and said he would gladly return it to the Arabs (Bermant 1994: 21).

On the secular side, a plethora of human and civil rights groups has grown up (Peace Now, ACRI, B'Tselem, Israeli Women against the Occupation, Women in Black, Yesh Gevul, Parents against Moral Erosion, and others [see, e.g. Hurwitz 1992: 197-208]). However, unlike the Gush, which has substantial facts on the ground, these organizations confine themselves to protest in words and demonstrations, most recently in processions from the grave of Yitzhak Rabin, whose murder has purified him of his crimes against humanity and virtually canonized him as the patron saint of the peace camp. His (reluctant) handshake with Arafat on the White House Lawn and signing of the 13 September 1993 Declaration of Principles proved to be Rabin's downfall. While for much of the world it symbolized a new hope and a new beginning, for the religious messianists and ultra-nationalists it spelled disaster, and the end of the dream of an undivided, full-blooded Jewish state on the west of the Jordan. Rabin the traitor, the obstacle to the divine schema, had to be removed.

Conclusion

Whereas modern universalistic thinking sees anti-Semitism as one form of social, legal and political discrimination to be addressed constitutionally within the structure of states and on the basis of civil rights, for Theodor Herzl the solution to the Jewish problem could not be found in making the host countries more tolerant and liberal, but only in the establishment of a state in which Jews could live in a purely Jewish land in full respect for their Jewish identity and 'apartness'. Although himself fully assimilated, he regarded the European countries as incapable of tolerating Jews, who were alienated by being a people apart and by their non-conformist practices. His refuge in nationalist colonialism eschewed a constitutional and civil rights' solution.

From its conception in the late 1890s to its implementation since, Zionism, although distinctive in some critical respects, was a political ideology, sharing much in common with nineteenth-century European nationalisms and colonialisms. In line with prevailing European racisms which predicated inferiority of all native peoples, Zionism determined to improve the lot of international Jewry at the expense of the indigenous population of Palestine. To achieve success, its programme required the support of major international powers, initially of Britain, and more recently of the United States. The existence of a friendly state in the strategically important Middle East would be of considerable value to the foreign policy interests of first Britain and then the USA.

Although the Zionist conquest of Palestine has many precedents (e.g. the European settlement in North America, or the British one in Australia and New Zealand), it had several unique features. The displacement took place within decades rather than two or three centuries. Secondly, the Zionist colonization took place after the heyday of European colonization, at a time when the European colonizing nations were beginning to respect the right to self-determination of indigenous populations and when the very notion of colonization was beginning to break down. Thirdly, most of the Zionist colonization has taken place in an age of mass communications, although until recently, it has managed to portray itself as an innocent victim reaping its just rewards. But, most distinctively, the Zionist colonial enterprise has widespread religious support, Christian as well as Jewish, and in most theological and religious circles is viewed as being consistent with biblical prophecy, or at least being no more than what the Jewish people deserve in virtue of the promises of God outlined in the Bible.

Much of the thrust in Zionism derives from a literalist interpretation of the biblical witness to land and of some of its messianic texts, with scant attention to the rights of the indigenes. However, as an agent of legitimacy in international law, the Zionist appeal to *Tanakh* for legitimation of its claims to Eretz Israel is not much more compelling than if the Portuguese and Spanish Governments today presented to the UN the bulls of Nicholas V and Alexander VI, which also claimed divine authority, in their bid to reclaim the lands of the New World (Lamadrid 1981: 346). In any case, no claim can be accorded an absolute status, but must be weighed up in conjunction with the claims of others.

With respect to the indigenous non-Jews of Palestine, one detects a disjuncture between the ideals of the preamble to Israel's Declaration of Independence (14 May 1948) and the real cost of the enterprise:

> The State of Israel will be open for Jewish immigration and for the ingathering of the exiles. It will foster the development of the country for the benefit of all its inhabitants: it will be based on freedom, justice and peace as envisaged by the prophets of Israel. It will ensure complete equality of social and political rights to all its inhabitants irrespective of religion, conscience, language, education, and culture; it will safeguard the Holy places of all religions and it will be faithful to the principles of the charter of the United Nations.

It would appear in some formulations of the Zionist victory that the indigenes should appreciate their passive path to redemption via the Jewish homecoming. There is no shortage of utopian idealizations of the promise of God's gift to the children of Israel: 'The union of people and land is intended to contribute to the perfecting of the world in order to become the Kingdom of God' (Buber 1973: 47). Whereas other nations who dispossessed indigenous people can legitimately be accused of robbery,

> Their charge against Israel is totally unjust for it acted under authority and
> in the confident knowledge of its authorization...No other people has ever
> heard and accepted the command from heaven as did the people of
> Israel...So long as it sincerely carried out the command it was in the right
> and is in the right in so far as it still carries it out. Its unique relationship to
> its land must be seen in this light...Where a command and a faith are pre-
> sent, in certain historical situations conquest need not be robbery (Buber
> 1973: 146).

For André Neher too, Palestine holds the key to Jewish existence. He
writes of a 'geo-theology' and its charm, and supports the view that
aliyah will foreshorten the redemption of the whole world and the
coming of the Messiah (1992: 22-23). But the spiritual and moral
tenets of the *Torah* must be obeyed, because otherwise the land will
vomit Israel forth, as it previously vomited the Canaanites, 'to whom
God had confided it in a moment of hasty imprudence' (Neher 1992:
20). The State of Israel is the agent of mass reconciliation: of Jews,
Christians and Muslims; of the sacred and the profane; and of Jews
who differ in their messianic expectations (1992: 27-29). The recon-
ciliatory impact of the return-to-Zion enterprise does not appear quite
so sanguine from my perspective as I write, overlooking the 'border'
checkpoint between Bethlehem and Jerusalem and surrounded by so
many signs of colonial plunder, as well as witnessing the daily humiliation of the indigenous population, which is made to experience
alienation and exile within its own homeland.

There is no doubt that the Jewish religious establishment, although
late in embracing Zionism, today fully supports its achievement. For
many religious Jews, the State of Israel is 'the most powerful collective expression' of Jewry and 'the most significant development in
Jewish life since the Holocaust' (Jonathan Sacks, Chief Rabbi of
Britain). Moreover, the religious wing is at the forefront of the
opposition to political 'compromise' (a euphemism for 'restitution')
with the Palestinians, with very few Orthodox rabbis supporting it,
and many at the vanguard of its destruction. It is a matter of concern
that religious Jews have little regard for the indigenes who have paid
the price for the establishment of Israel. But neither did Joshua in the
biblical narrative.

The rhetoric of the sacral discourse of the achievement of Zionism
is undermined by the reality of the catastrophe for the indigenous
population. The establishment of a Jewish state involved the eviction
of the majority of the Palestinians, the destruction of most of their

villages and the continual use of force and state terrorism, wars and military operations. The daily humiliation of the indigenous people and the litany of other atrocities casts a dark cloud over the achievement of the ethnocentric dream of nineteenth-century Jewish nationalist colonialists. What is most distressing from a moral and religious perspective is that the major ideological support for Zionist imperialism and the principal obstacle against treating the indigenous people with respect come from religious circles for whom the biblical narratives of land are normative. Already in 1913, the bad behaviour of Zionists towards the Palestinians made Ahad Ha'am fear for the future if Jews ever came to power: 'If this be the "Messiah": I do not wish to see his coming' (in Lehn 1988: 13).

Chapter 5

FABRICATING COLONIAL MYTHS

There are factors in the case of colonization which make the analysis of change much simpler than in most other cases of social transformation. Colonization results from the determination of a group to encroach upon a foreign terrain. The social transformation that follows is not the result of *laissez faire* policies, or of unpredictable changes in the body politic, but proceeds according to an overall plan which is put into place with some haste, reflecting the determination of the colonizers to alter radically the politics of the region in favour of the colonists.

Across the broad spectrum of colonial enterprises, one detects recurring attitudes towards the indigenous population. It was considered to be part of the natural wealth of the region, providing cheap labour etc. Where miscegenation was an option, the indigenous women were a resource to gratify the male colonizers and maintain the population. Where religious or cultural motivation was important, the natives became targets for fulfilling the mission of the colonizers, by spreading the 'superior' religion or culture of the homeland, thereby 'civilizing' the original inhabitants. When hostility was encountered, it was overcome, but, under the right circumstances, an accommodation was made.

Immigrant-settler societies were established in North America, South America, Australia, New Zealand, South Africa, Algeria, etc., and each had distinctive modes of dealing with the indigenous population. 'Frontiers of inclusion' included the original inhabitants in the enterprise, and initially this was the case in South America (Hennessy 1978: 147). On the other hand, 'frontiers of exclusion' excluded the original inhabitants from the new arrangements (for example, in North America and, except by way of using them as cheap labour, in South Africa and Zionist Palestine). Several motivations combined to

exclude the indigenes, and for those influenced by religious considerations, the biblical paradigm provided a ready justification for it.
The exclusivist tendencies in North America and South Africa have
been ascribed to the influence of the Old Testament in the Puritan
faith in the case of the former, and in the Dutch Reformed Church in
the latter (see Bastide 1972; Gerhard 1959; Hartz 1964).[1]

The Comparative Myths of Colonialism

The discourse of *comparative historiography* provides a framework
for discussing our examples of colonialism. *Parallel comparative
history* examines different historical cases, generally from quite disparate regions of the world (see e.g. Eisenstadt 1963). *Contrast comparative history* emphasizes distinctive features in disparate social
processes, allowing patterns of similarity to suggest themselves. In
general, it is assumed that each social complex (nation, empire, civilization) constitutes an intricate and unique socio-historical con-
figuration in its own right (see e.g. Geertz 1971; Lang 1975).
Predictably, there is an approach which, while respecting the speci-
ficity of each society, recognizes that the particularities of each
individual situation may suggest new historical generalizations.
Macro-causal analysis attempts to identify elements which are both
favourable and unfavourable to an hypothesis.

   I have analyzed each of the examples of colonialism independently,
to avoid overemphasizing those elements which fit in with a theory to
which one is predisposed. While no attempt was made to force them
into an undifferentiated sameness, patterns of similarity appear in all
four, as the following chart suggests.

---

1.   Algeria reflects an intermediate mode (Nora 1961). After it had been occupied
in 1844, the Europeans disallowed the traditional land titles of the Berber tribes,
since the primary determination of the settlers was to acquire their land and obtain
cheap Berber/Muslim labour (Pickles 1963: 23). The Muslims had the status of
colonial subjects, and by the time the process was over, the majority of the fertile
land was in the hands of European settlers (Gordon 1966: 51-52). The takeover was
justified in terms of the superiority of the settlers to the natives. Jules Roy, an
Algerian-born Frenchman sums up the situation as he saw it: 'One thing I knew
because it was told to me so often, was that the Arabs belonged to a different race,
one inferior to my own. We had come to clear their land and bring them civilization'
(Roy 1961: 17).

	Old Testament	Latin America	South Africa	Zionism
Chosen or privileged people	yes	yes	yes	yes
Racially superior	yes	yes	yes	yes
Frontiers of inclusion	no	yes	no	no
Extermination of indigenes	yes	limited	limited	limited
Displacement of indigenes	yes	limited	limited	yes
Corralling of indigenes	no	yes	yes	yes
Enslavement of indigenes	yes	yes	yes	yes
Miscegenation and intermarriage	no	yes	no	no
Religious motivation	yes	yes	yes	yes
Attempt at conversion of indigenes	no	yes	limited	no
Compunction	no	yes	yes	no

In each case, for example, the incoming society established itself through a violent injustice to the indigenous population. The Exodus–Conquest motif in the biblical narrative is unique in that it presents the Israelites as escaping from slavery into possession of another land. A case can be made for an analogous context for Zionism, except that the conquering immigrants did not hail from one oppressive context, and many came from societies in which there was nothing approaching slavery.

The modern examples do not display any grand unitary theory, such as one that ascribes the colonization to the imperative of the biblical paradigm. It is clear that the motivations and methods used, and the time-scale in which each colonization was effected differ. In particular, there was considerable variation in the role of religious and biblical motivation in the complex web of impulses propelling each enterprise. Nevertheless, despite such obvious differences, one detects similarities, both with respect to the intentions of the colonizing enterprise and the underlying world view by which it was justified.

A core element in the colonizing rhetoric is that the adventurous Europeans pioneered in a savage wilderness and brought civilization to it. Such myths disguise the truth that Europe's glory was gained at the expense of the tragedy of the indigenous populations. In rationalizing the subjugation and near-extermination of the indigenes, these myths stifle moral scruples and suppress embarrassing facts. Francis Jennings's description of the myths describing the invasion of North America are apposite to our discussion, and suggest that we are dealing with a stereotypical myth of colonialism.

> The basic conquest myth postulates that America was virgin land, or
> wilderness, inhabited by nonpeople called savages; that these savages
> were creatures sometimes defined as demons, sometimes as beasts 'in the
> shape of men'; that their mode of existence and cast of mind were such as
> to make them incapable of civilization and therefore of full humanity; that
> civilization was required by divine sanction or the imperative of progress
> to conquer the wilderness and make it a garden; that the savage creatures
> of the wilderness, being unable to adapt to any environment other than the
> wild, stubbornly and viciously resisted God or fate, and thereby incurred
> their suicidal extermination; that civilization and its bearers were refined
> and ennobled in their contest with the dark powers of the wilderness; and
> that it all was inevitable (Jennings 1976: 15).

Fabricating Colonial Myths

To compare colonizing enterprises is not to pretend to equate them.
While there are differences in the effects of colonization from one
region and period to another, one detects a uniformity in the mythology of conquest, which is expressed, with variations on the theme, in a
wide range of colonial enterprises. Typical elements cluster around
the presumption of a right to conquer and settle a land, for some
combination of the following reasons:

1. The land was in a virgin state or, in the case of an already
    inhabited land, habitation was irregular (the 'virgin land or
    wilderness' myth).
2. The people (to be) conquered were of an inferior status, and
    the colonizers enjoyed an inalienable right to resist opposi-
    tion from the indigenes (the myth of 'self-defence').
3. The mission to civilize or evangelize.
4. The enterprise was legitimized by appealing to such an
    unchallenged ideological motivation (e.g. to 'civilize' or
    evangelize the natives—the myth of 'purity of arms').

Although the colonizing enterprises pretended to altruistic motives,
invariably the colonizers benefited through wreaking havoc on the
indigenous populations (the Legacy—the myth of 'we deserve it').
Frequently, there were 'historical myths' which were specific to each
myth of origins (e.g. the Great Trek, in the case of South Africa).

We have already seen how these elements appear in the instances of
colonialism we have examined. It is instructive to present in 'parallel'
columns a selection of stereotypical perspectives from each.

1. *The 'Virgin Land or Wilderness' Myth.* Jennings postulates a 'standard conquest myth', whose core component is that the territory to be colonized was 'virgin land or wilderness' (1976: 15). This provides a justification for the colonizers, often retrospectively, guaranteeing the rights of people living there to stay put. A refinement of this myth is that, at most, the land was sparsely inhabited, often by unsettled tribes (bedouin or aboriginal), whose unsettled state deprived them of the rights that are accorded to those who have worked the land. The myth was used to justify the English conquest of North America,[2] and the Nazi conquest of Eastern Europe.[3] Hitler's *Lebensraum* policy was inspired by the conquest of North America. Although he indulged in the rhetoric of *Ostraum,* Hitler knew full well that Eastern Europe was overpopulated. His solution included the part extermination and part expulsion ('transfer of population') of the Slavs, with the remnant being confined to undeveloped enclaves ('we will isolate them in their own pigsties'), serving the German master race as a helot population. Meanwhile, millions of ethnic Germans would be relocated to the East, until 'our settlers are numerically superior to the natives'. Hitler saw himself in the line of European colonizers whose racial superiority conferred on them the right to dominate (in Finkelstein 1995: 93-94). Corresponding elements can be traced with respect to the Spanish-Portuguese conquest of Latin America, the Afrikaner conquest of southern Africa and the Zionist conquest of Palestine. The pretence that the land was 'empty' is an integral part of the colonizing myth. When it made no sense to pretend that it was empty, it became clear that its inhabitants were of a far inferior category:

---

2.   England was 'full' while North America was 'empty, spacious and void... Its few inhabitants run over the grass as do the foxes and wild beasts' (1622 author). Finkelstein (1995: 89-92) gives many examples of typical colonial attitudes in the conquest of North America. Recurring features allude to elements such as the following: the inadequate habitation by 'fierce savages' of the vast terrain, which was crying out for improvement by labour, and 'destined by the Creator to support a large population and be a seat of civilization, of science, and of true religion'.

3.   Eastern Europe was 'thinly settled', 'desert', 'desolate', etc. (Hitler). See Finkelstein 1995: 92-94, and his sources, pp. 197-98.

Latin America	South Africa	Palestine
There is no claim in the case of the mediaeval Spanish and Portuguese plunder of Latin America that the region was uninhabited.	The conventional account of the origins of the black southern Africans: The blacks started settling in the northern part of the country more or less at the same time as the first white people began settling at the southern tip of the country during the seventeenth century. The black settlements in South Africa were not purposive or permanent in the Western sense. As soon as one parcel of cultivated land was exhausted they moved on in search of virgin soil.	'A land without a people for a people without a land.' 'There is no Arab people living in intimate fusion with the country, utilizing its resources and stamping it with a characteristic impress: there is at best an Arab encampment' (Zangwill 1920: 104). 'A wild landscape devoid of trade and shade…where the inhabitants were strange and alien, wild like the land itself', and 'desolate under Arab rule' (Shapira 1992: 53, 214). There is 'a profusion of evidence' that Palestine was 'uninhabited' on the eve of the modern Zionist colonization (Peters 1984: 170).[4]

2. *The Myth of Racial Superiority.* Racism is a conception which is founded on the premise of physical and psychological inequalities between races, enabling one to distinguish between the 'aristocracy' and the 'rabble'. It served as the pretext for the ruthless exploitation, and sometimes extermination of indigenous populations in a range of areas which were subjected to colonialism. Invariably, the natives were considered to be inferior:

4.   Prime Minister Levi Eshkol, Prime Minister Golda Meir and Shimon Peres are on record along the same lines.

Latin America

South Africa

Palestine

In their pre-Christian phase, the Indians 'went about everywhere making war and assaulting people in order to sacrifice them, offering their hearts and human blood to the demons, in which many innocents suffered' (Fray Toribio, in Lockhart and Otte 1976: 241).
'The first and original inhabitants here in New Spain...lived as savages...They neither sowed nor cultivated the earth' (Fray Toribio in Lockhart and Otte 1976: 220-21).

The Afrikaner textbooks identified three principal races in pre-colonial southern Africa: Bushmen, who were true savages and were the oldest race in the region, Hottentots, who were slightly higher and came later from the north, and 'Kaffirs', who were barbarians rather than savages, and who originated in Asia and 'trekked' southward in comparatively recent times (Thompson 1985: 96-97).

Prime Minister Begin likened Palestinians to 'two-legged animals', and his successor Yitzhak Shamir compared a Palestinian to a 'fly' and a 'grasshopper', and declared that they were 'brutal, wild, alien invaders in the Land of Israel' (Neff 1993: 13).

'Because it is natural that prudent, honest and humane men should rule over those who are not, it follows that Spaniards have the perfect right to rule over the barbarians of the New World, who in prudence, intellect, virtue and humanity are as much inferior to the Spaniards as children are to adults, and women are to men. The barbarian races were wild and cruel, as compared with the Spanish who were a race of the greatest clemency' (Sepúlveda).

The Xhosa people were 'a race of monsters, who, being the unprovoked destroyers, and implacable foes of Her Majesty's Christian subjects, have forfeited every claim to mercy or consideration' and should have been exterminated (William Cornwallis Harris, in Thompson 1985: 88).

Expounding on the Jewish right to Palestine, Winston Churchill said: 'I do not agree that the dog in a manger has the final right to the manger, even though he may have lain there for a very long time. I do not admit...that a great wrong has been done to the Red Indians of America...I do not admit that a wrong has been done to these people by the fact that a stronger race, a higher grade race, or at any rate, a more world-wise race...has come in and taken their place' (in Ponting 1994: 254).

Latin America	South Africa	Palestine
'On the mainland they eat human flesh. They are more given to sodomy than any other nation... They are stupid and silly...They are brutal. They are incapable of learning...They eat fleas, spiders and worms raw...The older they get the worse they become...They become like real brutes' (Tomás Ortiz, in Todorov 1984: 150-51).	According to James Bryce, later British ambassador in Washington, not only had the black peoples made no progress, but the Afrikaners themselves were victims of the degeneration theory: severed from Europe for 200 years, they had gone backwards (in Thompson 1985: 94).	'Palestine is not so much occupied by the Arabs as over-run by them. They are nomads, who have created in Palestine neither material nor spiritual values...We cannot allow the Arabs to block so valuable a piece of historic reconstruction, so romantic a reparation to the sorely-tried race of the Apostles' (Zangwill 1920: 92-93).

3. *The Vision to Civilize or Evangelize*

Latin America	South Africa	Palestine
While the fundamental motive of the Portuguese-Spanish was their insatiable greed and ambition, the greatest ever seen in the world (Las Casas, in Dussel 1990: 41), the alleged theological motivation was the fulfilment of an 'ideal of Christendom'. The New world was to be civilized and evangelized.	Agents of civilization and evangelization, the heroic *voortrekkers* set out on the noble task of taming the wilderness, and bringing civilization to the natives.	'We should there [in Palestine] form a portion of the rampart of Europe against Asia, an outpost of civilization opposed to barbarism' (Herzl: 1896: 96).
The civilized Spaniards would bring the most salutary benefits to the barbarians, who hardly deserved the name of human being, converting them from being slothful and		'[The Jewish national centre] will be good for the world, good for the Jews and good for the British Empire. But we also think it will be good for the Arabs who dwell in Palestine, and we

Latin America	South Africa	Palestine
libidinous to being honest and honourable. They would be rescued from being irreligious and enslaved to demons to become Christians and worshippers of the true God (Sepúlveda).		intend that it shall be good for them, and they shall not be sufferers or sup- planted in the country in which they dwell or denied their share in all that makes for its progress and prosperity...' (Winston Churchill, in Palestine, March 1921, in Ingrams 1972: 119).

4. *The Myth of Legitimacy: The Religious Mandate*

Latin America	South Africa	Palestine
'Your highnesses...have seen fit to send me, Christopher Colombus, to the said parts of the Indies to see...what way there may be to convert them to our holy faith' (in Las Casas 1989-94: XIV, 41).	While there was some missionary activity, the Afrikaner society was more intent on preserv- ing its separate civilized condition than in 'evangelizing' the natives.	'Anyone who disputes Israel's right to the land of Canaan is actually opposing God and his holy covenant with the Patriarchs. He is striving against sacred, inviolable words and promises of God, which he has sworn to keep' (Schlink 1991: 22).
'My task has been and is to teach them Christian doctrine generally, con- veying it to them in their language...making tours and seeking to destroy the idols and idolatries' (Fray Pedro de Gantin, in Lockhart and Otte 1976: 213-14).		'The time has come for evangelicals to affirm their belief in biblical prophecy and Israel's divine right to the Holy Land' ('Evangelicals' Concern for Israel', Paid Advertisement, *Christian Science Monitor*, 3 November 1977).

The Legacy

Latin America	South Africa	Palestine
Humiliation of native cultures and religions.	Humiliation of native cultures and religions.	Humiliation of indige- nous population.

Latin America	South Africa	Palestine
'(a) Genocide through occupation…European diseases…excessive exploitation…causing the extermination of over seventy-five million… (b) Violent usurpation of our territories. (c) The fragmentation of our socio-political and cultural organizations. (d) Ideological and religious subjection' (Ecumenical Consultation, in Beozzo 1990: 79).	South Africa has the greatest recorded inequality of any country of the world, with two-thirds of the black population surviving below a defined minimum level, and nine million people completely destitute.	Creation of 714,000 refugees in 1948, and of 300,000 in the 1967 War. Plunder of Arab land. Economic exploitation. Political subservience.

Apartheid

Latin America	South Africa	Palestine
A continuous supply of cheap and docile labour was essential. The most telling device was to concentrate the Indian populations into *congregaciones*, or in Brazil into *aldeias* or villages. Ostensibly, this was to facilitate the work of evangelization, but in reality it aimed at ensuring that the whites could have their land. The indigenous people are confined to reserves, discriminated against in education, health and housing, and exploited in all ways possible (Richard 1990a: 64-65).	The Natives Act (1923) decreed that urban African 'locations' should be separated from the white towns. Segregation enabled the cities to function with black workers, but without their presence in numbers sufficient to disturb white domination, and was formally institutionalized in the *apartheid* laws. Under the terms of the Act, the Africans, although 67 per cent of the population, kept only 7.3 per cent of the land. For a while they were restricted to reserves, but since they were needed for cheap labour,	*Apartheid* means 'separateness' or 'apartness', which in Hebrew is *hafrada*, the term used in Israel to define the 'peace process'. Israel practises racial, ethnic and religious discrimination in the fields of residential segregation, job opportunity and political rights. Oslo II gives the Palestine National Authority (PNA) effective control over 4 per cent of the land, and limited administrative responsibility for 98 per cent of the Palestinian population of the West Bank. Movement between the zones under

Latin America	*South Africa*	*Palestine*
	the segregation spread into the white areas (Kimmerling 1983: 6 n.).	the PNA is restricted by the Israeli authorities. Note also the closure of Jerusalem to West Bankers and Gazans since March 1993, leading to economic strangulation, and social deprivation.
'You are all in mortal sin, and live and die in it, because of the cruelty and tyranny you practice among the innocent people. Say with what right and justice you keep these Indians in such cruel and horrible slavery. By what authority have you waged such detestable wars on these peoples, who were living on their own lands, inoffensively and peacefully, and exterminated such vast numbers of them with deaths and slaughter…so that you can seize and acquire gold every day' (Fray Antón de Montesinos, in Las Casas' account in *Historia de las Indias*, bk III, ch. 4)	'The existence of the coloured races is an immense benefit, as, by means of them, cheap labour is obtainable, and large agricultural supplies can be constantly procured; but Southern Africa, although its population chiefly comprises the descendants of stalwart nomadic races who have migrated from a northern part of the continent, is eminently a White man's country, where homes can be found for millions of the overflowing population of Europe' (Alexander Wilmot, in Thompson 1985: 93).	Before the *intifada* up to 100,000 Gazans crossed the Erez checkpoint to work daily in Israel. After the Gulf War, the number fell to some 56,000, and that number has fallen intermittently, down to some 13,000 in March 1996. Moreover, there have been some 300 days of total closure from the establishment of the PNA in May 1994 to March 1996.

Even if the arrangement in columns lacks a certain academic elegance, it does suggest the moral problematic in a striking, comparative fashion. Without pretending that 'parallels' indicate equivalence, there is a substantial similarity in underlying attitudes, and in specific techniques of colonization.

The Myths of Zionism

Although Zionism has much in common with the other forms of settler colonialism we have discussed, some aspects give it an unique position in the discourse. Even though nationalist colonialism is long out of vogue with liberal Western intellectuals, and is an object of disdain among Christian theologians, support for Zionism, at least up to recently, has been widespread. Its claims rest on a combination of divine right, unique historical claim and compelling need. The justification for the existence of a Jewish state includes appeal to the biblical mandate, to the historical right, to persistent diaspora longing, to the *Shoah*, to the decision of the United Nations, to the reality of military conquest, to the unbroken Jewish residence in the land, and so on. Since the relative value attached to each element of legitimation has varied at different stages and among different groups, it is naive to construct a composite legitimization by blending together the disparate components, reducing them to a form in which their unique identity is subsumed and their relative importance is undifferentiated.

Many Jews allege an unique derivative link between the biblical paradigm of conquest and Zionist settler colonialism today. If other forms of colonization could appeal to the alleged legitimization provided by the biblical mandate, the Jewish claim was unrivalled. Uniquely in the case of colonialism, Zionism appeals to an historical link between the settler population and the land to be settled: all Jews have an historical right to the land, in virtue of unbroken habitation there by Israelites/Jews, even when at times the Jewish population of the region was very small.

The Foundational Myths of the State of Israel

The early realization by the pantheon of its ideologues that the Zionist dream would require an Arab nightmare was carefully kept from the wider public. Moreover, after 1948, the history of events was scrupulously fabricated into foundation myths, involving 'the voluntary emigration of Arabs', 'making the desert bloom', and being 'the only democracy in the Middle East' etc. After the establishment of the State of Israel, Zionists began systematically to rewrite Palestinian history, legitimizing Jewish and repudiating Arab claims to the land:[5] the land had been virtually vacant for the 1800 years since the expulsion of the Jews; Arabs had lost any right to the land in virtue of having allowed it to become a wasteland; the new Jewish settlers had now redeemed it, and so on. Ben-Gurion claimed that on the eve of Zionist colonization, Palestine was in 'a virtual state of anarchy...primitive, neglected and derelict'. Jewish settlement 'revitalized' the land. The indigenous Arab population became the 'Arab problem' (Ben-Gurion 1971: xx, 25, 47).

One of the most successful propaganda campaigns in modern times has succeeded in masking the fact that the creation of the State of Israel resulted in the dispossession and dispersion of another people. According to Benny Morris, the official fabricated Zionist history of Israel claims:

1. Zionism's birth was an inevitable result of Gentile pressures and persecution, and offered at least a partial solution to the 'Jewish Problem' in Europe.
2. The Zionists intended no ill to the Arabs of Palestine. Zionist settlement alongside the Arabs did not, from the Jews' point of view, necessitate a clash or displacement.
3. However, Israel was born into an uncharitable, predatory environment. Zionist efforts at compromise and conciliation were rejected by the Arabs, and the Palestinians and the neighbouring Arab states, selfish and ignoble, attacked the Yishuv in 1947–48 with the aim of nipping the Jewish state in the bud.
4. The Arabs were far stronger politically and militarily than the Yishuv and were assisted by the British, but nonetheless lost the war.
5. In the course of the war, in order to facilitate the invasion of the Arab armies, the Arab leaders called upon/ordered Palestine's Arabs to quit their homes, this would lay the Jewish state open to charges of expulsion and physically clear the path for the Arab armies. Thus was born the Palestinian refugee problem (Morris 1990a: 4-5).

5.   As Whitelam has shown, biblical specialists, historians and archaeologists had long ensured that Palestinian history would not enjoy a place in Western academic discourse (1996: *passim*).

He might have added that the fabricated history claims that the land was empty (of significant people) and much neglected; that it was redeemed by Jewish labour, which made the desert bloom; that it never damaged, and indeed benefited the natives; that the Zionists acted alone, without the assistance of interested imperial powers; that the few unsavoury actions in 1947–48 were the result of the stresses of war; and that all its wars and invasions, and its actions against the Palestinians were purely defensive, and so forth.

That fabricated history, consistently taught to Israeli children, has shaped the minds of Israeli and diaspora Jews, and has moulded the perceptions of governments and much of the international community. It has taken some time for these foundational myths to be challenged. Simha Flapan considered seven foundational myths that have combined to mask the indisputable facts of history (1987). Avi Shlaim showed how the original goal of Zionism was the establishment of a Jewish state in the whole of Palestine, and that the acceptance of partition, in the mid-1930s as much as in 1947, was tactical, rather than a dilution of the Zionist dream: 'I don't regard a state in part of Palestine as the final aim of Zionism, but as a means towards that aim' (Ben-Gurion in 1938, in Teveth 1985: 188), a sentiment he made clear in a number of statements (see Morris 1988: 24; Shlaim 1988: 17). It is important to review the nationalist mythology.

Attitudes to the Indigenous Population
The determination of the Basle Congress in 1897—when the population of Palestine was 95 per cent Arab, and 99 per cent of the land was Arab-owned (Khalidi 1992: 17)—to establish a state for Jews in Palestine, without any regard for the indigenous population, marked the beginning of the Palestinian tragedy. Characteristic of the period, the intentions of the colonizers overrode every other consideration: Herzl's *Der Judenstaat* ignored the needs and rights of the indigenous people, and much of the Zionist public discourse proceeded as if Palestine were a *terra nullius*, or a land at the free disposal of the international community. Indeed, it was suggested that the project would be a bonus for everyone, including the surrounding states. But as early as November 1882, armed struggle was envisioned by at least some Jews. One of the Biluim wrote from Palestine:

> The final purposes…are to take possession in due course of Palestine and to restore the Jews…[to] political independence…It will be necessary to

> teach the young and the future generations the use of arms…The Jews, if necessary with arms in their hands, will publicly proclaim themselves masters of their own, ancient fatherland (quoted in Lehn 1988: 10).

In a series of letters and essays, the Ukrainian writer, Asher Zvi Ginzberg (Ahad Ha'am, 1856–1927)—who was present at the First Zionist Congress, but was disappointed with the Zionist programme, which strove to save the Jewish body but not its soul (Simon 1962: 39)—argued that it was neither realistic nor honest for Zionist leaders to envisage the establishment of a Jewish state. They should seek rather a Jewish settlement in Palestine, which could not be established without harmonious relations with the indigenous population, but would serve the cultural, spiritual and national needs of all Jews everywhere. In his *Emet Meeretz-Yisrael* (The Truth from Palestine), published in 1891 after his three-month stay in Palestine, he indicated the obstacles to large-scale Jewish colonization: the unavailability of large tracts of untilled but arable land and the attitudes of the Ottomans, who were opposed to large-scale immigration in Palestine. He emphasized that the indigenous Arabs showed no inclination to leave. In November 1913, he wrote to a settler in Palestine :

> I cannot put up with the idea that our brethren are morally capable of behaving in such a way to humans of another people, and unwittingly the thought comes to my mind: if it is so now, what will be our relation to the others if in truth we shall achieve at the end of time power in Palestine? And if this be the 'Messiah': I do not wish to see his coming (Ahad Ha'am in Lehn 1988: 13).

One detects already in Herzl the duplicity which was to become characteristic of Zionist discourse, producing 'a not-undeserved reputation in the world for chronic mendacity' (Sykes 1965: 26), both with respect to true Zionist intentions and the distortion of what was done in their execution, as we shall see. After Herzl's death in 1904, his private diaries were held by the Zionist movement, and until 1960 only edited versions were released in English. The earlier versions suppressed his plans (12 June 1895) to 'try to spirit the penniless population across the border, etc.' (Herzl 1960, 1: 88). Nevertheless, in a letter of 19 March 1899 to a concerned Jerusalem Arab, he exclaimed, 'But who would think of sending them [the non-Jewish population of Palestine] away? It is their well-being, their individual wealth, which we will increase by bringing in our own' (in Childers 1987: 167).

Herzl acknowledged that, reluctantly, the native population would have to be used for labour, especially when fever attacked the workers, a fate from which he wished to protect the Zionists.

The modern, secular Jewish state of Herzl's novel *Altneuland* (1902), writing of 1923 and for European consumption, was a haven of the liberal spirit and a blessing for the natives. To the visiting Christian, Mr Kingscourt, who had asked, 'Don't you look upon the Jews as intruders?' the Palestinian Rashid Bey, replied, 'The Jews have enriched us, why should we be angry with them. They live with us like brothers. Why should we not love them?' But in the same 1902, Herzl's general disdain of natives was obvious from his response to Chamberlain's protest that Britain could not support the Zionist proposal for a joint Anglo-Zionist partnership, since it was against the will of the indigenous population of Cyprus (Herzl's diary of 23 October 1902). Earlier in the entry for the same day, we read: 'Not everything in politics is disclosed to the public—but only results of what can be serviceable in a controversy.'

Similarly, while Ben-Gurion, Yosef Weitz and other Zionist leaders advocated 'transfer', they usually expressed their views in closed Zionist circles, and deleted these references in published protocols:

> Ben-Gurion...preached behind the closed doors of the Zionist Congress in 1937 the virtues of transferring Palestine's Arabs...but in the printed text of his speech solemnly expatiates on creating 'one law for the foreigner and the citizen in a just regime based on brotherly love and true equality...that will be a shining example for the world in treating minorities' (Benny Morris, 'How the Zionist Documents Were Doctored', *Ha'aretz*, 4 February 1994; see also Morris 1995).

Shabtai Teveth, Ben-Gurion's biographer, acknowledges the disjuncture between Ben-Gurion's public protestations and private aspirations:

> A careful comparison of Ben-Gurion's public and private positions leads inexorably to the conclusion that this twenty-year denial of the conflict was a calculated tactic, born of pragmatism rather than profundity of conviction. The idea that Jews and Arabs could reconcile their differences...was a delaying tactic. Once the Yishuv had gained strength, Ben-Gurion abandoned it. This belief in a compromise solution...was also a tactic, designed to win continued British support for Zionism (Teveth 1985: 198-99).

Moreover, as Lehn shows convincingly, despite its claims that no Arabs were evicted or disadvantaged by Jewish purchase of land, the

JNF insisted that the Arab tenants working on land which the JNF wished to purchase would be removed by the vendors as a condition for the sale (Lehn 1988: 55-57). The future Zionist leaders, schooled in the Herzlia Gymnasia in Palestine, had it drummed into their young hearts that 'the fatherland must become ours, *goyim rein*' (Menuhin 1969: 52).

The Myth of No Expulsions

The birth of the Jewish state caused the dispossession of some three-quarters of a million Palestinian Arabs, whether acknowledged to be intended by the Zionists or not. The myths of the benevolent and peaceful intentions of Zionism has been unmasked comprehensively by Masalha's study (1992), which reveals that the 'transfer' of the Arab population was supported by the whole pantheon of Zionist ideologues from the beginning, albeit in secret (see also Morris 1995). Moreover, the disjuncture between what actually happened and what the official Israeli records promulgated is striking. The official Israeli Government pamphlet on the refugee question, first published in 1953, states that the Palestinian Arabs were induced or incited to run away by express instructions broadcast by the President of the Arab Higher Executive (the Mufti) and surrounding Arab states. The charge has become a standard component of the Israeli myth of origins, despite the absence of corroborating evidence, and the presence of abundant proof to dispel it.

Even the report of the intelligence branch of the Israel Defence Force (IDF), 'Emigration of the Arabs of Palestine in the Period 1.12.1947–1.6.1948', ascribes the flight of 72 per cent of the Palestinian refugees (some 391,000 people in all during that critical period) to Israeli military force. Not only is there no mention of Arab broadcasts encouraging the temporary exodus of the Arabs, but the report stresses that the exodus of Palestinians was contrary to the desires of the Arab Higher Committee and the neighbouring Arab states: Arab broadcasts encouraged the population to stay put, issuing threats to stave off the exodus (see Hitchens 1988: 75). The myth is repeated to this day, despite the fact that already in London's *Spectator* of 12 May 1961, Erskine Childers revealed that in 1958, as a guest of the Israeli Foreign Office, he had requested to see the primary evidence for the charge that the Palestinians had been urged to flee by the Arab leadership. Despite claims of 'a mountain of evidence' and a 'wealth of evidence' no evidence, though promised, was produced then, or since.

The evidence customarily offered is a recourse of desperation. The allegation of an 'announcement made over the air' by the Arab Higher Committee to account for the flight of Arabs in the Deir Yassin 'incident' emanated from a Cyprus-based correspondent, who depended on an uncorroborated Israeli source. The contention that the Greek-Catholic Archbishop of Galilee had urged his flock to leave has been denied categorically by the Archbishop himself. Childers decided to check the substantial claim through the BBC, which had monitored all Middle East broadcasts throughout 1948, and a corroborating American monitoring unit. He found that

> There was not a single order, or appeal, or suggestion about evacuation from Palestine from any Arab radio station, inside or outside Palestine, in 1948. There is repeated monitored record of Arab appeals, even flat orders, to the civilians of Palestine *to stay put* (in Hitchens 1988: 77).

Moreover, the evidence for systematic Yishuv 'horror recordings' and 'psychological blitz' to clear the area of Arabs is abundant (see Childers 1987: 183-202).

Yitzhak Rabin, who presided over some of the most ruthless expulsions of the 1948 war, sought to perpetuate the myth that the expulsion of the Palestinians was brought about by Haj Amin Husseini's alleged call to the Arabs to leave in view of the forthcoming invasion by the Arab states (Finkelstein 1995: 195 n. 55). On 12 July 1948, after the slaughter of more than 250 Arabs in Lydda, Lieutenant-Colonel Rabin, head of operations, issued the order: 'The inhabitants of Lydda must be expelled quickly without attention to age…Yiftah (Brigade HQ) must determine the method.'[6] A participant in the 'death march' from Lydda recalls, 'I cannot forget three horror-filled days in July of 1948. The pain sears my memory, and I cannot rid myself of it no matter how hard I try' (Rantisi 1990: 23). Nevertheless, Israeli historians during the 1950s, 1960s and 1970s insisted that the inhabitants had violated the terms of surrender and 'were happy at the possibility given them of evacuating' (Morris 1990a: 2-3). Although Rabin's own acknowledgment that what happened in Lydda and Ramle had been 'expulsions' was excised from his text by Israeli Government

6. A similar order was issued for the expulsion of the inhabitants of neighbouring Ramle.

censors, to his embarrassment the *New York Times* later published
the offending passage (23 October 1979, Kidron 1988: 90-94).

Shapira devotes less than two pages to 'population transfer', and
justifies it in terms of the 'positive experience' between Turkey and
Greece, etc. without attending to the brutality such an enterprise
inevitably involves (1992: 285-86). Even the revisionist Benny Morris
confesses that, if pressed to evaluate morally the Yishuv's policies and
behaviour in 1948, he would be loath to condemn, and opines that
'any sane, pragmatic leader' would have done the same (Morris
1990b: 20-21). However, as Norman Finkelstein notes, a 'sane, pragmatic leader' is not necessarily a moral one (1995: 187 n. 8).

Israel's real, but publicly undeclared intentions are confirmed by
ongoing Israeli insistence on not allowing the Palestinians to come
back to their own houses and lands up to the present day. Whether
they left 'under orders, or pressure' or not, justice and international
law demand that their right to return on the cessation of hostilities be
honoured.[7] That Ben-Gurion's ultimate intention was to evacuate as
many Arabs as possible from the Jewish state can be deduced from the
range of methods he employed: an economic war aimed at destroying
Arab transport, commerce and the supply of foods and raw materials
to the urban population; psychological warfare, ranging from
'friendly warnings' to intimidation and exploitation of panic caused by
underground terrorism; and the destruction of whole villages and the
eviction of their inhabitants by the army (Flapan 1987: 92). After the
1967 war, IDF troops along the Jordan river routinely shot civilians,
men, women and children trying to slip back home (see McDowall
1989: 302 n. 109).

The Myth of 'Self-Defence'
Similarly, the myth of 'self-defence' has been exposed. Shapira argues
that the Zionist movement never intended to resort to force, but was
only driven to it by an accumulation of circumstances. She makes no
ethical distinction between the Zionist aim to transform Palestine into
a Jewish state and the indigenous Palestinians' determination to resist
it (Shapira 1992: 107-25). The conflict, then, was a clash of two

7.   'Israelis like to argue whether the Arabs escaped voluntarily or were expelled
by us. As if this made any difference. We could always have let them return after
the war' ('The 1948 Refugees Are the Original Sin of Israeli Society', *Haaretz*,
5 December 1993).

rights, more or less equal, a perspective which dilutes somewhat mainstream Zionist historiography with its assumption that the Zionist claim is stronger, if not absolute.

The appeal to a 'defensive ethos' was a public relations device, as well as an exercise in conscious self-deception. It assuaged both world opinion and the consciences of would-be immigrants and labour Zionists, who in principle were opposed to colonialism. However, from the beginning it was clear that Zionism was a conquest movement, whether, reflecting changing circumstances, through peaceful settlement or violence. No segment of the Arab population in Palestine would agree to assuming an inferior status to the Jews in their own land, and, *a fortiori*, to any arrangement that required them to abandon it. Recourse to arms sooner or later was inevitable, and was widely recognized from the beginning, whether by the minority revisionist Jabotinsky (author of *Homo homini lupus*—see Avineri 1981: 163-64) or the mainstream labour Zionist, Ben-Gurion (see Finkelstein 1995: 110).

The Myth of 'Purity of Arms'
This myth also has had to be abandoned in the face of the evidence. By 1948 the metamorphosis of the stereotypical Jew to becoming one capable of committing atrocities was unmasked. The former director of the Israel army archives, and other Israeli sources, confirm that in almost every Arab village occupied by Jews during the War of Independence, war crimes, such as murders, massacres and rapes were committed (see Finkelstein 1995: 110-12).

Zionism succumbed to the predictable paternalistic attitude of conquerors, branding the indigenous population with the stereotypical appellations reserved for 'inferior' colonized people (see Finkelstein 1995: 110-12). The socialism embraced by the Yishuv Labour leadership was that of Stalinist Russia, which legitimated the use of terror, the killing of the aged, women and children, the execution of suspected Jewish collaborators, the extortion of funds and acts of robbery, etc., during the Arab Revolt of 1936–39 (Shapira 1992: 247-49, 350), with the socialist end justifying the means.

Israeli war crimes did not end with the war of 1948–49. Rokach's *Israel's Sacred Terrorism* records the state terrorism against its neighbours, including civilian targets, during the 1950s. In an act of reprisal, 66 civilian men, women and children were deliberately killed by troops in the West Bank village of Qibua on 14 October 1953, when their homes were demolished over their heads. While officially denied by the Israeli Government at the time, it was later proved to be the work of Unit 101, a special forces battalion of the regular IDF, designed to carry out cross-border reprisal raids, and under the command of Ariel Sharon, subsequently Israel's Defence Minister, and Minister of Infrastructure in the Likud-led government of 1996. Moreover, between 1949 and 1956 some 3000–5000 unarmed civilians were killed by the IDF without compunction (McDowall 1994: 35).

After his investigation of the IDF's behaviour, Benny Morris suggested that it

> ...reflected a pervasive attitude among the Israeli public that Arab life was cheap (or, alternatively, that only Jewish life was sacred)...The overall attitude, at least down to 1953, seemed to signal to the defence forces' rank and file that killing, torturing, beating and raping Arab infiltrators was, if not permitted, at least not particularly reprehensible and might well go unpunished (Morris 1993: 166).

McDowall notes that, while sadistic racism exists in all armies, the real issue is how vigorously senior commanders enforce discipline and punish offenders (1994: 36). The IDF committed several atrocities which were covered up and denied, for example, that of 49 civilians in Kafr Qasim in October 1956 (McDowall 1989: 204), and of over 500 men in Khan Yunis and Rafah some days later (see Cossali and Robson 1986: 17-18; Locke and Stewart 1985: 6). Reprisals in which civilians were foreseeably the primary victims include the killing of 18 civilians in Samu (West Bank) in 1966, and air attacks on Irbid (Jordan, 1968, 30 civilians killed), Abu Za'abel factory (Egypt, 1970, 70 civilians killed), Bahr al Baqr (Egypt, 46 civilians killed), and Beirut (1981, over 200 civilians killed) (McDowall 1989: 302 n. 106).

The Israeli daily, *Ma'ariv* (2 August 1995), exposed serious war crimes committed in 1956 (the killing of some 140 Egyptian prisoners of war, including 49 Egyptian workers, in cold blood) by the elite paratroop unit 890, led by, and on the orders of Rafael Eitan, who later became the IDF Chief of Staff and subsequently founded and led the *Tzomet* Party. Israel's self-perception as morally superior in its purity of arms was further rocked by the revelation of army veteran and former Labour MK, Michael Ben-Zohar, that he had witnessed the fatal stabbing of three Egyptian PoWs by two Israeli chefs during the 1967 June War. Military historian and former MK, Meir Pa'il, knew of many instances in which soldiers had killed PoWs or Arab civilians. Prime Minister Rabin regretted that 'things have been said so far. I won't add anything to this' (*Jewish Chronicle*, 18 August 1995, p. 1).

More recently, the racism inherent in Zionism reached unacceptable levels in the ideology and practice of the late Meir Kahane. The slogan 'Death to the Arabs' was heard widely and appeared on Hebrew graffiti, for example, on the wall of the Fifth Station on the *Via Dolorosa* for a number of years. There was considerable concern for the inroads of racism into Israeli culture, with soldiers who, exposed to the history of the *Shoah*, were planning all sorts of ways to exterminate Arabs: 'Too many soldiers were deducing that the Holocaust justifies every kind of disgraceful action' (IDF Education Corps officer, Col. Ehud Praver, in Segev 1993: 407).

Both within Israel and outside comparisons were made between the Israeli army and the Nazis.[8] The well-known songwriter, Dan Almagor wrote, 'We had better start preparing ourselves and the glass booths in which we will sit when they judge us for what we did to the Palestinian people' ('I Regret', in *Yerushalaim*, *Yediot Aharonot*, 16 December 1988, p. 23, quoted in Segev 1993: 410).

Avraham Shapira's *The Seventh Day* (1970), an oral history of the June 1967 war, based on interviews with soldiers, highlights the attitudes of the soldiers for whom the moral problematic was not what the war did to the victims, but what it did to the Israeli soldiers. The Israeli soldier was the war's salient victim, and the one deserving of pity. Such exercises in self-extenuation and self-exculpation prevent the perpetrators from recognizing themselves as murderers, and settle for presenting themselves as tragic figures and objects of pity. Such

8.   Yeshayahu Leibowitz introduced the term *Judeo-Nazis* in protest against the Israeli attack on Lebanon, and in some circles the term *Asken-Nazis* was being hurled as a sign of ethnic tension. The Moledet Party was described as *neo-Nazi*. After a Tel Aviv judge sentenced a Jewish citizen to six months of public service for killing an Arab boy, Professor Zeev Sternhell, a Hebrew University expert on the history of fascism stated, 'The end came to German democracy not on the day the Nazi militias killed their first leftist demonstrator but when a Nazi was sentenced to three months in prison for the same offence for which a Communist was sentenced to three years' ('Banai, Struzman, Farago', *Hadashot*, 2 June 1986, quoted in Segev 1993: 410).

self-righteous and sanctimonious piety substitutes sentimental self-pity for genuine moral concern for the suffering which the self has inflicted on the other, all in the name of public duty (see Finkelstein 1995: 114-20).[9]

Adjudicating between Conflicting Rights

From the beginning of the modern Jewish settlement in Palestine, Jews had to experience some unease on being confronted by the reality that their coming to Palestine with Zionist zeal immediately established conflict with the indigenous Arab population: 'I feel that someone lived in this house before we came' (Y. Geffen, *Ma'ariv*, 11 August 1972, in Kimmerling 1983: 183). If convinced of his own claims to be there the Jew had to contend with the Palestinian counterclaim.

There were six major tendencies among Zionist groups on how to deal with the indigenous Arab community: as relatives, natives, Gentiles, Canaanites, as an oppressed class, and, finally, seeing the Arabs and Jews as two national movements (see Kimmerling 1983: 184-89). Seeing the Arabs as relatives, fellow Semites who resembled the forefathers of Jews, made them worthy of respect in the view of many of the early settlers. Viewing them as natives, which though seldom acknowledged in public became one of the most widely shared perceptions among Jews, led to the realization that Zionism could be achieved only by force. Regarding the Arabs as Canaanites, and the Zionists as descendants of the biblical children of Israel imported into the discourse the biblical mandate to take over the land and to purify it of its idolatrous practices. Weighed against the divinely-given right of the colonizers, the rights of the local population had no validity. Views of this kind were accentuated in the wake of the 1967 War and the rise of Gush Emunim, with its policy to flood the Occupied Territories with so many Jews that Arab autonomy therein would never be possible.

Kimmerling's suggestion that the estimation of the early Zionist settlers that the Palestinian Arabs were an oppressed class who were in the shackles of the feudal, exploitative pre-capitalistic regimes does not square with the policies of the JNF. Those who saw the growth of an Arab national movement as a challenge to the Jewish one

---

9.   Invariably, when I question an Israeli soldier about his behaviour, and ask whether he experiences any moral perturbation about his activities, I get the answer, 'I am only doing my duty.'

determined to abort it as soon as possible. On the other hand, those who saw it as inevitable proposed various patterns of territorial division, and division of political authority (see Kimmerling 1983: 184-89).

While it is instructive to discuss such Zionist ideologies, because of the typical disjuncture between the public ideology of Zionism and its practice, it is more relevant to evaluate what actually happened. If Ben-Gurion's claim in 1928 that,

> According to my ethical beliefs, we do not have the right to deprive even a single Arab child, even if by means of that deprivation we will achieve our goal. Our work cannot be built upon the deprivation of even a single person's rights.

reflected his real views, his actions later witness to an accelerated moral collapse. It is more likely that they were only the public part of the double discourse of Zionism, which hid the sordid elements of its programme from public discussion. Jabotinsky, in any case, attributed such sensibilities to 'only those with crippled spirits, with a diaspora psychosis' (in Kimmerling 1983: 189).

The argument from the compelling need of Jews to settle in a Jewish state does not constitute a right to displace an indigenous population. And, whether intended from the start or not, the moral problematic arises most acutely precisely from the fact that Zionism has wreaked havoc on the indigenous population, and not a little inconvenience on several surrounding states.

The 'historical right' is considered to be so obvious as to require no demonstration. Today's Jews, from anywhere on earth, are widely presumed to be the descendants of the ancient people of Israel, while the Palestinian Arabs are interlopers. Historically, however, the Palestinian Arabs are likely to have been descendants of the inhabitants of the region when, according to the biblical narrative, the children of Israel settled there towards the end of the Bronze Age. Palestine, at least since that time, has been multi-cultural and multi-ethnic. We know that some Palestinian Jews became Christians, and that some of them in turn became Muslims. Ironically, many of the forebears of Palestinian Arab refugees may well have been Jewish.

The appeal to Jewish forebears who were buried there, and Jewish blood which had fertilized the land, etc. are of the order of the Nazi justification of their conquest of the East on the basis of it having been inhabited by Germans in primeval times, and that it had been fertilized by the most noble ancient German blood. Finkelstein argues that

Zionism's 'historical right' was neither historical nor a right: not historical because it denied 2000 years of non-Jewish habitation of
Palestine, and 2000 years of Jewish habitation elsewhere, and not a
right, except in terms of the Romantic mysticism of blood and soil
(1995: 101).

The 'Right to Return'

This is among the major claims to justify the establishment of the
Jewish state in Palestine. The *Law of Return* permits any Jew in the
world to settle in Israel. However, in the wider world, the right of
return operates only when an appropriately defined community has
been subjected to recent expulsion. Such an understanding is a *sine qua
non* of orderly international behaviour. In order to establish a right to
return, all the Jews of the world, from Siberia to Johannesburg,
would have to constitute a clearly defined community which could
demonstrate its collective recent expulsion from its territory. But
there never was a definable, single Jewish community which was
exiled at one time, or over a definite period, and which awaited its
opportunity to return. In the course of history, many Jews emigrated
from Palestine, by no means all by forcible exile.

The moral case for return is undermined by the time-span between
the act of expulsion and the determination to resettle. A right to
return dissolves into desuetude as the time-span between expulsion and
the determination to re-settle or reclaim the homeland exceeds reason-
able limits. If there were no time limits on the right to return, international order would collapse. To concede the legitimacy of a Jewish
Law of Return would open the floodgates for bizarre returns to ancestral homes at the expense of people in place for thousands of years.

In customary international law, no group has a right to conquer and
annex the territory of another people and expel its population.
Moreover, a people's return to the land from which it has been
expelled is a right under customary international law. This right has a
universally valid moral quality, and obtains for all peoples which
experience expulsion. The exiled Palestinians constitute a quintessen-
tial example of a people with a right to return, since, in 1948, a
clearly identified population was expelled by their Zionist conquerors,
and has never renounced its rights—many still possess their title deeds
to land, and even the keys of their homes. Diaspora Jews could never
have a right to immigrate into Palestine unless these Palestinians

surrendered to them their right to return. Moreover, Jewish claims of a right to return have no measure of justice and morality, and rely only on legislation which lacks moral coherence, and which receives its force exclusively from conscienceless power. While conquest and war are effective agents of annexation, they are not instruments of legitimacy in the modern world.

Appeal to the needs of Jews runs the risk of elevating the perceived needs of Zionist Jews to an imperative that does not have to contend with the demands, needs or rights of any other people or national community. In such a unique discourse, Zionism defines universal morality exclusively in its own terms. In reality, Zionism cannot deal comfortably with moral discourse. The establishment of the State of Israel itself was possible only on the basis of land expropriation and massive expulsion. No amount of legal acrobatics could ever justify its behaviour towards the indigenous population. From that point on, the exercise of legal power could only consolidate and amplify the foundational immorality. The advancement of the Zionist dream could only corrupt the normal discourse of jurisprudence, which, instead of being an instrument of morality, would merely compound the original crime.

The Shoah *and Jewish Nationalism*
The organized transfer of Jews from villages, towns and cities all over Europe to Nazi concentration camps resulted in the murder of at least six million Jews (Gilbert 1982: 244-45).[10] Only some 1.6 million Jews who were in Europe in September 1939 survived until May 1945, and of these some 300,0000 endured the concentration camps (Gilbert 1982: 242-43). Frequently, the *Shoah* alone is presented as a justification for the establishment of a Jewish state (e.g., W. Davies 1991: 120). Moreover, in some quarters Arab opposition to the establishment of the state was considered to be continuing the Nazi genocide (e.g. Manès Sperber's *Than a Tear in the Sea*, 1967: xiii), a sentiment which Emil Fackenheim quotes, apparently with approval (1987: 400). The *Shoah* argument is critical in Israel. Appeal to it does not draw on the Jewish attachment to the land of Israel, but rather that

10. At the outbreak of World War II there were almost 17 million Jews, of whom 8 million lived in Eastern Europe and some 5 million in the Americas. The Jewish population in Eastern Europe was the largest increasing one, and was also responsible for the increase in numbers elsewhere (Halpern 1969: 6-7).

(a) the *Shoah* is an unique event in history, in that what happened to the Jews never happened to anyone else;[11] (b) not only did the Gentiles not aid the Jews, but they assisted in their mass murder—hence, Jews cannot ever rely on the *goyim* for protection; (c) a Jewish nation state is the only protection against another holocaust.[12] One of the features of the *Shoah* as an *apologia* for the establishment of a Jewish state is that no attention is paid to the cost to the Palestinians. Indeed, since all the *goyim* are potentially anti-Semites, and even potential murderers of Jews, it might be necessary to cleanse Palestine ethnically and expel the enemies within the gate.

The 'Holocaust Theology' of Elie Wiesel, Emil Fackenheim and Rabbi Irving Greenberg and others posits the perceived needs of Jews as constituting a moral absolute, without any reference to the legitimate needs of the Palestinian people, who function only in terms of their perceived threat to the survival of the Jewish people. Its absorption in 'what is good for the Jews' precludes a critical history of Zionism or of Israeli state policy. In failing to deal meaningfully with the fact that Israel's success has been brought about by the humiliation of another people, Holocaust theology eludes the moral imperative of confronting the realities of the formation of the Jewish state and its policies since 1948. The plight of the Palestinian people undermines the force of Holocaust theology, with its portrayal of an innocent, suffering people in search of security and freedom.[13]

The Myth of the Unique Historical Claim
The status of the land of Israel in religious Jewish thought derives from the covenant between God and his people. But one must caution against the assumption that diaspora attachment to the land is virtually

11. Fackenheim discusses whether the Holocaust was *unique*, or only *unprecedented*, and concludes that it was both (1987: 400).

12. The Masada myth was fabricated as a glorious example of Jewish heroism which would bolster the spirit of the 'Never Again' defiance. Nachman Ben-Yehuda has shown how the mythical narrative was consciously invented, fabricated and supported by key entrepreneurs and organizations in the Yishuv. It was constructed as a central national symbol of heroism for the new secular Zionist culture during the period of nation building since the 1920s and since the establishment of the state after 1948 (1995: 307-309).

13. Moreover, the tragedy of the *Shoah* is employed to serve overt political intentions: see Beit-Hallahmi 1987: ix-x; Phillip Lopate and Avishai Margalit, in Ellis 1990: 196 n 2; 34.

equivalent to the intentions implied in political Zionism. Many assume that the implementation of the goals of political Zionism was the fulfilment of the ideals of world-wide Jewry from the earliest times to today. According to this reading of events, all Jews had been forcibly dispersed at one time, and Zionism had brought them back. Historical realities, however, do not support such an analysis.

Certainly there were forced expulsions.[14] However, it was never easy to reconcile the view that exile was the punishment for sin with the reality that many Jews remained in Babylon after the return to Zion in 538 BC, and with the existence of a widespread Jewish diaspora in the Hellenistic period. It was held in antiquity that the 'ten tribes' had never returned from exile in Babylon (e.g. Josephus, *Ant.* 11.5.2 (133); *4 Ezra* 13.39-47; *m. Sanh.* 10.3.5). Even the return of the tribes of Judah and Benjamin is unlikely to have been total. Documents from the Persian period show clearly that Jews remained on in Babylon (see, e.g., Bickerman 1984).

Voluntary emigration of Jews from Palestine into the areas bordering on Palestine and into the cities of the so-called civilized world was widespread in the Hellenistic-Roman period. Part of Alexander's plans to extend Hellenistic culture was to encourage the foundation of new cities and new people to settle in them. Such settlers were granted various privileges and even citizenship. Jews answered the call in considerable numbers, going to Syria and Egypt, especially Antioch and Alexandria, and to other newly-founded Hellenistic cities. Jewish voluntary emigration extended to Mesopotamia, Media, Babylonia, Dura-Europos, the Arabian Peninsula, Asia Minor, the North Coast of the Black Sea, Cyrenaica, Africa, Macedonia and Greece, the Greek Islands, the Balkans, Rome, Italy, and in the Christian period also to Spain, Gaul and Germany. An abundance of evidence witnesses to a widespread Jewish diaspora (1 Macc. 15.22-23; the *Sib. Or.* 3.271; Strabo, according to Josephus, *Ant.* 14.7, 2 [115]; Josephus, *Wars* 2.16.4 (398); 7.3.3 (43); Philo, *Flacc.* 46 and *Leg. Gai.* 281-82; Acts 2.5-11; etc.). There were colonies of Jews throughout most of the

14. Hebrews were forcibly deported by the Assyrians (721 BC), the Babylonians (586 BC), Artaxerxes Ochus (345-343 BC?), and Tigranes (83-69 BC). The Romans carried off hundreds of prisoners of war to Rome after the conquest of Jerusalem by Pompey in 63 BC (Schürer 1986: 3-6). Deportation also followed the defeat of the Jewish Rebellion (66-70 AD) and that of Bar Kochba (135 AD).

inhabited world, as known by people in the West. However acute the theoretical question of whether religious Jews could live other than in the land of Israel, the communities of Jews who settled throughout Europe, North Africa and east of Palestine gave a pragmatic answer. Whatever the degree of attachment to the homeland, there is no evidence for a longing sufficiently vigorous to induce more than a handful of Jews to 'return' even when the circumstances in the diaspora were difficult.

In the Deuterocanonical Old Testament and the Apocrypha (the Apocrypha and Pseudepigrapha), one finds some of the same attachment to the land that one encounters in the Old Testament, although notably less frequently.[15] One finds also the promise that God would restore his people to the land (*Pss. Sol.* 17.26-28). In the end, God will protect only those who live in Israel (2 Bar. 9.2), the land will aid redemption (2 Bar. 1.1) and becomes 'holy' because God draws near it (*4 Ezra* 9.7-9). Finally, it is in the pleasant land of Israel that the throne of God will be erected (*1 En.* 90.20).

However, Halpern-Amaru has shown how the biblical traditions of land were rewritten to reflect the historical contexts and contemporary interests of the authors. In each of her four examples, she shows how the author reconstructs the narrative, so that the land no longer functions as the key signature of covenantal history, and develops new narratives which de-emphasize the theological significance of land. In *Jubilees* and *The Testament of Moses* the rewriting is eschatological, while in *Pseudo-Philo* and Josephus's *Antiquities* it is historically oriented. In each reworking of the tradition, the concept of Covenant is reformulated so that some promise other than land assumes the pivotal position (Halpern-Amaru 1994: 116-17).[16]

---

15. The term *holy land* appears in a number of texts (e.g. Wis. 12.3; 2 Macc. 1.7; *Sib. Or.* 3.266-67). The land is *good/beautiful* (e.g. Tobit 14.4, 5; *Jub.* 13.2, 6), a *pleasant and glorious land* (e.g. *1 En.* 89.40), *extensive and beautiful* (*Ep. Arist.*, line 107). It is the land *of promise* (e.g. Sir. 46.8; *Jub.* 12.22; 13.3; 22.27). One notes other reflections of earlier biblical values: failure to observe the demands of Yahweh is incompatible with occupation (*Jub.* 6.12-13); the circumcized will not be rooted out of the land (*Jub.* 15.28), and the original Israelite conquest was due to sins of the Canaanite inhabitants.

16. 'A meeting ground between theology and history, religion and politics, the Land concept has been exaggerated, minimized, allegorized, idealized, rationalized, and polemicized. In the expansionist era of the Hasmoneans the biblical Land idea was formulated in geo-political terms. With the growth of large diaspora

In the Dead Sea Scrolls we detect the persistence of attitudes to the land we find in the biblical books. It is in the land that the members of the community practise truth and righteousness and maintain faithfulness (1QS 1.5; 8.3). Part of the task of the Qumran community was to cleanse the land, which the Temple sacrificial system had sought in vain to accomplish, in order to render it acceptable to God (1QS 9.3-5). Sin leads God to hide his face from the land (CD 2.9-11), and causes the land to be desolate (CD 4.10). In the final war, the sect, the true Israelites, would occupy the land, and would fight a holy war against the Gentile lands (1 QM 2).

After the devastation of the land in 70 AD, so many Jews were leaving, especially for Syria, that the rabbis feared the land would be depopulated, and began to extol its virtues. For the rabbis, the land was simply *ha'aretz*, and other lands were 'outside the land'. It required only the application of a rigid reading of the biblical text to recognize that an authentic Jewish life would be possible only in the land of Israel, centred on the Temple in Jerusalem. Many of the *mitzvot* could be observed only in the Land of Israel, for example, the laws of sabbatical and jubilee years, the tithes and offerings to the priests and the rituals dealing with the Temple. Only in such a kingdom could it even be possible to live a fully Jewish life consistent with the demands of the *Torah*. For that reason it could be said of a Jew living among the *goyim* that 'he is like one who has no God' (*b. Ket.* 110b). When the Temple was destroyed, God could not be worshipped adequately.

After the failure of the Bar Kochba revolt, movement from the land increased. The Jewish sages faced a dilemma. On the one hand, they had to try to prevent the total abandonment of the land, while on the other they had to devise a *modus vivendi* with the diaspora which would authenticate Jewish living outside the land. The rabbinic exaltation of the land had its roots in the Old Testament (e.g. Lev. 19.23;

communities in the early rabbinic period, it became a spatial benchmark for the development of Jewish law. And, displaced from its central position in Jewish thought in the course of diaspora history, it was then transformed in idealized form into a temporal symbol of redemptive hope. Nineteenth-century political Zionism retranslated the concept into a signpost of cultural and political normality; and the return to sovereign nationhood in the twentieth century provoked renewed efforts to determine its religious significance. The interpretive encounter with the biblical concept of Land has not ended' (Halpern-Amaru 1994 : 1-2).

23.10; 23.22; 25.2 and Deut. 26.1; Num. 35.9-10; Deut. 4.41-42; 19.1-2), and since so much of the *Torah* dealt with the land, it would feature prominently even after dispersal. The sages repeated the biblical themes of the land of Israel and tended to idealize them. Constant reference to the ritual patterns endowed the land of Israel with almost mystical significance. It became an imagined place, and longing for it took the form of that nostalgia for 'Paradise' that one finds in many diaspora communities.

One-third of the Mishnah is connected with the land. Most of the first division, *Zeraim* (Seeds), of the fifth division, *Kodashim* (Holy Things), and of the sixth division, *Toharoth* (Purities) deal with laws concerning the land, and there is much besides in the other parts. Rabbi Simeon b. Yohai (140–165) said that the Holy One gave Israel three precious gifts: The *Torah*, the land of Israel and the World to Come (*b. Ber.* 5a). While 'the land of Israel is holier than all land', the tenth degree of holiness is the sanctuary: 'The Holy of Holies is still more holy' (*m. Kel.* 1.6-9). The degree of holiness of the land derives from the extent of its association with the enactment of the Law. A fundamentalist reading of the *Torah* legislation on land matters would suggest that Jewish sanctity was only fully possible in the land, and that exile was an emaciated life (see Davies 1991: 26). However, such attitudes to religion and morality reflect a failure to adjust to radically changed circumstances.

While the rabbis prescribed the recitation of the Eighteen Benedictions (the *Tefillah*, or *Shemonei Esreh*), which became a core element of the Jewish liturgy, the emphasis was on the Temple rather than just the land: 'Zion the abiding place of Thy glory, and towards Thy temple and Thy habitation' (Benediction 14; see also 16, 18). This is also the case in the Siddur Benediction 18. The prayers were to be said facing Jerusalem, or at least orienting the heart towards the Holy of Holies (*m. Ber.* 4.5).

The Jewish liturgy played a critical role in keeping alive the attachment to the land. The annual Liturgy of Destruction, ending on the ninth day of Ab (*Tisha be-Av*), is given over to fasting for the annual commemoration of the devastation of the land, Jerusalem and its Temple. On that day, the prayer begins, 'O Lord God, comfort the mourners of Zion; Comfort those who grieve for Jerusalem', and ends with, 'Praised are You, O Lord, who comforts Zion; Praised are You, who rebuilds Jerusalem.' See also *m. Roš Haš.* 4.1-3 for the centrality of Jerusalem. That Jerusalem established the time for world-wide celebration of the Jewish festivals, and that all synagogues faced Jerusalem added to its importance.

The Tannaitic and Amoraic sages were wary of political attempts to re-establish the kingdom of Israel on its own land. However, devoted and intense religious concern for the land/Temple remained part of the communal consciousness of Jews. The last revolt of Jews in the Roman Empire in the hope of re-establishing a Jewish state occurred after the anti-Jewish statutes of Emperor Justinian (483–565 AD). Later, Nehemiah, a messianic figure, reigned in Jerusalem in the period 614–17. With the Arab Conquest in 639, and the building of the Mosque of Omar on the site of the temple (687–91), Jewish devotion to the land was reflected in voluntary individual pilgrimages and immigrations rather than in political activity for the establishment of a state.

The Law demanded that every male should make pilgrimage to Jerusalem at Passover, Feast of Weeks and Tabernacles (Exod. 23.14-17; see Deut. 16.1-17). During the Second Temple period even diaspora Jews sought to observe the pilgrimage (e.g. *m. Ta'an.* 1.3). Philo has left a record of his attachment to the Temple in Jerusalem, and describes world-wide pilgrimage to it (*Spec. Leg.* 1, the MSS insert *Of the Temple* 67-70). After the destruction of the Temple in 70 AD, however, pilgrimage reflected the devotion of Jewish pilgrims to the worship at the site of the Temple. Invariably such pilgrimages to the Wailing Wall became occasions of lamentation.

The polarity of the relationship of diaspora Jews to the land is reflected in two contrasting standpoints of the poet Jehuda Halevi (c. 1075–1141) and the great post-Talmudic spiritual leader, Moses Maimonides (1135–1204). In his *Kuzari*, Halevi showed how exile had severed the links between the *Torah*, the people of Israel and the land of Israel, which would be mended only with the coming of the Messiah. He lamented his separation from Zion: 'My heart is in the East, and I am at the edge of the West…it would be glorious to see the dust of the ruined Shrine' (*Libbi bemitzrach,* in Carmi 1981: 347). Invariably his lament is related to the devastation of the land and of Jerusalem in particular (see his Zion poems, and in particular *Sion, halo tishali*, which was included in the liturgy of *Tisha be-Av*, in Carmi 1981: 347). The main strands of Hebrew thought affirmed the centrality of the land, the city of Jerusalem and its Temple, and for

Halevi also, the land of Israel marked the threshold between the human and the divine spheres.

Halevi considered that every Jew must make every effort to go to the land of Israel to observe the commandments there. In several poems he imagines his voyage. In 1141, at the age of 65, he left his family in Spain and headed for the Levant (see his *Hava mabbul*, in Carmi 1981: 352). Whether he visited Jerusalem or not we do not know. We do know that his tomb in Lower Galilee was seen within some 20 years of his death by Benjamin ben Jonah of Tudela, the first mediaeval Jewish writer of whose travels we have a detailed record (Adler 1894).

By contrast, for Maimonides, who followed the later prophetic and *halakhic* sources, the land of Israel was of itself no different from other lands. However, historically speaking, it was distinctive because it was sanctified by the commandments and by events of Israelite history. Maimonides passed through the land of Israel on his way to Egypt but lived his entire life in the diaspora. Similarly, Benjamin of Tudela spent an extended period away from Spain, which he left in 1160, going as far as Syria, Palestine and Persia, and returning to Spain in 1173. His account reflects his interest in what we might call inquisitive journeying rather than in what religious people call pilgrimage.

The fate of living in different parts of the Jewish diaspora assumed dreadful proportions in several places during the period of the Crusades. In an anonymous poem, 'Come with us', the smitten daughter of Zion is invited to join in the march to the Holy Land (Carmi 1981: 368-70). David bar Meshullam of Speyer called on God to avenge the mass suicides in Speyer during the First Crusade (1096) (Carmi 1981: 374-75), and the poems of Ephraim of Regensburg (1110–75) reflect the horrors of the Regensburg massacre of 1137 and of the Second Crusade (1146–47). *Sefer Zekhira* of Ephraim of Bonn (1132–1200) records the decrees and persecutions of the Second and Third Crusades, and his lament for the massacre of Jews at Blois (1171) ends with the hope of being rescued and paying homage to God in Jerusalem (Carmi 1981: 385). A feature of the poetry of lament in this period is the presentation of massacres as a sacrificial ritual, the offering of the unblemished and willing lamb.

Shalem Shabazi (d. after 1681), the foremost Yemini poet, reflects on the messianic expectations of Jews, especially in the wake of the persecutions of 1679–81: 'When will He give me leave to go up and make home within the extolled gates of Zion? Morning and evening I call to mind the Princess [the Shekinah]' (Carmi 1981: 487). And again, 'My Beloved…will assemble all my kind and righteous tribes, and Israel will rise to greet the dawn in Zion's gates' (Carmi 1981: 488).[17]

With regard to Jewish religious settlement in the land, Rabbi Moses Ben Nahman (Ramban, 1194–1270), the highest religious authority of his time in Spain, emigrated to Palestine in 1267 and was active in founding *yeshivot* and synagogues in Acre and Jerusalem. In 1286, Rabbi Meir of Rothenburg sought to lead a number of Jews from the area of the Rhine to Palestine. In 1523, a messianic movement led by David Reuveni aimed at a return to the land and attracted the interest of communities in Egypt, Spain and Germany. In 1772–80, Rabbi Nahman of Bratzlov journeyed to the land and judged that what he had known before was insignificant, and that simply by direct contact with the land 'he held the Law whole'. He achieved this merely by stepping ashore at Haifa. He desired to return immediately, but under pressure went to Tiberias, but never to Jerusalem. The Maharal of Prague (Rabbi Yehuda Liwa of Loew—Ben Bezalel, 1515–1609) did not urge the establishment of a state in Israel, leaving that to God, who would come in his own good time (Lev. 26.44-45) (Davies 1991: 33).

Under the influence of Rabbi Elijah Ben Solomon Salman of Vilna (the Vilna Gaon), a number of groups went to Safed in 1808 and 1809 and saw themselves as representatives of all Jews, and considered themselves justified in appealing to other Jews for help. Some, such as Rabbi Akiba Schlessinger of Pressburg (1837–1922), were driven to go to the land, it being more and more difficult to live according to the *Torah* in an increasingly secular Europe.

W. Davies identifies Jewish movements of escape from modernism and secularism with the Zionist movement (1991: 34): Jews who had abandoned their religious and national identities to become 'normalized' in Western society subsequently became disillusioned and returned to the tradition they had shed. However, to do so both in religious and national terms was too much, and instead of returning to religious roots, they turned to 'nationalism', socialism and

---

17. The extant poetry, of course, also reflects the themes of poets of all periods, especially those dealing with the attraction of love (cf. the love poems of Immanuel of Rome, c. 1261–c. 1332, the 'emperor of poets').

romanticism, regarding their religion as a fossilized survival. For those nineteenth-century secular Jews who ultimately became Zionists, 'religious devotion to the land symbolized all that was particularistic, "scandalous", and nonassimilable in Judaism' (Davies 1991: 35 n. 17). Nevertheless, Davies postulates a certain consistency between the religious longing for the land and Zionist nationalism.

Conclusion

Although the practice of settler colonialism is distinctive in each case, we have seen that stereotypical attitudes to the indigenous people obtain in the ideologies we have examined. Invariably for colonization to take place, the colonizer had to be technically, materially and militarily more developed than the colonized. By the criteria of the colonizer, these qualities conferred superiority, 'natural' or 'racial', and justified 'the insatiable progress of our race'. The colonizers seldom considered the impact of their enterprise on the indigenous population, and either ignored it or knew what was best for the natives, and arrogated to themselves the right to be overseers of their destiny, whether in reservations, *congregaciones, aldeias, Bantustans* or Zones A of the PNA.[18] In the Eurocentric version of world history, in which 'the World is discovered by Europeans', even the most problematic achievements could be explained: 'The effect of the slave trade on Africa was undoubtedly harmful. Yet the balance was not altogether unfavourable. The Portuguese, for example, introduced a variety of new fruit and vegetables' (Williams 1962: 41).

Consistent with the practice in virtually all nations and political movements, the historiographers of Zionism and the State of Israel fabricated a history along the lines discussed above. Having forged a myth of a perennial Jewish longing to abandon the *galut* and establish a Jews-only state in the ancestral homeland, they posited it as the norm in every generation (the *Myth of the Unique Historical Claim*), even

18. In the nineteenth-century US also, the government adopted a policy of 'population transfer' of hundreds of thousands of Indians from their own land into reservations. Such an act required no further justification than that provided by the obvious superiority of the white man over the Indian. Moreover, any semblance of moral culpability for the action was removed by naming the operation 'The Manifest Destiny'. See Dee Brown's *Bury my Heart at Wounded Knee* (1981) and in particular p. 31 for an insight into 'Manifest Destiny'.

though such an aspiration did not appear in Jewish circles until the rise of other nationalisms in nineteenth-century Europe. The aspiration to establish a nation state in Palestine made no appearance in Jewish history between the defeat of Bar Kochba's revolt in 135 AD and the advent of nineteenth-century European nationalism. In fact, Jewish longing for the land was akin to the longing for a lost paradise of Temple ritual. In religious circles, the exceptional nationalistic views of Rabbis Kalischer and Alkalai ran in the face of the Orthodox establishment. Zionism depended on no religious sensitivities and was consistently opposed by the religious establishment, and the major Zionist ideologues despised religion. The rich diversity of pre-Zionist Jewry should not be forged into an inevitable linear progression to one agreed ideology, be it Zionism or some other. The fabricated proto-Zionist myth of the pre-history of political Zionism not only distorts the truth of history but perverts present-day Jews' perception of themselves, their origins and their destiny.

The amassing of texts from different periods and places, reflecting a certain alienation from the Holy Land and a discomfort in the diaspora, does not amount to evidence of a perennial and ubiquitous persecution of Jews (the *Myth of Perpetual and Ubiquitous Alienation and Persecution*). As the survival of Jews shows, the peril was neither everywhere nor at all times. There were golden ages in the diaspora, as well as dark ones. Indeed in 1950–51, Ben-Gurion felt obliged to sanction the bombing of synagogues and other Jewish buildings in Baghdad to engineer the *aliyah* of Jews from Iraq—an immensely successful campaign which drove some 105,000 Jews to flee the country with no choice of destination other than Israel, leaving only some 4000 behind (Shiblak 1986: 127).[19]

Diaspora longing for the land of Israel was invariably linked to Temple worship. While many volumes of the literature of 'classical

19. Agents of the Israeli Government spread the fear of anti-Semitism into the Iraqi Jews by blowing up synagogues (e.g. the Mas'uda Shemtob Synagogue on 14 January 1951), firms owned by Jews (May and June 1951) and other places frequented by Jews, as well as the US Information Centre in Baghdad (March 1951), in order to gain support for the Zionist cause in the US. The bombing campaign, carried out with the personal knowledge of Yigal Allon and David Ben-Gurion, was sustained over a period of time in order to ensure a mass exodus of Iraqi Jews to Israel: 'Every time fears would abate, a new bomb shattered the feeling of security, and the prospect of staying on in Iraq seemed gloomier' (Shiblak 1986: 124).

Judaism' discuss the Temple and its animal sacrifices, there is little on the town of Jerusalem. Moreover, it is the Temple and its sacrifices which are constantly referred to in Jewish prayers. However, attachment to the Temple rituals, the desire to rebuild the Temple and restore its animal sacrifices must take account of realities. *Ha'aretz*'s Passover Eve supplement ('The Holy Butcher Shop', 14 April 1995) shocked its readers with its description of how the Temple functioned with animal sacrifices etc. The ritual of priests skinning and dividing the animals, and the stench from the daily burning of hundreds of sheep and bulls as sacrifices and so on would temper the nostalgia for the earthly Jerusalem that is at the heart of diaspora longing.

Pilgrimage to Jerusalem also was motivated by attachment to the site of the Temple. The exclamation, 'Next year in Jerusalem' was in anticipation of a pilgrimage to the site of the Temple and not a proto-Zionist aspiration to establish a colonial settlement. Spiritual and emotional attachment to the land should not be confused with wishing to live there, and less with the desire to control it politically, especially at the expense of the indigenes. Essentially, pilgrims visit a place and return home.

Before the nineteenth century, there is little evidence that Jewish longing could be assuaged by recourse to settler colonialism. In the Bible itself, the land of Canaan is the Promised Land, 'the acquisition of which involves a moral and religious problem and to the possession of which a moral condition applies' (Schweid 1987: 535). Schweid's moral and religious problem is solved, however, because it is a land whose 'previous inhabitants lost their right to it because of their sins, and the Israelite tribes will continue to reside in the land only if they will be just' (1987: 535-36). It is not just to attribute such a cavalier morality to generations of diaspora Jews who give no attestation to such views.

In their determination to present an unblemished record of the Zionist achievement, the historiographers of Zionism and the State of Israel rewrote not only their history, but the documents upon which such a history were based. Morris analyzes the disjunctures between the handwritten diaries of Yosef Weitz and the sanitized published version, and the clear evidence of extensive self-censoring in Ben-Gurion's diaries. The propagandistic intent is evident, particularly in removing references to the 'transfer' intentions of the Yishuv, as reflected in the meetings between Weitz and Ben-Gurion. In his sanitized version of the conquest of Arab villages, Ben-Gurion makes no reference to massacres, rapes and expulsions, and presents the massive looting of the towns and villages as the only 'moral shortcoming' of Israeli behaviour (Morris 1995: 56-57).

Weitz also 'laundered' the diaries of Yosef Nahmani, removing all reference to massacres in the 'stenographic' records of meetings, and all citations of Nahmani's consistent criticism of the aggressiveness and wanton cruelty of the Haganah, who, on orders from their command, refused to negotiate with the Arabs, who 'only want peace' (Morris 1995: 54). Weitz omits any reference to Nahmani's dismay at the behaviour of the Haganah in Tiberias in April 1948 ('Shame covers my face and [I] would like to spit on the city and leave it'), and to his horror at the rape of women and the massacre of 56 peasants in Safsaf, after the town had raised a white flag, and the massacre of 67 men and women, also after surrender, in Saliha (p. 55). Nahmani had asked in his diary, 'Where did they come by such a measure of cruelty, like Nazis?' but no such embarrassing records appear in Weitz's extracts. All references to comparisons made by Jews between the behaviour of IDF units in operations Hiram and Yoav and Nazi behaviour in occupied Europe disappear from the official 'stenographic' records (pp. 55, 59). Morris considers the fabricators of propagandistic Zionist history to be among the most accomplished practitioners of this strange craft of source-doctoring (1995: 44). The aim was to hide things said and done and to bequeath to posterity only a sanitized version of the past (the *Myth of No Expulsions*, and the *Myth of Purity of Arms*).

One of the most significant effects of a pan-Zionist reading of Jewish history is the reduction of the rich diversity of Jewish historical experience to one kind of ideological drive which emphasizes some of the most ignoble and regressive elements of Jewish tradition, namely those which glory in a separation from the nations and a determination to carve out the destiny of a Jewish state irrespective of the cost to others. These dispositions which derive from an ethnicist and xenophobic nationalism and are premised on attitudes of racial dominance and exclusion do not advance the goal of other traditions within Judaism, such as that inviting the Jewish community to be a light to the nations.[20]

20. 'In this nuclear age, when the movement towards Christian unity and

This rewriting of Jewish history has gone hand in glove with the myth which propels Zionism and catapults to the zenith of Jewish aspirations a single phase of its history that is very recent, and one that in all likelihood will not endure. It will not endure, in the same way that tyrannies collapse eventually, usually under the weight of a combination of internal tensions which spring from ideological contradictions, and external ones which will not tolerate or support such oppression indefinitely.[21] Pre-Zionist Judaism deserves to be assessed on its own terms, and the whole of Jewish history must not be allowed to be dominated by the combined forces of nineteenth-century imperialist and colonial-nationalist tendencies and the disaster inflicted on European Jewry by the racist policies of the Third Reich.

Fundamentally, the Jewish claim to return rests with the Bible, since there is no other convincing moral ground supporting it. What most distinguishes the wholesale foundational plunder which Zionism perpetrated on the indigenous Palestinians is the fact that it is generally regarded favourably in the West, and in most theological and religious circles is viewed as being no more than what the Jewish people deserve in virtue of the promises of God outlined in the Bible. The Bible is a *sine qua non* for the provision of alleged moral legitimacy, and without it Zionism is a discourse in the conquest mode, as against a moral one. The Bible read at face value provides not only a moral

supranational unity is sweeping the world, the Jews of the world, through indoctrination with the regressive political Zionist philosophy, are being dragged back ideologically into the old, dark east European ghettos, where self-segregation and cultural isolation once reigned supreme' (Menuhin 1969: xiv).

21. The demographic factor alone bodes ill for the maintenance of a Jewish state. Even with a negative migration balance (i.e. more leaving than returning) of 159,300 for the West Bank and 113,200 for the Gaza Strip for the period 1967–92, the population growth rate in both areas, respectively 4.2 and 5.3 per cent, has yielded Arab populations of 1.05 million in the West Bank, 155,500 in East Jerusalem and 716,800 in the Gaza Strip in 1992. Population increases of that order will ensure that the Jewish majority in Mandated Palestine will soon be overturned. Ironically, the relatively greater oppression of Palestinian Arabs in the West Bank and the Gaza Strip over against that in East Jerusalem has added to the increasing birth rate (see Sabella 1996). Moreover, the tension between the religious-ultra-nationalist coalition and those espousing a Western-like democratic state is likely to increase, perhaps to the point of civil war. Externally, Israel will never be secure unless it establishes moderate relations with its Arab neighbours and makes some restitution to the Palestinians for its colonialist plunder.

framework which transposes Jewish claims into a divinely sanctioned legitimacy, but postulates the taking possession of the Promised Land and the forcible expulsion of the indigenous population as the fulfilment of a *mitzvah*. One could scarcely imagine that the Messianic Age would open with colonial plunder.

Part III

COLONIALISM AND THE BIBLICAL EVIDENCE

Chapter 6

REINTERPRETING THE BIBLICAL EVIDENCE:
LITERARY AND HISTORICAL QUESTIONS

Because of the foundational significance of the biblical land traditions in colonial enterprises, it is appropriate to re-examine these narratives. Throughout the history of Christianity and Judaism, the Synagogue reading of the *Torah* and the Church reading of the Old Testament related the narratives to the period of the characters within the story as though they were dealing with simple historical records of the past, rather than to the time of composition several centuries later. While the biblical narrative which has fuelled colonial enterprises is considered in both Synagogue and Church to communicate basically reliable historical information, the most recent critical scholarship on the Pentateuch and the so-called deuteronomistic history is divided between those who argue for a sixth–fourth-century BC time of composition and those who contend that it was written in the third–second century BC. There is, then, a major time lapse between the alleged events and their narration, giving rise to questions of historicity, literary form, authorial intention and interests. Sixth–fourth-century BC literary accounts should not be presumed to reflect accurately the social conditions of the 'Patriarchal period', nor of fourteenth–tenth-century Palestine. Moreover, the biblical narrative contains only one aspect of the wider picture.[1]

The Patriarchal Narratives

The patriarchal stories of Genesis have great imaginative power, and are deeply embedded in western culture. Moreover, the account of the

1. Philip Davies distinguishes between three Israels: biblical Israel (literary), historical Israel (the real origins of the people) and 'ancient Israel' (what scholars have constructed out of an amalgamation of the other two) (Davies 1995: 11).

promise of land to Abraham and his descendants is read as though it were a record of what actually happened. While acknowledging the text as powerful literature, the quest into what happened in the past is critical for an assessment of the text and of its later appropriation. Literary answers to questions of history are no better than historical answers to questions of literary form.

The following picture emerges from a simple reading of the patriarchal narratives. After Genesis 1–11 presents its perspective on the origins of the universe, the world, its animals and human beings, the focus changes from the many peoples of the earth to one. Abram is brought on to the stage of human history (Gen. 11.28) and another beginning is ushered in: 'I will make you a great nation' (Gen. 12.2). The Covenant with Abraham involved leaving his own land and going to the land of promise, the land of Canaan (v. 5). The Lord promises to Abram and his heirs forever all the land that his eyes can see (Gen. 13.12-14), from the river of Egypt to the Euphrates (Gen. 15.1-18). Hagar is to bear Ishmael (Gen. 16.10-12), but God will maintain his covenant with Isaac rather than with Ishmael (Gen. 17.15-22). The contract was renewed between God and Isaac (Gen. 26.2-4). Isaac's son, Jacob, was to live in the place promised to Abraham (Gen. 28.1-4), while the other son, Esau, was to live in Edom (Gen. 32.4), etc. Genesis 11.27-50.26, then, deals with the origins of the Israelite people, through its ancestors, Abraham and Sarah, down to the death of Jacob and Joseph in Egypt. The remainder of the Pentateuch concentrates on the affairs of this one nation.

The Book of Genesis: Literary Critique
The colonialist appropriation of the Chosen People–Promised Land paradigm reflects the widespread view that one is dealing with historical pericopae. Until recently, historians of Israel and Judah invariably viewed the biblical text as providing a firm historical basis and considered their authors to reflect on past events and on their causal relationships (e.g. Orlinsky 1985: 45). In many respects they did little more than provide a paraphrase of the biblical text, which they adhered to with only thinly veiled apologetics and special pleading (see Garbini 1988: 1-20).

However, several factors combine to suggest that the patriarchal narratives are a literary fiction. Let us consider the historicity of the Abraham cycle, since it is within that material that we encounter

God's original promise of land and progeny. The fact that the name *Abram* is widely attested in Mari, Ebla, Ugarit, Egypt and Cyprus, among others is little help in determining the historicity of the biblical person (Ahlström 1993: 181). The Genesis narrative tells us that Abraham and his clan came from Ur of the Chaldeans to Haran in upper Mesopotamia and thence to Canaan (Gen. 11.31), abandoning a sophisticated lifestyle for that of a semi-nomad, and possessing only the cave of Macpelah in Hebron, which he purchased from a Hittite as a burial place (Gen. 23). The promise of the land to Abram and his descendants (Gen. 12.6-7) is repeated again and again (Gen. 13.14-17; 15.18-21; 17.5-8; cf. Gen. 26.3-4; 28.4, 13-15; 50.24), and recurs in each of the other books of the Pentateuch (Exod. 2.24; 33.1, etc.; Lev. 26.42; Num. 32.11; Deut. 1.8, etc.).

Since the patriarchal narratives do not provide information which can be dated by synchronization with a fixed chronology derived from extra-biblical sources, one is left with attempting to date the events on the basis of conformity between the lifestyle depicted in the narratives and that portrayed in material from surrounding cultures. Scholars have argued that the semi-nomadic lifestyle portrayed in Genesis resembles that of the alleged migrations of 'Amorites', as reflected in the archaeological evidence and in the documents from Mari, fixing the patriarchs in the Middle Bronze I period (2000–1800 BC). Others have placed them in the Late Bronze Age (1550–1200 BC) on the basis of similarities with the social customs of the texts from Nuzi.

But several factors suggest a late dating for the Abraham narrative. The designation *Ur of the Chaldeans* as the place from where Abram and his family came (Gen. 11.31) is an anachronism: the Chaldeans do not appear on the world scene before the ninth century BC,[2] and gave their name to the region no earlier than the eighth or seventh century BC. The phrase, *Ur of the Chaldeans*, does not occur again until Neh. 9.7, which could suggest that the Abraham narrative is much later than the time suggested by the material of the narrative. Moreover, Beer-sheba, which figures in Isaac's life, did not exist before the early Iron Age. Likewise, whereas Abraham and Isaac are both said to have had dealings with the Philistine king, Abimelech of Gerar (Gen. 20 and 26), the Philistines were not known in Palestine before 1200 BC.

---

2. The Akkadian term *matkaldu* occurs no earlier than the first half of the ninth century BC (see Ahlström 1993: 30).

Again, the camel was not used as a beast of burden before the end of the second millennium BC. Furthermore, the fictional nature of the Abraham narrative in Genesis 14 is clear (Ahlström 1993: 184-86). The presence of anachronistic elements within the narrative opens up the question of its historicity, its literary character and of its period and circumstances of composition.

Abraham, History and Tradition

Already in 1885 Julius Wellhausen had concluded that we have no historical knowledge of the patriarchs, and that Abraham was more likely a free invention of unconscious art rather than a historical person. More recent scholarship has shown convincingly (*pace* Goldingay 1983; Millard 1983) that the patriarchal narratives contain no reliable evidence for the period depicted in the narrative, but are literary fictions composed at a later period to address the context of the day. In 1974, T. Thompson evaluated the major scholarly reconstructions between 1920 and 1970 and challenged their efforts to establish the historicity of the patriarchs on the basis of extra-biblical resonances. He showed that the tradition of Abraham's journey from Ur of the Chaldees to Canaan by way of Haran is unhistorical and is a reconstruction based on several originally independent and conflicting traditions, and that the biblical chronologies are not based on historical memory, but on a very late theological schema that presupposes a very unhistorical world view. He dismissed as fundamentalist the efforts to use the biblical narratives for a reconstruction of the history of the Near East (1974: 315).

Thompson initiated a serious reinterpretation of our understanding of second-millennium Palestine and of the Genesis narratives. Independently, Van Seters's study showed that an early dating of the allegedly corroborative extra-biblical material and the supposed antiquity of the patriarchal narratives were untenable (1975: 121). Moreover, he argued that the central Yahwist tradition of the Pentateuch (*J*) sprang from the exilic, or post-exilic periods, rather than from that of the early monarchy. The fact that Abraham is referred to as an individual only in the exilic texts (Isa. 51.2; Ezek. 33.24), and that, with the exception of Josh. 12.3-4, 12, the pre-exilic parts of the Old Testament make no mention of the incidents associated with Abraham, Isaac or Jacob suggests that the stories used by the author of Genesis may be no earlier than the period of the Babylonian exile (Whybray

1995: 49-50). The fabrication of a family history based on various stories about legendary figures about whom the extant pre-exilic literature is vague constituted a 'national' tradition of a single family which in four generations had branched out into the 'twelve tribes of Israel'.

Most of the genres of biblical literature have their counterparts in the literature of the Ancient Near East. However, we look in vain for any analogue either in content, or even in form to the material in Genesis 12–50, and to the accounts of the Exodus and the conquest of the land. While we have evidence of cultures which trace their origins back to the Late Bronze Age, and have analogues, particularly among the Greeks and the Romans, of peoples tracing their origins back to a legendary past, analogues of the Hebrew extended patriarchal narratives do not exist outside of the Jewish and Greek world. Garbini suggests that the Philistines, direct heirs of the Aegean and Anatolian culture, were responsible for introducing this Greek genre into a Hebrew setting (1988: 85-86).

The role of ancestors in the foundation of Greek cities resembles aspects of the patriarchal traditions. Weinfeld focuses on the Aeneas–Abraham analogy (1993: 1-21). Garbini suggests that the Israelites had Abraham born in Mesopotamia in the same way as the Romans traced themselves to the Trojan hero Aeneas (1988: 80). In both cases, the pattern is established in stages: a man leaves a great civilization and is charged with a universal mission; there is a gap between the migration of the ancestor and the actual foundation, etc.:

Father Aeneas (*Aen.* 2.2) leaves famous Troy with his wife, his father and his son,	Father Abraham (Isa. 51.2) leaves Ur of the Chaldaeans with his wife and father (Gen. 11.28-31; 15.7; Neh. 9.7),
and stays for a while in Carthage (which later becomes Rome's great enemy). His son, Ascanius reaches Lavinium (*Aen.* 1.267-69) and Alba-Longa.	stays for a while in Aram (which later becomes Israel's enemy) and reaches Canaan, the land of promise,
His descendants reach Rome which is destined to rule the world (*Aen.* 1.57-59; 286-88; 3.97).	out of which his descendants will rule other peoples (Gen. 17.5; 27.29; 49.10).
Aeneas is told that the gap will be 333 years (*Aen.* 1.270-72).	Abraham is told that the gap will be 400 (Gen. 15.13) or 430 years (cf. Exod. 12.41).

The gap is filled by introducing a long dynasty. In the case of the Israelites, the Genesis traditions of nomadic ancestors and their worship of El in Canaan were adopted from peoples who lived in the region before the settlement of the Israelite tribes. The pentateuchal traditions attest that the Patriarchs did not know Yahweh, the national God (Exod. 6.3-5). The stories about Jacob may come from the Canaanites also—the name *Jacob* is similar to that of a prince of the Hyksos dynasty, *Yaqob-hr* (Weinfeld 1993: 8-9). Weinfeld draws attention to the similar language used in the depiction of Abraham and David and argues that Abraham is a retrojection of David, as pious Aeneas was a retrojection of pious Augustus (1993: 9-11).

The Significance and Provenance of the Abraham Narrative
The focus of the patriarchal 'history' is set out in Gen. 12.1-3, wherein Abram is commanded to leave his country and move to where he will gain both land and posterity. However, neither Abraham nor any of the patriarchs ever owned the land—it was the land of the Canaanites (Gen. 12.6; 13.7) and others (Gen. 23)—but were merely resident aliens (Gen. 23.4; 35.27). Indeed, the book ends with Joseph being put in a coffin in Egypt (Gen. 50.26), with the result that the patriarchal narrative begins with a patriarch away from the land of promise and ends with another in Egypt. While the promise of progeny is fulfilled within the narrative, that of being a famous nation which would be victorious over enemies (Gen. 12.2-3; 17.2-5, etc.) remained to be fulfilled. The dying Joseph assured his brothers, 'I am about to die; but God will surely come to you, and bring you up out of this land to the land that he swore to Abraham, to Isaac, and to Jacob' (Gen. 50.24).

The accounts relating to the patriarchs are distinctive in that, in general, they do not provide information of a historical kind. Instead we have a succession of family events and highly charged religious episodes, with Abraham functioning as an example of faith. The 'facts' of the patriarchal narratives are virtually outside time, with the result that the incidents have been dated variously within the range 2500–200 BC. It was not necessary for the narrator to have precise information about the past, since his purpose was not to write a detached history, but to insert material about the past of the archetypal patriarchal figures who moved against a background which is outside historical time into a construction which suited his intentions and his perceptions of what was best for his readership at the time of final composition (Garbini 1988: 15), perhaps during the Babylonian exile.

The exiled Judahites employed the patriarchal narrative of a mythical and legendary past to affirm their right to represent all Israel, making Abraham the ancestor of Jacob and the recipient of the divine promise. This promise repudiated the monarchy which, in general, they judged to have failed them and vested the divine relationship with the whole people. By situating the origin of Abraham in Ur, the exiles could ingratiate themselves to their new rulers.[3] This tracing of origins finds an analogue in the mythical and legendary past which Rome created for itself not long after. Ahlström argues that the Abraham tradition reached its final redaction after the Babylonian Exile, when the right to the land was denied to the returnees. The absence of reference to the figure of Abraham in the so-called deuteronomistic history and in most of the pre-exilic prophets supports the post-exilic dating (Ahlström 1993: 182).

The present Mesopotamian form of the Abraham narrative, with its insistence on his ancestorship of not only the Israelites and Judahites, but also of the Arabs through Ishmael (Gen. 25.12-18), of the Aramaeans through Jacob and his mother Rebecca, of the Moabites and the Ammonites through Abraham's nephew, Lot, and the Edomites through his grandson Esau (Gen. 25.25; Deut. 2.4-7), had as its purpose the projection of most of the west-Semitic world and its peoples as the descendants of Abraham. Abram's wanderings were the means through which the kinship of all the west-Semitic peoples could be established. Abraham was the ideal ancestor of the peoples of Israel and Judah. When the post-exilic community was in distress, the people's prehistory was idealized. Abraham represented a former 'golden age' (see Ahlström 1993: 184-87).

---

3.   Garbini suggests that Ur of the Chaldeans and Haran were inserted to situate Abraham in Mesopotamia and Syria in the time of the Babylonian ruler, Nabonidus. The two cities contained the most important sanctuaries of the cult of the moon god Sin, of whom Nabonidus was a fervent adherent. Thus, the Judahites in exile in Babylon were able to posit an original link between themselves as exiles and the king they served. This gave them a way of declaring themselves 'fellow-countrymen' of Nabonidus (Garbini 1988: 77-78). The narrative of the migration of Abram, then, found a realistic context in the Babylon of Nabonidus. The promise of numerous descendants (Gen. 15) was the king's prerogative in the ancient Near East. Garbini argues that the Genesis text is consistent with the anti-monarchy sentiments reflected in Isa. 55.3 and Ezek. 34.9-10, which are products of exilic, Babylonian Judaism and dates the Genesis text to around 500 BC.

It is likely that there were earlier traditions about Abraham, such as that concerning Sodom and Gomorrah, on to which other ones, for example, those concerning Jacob, were added during the Babylonian captivity. The ubiquitous Jacob of the narrative (in the south, in Transjordan, in central Palestine and in the north) made him a suitable eponymous ancestor of all Israel, as father of the twelve eponymous ancestors of the twelve tribes. Despite the prominence given to Jacob, pre-eminence was given to Abraham, the progenitor of the nation (Exod. 2.24; 4.5; 32.13; Ezek. 33.24; Mic. 7.20), perhaps because of the fact that his 'activities' in the southern kingdom of Judah made him a favourite with the Judahites who united the traditions, perhaps in the exile. In that scenario, the patriarchal narrative as we have it represents the narrator's redaction and interpretation of the traditions available to him, which he published in conformity with his assessment of affairs. He wrote in support of the Babylonian Jews' repudiation of the royal ideology and to affirm the authenticity and even supremacy of the Judahite theology of Babylon, thereby giving birth to Judaism (cf. Garbini 1988: 85).

The Pentateuchal Narratives

The synchronic fashion of reading the Pentateuch concentrates on the completed text, bypasses questions of historicity and focuses on its religious value (see Childs 1976: 73; Prudký 1995; Whybray 1995: 133-43). The text narrates the history of Israelite origins from creation to the end of the patriarchs (Genesis) and through the period of slavery in Egypt to Moses' meeting God on Sinai (Exod. 1–19). After the laws of the covenant are delivered to Moses (Exod. 20–Num. 10.10), the children of Israel advance from Sinai to the border of the Promised Land (Num. 10.11–36.13), where the laws are recapitulated for the new conditions of living in the land (Deut. 1.1–33.29). The pentateuchal narrative is followed by the account of the people entering and settling the Promised Land (Joshua, Judges), changing their method of government from tribal rule to kingship (1–2 Samuel), and, finally, by an account of life under the kings down to the time of the Babylonian Exile (1–2 Kings).

It is possible to discern a certain development in the five books. God created the world and humanity failed him (Gen. 1–11), but, by way of a new start, God chose a single people to be faithful and to teach the nations (Gen. 12–50). This people learned the ways of God through suffering, after which followed their deliverance (Exodus). The people became God's holy people (Leviticus and Numbers 1–10) to be led to a Promised Land (Num. 10–36), which they would retain only on condition of fidelity (Exod. 20.12; Deut. 4.40; 5.16, 29-30; 8.1-9; 11.8-21). The Israelites were to dispossess the indigenous inhabitants because of their wickedness and in order to fulfil the oath that the Lord made to Abraham, Isaac and Jacob (Deut. 9.5; cf. Deut. 7). If the greatest gift of the covenant was to live in peace and prosperity in the land, the greatest punishment for violating the covenant would be to suffer the loss of the land (Deut. 4.25-31; cf. Deut. 32.26, 46-47). The land was 'holy' (separate) because Yahweh dwelt in the midst of Israel (Num. 25.34). The Holiness Code, Lev. 17-26, emphasizes this aspect. The land itself had vomited out the earlier inhabitants, and would do so again, if the Israelites committed abominations and defiled it (Lev. 18.24-30). Among the prohibitions were harlotry (Lev. 19.29), shedding blood (Num. 29–34; Deut. 21.6-9), allowing a corpse to hang on a tree (Deut. 21.22-23) and remarriage (Deut. 24.1-4).

The Question of Sources
Abandoning the presumption of the Mosaic authorship of the Pentateuch, the classical Documentary Hypothesis of Wellhausen attempted to account for its composition by postulating earlier small units which were gradually combined to form written sources. A writer in Jerusalem, the *Yahwist (J)*, wove existing traditions into an account of Israelite history down to the high point of the united kingdom under Solomon (c. 960–920 BC), which constitutes the bulk of the Pentateuch. After the break-up of the united kingdom, a writer in the northern kingdom, the *Elohist (E)*, wrote a corresponding account of Israelite history. On the collapse of the northern kingdom in 721 this was brought south, and a merged version of the history was composed, uniting both traditions *(JE)*. During the reform of King Josiah in 621 BC (2 Kgs 22–23), Deuteronomy was composed as a collection of laws *(D)*, which, with its stress on the covenant, caused some rewriting of the *JE* history. After the exile and the resettlement in Judah a new renewal movement grew, which, as it was dominated by the priests, drew up a body of legislation which stressed the appropriate conditions for worship and the construction of a holy nation,

the *Priestly* tradition (*P*). This was later merged with *JE*, giving one comprehensive account of the people's origins.

Moreover, a general scholastic consensus developed that there were four main stages of composition of the larger biblical material from Genesis to Kings, beginning perhaps in the tenth century, and not reaching its final state until perhaps the second century BC. These documentary hypotheses questioned the acceptance of the historicity of not only Genesis 1–11, but of the patriarchal stories and the Mosaic traditions, and argued that while the four discrete sources contained valuable information on the periods of composition, they were of little value for reconstructing the early history of Israel. Subsequent scholarship departed from the notion of *J*, *E* and *P* as independent, coherent documents and instead suggested that the traditions from which the documentary sources derived were largely folkloric and legendary oral material, long antedating their literary composition. Nevertheless, conservative reaction to the de-historicization of the biblical narratives implied in the Documentary Hypothesis insisted on the historicity of core events at the heart of the literary accretions within the biblical texts, including within the patriarchal narratives. In that way the alleged historicity of the kernel of the patriarchal narratives was salvaged, with the oldest traditions (*J* and *E*) likely to be closest to the historical core of Israel's earliest history. W.F. Albright championed the situating of the patriarchal narratives within a specific Near Eastern historical period, thereby affirming their essentially historical character.

However, the classical documentary four-source hypothesis has come under terminal strain (Blum 1990; Rendtorff 1977; Schmid 1976; Van Seters 1975). Several scholars question the very existence of the *J* tradition, and the available evidence does not support the claim that *E* was an autonomous tradition. In addition, there is disagreement about the nature and range of the 'deuteronomic' component in Genesis to Numbers. Moreover, there is discussion about whether *P* should be regarded as an originally independent source or a revision of an earlier non-priestly composition (Vervenne 1994: 246). Several scholars conclude that up to the sixth-century exile at the earliest, there was no 'Pentateuch' as such (see Whybray 1987: 221).[4]

4. Blum, for example, rejects independent and parallel sources for Genesis–Deuteronomy and suggests that it results from two post-exilic compositions which united a pre-priestly composition of deuteronomic type (*KD*) and a writing of the

Diachronic Concerns

The tendency to concentrate on the final form of the pentateuchal narrative and the so-called deuteronomistic history (from Deuteronomy to 2 Kgs 25, with, perhaps, Genesis–Numbers added later as an introduction [Mayes 1983: 139-49; Rendtorff 1990: 200]) evades the problems which are posed by a consideration of the mode of composition of the work. However, in approaching documents from antiquity, one should seek to discover what happened in the past, how the 'events' were understood and what the intention of the author was (see Ahlström 1993: 19). In addition, one must pose literary questions of the genre, the sources and their use and the *Tendenz* of the author(s) of the material. Such queries are frequently evaded in favour of a historicist reading of the biblical text, which is justified in virtue of its supposed benefits for faith.[5]

There is considerable reluctance to apply the usual criteria of investigation to documents which deal with matters of religious faith, and resistance to abandoning the sure ground of the historicity of the biblical accounts of the promise of land and the subsequent settlement in Canaan etc. But, as has been shown comprehensively by T. Thompson (1974) and others, the pentateuchal narratives cannot serve as a guide to what happened in the early Israelite period, and one must seek a better explanation of the material. Suzanne Boorer's study examines the motif of the promise of land in the Tetrateuch, in Deuteronomy, in Joshua–Kings and Jeremiah, and concludes that the motif was peculiar to the narrowly defined circles of thought of a deuteronomistic school (1992: 37). She argues that the promise of land as oath entered the Pentateuch gradually through a dynamic process of redaction, with the result that the ongoing reflection makes it difficult to discover a single meaning for the land motif.

The idea of the land which is to be possessed dominates the book of Deuteronomy from beginning to end and forms the theme both of the

priestly school (*KP*). The Pentateuch was a historical compromise between two different tendencies (*KD* and *KP*), represented by two dominant groups in the community of the second temple. The 'final form' was a complex amalgam which could not be the product of a single intention (Blum 1990: 5, 102-104; see López 1994: 50).

5. It is not enough to say of a text such as the crossing of the Jordan with dry feet (Josh. 4.21-22), 'That is a datum of faith'. An assertion of faith is not an adequate response to a literary, or historical or archaeological question (see Hemelsoet 1995).

laws and of the paraenetic discourse.[6] At the surface level, the purpose of the deuteronomic commandments is to lay down the new style of cultus and way of life for the radically changed circumstances arising from the settlement: 'When you come into the land which Yahweh your God gives to you, then you shall...' (see von Rad 1966: 90-91). In a literalist reading the book appears to sanction a policy of the ethnic cleansing of the indigenous Canaanite population to make way for God's chosen people (Deut. 7.2). The possession of the Promised Land was to be carried out through the genocide of the resident people and not simply by dispossessing them (e.g. Deut. 20.16-18). As we shall see, the available evidence does not support the execution of any such widespread and violent intrusion by the 'Israelites', which invites one to construct a more likely scenario for the biblical texts.

A plausible context for the composition of Deuteronomy is to see it as the blueprint for a fresh start for one of the waves of exiles returning to Palestine from Babylonia, rather than a record of what happened before 'the entry of the Israelites into the Promised Land some seven hundred years earlier'. The priestly-prophetic author of Deuteronomy encourages the returning exiles to set foot on the land of their ancestors again. This confessional community is encouraged to pursue zealously the purity of its exclusive faith, disdainful of the inhabitants they encounter on their return (Mayes 1981: 113). The returning exiles are addressed in the manner of the Moab generation listening to Moses (Deurleo 1994: 46). The reform community consisted of those who took to heart the words of this book (30.1), identifying with the Moab and Horeb generation. The central theme of Deuteronomy is a call to the service of the one God by an elect people centred around one sanctuary, through obedience to the law in the land which God has given (Mayes 1981: 57-58).[7]

---

6.   The land is a critical factor in the redemption to which Israel has been brought. That God has given the land occurs in all parts of the book (e.g. 1.36, 39; 3.18; 15.17; 16.20; 17.14; 18.9; 19.8; 26.9; 27.2; 28.8; 34.4, etc.—see further Plöger 1967: 134-126). Yahweh also gives cities (13.13; 20.16), gates or towns (16.5, 18), peoples (17.6), nations (19.1), booty (20.14), rest and inheritance (12.9), blessing (12.15), herds and flocks (12.21), sons and daughters (28.53) and strength to get wealth (8.18) (see Miller 1969: 453).

7.   The central issue in the theology of Deuteronomy is belief in the one God. The tetragrammaton occurs no less than 561 times in the book; note also the monotheistic statements of the book (especially Deut. 4.35, 39; 6.4; 7.9; 32.39).

In the framework to the deuteronomic legislation, especially in Deut. 4.25-31 and 30.1-10, the curse of the law which Israel would experience in exile would be succeeded by the blessing of renewal and restoration. This perspective reinforced the belief that exile from the land was the greatest form of punishment, a theme reinforced by the prophets, and the experience of the nation of Israel, that sin and exile were synonymous and intimately linked. Very little in Deuteronomy suggests a spirit of preparedness to cohabit with the wider world in a spirit of respect for the surrounding cultures—exceptions being the concession of accepting third generation Edomites (Deut. 23.4-9), marriage with a foreign woman taken captive in war (Deut. 21.10-14) and the care for the *ger*, the foreigner in Israel's midst (Deut. 14.29; 16.11, 14, etc.). Deuteronomy looks rather like a constitution suited to the religious ghetto, for religious zealots for whom the worship of God and the study of his law appear to be the only worthwhile human activity, which may be carried out in ways which appear to be disdainful of the wider world. The deuteronomistic theology reflects an intensity of relationship between one national people and their tribal God. Such a theology will attract only the introspective and xenophobic members of the 'national' group.

The 'Israelite' Conquest–Settlement Narratives

While it is unanimous in affirming that Israel was not native to the land, but arrived from outside and conquered it, the Bible has two contrasting and in many respects contradictory accounts of the Israelite settlement of Canaan.[8] If Joshua 1–12 suggests an almost complete and violent conquest, Judges 1 (cf. Josh 15.13-19, 63; 16.10; 17.11-13; 19.47) narrates a partial conquest and gradual consolidation

---

8. Historically, the term 'Canaan' referred to the Bronze Age territory of Palestine and 'Canaanites' to its inhabitants. The terms are radically transposed centuries later in the biblical tradition, in which the 'Canaanites' are perceived to constitute the population of pre-Israelite Palestine and to have an *ethnic* coherence. T. Thompson suggests that the name 'Israel', first attested in the Merneptah inscription of the late thirteenth century, may also at that period refer to a region (1992: 139). The Bronze Age is divided into the Early Bronze Age (3200–2000), the Middle Bronze Age I (2000–1800), Middle Bronze Age II (1800–1650), Middle Bronze Age III (1650–1550), Late Bronze Age I (1550–1400), and Late Bronze Age II (1400–1200).

in the land.[9] As well as conveying religious import, these conflicting accounts pose historical and literary questions. The discovery of what really happened in the 'Israelite'[10] conquest–settlement, as well as satisfying legitimate curiosity about the past, has considerable theological and ethical implications, lending biblical authority either to violent conquest or to gradual infiltration and relatively peaceful settlement. In a number of places the biblical narratives give evidence of Israelite bad conscience at dispossessing others.[11]

Two primary sources, archaeological and literary (biblical and extra-biblical), are available to the historian of Syro-Palestine, and these are supplemented by insights from geography, sociology, anthropology, historical linguistics, Egyptology, Assyriology, etc., each of which disciplines has developed independent methodologies. Until recently, biblical interpretation has occupied the centre stage of the discussion of Israelite origins, with all other evidence being in its service.[12] The

9.   Weinfeld suggests that the traditions which set Joshua at the head of the conquest may have been created in the sanctuaries in the north, while in the account in the southern kingdom of Judah Joshua is missing (1993: 154).

10.   It is important to respect the multifarious meanings of the term 'Israelite' and to avoid the anachronism of identifying the name in the post-exilic context of the biblical narrative with a putative reality in the Iron Age. The archaeological evidence from Iron I Palestine does not justify the use of the term 'Israelite'. It could be used in Iron Age II if it could be shown that the regional state of 'Israel' was distinctively 'Israelite'. Correspondingly, the term 'Canaanite' is inappropriate for those periods also, since it implies a regional and often ethnic unity among the inhabitants of Palestine which is contradicted by the available evidence. The post-exilic biblical polarity between 'Israelite' and 'Canaanite' should not be imposed on the earlier period, especially since all the available evidence from the region contradicts it. The Iron Age Period is divided into Iron Age IA (c. 1200–1125); Iron Age IB (1125–1050); Iron Age IIA (1050–900); Iron Age IIB (900–800); Iron IIC (800–540); while Iron III (540–332) is usually called the 'Persian Period'.

11.   E.g. Josh 24.13 (Israel did not develop the land), Josh 24.8 (the land is called 'of the Amorites'); Judg. 11.19-21 (dispossession affirmed); cf. 2 Sam. 7.23; Num. 33.50-52. The conquest is justified because of the inhabitants' iniquity (Deut. 9.4-6; 18.9-14; 22.2-4—cf. Pss. 44.3; 105.44). Bad conscience over the dispossession of others, or the need to justify it is reflected as late as the turn of the first century (1 Macc. 15.33). Coexisting with this strain is the persistent view that the land belonged to Yahweh (e.g. Num. 26.55; Ezek. 47.13-14), and cultic offerings were to be made in acknowledgment of his ownership (Exod. 22.28; Lev. 18.24, etc.).

12.   See Coote and Whitelam 1987: 13. In Whitelam's estimation, the history of

biblical narratives concerning thirteenth and twelfth centuries BC Palestine show little historical knowledge of the political scene. The reader learns nothing of Egypt's rule over the country, nor of the garrison cities and Egyptian temples. There is no mention of an Egyptian campaign, nor of Merneptah's destruction. In fact, no Egyptian pharaoh is mentioned by name before Shoshenq (Shishak) marched through Palestine in the fifth year of Rehoboam's reign (1 Kgs 14.25). It is possible, of course, to account for this by proposing that annalistic writings did not occur before the emergence of the monarchy (Ahlström 1993: 347). The biblical accounts reflect particular perspectives, and the context and authorial intent, as well as the genre of the narratives must be respected.

Throughout this century there has been intensive study of the 'Israelite' settlement in Canaan. Archaeologists place it within the period of the Late Bronze–Early Iron Age transition, invariably appealing to an alleged sharp break between these two cultures. This has resulted in a number of models of Israelite settlement, each of which bears a particular relationship to the biblical text and suggests a different evaluation of the nature and theological significance of the event. Two of the three major models, *nomadic infiltration* and *large-scale invasion*, postulate substantial intervention from outside, while the third proposes the hypothesis of a mainly internal peasants' withdrawal from, or revolt against the Canaanite cities.[13]

Nomadic Infiltration Model
The nomadic infiltration model, associated with the 'German School' of Alt (1953a, 1953b, 1966), Noth (1960) and Weippert (1971, 1979) was first proposed in the 1920s and 1930s. Alt distinguished between two types of society in Palestine in the Late Bronze period. The

ancient Palestine, particularly from the thirteenth century BC to the second century AD has been merely a backdrop to the history of Israel, Judah and Second Temple Judaism, with ancient Israelite history being viewed as the domain of religion or theology rather than of history. The driving force within biblical studies has been the search for ancient Israel as the taproot of Western civilization and the antecedent of Christianity, and, more recently, has been reinforced by the foundation of the State of Israel, with Israeli scholars searching for their own national identity in the past (Whitelam 1996: 2-3, 119).

    13. In the following overview of the models the convenience of grouping scholars within particular schools conceals the often substantial differences between members of the same 'school'.

pharaoh exercised power vicariously through vassal 'petty' princes who governed a number of small 'city-states' centred on a town mainly in the coastal lowlands. Life in the highlands was less developed due to the lack of good arable land. Alt considered that the geographical and historical setting of the patriarchal narrative was altogether fictional, and that the roots of the pre-settlement 'Israelites' were outside of Palestine. In contrast to the settled 'Canaanites', the pre-settlement 'Israelites' were pastoralist nomads, or semi-nomads, in search of land, who, in accordance with their natural migratory movement, infiltrated gradually into the sparsely populated hill country of Canaan. These nomadic groups migrated annually between the winter pastures in the steppes east of Palestine and the summer pastures in the central hills of Palestine. Gradually, they settled more permanently, and as they grew in numbers they began to put pressure on the land of the Canaanite city-states in the valleys. The peaceful settlement was facilitated by the dissolution of the Bronze Age cities by c. 1200 BC (Weippert 1971: 133).

The political map of Palestine[14] changed on the collapse of Egyptian power at the end of the Late Bronze Age, leaving some six states in the area. Alt assumed that the shift in power could be explained only by recourse to external influence. The band of nomadic foreigners called 'Israelites' associated with each other through the bonds of a sacral confederation of tribes, with Yahweh, the non-Canaanite god being worshipped at a special cult centre. Alt's cultic amphictyony developed into a political league which was finally replaced by a monarchy. Central to Alt's reconstruction was his alleged polarity between 'Canaanite' and 'Israelite' culture, coinciding with the supposed contrast between Palestine's Late Bronze ('Canaanite') 'city-states' and the Iron Age ('Israelite') 'nation-state'.

The relatively peaceful infiltration of various tribes into the unoccupied hill country later became a militant one. An increase in

14. The name 'Palestine' does not imply that the region constituted a socially, politically or economically homogeneous entity which evolved in a coherent and consistent fashion independent of its wider context. 'Palestine' was fragmented ecologically and geographically into a number of distinct, isolated cultural sub-regions. The regional disparities were so decisive that in the period preceding Assyrian imperial domination Palestine consisted of small, largely independent petty chieftainships and was a 'heartland of villages', a domain of scrub farmers and shepherds rather than of kings and emperors (Thompson 1992: 191, 187, 193-94).

population followed by expansion of their territory to include the
lowlands caused conflicts with the Canaanites through limited military
campaigns, which is reflected in the account in the book of Judges.
Because the 'Israelites' were not able to eliminate all the 'Canaanites',
religious and cultural problems became the order of the day. These
small-scale military exploits eventually inspired the legendary material in Joshua and Judges. While cities such as Hazor and Luz/Bethel
were destroyed, the bulk of the material in Joshua is fictional and is a
series of aetiologies composed to account for names, customs and
ruins. The fruit of the change was the development of a national consciousness and the construction of 'nation-states'. For Alt, the sweeping away of the 'city-state' system by Israel and Judah was the defining
moment in the history of the region. The entry of the 'Israelites' into
Palestine paved the way for the ultimate achievement of David and
Solomon, an achievement beyond the capabilities of the indigenous
population (1966: 160).[15]

Large-Scale Invasion
In sharp contrast, the 'American School' of Albright (1935, 1939),
Bright (1956, 1981) and Wright (1962), joined by some Israeli scholars (Aharoni 1979: 200-29; Malamat 1979, 1982; Yadin 1979, 1982),
argued that the archaeological evidence supported the essential historicity of the account of a unified, violent large-scale invasion and
conquest by 'Israelite' nomads led by Joshua, which destroyed several
Canaanite cities in the process (Josh. 1–12). Hazor, Debir, Lachish and
Luz/Bethel had been destroyed in the thirteenth century BC, and
Albright maintained that the strata above the levels of destruction witnessed to a new material culture, which he attributed to the Israelites
of the Iron Age period.
   However, several arguments converge to conclude that the account
in the book of Joshua is not a record of what actually happened, and
that to attempt to harmonize the narrative with the real history of
origins would be in vain. Albright's reconstruction lacked convincing
archaeological evidence from the Late Bronze Age period. The fact

   15. Whitelam claims that the source of Alt's insight was the increasing Zionist
immigration into Palestine, which was under way as Alt engaged in his research
(1996: 76). Volkmar Fritz argues for a variant of the infiltration hypothesis, which he
calls *the symbiosis hypothesis* (1981; 1987).

that Jericho,[16] Ai, and Gibeon and Heshbon in Transjordan did not exist as walled cities in the thirteenth century BC makes the conquest model unacceptable. While Hebron (Judg. 1.8) and Debir (Judg. 1.13) were destroyed in the thirteenth century BC, and Lachish, Tel Beit Mirsim and Gezer were destroyed c. 1200 BC, no evidence requires that these destructions were carried out by the 'Israelites'. Moreover, archaeologists were finding it increasingly difficult to identify as peculiarly 'Israelite' the early Iron Age strata, raising the question as to whether the 'Israelites' and the 'Canaanites', diametrically opposed in Albright's reconstruction of history, were ethnically distinct peoples.

Peasants' Revolt
The 'German' and 'American' models share the view that at the beginning of the Iron Age there was a large-scale entry of people (later called 'Israelites') into the central hill country of Canaan, whether through relatively peaceful nomadic infiltration (German) or through invasion (American). George Mendenhall rejected the hypotheses of a large-scale influx of outsiders into Canaan. He claimed that the late Bronze Canaanite city-state system was a brutal, oppressive and dysfunctional structure which dominated the whole of Palestine and Syria. The *'apiru* of the Amarna letters were homeless and stateless indigenous Canaanite peasant malcontents who revolted against Egyptian exploitation.[17] These large population groups withdrew, not physically and geographically, but politically and subjectively from the existing political regimes and gave their allegiance to Yahweh, the overlord of a small group of slaves who had escaped from Egypt. This found a sympathetic resonance among the indigenous Canaanite peasants, who had been subjugated and exploited, and inspired the *'apiru* to create a 'religious federation' of Yahweh-covenanters, who

16. Kenyon reopened the Jericho excavation in 1952 and established that the Tel es-Sultan mound was in an almost complete state of abandonment for all conceivable periods of the biblical account of the occupation, from 1500–c. 860 BC.

17. Many of the 350 texts consist of letters written by Syro-Palestinian leaders to Egypt or copies of letters written from Egypt to local rulers within the Egyptian empire in the Late Bronze period, mostly in the reigns of Pharaohs Amenophis III (c. 1414–1397 BC) and Amenophis IV (c. 1379–1362 BC). In one, Abdu-Heba of Jerusalem writes that 'The Apiru plunder all the lands of the king…All the lands of the king, my lord, are lost!' (ANET 487-88).

rejected the social and religious system of Late Bronze Age Canaan (Mendenhall 1962: 72-73).[18]

Mendenhall's views were carried further by Norman Gottwald, who also emphasized the non-nomadic character of Israel's origins and proposed a class warfare model of a socialist proletarian revolution. He viewed the Canaanite city-state initially in feudalistic terms, with an 'elite' aristocracy lording it over an oppressed 'peasant' class (1979: 212). The group of slaves which had fled from Egypt, having made a covenant with Yahweh in the desert, settled in Canaan (1979: 211). Whereas the inhabitants of Canaan had El for their god at first, they adopted Yahweh at Shechem (Josh. 24), who thus became the god of a new society of revolutionary covenanters, the 'Israelites' (1979: 564-66).

Gottwald added a novel element, blending abstract sociological theory with historical reconstruction. Unlike Mendenhall, who regarded the Israelite society as an apolitical 'religious federation', Gottwald, using Marxist categories, emphasized the relations of power and the demands of the peasantry in their fight against their Canaanite oppressors. Working within the paradigm of Alt's model of a shift in power from the 'city-states' in the plains to the 'national states' in the hills, Gottwald stressed the revolutionary aspect of the transition from an oppressed proletariat to a relatively egalitarian society. Archaeological evidence confirms that hundreds of settlements throughout Palestine, unoccupied in the Bronze Age, were settled peacefully, beginning at the end of the thirteenth century and continuing for two centuries. This egalitarian society, bonded together on the basis of social revolution, continued to wage war on the Canaanites until the unification achieved by King David.

Each of the three models has had its advocates and critics (see Gnuse 1991; Ramsey 1981). The similarity between 'Israelite' and Late Bronze Canaanite culture argued against both the 'German' and 'American' views that the Israelites were aliens. The violent conquest model was criticized for its apologetic attempts to verify the biblical text by recourse to archaeology. Moreover, the destruction of the

18. More recent study of the *'apiru* of the Amarna letters sees the term as referring to the social status of groups who, because of the collapse of their economic circumstances, were relegated to the fringes of society and were in conflict with local rulers rather than to any specific ethnic group in Palestine. There is no reason to suspect continuity between these groups and the post-exilic biblical term *'ibrim.*

Canaanite cities was accounted for more readily at the hands of Egyptian campaigns, or by those of the invading Sea Peoples: the cities were not destroyed at the same period, and several cities cited in the Joshua's conquest narrative were not inhabited in the Late Bronze–Early Iron Age transition (e.g. Kadesh-Barnea, Arad, Jericho, Ai).

In addition to the weakness of the absence of any historical evidence for such a social revolution, Gottwald's attempt to expand Alt's model of Israelite origins presents too many methodological problems.[19] The proponents of the peasant revolution model, then, have not provided compelling evidence for such a revolution in 'ancient Israel', and the imposition of modern social theory and anthropological and sociological models is no substitute for the more pedestrian requirements for unique evidence demanded by a truly scientific historiography.

Two recent developments contribute to the assessment that each of the three models is an invention rather than a description of an ancient past. Literary and source criticism of the Pentateuch and the so-called deuteronomistic history of Genesis–2 Kings casts serious doubt on the validity of using these late traditions for the historical reconstruction of a much earlier past. Secondly, the accumulating archaeological data from single-site excavations and regional surveys conflict with the claims of the biblical narrative (see Finkelstein 1990: 37-84; Mazar 1990: 328-38). Running consistently through the theories which respect the archaeological evidence is the affirmation that the Late Bronze–Iron Age transition was marked by peaceful, indigenous change, giving a picture which is very much at variance with the biblical narrative.

Israelite Settlement as a Peaceful Internal Process
Anticipating recent discussion, de Geus argued that the 'Israelites' were indigenous to the territory for centuries before the 'conquest' (1976: 123-27), and constituted a settled rather than a nomadic society (129-30). They were united on ethnic grounds and were settled highlanders who used tribal nomenclature in varying fashion (172). Subsequently,

19. See Thompson 1992: 58-59, who adds that what is amazing about the 'models' of Mendenhall and Gottwald is not that their theories were unsupported by evidence, but that, lacking evidence, they were ever proposed (1992: 405). Gottwald's reconstruction of Israelite origins suffers from the absence of a credible account of the nature and origins of the Canaanite city-state culture which is consistent with what we know of it, and from a misrepresentation of Marx's account of 'Asiatic modes of production' (see T. Thompson 1992: 51-57).

the 'new search' for ancient Israel of the mid to late 1980s has yielded a crop of new works which question the appropriateness of using the much later biblical traditions as evidence for the alleged Israelite origins in the Late Bronze–Iron Age transition.[20] They emphasize the indigenous nature of 'Israel' in the Palestine of the period of transition, since the numerous reports on site excavations and surveys stress the continuity between Late Bronze Age material culture and that of the Iron I settlements. This points to indigenous development rather than what came from the settlement of outsiders.

Unfortified highland villages rather than walled cities have become the target of archaeological investigation, whose findings have emphasized the similarities between Israelite and Canaanite culture. The peaceful nature of the unfortified village settlements is obvious. Moreover, the highland villages betray such similarity with the culture of the lowland Canaanite cities (in pottery, farming techniques, tools and construction patterns, etc.) that they are considered to have been an outgrowth of lowland urban culture. In this interpretation of the evidence, the Canaanites who peacefully withdrew from their cities and moved to the highlands gradually evolved into Israelites (Gnuse 1991: 60). For Ahlström, the term 'Israel' was a place name, deriving from the Canaanite divine name El (1986: 6-9), which was applied to a people only with the rise of the united monarchy, and in post-exilic times assumed religious connotations. Ahlström explains the continuity of culture between the lowlands and the highlands by proposing that the highland people withdrew from the lowland cities due to the violence perpetrated by the Egyptians and the Sea Peoples (1986: 6-9, 18-36, 58-61). While most of the highland villagers were Canaanite, he allows for the entry of some foreigners from the south and east, who brought the worship of Yahweh with them (1986: 7-8, 92-94).

Variants of the model of peaceful withdrawal from the lowlands have been advocated by Meyers (who postulates war and plague as reasons for withdrawal), Soggin (who suggests that it was to avoid heavy taxation) and many others. Several scholars consider the Israelites to have been indigenous to the highlands before the collapse

20. E.g. Lemche (1985, 1988), Ahlström (1986, 1993), Coote and Whitelam (1987), Finkelstein (1988, 1990), T. Thompson (1987, 1992). Thompson 1992 evaluates recent scholarship and outlines the future task of constructing an early history of the Israelite people free of the constraints imposed by a mistaken understanding of the biblical narrative as historiography.

of the Canaanite city states. Some Canaanites did withdraw from the urban centres, but the majority of the highlands population derived from the settlement of pastoralist nomads from the Canaanite valleys, who were ethnically distinct from the Canaanites but enjoyed close cultural links with them (see Gnuse 1991: 109; Hopkins 1987: 191; Kochavi 1985; Mazar 1985; Stager 1981: 1; 1985a: 84; 1985b: 3).

Finkelstein's synthetic survey of archaeological remains from the early Iron Age period, both in the highland and in the lowland settlements in Palestine radically changes our perception about Israelite origins (1988a). His model of *internal nomadism* proposes that the Israelites were 'enclosed nomads' who lived within the land of Canaan throughout the Late Bronze Age (1550–1200 BC) in close proximity with the urban centres without settling down. With the collapse of the cities, economic factors, such as the need to produce grain and so forth, forced them to settle. Initially, they settled in the Ephraimite highlands and spread north into Galilee, westward into the central highlands and southward into Judah (Finkelstein 1988a: 324-35), developing horticultural as well as agricultural skills. With increasing population, they expanded into the lowlands, which brought them into violent conflict with the inhabitants there, which perdured until the consolidation of their position under David. Finkelstein's excavations at Shiloh and elsewhere on the highlands convinced him, as it has convinced others, of the continuity between Canaanite and Israelite culture in Iron Age I.

Finkelstein attempts an historical overview of the whole process (1988a: 315-22). Following Rowton's model of *enclosed nomadism*, he asserts that before the domestication of camels, pastoral nomads were constrained to live in close proximity to settled areas. The nomads exchanged livestock, meat and skins for grain, horticultural produce and manufactured goods (1988b: 36). These pastoral nomads ('proto-Israelites') were in the land as early as the Middle Bronze Age II (1750–1550). The highlands, he argues, were the first to be occupied in times of prosperity and the first to depopulate in difficult times. While the Middle Bronze Age IIb (1750–1650) was a period of prosperity that of Middle Bronze Age IIc (1650–1550) was one of decline. In fact the entire Late Bronze Age (1550–1220) was an era of decline on both sides of the Jordan. Egyptian wars and crippling taxation policies led to the further decline of the highland villages and to a withdrawal into nomadism (1988a: 339-43).

According to Finkelstein, as a result of the collapse of lowland urban centres, people began to settle down in the highlands as early as the thirteenth century BC, beginning a process that would ultimately lead to the formation of a state (1988b: 41-45). The settlement process was a gradual and peaceful resedentarization, until the settlers came into conflict with Canaanite centres (1988a: 348-51). The biblical account is a much later reinterpretation of the process (1988a: 337). However, central to Finkelstein's reconstruction is his postulate that the Iron Age settlement of the hill country and Galilee was 'Israelite', as distinct from the lowland 'Canaanite' culture, a conjecture whose driving force may be the later biblical historiographers' insistence on an 'ethnic' distinction between the two.

According to Lemche, Israel's origins lie firmly within Canaanite culture, with the Israelites being in continuity with the Canaanites in culture, ethnicity and religion (1985: 66-76). A certain distinctiveness from Canaanites gradually developed over a period of time, which was based on socio-economic rather than ethnic factors. The peasants of Canaan, among whom one counts the *'apiru* and other landless people, evolved into the Israelites in a gradual process which reached its completion only in the time of David, when Israel manifested a conscious unity for the first time (Lemche 1985: 295).

Stiebing stresses climatic factors in accounting for the historical process (1989). Dry conditions and drought between 1250 and 1200 BC caused population decline in the Mediterranean region, leading to lowlanders abandoning the cities and withdrawing to the highlands. With more moist conditions, the population increased from 1000 BC on, leading to the creation of a monarchical state. Israel, then, was created, not by the introduction of new peoples, but by a natural increase in population due to favourable climatic and agricultural conditions. Coote and Whitelam attribute the rise of Israel to a repeating cycle of hinterlands developing in periods of economic prosperity and being able to absorb the populations from the lowland cities when these collapse (Coote and Whitelam 1987: 129). Flanagan also rejects any notion of conquest, infiltration or revolt and stresses the lack of unity prior to David, affirming that the rise of David marks the true cultural and religious unification of Israel (1988: 166). State formation was due to natural population increase more than to settlement of lowlanders. The archaeological evidence, then, suggests reconstructions which stress the indigenous nature of the changing population patterns and continuity of culture. It offers no support to a model of aggressive intrusion from the outside.

Regional Diversity and Ethnic Identity
The ethnic unity of the inhabitants of any Palestinian region is unlikely, given the movement of peoples throughout the whole of the eastern Mediterranean world and Palestine at the turn of the millennium. Moreover, climatic changes profoundly changed the settlement patterns. Regional surveys reveal that during the Late Bronze dry spell, the well-watered lowlands suffered a loss of many small villages, and the diminished population consolidated itself in the larger towns. The great Mycenaean drought in the transition to the early Iron Age brought a deepening economic depression which led to a widespread dispersal of the lowland population into a large number of smaller settlements. In the uplands, the climatic stress caused the widespread collapse and abandonment of sedentary village agriculture and gave birth to a complex of small village settlements in the central hills during Iron Age I (Thompson 1992: 302-303).

Such economic conditions were not conducive to constructing a unified 'national' order. Moreover, the pluralized and multi-linguistic diversity of the region acted against a centralized unified 'national' social structure. The collapse of Egyptian hegemony in the region did not lead to 'national' unity but rather to centrifugal competition between the Iron II cities and their hinterlands (e.g. Ashkelon, Gaza, Hazor, Gezer, Lachish, Megiddo, Jerusalem, etc.). Indeed the archaeological evidence precludes any transregional political structures in the highlands and any coherent sense of unity of the population prior to the building of Samaria (Thompson 1992: 306-307, 409-12). The Late Bronze–Iron I transition is not sufficient of itself to account for the distinctiveness which was to develop into the unique character of the 'Israelites' of the exilic period. The Iron II (Assyrian) period was critical in generating this 'national' identity.

Unless one postulates the displacement of the entire indigenous population by the entry of an altogether foreign society into Palestine, such as that broadly predicated in the Joshua narrative, the search for Israelite origins must respect the diversity of the indigenous population of the region. The political entities of the regional states of Israel and Judah, which emerged as part of the new order of the Assyrian Empire, incorporated a wide range of diverse groups. The new Iron

Age I–II settlements in the Palestinian hill country accommodated descendants of the inhabitants of the Late Bronze highland towns, economic refugees from the lowlands devastated by drought, indigenous non-sedentary pastoralists of the region, transhumant pastoralists from the steppe and possibly some of the immigrants from coastal Syria, Anatolia and the Aegean. Moreover, the establishment of the regional state of Judah added to the population mix, since it now included within its territory the indigenous population of the Shephelah with its roots in the Bronze Age, some admixture from the southern coast of Philistia, the mixed population of steppe dwellers, the Arabs associated with overland trade in the northern Negev, the long-standing population of the Jerusalem saddle and Ayyalon Valley and the multicultural population of Jerusalem itself. The predication of Israelite *ethnic distinctiveness* at this period is illusory, a fact reflected in the complexity of linguistic differentiations and affiliations within Palestinian languages and dialects in the first millennium (see Thompson 1992: 334-37).

The Bible's portrayal of a United Monarchy during the tenth century is an unlikely scenario, since the conditions for such regional power did not exist until the expansion of the Assyrian Empire. The advent of the Assyrians converted the state of Israel into the province of Samaria and contributed further to a mixture of population. Population transfer was part of the process of Assyrian imperial control, as it had been in Ancient Egypt, Babylon and the Hittite world early in the second millennium. It was the purpose of the Assyrian king to bring all peoples under the universal authority of Ashur. Mass deportation of subject populations took different forms (one-way deportations to Assyrian cities; deportations to areas from which others had been deported; and the scattered settlement of a transferred population to a variety of places), and in all may have resulted in the dislocation of over a million people.[21] With the fall of Samaria, much of Israel's population was resettled in Assyria, Media and Northern Syria, and partially replaced by groups from Northern Syria, Babylon,

---

21. The reasons for the deportations were varied (punishment for resistance; staving off rebellion; creating dependent and therefore loyal subjects; military conscription; slave labour, etc.), but also, in some cases at least, deportation offered an improvement in the living standards of those deported, giving them freedom from their former oppressors, and land, property and protection in the new place of settlement (Oded 1979: 47-48).

Elam and Arabia. Although Jerusalem survived Sennacherib's assault, he claims to have deported parts of the population of 46 villages of Judah.

The transfer of population was continued by the Babylonians and Persians, who inherited Assyria's well-established imperial structures. Population deportation and replacement by foreign peoples throughout Judea followed Nebuchadnezzar's destruction of Jerusalem. The Persian texts, in particular, represent Cyrus as understanding the restoration of the peoples and their gods as the primary function of empire. His successors determined to centralize their control by a 'restoration' of the indigenous traditions of subject peoples (see Thompson 1992: 346-51, 418). This period is the most likely context for the biblical narrative of Genesis–Kings.

The Literary Form of the Accounts of Israelite Settlement of the Land
The biblical accounts of the changes in the Late Bronze–Iron Age transition present a picture with which the abundant extra-biblical evidence, archaeological and textual, does not cohere. Moreover, it is surprising that Joshua, whose part in the conquest is central, occupies so little attention in the Bible.[22] In addition to the difficulties of harmonizing the archaeological evidence with the narrative of Joshua, other factors suggest that the account is something other than a record

22. He is a minor figure in the Pentateuch and is not counted among the heroes of the early history of the people. Exod. 18.8 brings him on stage as Moses' military assistant and elsewhere as his companion (Exod. 24.13; 32.17). He is subordinate to Caleb in Num. 14.24, 30, and a secondary figure in Num. 13.18 and Deut. 32.44. Even in Deuteronomy his role is minor. 1 Sam. 12 names Moses and Aaron (vv. 6-8), Jacob (v. 8), Jerubbaal and Barak, Jephthah, Samson (v. 11) and Samuel (vv. 18-22). Nehemiah 9 recalls Abram–Abraham (v. 7) and Moses (v. 14). Joshua is not mentioned in Ps. 105, which names Abraham, the children of Jacob (v. 6), Isaac and Jacob (v. 9), Joseph (v. 17) and Moses and Aaron (v. 26). Ps. 106 names Moses and Aaron (v. 16) and Phinehas (v. 30). Moreover, the exploits for which he might be especially remembered (the fall of Jericho, the capture of Ai, the division of the land and the covenant at Shechem) are not mentioned elsewhere in the Bible. Even in the so-called deuteronomistic history (apart from the book of Joshua), reference to Joshua is scant (Judg. 1.1; 2.6-9; 1 Kgs 16.34). In the post-exilic period he is mentioned only in 1 Chron. 7.27 (without comment), and only briefly in Neh. 8.17. It is only in the late period that Joshua and his deeds are mentioned in some detail (Sir. 46.1-8; cf. 2 Esdr. 7.37; 1 Macc. 2.55, as well as Acts 7.45 and Heb. 4.8).

of what happened in the past. Younger's comparison with conquest accounts in Assyrian, Hittite and Egyptian suggests that Joshua 9–12 is structured on a transmission code similar to that of ancient Near Eastern royal inscriptions (1990: 253-65).

More generally, several arguments force one to question the historical reliability of the Genesis–Joshua traditions. The predication of a 'Golden Age' in the remote past in which people enjoyed intimacy with the deities and lived to fabulous old age is a commonplace in antiquity. The primacy of the divine activity within human affairs, frequently in the form of miraculous interventions, is characteristic of ancient literature in general. The Genesis–Joshua narrative is replete with conventional story-telling techniques (see further Miller and Hayes 1986: 58-60). Faced with a range of historical improbabilities, the critical historian, sensitive to the relationship between the biblical narrative and historicity, seeks to construct a history of origins based on all available information, literary and archaeological, and also a scenario which accounts for the creation of the narrative of origins.

Developments within general historical scholarship confirm that all historiography is ideological (e.g. Veyne 1984: 31-46; White 1978: 121-34). Genesis–2 Kings (creation to exile) is a fabricated history of origins using all available sources, including folk traditions and legends, which consolidated group identity in the present by fashioning its imagined origins in a distant past. This literary creation, reflecting the religious perspectives of the writer(s), invoked the God of the patriarchs, the wilderness and conquest, and the golden age of a putative united monarchy. It postulated unique religious origins for the people in their having been chosen by and invited into covenantal relationship with Yahweh, from which derived their religious traditions (*Torah*, religious festivity, priesthood, etc.), as well as the legitimacy of their possession of the land of Canaan (Gen. 12–Deut. 34). This was done within the broader framework of the origins of other peoples and of the other elements of the cosmos (Gen. 1–11). The progenitors of the newly emerging society had taken possession of the land promised by Yahweh and consolidated their control over it (Joshua and Judges), but their kings failed to watch over their kingdoms (1 Sam.–2 Kgs).

The hypothesis that Genesis–2 Kings constitutes one literary work which reworked earlier traditions, and the recent concentration on the literary character of the biblical narratives (e.g. Alter and Kermode

1987; Exum and Clines 1993) have deflected attention from the question of historicity and helped to focus scholastic attention on authorial *Tendenz*. Some see Genesis–Kings as punctuated by a quartet of themes: the apostasy of the people; an invitation to repentance; a determination to obey; and a guarantee of salvation. However, while the individual elements of the composition have been combined to give the finished literary product a certain unity and coherence, leaving many 'rough edges', the dissonances in, and composite character of the Genesis–Kings narrative are well recognized.[23] The presence of variants and repetitions, as well as what appears to be the imposition of a structure which is built on a chronological succession of biographies of heroes (Adam, Abraham, Moses, Joshua, *et al.*), should alert the reader to the reality that multiple, diverse theologies and perspectives exist side by side within the text (see Thompson 1992: 353-69). This calls into question the notion of a single hand with an univocal ideological tendency. Insistence on a fixed, unitary theology and motivation of the deuteronomistic author reflects more the aspirations of the modern reader familiar with finely chiselled modern books with their redactional consistency than the reality of the achievement of the deuteronomistic tradent. The coexistence within the so-called deuteronomistic history of a variety of conflicting perspectives should caution against easy assumptions that selective coherent patterns discerned by a modern reader constitute the ideological *Tendenz* of the author.

Period of composition
Most scholars agree that the major part of Genesis–Kings is a product of the seventh century, during the reign of King Josiah, but revised in the light of the cataclysmic events of the fall of Jerusalem, the collapse of the monarchy and the destruction of the Temple in 586 BC and the subsequent exile to Babylon (e.g. Blum 1990; Van Seters 1975). Moreover, some recent scholarship argues for a later date for the final redaction: Lemche (1991) and T. Thompson (1974: 10; 1992: 356), Garbini (1988: 176-77) in the Hellenistic Period, with P. Davies

23. For example, for our purposes, was Hebron captured by Joshua (Josh. 10.36)? or Caleb (Josh. 15.13-14)? or by Judah (Judg. 1.9-10)?; if Joshua conquered the whole of Canaan, destroying its inhabitants (Josh. 10.40-42), and settling the tribes in the allotted places (Josh. 13-22), how does one explain the account in Judg. 1 which describes ongoing struggles between the Israelites and the Canaanites?

(1995: 149-55) suggesting the Hasmonean period for the 'normativization' of the writings.

The so-called deuteronomistic writer(s) attempted to explain the trauma of the destruction and exile through the medium of not only recent history, but of that of the distant past as well. History was considered to provide causal explanations for current disasters in an intimate, paradigmatic causal link between the past and the present (Lemche 1995: 182-83). This was not history in the Ranke sense of nineteenth-century European historiography, with its attention to what really happened, but an attempt to give a theological interpretation of the past according to particular theological standpoints. Rather than lay the blame for the devastation at the feet of their God, the reason they propose for the collapse of their vital institutions was the failure of the people to be faithful to the covenant. While the monarchy material preserves traces of historical events which really happened, the Hexateuch component is mythical and legendary.

It is difficult to be precise about the date of the final composition of the book of Joshua. It has been suggested that it is a series of fictions which were created in order to create an all-Israel identity after the 722 fall of the northern kingdom (see further Lemche 1985: 206-85). Others argue that it was produced in the seventh century, during the reign of Josiah, and revised during the exile in the light of the events of 586 BC. The historical Joshua, an Ephraimite (Josh. 19.50; 24.30), was perhaps a local hero who became the locus for the deuteronomistic ideal reconstruction of early Israel. The biblical Joshua is to a large extent a literary creation, a carbon copy of Moses, and, as the ideal Israelite leader, a prototype of the ideal kings, David, Hezekiah and especially Josiah (Nelson 1981a: 124; 1981b: 540). The book of Joshua attributes everything to its hero, just as all the laws are attributed to Moses. The book is a type of historical-theological fiction, presenting a picture of the ideal Israel under ideal leadership, with the profound conviction that obeying the Law was the sure way of maintaining possession of Yahweh's land (Coogan 1989: 112). Garbini argues that the book of Joshua reflects a historical situation markedly later than the exile and an ideology which it is difficult to date before the third century BC (Garbini 1988: xv).

The portrayal of Israelite origins in the pentateuchal traditions and in the deuteronomistic history are best evaluated in terms of the period of their composition. The decision of Nabonidus to 'restore' the lost cult of *Sin* (the stelae of Nabonidus and his mother) suggests to Thompson a comprehensive context for the composition of Genesis–Kings. Nabonidus strove to bring people from Babylon, Syria and Egypt to share in the restoration as citizens of and heirs to the forgotten traditions of Haran. *Sin* was identified with the God of heaven, the ultimate divinity of the neo-Babylonian world. In the deportation policy perfected by the Persians, Marduk called upon Cyrus to restore both gods and peoples to their homes (cf. 2 Chron. 36.22-23; Ezra 1.1-4; cf. Isa. 45.1-25). 2 Chron. 36.22-23 and Ezra 1.1-4 identify *elohe shamayim* with Yahweh, the name of the long-neglected indigenous god of the former state of Israel. Ezra put Cyrus in a role analogous to that of Nabonidus: Cyrus was charged with 'restoring' the ancient cult of Yahweh at Jerusalem and 'returning' the exiles to their former 'homeland'. Thompson asserts that we are not dealing with returned exiles being restored to their former homeland and the worship of their ancestral god, but with the creation of a new people with a new cult, centred on a new temple administered by the Persian administrator (Neh. 1–11). Whoever these people who were to be transported to Palestine were, they certainly were not the Israelite population of long-lost Israel returning to '*Eretz Israel*' from bitter exile. Continuity with the past was provided in Ezra's narrative by the device that the 'returnees' brought with them the great treasures of the old temple of Yahweh (Ezra 1.5-11; cf. Dan. 1.2; 5.2-4), although, according to other formulations, these treasures had long been looted and broken up (2 Kgs 24.13; 25.13-17; cf. 2 Chron. 36.19 [see Carroll 1992: 81]). With the help of the Persians, these people deported from Babylon and other areas of the new empire determined to establish the cult of *elohe shamayim*, the very essence of the divine throughout the empire, but who, in *Palestine*, went by the name *Yahweh* (Thompson 1992: 418).

The imposition of this new centralized administration, centred on the worship of Yahweh in a restructured Jerusalem, posed a substantial threat to the order of the indigenous people in Palestine, long accustomed to the previous Assyrian and Babylonian systems (see Ezra 4–6). Carroll argues that the second Temple community was to be constituted by 'the people of the deportation' only, the 'good figs' who had been deported with Jechoniah (597 BC): they only were 'the sacred enclave', 'the holy community' which must keep itself apart from the people of the land. 'Much—in some sense perhaps *all*—of the literature of the Hebrew Bible must be regarded as the documentation of their claims to the land and as a reflection of their ideology' (Carroll 1992: 85; cf. Thompson 1992: 419). The propagandistic Persian vocabulary of 'restoration' and 'return' should not be used to underpin the categories of *pre-exilic*, *exilic* and *post-exilic* as accurate delineations of the history of 'Israel'. The formers of the biblical tradition, by putting themselves within the category of those 'redeemed' from exile, identified themselves with the victims of the Assyrian and Babylonian deportation practices. The pre-exilic period of a lost Jerusalem and Judah and Samaria and Israel, then, became a lost glory to be restored.

Whatever coherence or 'national ethnicity' Palestine had ever developed, it did not survive the dislocations and displacements of the sixth century.[24] 'The Iron Age population of the Palestinian highlands entered the Persian period radically transformed' (Thompson 1992: 415):

> By the end of the sixth-century, *Palestine* was without unity or any meaningful coherence. Ethnically, linguistically, religiously, economically and politically it lacked cohesion. Its elite had been transported to serve imperial aims, and the core of its populations was scattered and divided among incoherent groupings of indigenous and resettled peoples (Thompson 1992: 421).

The literary paradigm of the 'Babylonian Exile' provided a context for the self-understanding of the people of Yahweh as a saved remnant.[25] The trauma of exile gave the identity of 'Israel' to the newly-formed tradition. In the Persian period, the new people acquired the identity of 'Israel' through association with this remnant, whether

24. The terms *ethnicity* and *nation*, although widely used in the discipline, are of dubious value. The concept of *ethnos* is a political rather than anthropological aspect of human society—a fiction created by writers (T.L. Thompson's paper, 'Hidden Histories and the Problem of Ethnicity in Palestine', delivered at the Jerusalem Day Symposium, Amman 1996—to be published). The application of the term *nation* to the societies of the Bronze and Iron Ages is an anachronism. Moreover, the concepts of *nation* and *nationality* themselves are cultural artefacts with roots in eighteenth-century Europe. Indeed, the term *nationalism* was not used widely until the end of the nineteenth century (Anderson 1991: 4).

25. The inclusive monotheism of the *Torah* corresponds to the Babylonian heavenly supreme deity (*Sin* at Haran) and the Persian universal God of heaven and creator of all (*Ahura Mazda*). Under Xerxes, the inclusivity yielded to exclusivity, which is echoed by the nationalistic proclivities of a later Yahwism.

one's ancestors came from Babylon, Nineveh or Egypt, or had always been in Palestine:

> To identify with the true Israel was to assert one's roots in exile, and
> through it in the lost glory of the Davidic empire, in the conquest with
> Joshua, in the wilderness with Moses, in the exodus from *Egypt*, as a *ger*
> with Abraham and with *Yahweh* at creation (Thompson 1992: 422).

The linguistic and literary reality of the biblical tradition is folk-loristic and corresponds to no reality at any period of history:

> The concept of *benei Israel*: a people and an ethnicity, bound in union and
> by ties of family and common descent, possessing a common past and
> oriented towards a common futuristic religious goal, is a reflection of no
> sociopolitical entity of the historical state of Israel of the Assyrian period,
> nor is it an entirely realistic refraction of the post-state Persian period in
> which the biblical tradition took its shape as a cohering self understanding
> of *Palestine's* population. It rather has its origin and finds its meaning
> within the development of the tradition and within the utopian religious
> perceptions that the tradition created, rather than within the real world of
> the past that the tradition restructured in terms of a coherent ethnicity and
> religion (Thompson 1992: 422).

Conclusion

Twentieth-century biblical scholarship has shifted from viewing much of the biblical narrative as simple history to concentrating on its authors as historiographers, whose reconstruction of the past reflected their own religious and political ideologies. However, no amount of special pleading is sufficient to justify the classification 'history' for the biblical narrative of Israelite origins. *Pace* Brettler's strained attempts to retain the term for much of the biblical narrative (1995: 10-12), no 'didactic history' which 'patterned the past after the present', or even fabricated the past for allegedly honest paraenetic motives should be confused with the discipline of history whose criteria are accuracy and adequacy of portrayal of the past, independently confirmed where possible.[26] History proper must be distinguished

---

26. Brettler argues that the Chronicler wrote a type of 'didactic history' which 'patterned the past after the present', in which what might be learned from the event or pattern rather than the historicity of the event itself was important. Such a work ought to be read in terms of the meaning which the narrative conveys rather than as a record of past events (1995: 41). Brettler is at pains to retain the biblical writers within the category of historians. Although the Deuteronomist modified and diverged

from a series of ideologically motivated assertions about the past (cf. Thompson 1992: 404-405).

Biblical scholarship can include Genesis–Kings within the genre of historiography only by a tortuous expansion of the definition. Such a designation confuses the world of historiography, which deals with the true and real past with that of fictional literature which reflects the conceptual world of the author. Genesis–Kings, which preserves fragmentary sources emanating from many authors reflecting diverse ideologies and retaining seemingly disharmonious tale variations, does not merit the genre of self-conscious historiography as understood in antiquity or today. The so-called deuteronomistic tradent appears to have been driven by an antiquarian's desire to preserve the diversity of what was old while giving it a loosely chronological catalogue of a sequence of great periods (see Thompson 1992: 373-78).

The rejection of the historicity of the patriarchal narratives in the seminal works of T. Thompson (1974) and Van Seters (1975) is now part of the scholarly consensus that the narratives do not record events of the patriarchal period, but are retrojections into a past about which the writers knew little, which reflect the authorial *Tendenzen* at the later period of composition. The pentateuchal narratives are best understood as common traditions of Judah sometime after 600 BC. They should not be used as historiographical sources for the period before 1000 BC (Lemche 1985: 385-86) and should be used only very rarely for the period of the monarchy itself (Thompson 1992: 95). While ancient Israelite historiographers may not have been much different from the later Jewish rabbis, for whom 'there was no question more meaningless or boring than the purpose and usefulness of an exact description of what actually transpired' (Moshe David Herr, in Brettler 1995: 2), the questions concerning what, or whether God's promise of land to an Abraham and his descendants actually happened are of critical importance.

Against the background of the virtually unanimous scholarly scepticism concerning the historicity of the patriarchal narratives, it is unacceptable to cleave to the view that God made the promise of progeny and land to Abraham after the fashion indicated in Genesis 15. Literary and historical investigation make it more likely that such

from his sources radically and 'fabricated' history, he is excused because he honestly believed his ideology, and is conceded to be 'writing history like all other historians' (1995: 78).

promises emanated from within the ideologies of a much later period, perhaps that of the attempt to reconstitute national and religious identity in the wake of the Babylonian exile. Nevertheless, despite their legendary character, both Church and Synagogue continue to treat the patriarchal narratives as though they were a record of what actually happened. The scholarly community for its part evades the problem by contenting itself with studying the texts rather than the events which lie behind them (see Brettler 1995: 1-2; Neusner 1990: 247; cf. Thompson 1992).

Much of the scholastic reaction against viewing the Abraham narrative as late and largely legendary is motivated by 'confessional' considerations.[27] This disposition springs from a fear that any deviation from 'historical' truth is a dilution of, and derogation from religious truth, as if history (in the sense of a record of what really happened) were the only literary genre worthy, or even capable of communicating religious truth.[28] It is as if factual history were the only genre which could validate a religious appreciation of the narrative of the call of Abraham and the promise of progeny and land: Christian faith and Jewish belief demand no less. However, an authentic biblical faith must respect the variety of literary forms of the biblical *narrative* and acknowledge that the narrative of the folkloric and legendary 'events' of the past functions as an honourable medium for the communication of truth, albeit not historiography. To abandon one's attachment to the historicity of the events of the narrative in the light of compelling evidence is not to forsake belief: 'To learn that what we have believed is not what we should have believed is not to lose our faith' (Thompson 1974: 328).

The narrative of the book of Deuteronomy does not care much for the indigenous population. The notion of the land as the gift of God must reckon with the fact that, invariably, one takes the land from its original inhabitants. The dream of colonizers customarily exacts a nightmare for the indigenous population and, *pace* P. Miller (1969:

27. 'Without Abraham, a major block in the foundations of both Judaism and Christianity is lost; a fictional Abraham...could supply no rational evidence for faith...Inasmuch as the Bible claims uniqueness, and the absolute of divine revelation, the Abraham narratives deserve a positive, respectful approach; any other risks destroying any evidence they afford' (Millard 1992: I, 40).

28. E.g., 'Si la foi historique d'Israel n'est pas fondée dans l'histoire, cette foi est erronée, et la notre aussi' (de Vaux 1965: 7).

465) and others, it is not morally acceptable to predicate the land as one's own even 'by the grace of God'. It is some comfort to be rescued from a literalist reading of Deuteronomy, since such a reading predicates a god who shares the predictable dispositions of a ghetto community in an exclusivist, ethnicist, xenophobic and militaristic fashion. While modern biblical scholarship is united in concluding that the narrative of the Pentateuch does not correspond to what actually happened (Whybray 1995: 141), it is not acceptable to allow the narratives to escape an evaluation based on criteria of morality, especially in the light of the use to which they have been put. Subsequent use of the pentateuchal narrative and the so-called deuteronomistic history, especially in the liturgy, invites new generations of hearers/readers to embrace the values of separateness appropriate to (a section of) the Israelite community. One would hope that the generations of participants in the liturgy would be stimulated by these texts rather less energetically than were the Crusaders, the mediaeval theologians justifying the conquest of the New World, the Pilgrim Fathers, the South African Calvinists and, most recently, the more enthusiastic religious Zionists.

A historiography of Israelite origins based solely, or primarily on the biblical narratives is an artificial construct determined by certain religious motivations obtaining at a time long post-dating any verifiable evidence of events. The way forward is to write a comprehensive, independent history of the Near East into which the Israelite history of origins should be fitted. While there is nothing like a scholarly consensus in the array of recent studies on Israel's origins,[29]

---

29. In their attempts to construct a history of Israel, Soggin (1984) and Miller and Hayes (1986) mark a departure from the confidence of earlier scholarship in their scepticism concerning the historicity of the biblical traditions of the pre-monarchic period. They question our ability to say anything sure about Israel's origins and concur in the judgment that little can be learned from the Bible on the subject, and, in particular, that the traditions of Genesis–2 Kings are of limited use for that purpose. At the level of reception, the societal contexts of modern historians of Israelite origins are reflected in their work. One detects in German historiography of Israel a preoccupation with the nation state after the model of Bismarck's unification of Germany. In American scholarship, the recent history of the 'pilgrim fathers' stressed the model of a chosen people in search of a promised land. In the case of Israeli historiographers, these emphases find an echo in terms of the origins of the modern State of Israel. In all three regions, the stress has been on Israelite unity and the role of leading personalities (see Coote and Whitelam 1987: 173-77).

there is virtual unanimity that the model of tribal conquest as narrated in Joshua 1–12 is untenable (see, e.g., Thompson 1987: 11-40). Leaving aside the witness of the Bible, we have no evidence that there was a Hebrew conquest. Moreover, there is a virtual scholarly consensus that the biblical narratives which describe the conquest–settlement period come from authors writing many centuries later than the 'events' described (whether in the exilic, or post-exilic periods), who had no reliable information about that distant past.

The Exodus–Settlement accounts reflect a particular genre, the goal of which was to inculcate religious values rather than merely present empirical facts. The modern historian must distinguish between the actual history of the peoples and the history of their self-understanding. The archaeology of Palestine must be a primary source for tracing the origins of Israel, and it shows a picture quite different from that of the religiously motivated writings (Ahlström 1993: 28-29). The archaeological evidence points in an altogether different direction from that suggested by Joshua 1–12. It suggests a sequence of periods marked by a gradual and peaceful coalescence of disparate peoples into a group of highland dwellers whose achievement of a new sense of unity culminated only with the entry of the Assyrian administration. The Iron I Age settlements on the central hills of Palestine, from which the later kingdom of Israel developed, reflect continuity with Canaanite culture, and repudiate any ethnic distinction between 'Canaanites' and 'Israelites'. Israel's origins were within Canaan not outside it. There was neither invasion from outside nor revolution within. Moreover, the 'Israel' of the period of the biblical narrative represented a multiplicity of ethnic identities, reflecting the variety of provenances in the Late Bronze–Iron Age transition and that brought about by three waves of systematic, imperial population transfer and admixture (Assyrian, Babylonian and Persian). The predication of Israelite *ethnic distinctiveness* prior to the Persian period is illusory, and the unity of the biblical *benei Israel* is a predilection of the biblical authors rather than the reality reflecting a commonality of ethnic identity or communal experience.

The contemporary needs of the final redactors of the biblical narrative determined and dominated their ideological stance, which we may wish to call religious or pastoral, and issued in an ideal model for the future which they justified on the basis of its retrojection into the past of Israelite origins, the details of which only the surviving conflicting folkloric traditions provided. If we excuse the biblical writers for their misrepresentation of the past on the basis of their paraenetic motives for their own circumstances, we ought not to be equally indulgent with theologians and Church–Synagogue people for whom the evidence of what happened in the past is more reliable. The legendary account of Joshua 1–12 offers no legitimizing paradigm for land plunder in the name of God, or by anyone arrogating to himself his authority. Indeed, the extra-biblical evidence promotes a respect for the evolution of human culture, rather than for a process that can deal with change only by way of violent destruction.

While generations of religious people have derived both profit and pleasure from the retelling of the biblical stories, the victims of the colonialist plunder we have examined are likely to be less sanguine in their attitude to the texts, and would welcome any attempt to distinguish between the apparent ethnocentricity of the God of Genesis–Kings and the paranaetic and political intentions of authors writing much later. A major epistemological question arises. Do texts which belong to the genre of folkloric epic or legend, rather than of a history which describes what actually happened, confer legitimacy on the 'Israelite' possession of the land and on subsequent forms of colonialism which looked to the biblical paradigm, understood as factual history, for legitimization later? Does a judgment which is based on the premise that the genre of the justifying text is history in that sense not dissolve when it is realized that the text belongs to the genre of *myths of origin*, which are encountered in virtually every society, and which, as we have seen, were deployed in the service of particular ideologies?

Chapter 7

REHABILITATING THE BIBLE:
TOWARDS A MORAL READING OF THE BIBLE

The Land in Modern Biblical Scholarship: Status Quaestionis

When one considers that there are some 1705 references in the English Bible to *land*, it is surprising that the theme has attracted so little scholastic attention. In his 1943 pioneering essay, Gerhard von Rad noted that despite the importance of the theme in the Hexateuch, no thorough investigation of it had been made (1966: 79). But even by 1962 *The Interpreter's Dictionary of the Bible* had no article on the theme. *The Peake Commentary* (1962) has two references to the land in its index. Kittel-Friedrich's *Wörterbuch* allots just four pages to the theme. The index of *The New Jerome Biblical Commentary* (1989) lists only three places in which the theme is dealt with. However, W.D. Davies and Walter Brueggemann have written major and influential works on the subject.

Davies's 1974 study was written at the request of friends in Jerusalem, who just before the 1967 war, urged his support for the cause of Israel (1982: xiii). His second was written under the direct impact of that war: 'Here I have concentrated on what in my judgement must be the beginning for an understanding of this conflict: the sympathetic attempt to comprehend the Jewish tradition' (1982: xiii-xiv). Its updated version was written because of the mounting need to understand its theme in the light of events in the Middle East, culminating in the Gulf War and its aftermath (1991: xiii). While Davies considers the topic from virtually every conceivable perspective in his 1974 and 1982 works, little attention is given to broadly moral and human rights' issues.[1]

---

1.   Consistent with virtually all biblical scholarship, Alfaro's survey (1978) does not deal with the moral question of the fate of those already inhabiting the land.

From his own experience of urban life in the USA, Walter Brueggemann sees human culture in search of a place and the Bible as concerned primarily with being displaced and yearning for a place (1977: 2). Land is a central, if not *the central theme* of biblical faith, and might be a way of organizing biblical theology (1977: 3). Brueggemann's reading of the Bible is refracted through a concentration on *the land*. The significant moment before entry into the Promised Land is an occasion for a profound pause: the gift of the land is *sola gratia* (p. 48). He bypasses the treatment to be meted out to the indigenous inhabitants. At one point he affirms, 'What is asked is not courage to destroy enemies, but courage to keep Torah' (p. 60), avoiding the fact that in the biblical narrative 'keeping Torah' involves accepting also its xenophobic and destructive militarism. Yet he acknowledges that 'the land of promise is never an eagerly waiting vacuum anticipating Israel. It is always filled with Canaanites' (p. 68). He evades the moral issue, however, by assuring us that that is how the promise comes.

For Brueggemann Judaism's attachment to the land could find expression only in the formation of a modern nation state, of whatever complexion. While he appears to concede 'Arab' rights and grievances in theory, he shows no appetite for addressing them. He does not offer any critique of the moral character of the values implied in the biblical account. Murder, killing, destruction, expulsion and generally horrendous human suffering are the inevitable price one pays in pursuit of the goals in which the biblical narrative of land is set, when read in a naively literalist way. In such a reading, the divinely approved, divinely mandated outrages keep the name of the tribal god alive, but at the cost of the death of a God whose morality transcends the particularist, the ethnicist, the xenophobic and the militaristic.

W. Davies accepts as epistemologically tenable the view that what Jews believe to have happened constitutes a fact of undeniable historical and theological significance. That belief itself, he claims, has become a historical datum: 'Its reality as an undeniable aspect of

Orlinsky bemoans the neglect of *the land* in treatments of the biblical concept of covenant (1985) and treats the biblical text as though it were a record of what actually happened. He pays no attention to the indigenous inhabitants. His study proceeds with significant attention to questions of Hebrew syntax, but with none to questions of morality and ethics.

Judaism cannot be ignored' (1991: 97). The promise of land was so reinterpreted from age to age that it became a living power in the life of the people. What was important was its formative, dynamic, seminal force in the history of Israel, rather than its historicity. The legend acquired its own reality (1991: 5-6). The sense of possession became a determinative reality, whether or not the gift of land ever had any historical support. In other words, whether or not the land was ever promised by God, the narrative and its underlying traditions justify such an ascription.

Davies traces the theological conviction that there was an unseverable connection between Israel, the land and its God from the early Israelite period to the modern. He does acknowledge that the very discussion of the land theme would not have been possible but for the conscious and unconscious pressure of Zionism. However, he insists that neat dichotomies between the religious and political factions in Zionism are falsifications of their rich and mutually accommodating diversity. He claims that the often silent but ubiquitous presence of the religious tradition won the day. He concludes, 'To understand the secular character of Zionism and to overemphasize its undeniable religious dimensions is to lay oneself open to the temptation of giving to the doctrine of The Land a significance which in much of Judaism would be a distortion' (Davies 1991: 76).

Davies deals with the criticism that 'the land' as *a piece of real estate* is anachronistic and a superstition unworthy of serious consideration. He has no sympathy for those who hold that the land, together with the other doctrine of 'chosenness/election', are especially primitive expressions of the unacceptable particularism of the Jewish faith. He defends the Jewish claim to territory because, without such territory, there is a loss of security, stimulation, identity and political self-determination. Christianity, he claims, substituted for the holiness of place the holiness of Christ, with life 'in Christ' replacing life 'in the Land' as the highest blessing (Davies 1991: 90). He does not appear to have been swayed by the view that the way of *Torah*, in the emerging rabbinic movement, enabled each individual to bring holiness into daily life, no longer by means of the Temple. There was a conscious discontinuity: *Torah* was the basis for a new piety. Davies bemoans the spiritualization of the notion of land in both Christianity and Judaism and lauds the sense of rootedness which the materiality of the concept keeps alive.

Davies excluded from his concern, 'What happens when the understanding of the Promised Land in Judaism conflicts with the claims of the traditions and occupancy of its other peoples?' He excuses himself by saying that to engage that issue would demand another volume (1991: xv), without indicating his intention to embark upon such an enterprise. Similarly, at the end of his 1981 article (p. 96), he claimed that it was impossible to discuss that issue. His 1991 work does include a symposium in which Krister Stendahl saw Zionism as a liberation movement, and the State of Israel as the fulfilment of biblical promise (in Davies 1991: 111-12). Arthur Hertzberg insists that Judaism cannot survive in its full stature in the diaspora, since the bulk of the 613 *mitzvot* can be observed only in Israel. That religious insight, he claims, is the prime source of modern Zionism (in Davies 1991: 106). R.J. Zwi Werblowsky also gives no indication of moral perturbation deriving from the implications of the *Torah*-driven piety implied in Zionism. David Noel Freedman hints at Davies' omission of the moral dimension of the treatment of the subject:

> Even the longed-for guidance for the thinking of serious people, puzzled and disturbed by the apparent historical consequences of the doctrine of The Land in the lives of peoples and lands in the Near East today, almost a re-enactment of the first Exodus, conquest, and settlement, may be too much to ask (Freedman, in Davies 1991: 104).

Kenneth Cragg gets to the heart of the moral predicament. He points to the perpetual crisis which arises when the granting of covenanted territory to a covenanted people through a covenanted story conflicts with the identity of other inhabitants, to which Davies refers only at a tangent (in Davies 1991: 101).

For Jacob Neusner, the obsession with the land in Genesis to Joshua and the principal historical and prophetic books is explained by the fact that they all reached their final form outside the land and in consequence of the loss of the land. But the Babylonian Talmud makes it clear that one can practise the holy way of life anywhere, any time. Neusner's contrast between the Babylonian Talmud and the theology of the Mishnah, from which it derives, is telling. Whereas for the Mishnah, 'Israel can be Israel only in The Land of Israel' (in Davies 1991: 108), the Babylonian Talmud ignores the whole of the Mishnah's repertoire of laws on cultic cleanness (except for the one on woman's menstrual uncleanness), as well as the first division of the Mishnah on agriculture. In transmitting the Mishnah, the great sages of Babylonia converted it into something relevant for the diaspora. Neusner adds that American Jews today, faced with the claim that normality is to live in the land and abnormality is to live abroad, do what they want, amiably professing feelings of remorse and guilt (Neusner, in Davies 1991: 109).

It is left to J.S. Whale to bring the moral question to the fore. His criticism of Davies's indifference to the fate of the people who have to pay the price for Israelite and Israeli seizure of the land is as devastating as it is polite. He notes that Davies 'must know that conquest is always cruel, even when perpetrated by God's Elect; and that empire is always huge robbery, whether Roman or British, Muslim or Christian' (in Davies 1991: 116).

Davies added further reflections in response to the symposium. To the criticism that he had not given due attention to the Holocaust, he affirms that he justifies the State of Israel in terms of the Holocaust (Davies 1991: 120). One wonders where the logic of his biblical thesis would have led had the Holocaust not occurred. Davies acknowledges that the land is not an absolute value in Judaism, and that the zeal of devotees may be tempered by appeal to the primacy of the sanctity of life within Judaism. However, he does not allow that principle to express itself further. He settles for an accommodation of the two people and a compromise as an utter necessity: land can be traded for peace (Davies 1991: 130). But one must question how his earlier logic could allow such a derogation from the divine mandate.

Davies takes the establishment of the pre-1967 Jewish State of Israel in his stride. Only the post-1967 occupation is a problem. The colonial plunder associated with the foundation of the State of Israel is above reproach and appears to enjoy the same allegedly divinely sanctioned legitimacy and mandate as the Joshua-led encroachment on the land. One wonders whether Davies would be equally sanguine had white, Anglo-Saxon Protestants or Catholics been among the displaced people who paid the price for the enactment of the divine mandate. He shows no concern for the fundamental injustice done to the Palestinian Arabs by the encroachment on their land by Zionists and for the compensation that justice and morality demands. Despite the foundational plunder of 1948, Davies writes as if there were now a moral equivalence between the dispossessed Palestinians and the dispossessor Zionists.

Davies moves smoothly from the religious motivation to live the fullness of the *Torah* in the land of Israel to the conclusion of the legitimacy of establishing a state, with all that that implies, especially in an area already inhabited. Nor does the behaviour of the State of Israel towards the Palestinian Arabs, both in the Occupied Territories and Israel itself, and towards those it expelled from their homes mute his sense of Bible-based propriety. He is guided by the principle that whatever is apportioned to the people of Israel in their foundation documents requires no further justification.

Davies concedes that things have changed with the emergence of the State of Israel. The Zionists, he agrees, superseded the intentions of the 'Lovers of Zion', who, having a 'mystical' relationship to the land, were indifferent to whoever would assume political and military responsibility for it. But he does not allow the clear evidence of colonial Zionism to shake his fundamental satisfaction with his major thesis, thereby playing down the real gap between his romanticized biblicism and the reality of the disruption and social upheaval that always attends 'ethnic cleansing'. While Davies's theology of land is forced into confrontation with some of the realities of its implications today, his sensitivity to issues of human rights and international law and to the wider international political scene is not impressive. His overall, somewhat confused position may be summed up as follows:

1. The State of Israel is justified in terms of the Holocaust.
2. Compromise is an utter necessity to accommodate the two people (but, one might ask, by what biblical authority?).
3. Only the post-1967 occupation is a problem—the dislocation of 1948 is accepted.
4. The desired life in the land has been possible only with the aid of the despised life outside it.
5. Loyalty to the *Torah* is more precious than even the blessing of living in the land—faith outside the land is possible, but not outside the *Torah*.

Davies does not deal with the question of the dimensions of the land.

A number of items distinguish the scholastic treatment of the land. The most distinctive aspect of the discourse is the virtual absence of any sensitivity to the moral questions involved in one people dispossessing others. The conventional discourse suffers from other serious limitations:

1. Its writers settle for a synchronic reading of the biblical text that does not address the significance of its provenance and literary evolution.
2. They appear to accept on this one issue that the literary genre of the biblical treatment of the origins of Israel is history—a view which runs in the face of all serious scholarship.
3. They do not differentiate between the different stages in the life of 'the people of Israel', for example, before occupation of Canaan, during the period of the monarchy and before, during and after exile.
4. They assume in most cases that one is dealing with a homogeneous people of Israel, ethnically, culturally and religiously one at all periods.
5. They consider the biblical attitudes towards the land to be above moral reproach, and make no value judgment on them.
6. They assume that the attitudes to land portrayed at one (biblical) period have an automatic currency for quite a different one; in particular, that they automatically transfer to that specific form of attachment to land which we know as Zionism.

A more acceptable academic discourse requires that each of these limitations be addressed with a particular sensitivity to moral issues and a certain concern for the dispossessed. In the light of the biblical exegesis discussed above, one speculates as to the relationship between epistemology and the formation of character. A faith nourished on the Bible as understood by the prevailing biblical scholarship conflicts with universally agreed perspectives on human dignity and rights.[2]

The failure to distinguish between the biblical narratives as story and as history in the sense of informing about the past is no longer acceptable. Scholars must abandon the security of considering the biblical narrative as 'history', accept the consequences of respecting the

2. I shall discuss elsewhere the place of the Bible in the mainstream Christian Zionism of Reinhold Niebuhr (see Fox 1987), Franklin Littell, Paul van Buren and John Pawlikowski *et al.*, and the biblical hermeneutics of Evangelical Christian Zionism (see Wagner 1995). I shall discuss also the challenge to Zionism posed by Jewish scholars, for example, Moshe Menuhin (1969), Yeshayahu Leibowitz, Elmer Berger, Uri Davis, Marc Ellis and Deena Hurwitz (1992), and within Christian theological circles (e.g. Ruether and Ruether 1989; Ruether 1990), as well as from Palestinian Liberation theologians (e.g. Ateek 1989; Rantisi 1990).

new evidence about the past and attempt to reconstruct religious doctrine which respects that evidence. Living with the imprecisions of a reconstruction of the past is preferable to the security of embracing a fictitious and unsustainable fabrication of it, particularly one which legitimates colonial plunder. It will not be possible to put the old paradigm of the unity of Bible and history together again (Thompson 1995: 697-98), and we shall have to learn to live with ambiguity (Redford 1992: 311). Any reconstruction of the Israelite past must distinguish between the 'historical Israel' and 'biblical Israel', respect the archaeological evidence and give due weight to the nature of the biblical narrative, recognizing the ideological intentions of the authors. The heated nature of the debate about possible reconstructions of 'ancient Israel' reflects the reality that one is not dealing merely with objective scholarship in search of an elusive past, but that one is enmeshed also in discussion about the legitimacy of developments in Palestine in our own time (see Whitelam 1996: 71-121).

Any discussion of the Bible must allow for a moral critique which respects the discourse of human rights and international law to which our generation is accustomed. I can only indicate here some ways forward. But first we must acknowledge the problem.

The Moral Problem of the Land Traditions of the Bible

The indigenous peoples in the three regions we have examined have no doubt about the link between religion and oppression and reserve particular criticism for the Bible. The representative Andean and American Indians who presented an open letter to Pope John-Paul II when he visited Peru left him in no doubt about their assessment of the role of the Bible in the destruction of their civilization. They asked him to take back the Bible and give it to their oppressors.[3] A saying in South Africa sums up a popular appraisal of the Bible in the oppression of its indigenous population: 'When the white man came to our country he had the Bible and we had the land. The white man said to us, "Let us pray". After the prayer, the white man had the land and we had the Bible.'

The Palestinian theologian Naim Ateek reflects that whereas one looks to the Bible for strength and liberation, it is used by some

3.   Columbus regarded the discovery of the New World as a fulfilment of the prophecy of Isaiah (Isa. 60.9, in Bonino 1975: 4-5).

Christians and Jews in a way which offers Palestinians slavery rather than freedom, injustice rather than justice, and death to their national and political life (1989: 75). He notes that, since the establishment of the State of Israel, which was a seismic tremor that shook the very foundation of their beliefs,

> The Old Testament has generally fallen into disuse among both clergy and laity, and the Church has been unable to come to terms with its ambiguities, questions, and paradoxes—especially with its direct application to the twentieth-century events in Palestine. The fundamental question of many Christians, whether uttered or not, is: How can the Old Testament be the Word of God in light of the Palestinian Christians' experience with its use to support Zionism? (1989: 77-78).

The problem has been noticed in Asia also.[4]

Acknowledging the Problem
It is undeniable that terrible injustices have been committed through processes of colonialism, and, as we have seen, biblical and theological discourse has been a vivifying component in propelling them. What response is possible? One of the features of the deployment of the Bible as a legitimation for colonialism and exploitation is the absence of serious consideration for the victims of such activity. The Canaanites did not have the right to continue to occupy a region which they had profaned with their idolatry and abominations (Deut. 9.5; cf. Deut. 18.9-14; Lev. 18.24-25; 20.22-24), which justified the violence against them.

There exists within the Bible a degree of violence and praise of violence that is surpassed by no other ancient book (see de Ste Croix, in Said 1988: 166). The existence of such texts within Sacred Scripture is an affront to moral sensitivities. The Holy War traditions, and especially that of the *herem*, pose an especially difficult moral problem (Niditch 1993: 28-77; see Barr 1993: 207-20; Hobbs 1989; Lind 1980). The ban requires that the enemy be utterly destroyed as a

---

4.   Pui-lan Kwok notes the controversial, ambivalent, and often conflicting status of the Bible in Asia. During the nineteenth century it was an integral part of the colonial discourse, legitimating an ethnocentric belief in the inferiority of the Asian peoples and the deficiency of Asian cultures. Ironically, the same Bible has also been a resource for Christians struggling against oppression in Asia. Kwok judges that one of the reasons why, after centuries of missionary activity, only some 3 per cent of Asians are Christians is the link between Christianity and colonialism (1995: 1-2).

sacrifice to the deity who had made the victory possible. This portrays God as one who cherishes the sacrifice of the crown of his creation. Moreover, the killer is not only acquitted of moral responsibility for his destruction, but acts under a religious obligation. The ban both reduces the nature of the crime and exonerates the culprit. It is little consolation to the victims of unsolicited slaughter that their killing is an act of piety which redounds to the glory of God and advances the sanctity of the perpetrator. For many modern readers, clothing such activity in the garment of religion and piety adds to the problematic.

'Ancient Israel' did not invent such perspectives, nor were they left unchallenged within Israelite moral reflection, as the variety of (war) traditions within the biblical text itself makes clear.[5] The ban tradition is appealed to in support of the deuteronomistic ethic, which emphasizes the priestly values of separating the good from the bad etc. These authors, of course, had no intention of applying the letter of their war traditions, nor were they in any position to do so. Their real interest lay in promoting the ideal that the 'Israelites' should separate themselves from the impurity of others, a relatively innocuous, if not particularly attractive disposition. Had these authors used a less morally problematic metaphor than the ban, colonized peoples up to the present time might have been saved some of the racist outrages inflicted

---

5. In the priestly ideology of war recounted in Numbers 31 there is a variant of the ban paradigm. Here one encounters perspectives on justifying killing or not killing in war. In this circle, one becomes engaged in the symbolic world of the priests, in which everything is weighed in terms of the duality of clean (us) and unclean (them), with special attention to sexual status. In addition to incorporating the notions that the cause of war is holy and that its execution is of the order of a ritual, the overall ideology of war, however, involves the realization that killing brings on defilement, from which one must be purified (see Niditch 1993: 78-89). This ideology tries to have it both ways: killing the 'Other' is a divine mandate, but at the same time is a defiling activity. Niditch also discusses the bardic tradition of war, in which the activity is equated with a 'sport' in which heroes and fair play feature prominently (1993: 90-105). 'The chivalric texts of the Hebrew Bible impose a patina of noble order on the chaos that is real war' (p. 103). She examines the ideology of tricksterism in war, in which the weak justify their indiscriminate fighting on the grounds of the justness of the trickster's cause (1993: 106-22). The ideology of expediency applies to those war situations in which the powerful consider themselves to be justified in exercising extreme brutality with God's blessing (1993: 123-33). Finally, Niditch examines the ideology of non-participation, by which the powerless leave the fighting to be done by way of a miraculous divine intervention (1993: 134-49).

upon them, fuelled by a simplistic reading of these traditions.

The sermon of Cotton Mather, delivered in Boston in September 1689, charged the members of the armed forces in New England to consider themselves to be Israel in the wilderness, confronted by Amalek: pure Israel was obliged to 'cast out [the Indians] as dirt in the streets', and eliminate and exterminate them (Niditch 1993: 3). Roland Bainton provides numerous examples from the period of the Crusades (1960: 112-33) up to such eighteenth-century preachers as Herbert Gibbs who thanked the mercies of God for extirpating the enemies of Israel in Canaan (i.e. Native Americans) (1960: 168). Niditch observes:

> This ongoing identification between contemporary situations and the warring scenes of the Hebrew Bible is a burden the tradition must guiltily bear. The particular violence of the Hebrew Scriptures has inspired violence, has served as a model of and model for persecution, subjugation, and extermination for millennia beyond its own reality. This alone makes study of the war traditions of the Hebrew Scriptures a critical and important task (Niditch 1993: 4).

It is some consolation that some passages of the Bible reveal a sense of guilt and remorse at the occupation of what belonged to others (see, e.g., Josh. 24.13; 1 Macc. 15.33-34). Nevertheless, in the biblical legend, whatever rights the Canaanites had in terms of the prevailing international order evaporate in the pens of some of the biblical theologians. In the biblical narrative, religion defined the terms of discrimination, leaving the believers with all the rights and unbelievers with none.

There are major errors involved in a naive interpretation of the Bible, and every effort must be made to rescue it from being a blunt instrument in the oppression of one people by another. A major problem with some of the traditions of the Old Testament, especially those concerned with the promise of land, is its portrayal of God as what many modern people would regard as a racist, militaristic xenophobe, whose views would not be tolerated in any modern democracy. People with moral sensitivities and concern for the dignity of other peoples will question the kind of biblicism which sees the core of biblical revelation to be frozen in the concepts of Chosen People and Promised Land, when the application of such views can have such morally questionable outcomes as discussed here. If a naive interpretation of the Bible leads to such unacceptable conclusions, what kind of exegesis can rescue it?

The Impact of Reading the Bible

The Bible is the most important single source of all (English-language) literature, and its influence on our culture has been so pervasive and profound that in order to understand ourselves we must deal with its strange and yet familiar past (Alter and Kermode 1987: 1-2). Over the last ten years there has grown up a range of approaches to the criticism of 'the biblical text' which move away from historical-critical criticism, which has dominated the discipline since the Enlightenment (see Parsons's survey, 1992). However, the claim of Alter and Kermode that the Bible achieves its effects by means no different from those generally employed by written language (1987: 2)—an assertion made without recourse to any sophisticated study of how the Bible actually functions, whether in the secular or religious academic context, the liturgical and para-liturgical one, or the marketplace—is not borne out by my study and is erroneous.

The *Literary Criticism* of the Bible applies the normal techniques of the discipline, which derive from the experience of reading books written by single authors for individual readers. The results which obtain in the case of normal secular literature are likely to be a poor guide to appreciating the pervasive, constitutive influence of the Bible on those who engage in the variety of encounters with it. Moreover, the presumption that the place and significance of the Bible are uniformly understood and find an agreed universal position within a shared discourse must be abandoned. The quite different predispositions towards, and uses of the Bible within the various Christian and Jewish traditions are not generally acknowledged, and are hidden within such confused phrases as *the Judaeo-Christian tradition* and *sharing the same Bible*.

Roman Catholics, for example, tend to situate the Bible within a wide tradition which incorporates 2000 years of Christian reflection and practice. In the Reformed Christian traditions, there is a tendency to accord the Bible the status of the supreme source of religious insight, and to regard it as the only primary text, and often the sole norm of belief and practice. When an extract from the Bible is read in the Christian assembly it is invariably a part of the drama of re-enactment of the saving acts of Jesus. In the Christian Eucharistic assembly in particular, when the texts re-present the Word, the drama of the liturgy moves on to the offering of gifts, the great Prayer of

Thanksgiving, with its focus on the Passion, Death, Resurrection and Future Coming of Christ. The re-proclamation of the biblical text in a liturgical context ought to be followed by actions to avoid meriting the exhortation of a preacher of an earlier generation, 'Be doers of the word, and not hearers only, deceiving yourselves' (Jas 1.22).

Within the Jewish rabbinic tradition, the Bible read in the synagogue is understood within the framework of the Oral Tradition (*Torah she be'al peh*) learned in the *beit midrash* (the house of interpretation). Although the *Torah* and certain prophetic readings constitute an integral part of Jewish liturgy, these texts are dealt with within an interpretative culture, of which the Talmud, the commentaries (e.g. of Rashi), and the Responsa Literature (incorporating questions and answers from the mediaeval period until today) are the frameworks. Within the culture of Jewish employment of the Bible, the text is given its significance only within the terms of the hermeneutics of the relevant Jewish community and as part of the expression of Jewish religious identity. For a religious Jew, the Bible is an ongoing living text, employed in daily prayers and in the Jewish festivities, whether at home or in the synagogue.

The elevation of the biblical text from being literature to being canonical Scripture ensures that in both the Jewish and Christian experiences the Bible functions as a foundational strand within a more complex matrix, involving both the biblical text as narrative and a range of *meta-narratives*. Failure to appreciate the critical difference between an ordinary reader's disposition before a literary text and a Jew's or Christian's disposition in the face of the biblical text leads to a fundamental misunderstanding of what is in fact taking place. One is not dealing merely with the pre-understanding (*Vorverständnis*) of a biblical text, but with the much more pervasive *through-understanding* of the text, that is, the consolidation of one's understanding of the text due to the ongoing encounter with it. One must also acknowledge the after-effects of the encounter with the biblical text—what I suggest we call the *after-understanding*.

The impact of the biblical text on the psyche of people is much more pervasive than any analogous practice from secular literature. Only religious texts, used liturgically as part of the public worship of the believing community, for example, the *Qu'ran* or the Sikh Scriptures, are treated in a remotely comparable fashion with that meted out to the Bible. These religious texts have an altogether higher authority, which derives to a large extent from their alleged divine provenance.

The Divine Provenance of the Bible

In religious and many secular circles in the West and elsewhere, the Bible is considered to be a fundamental source for the construction of a high morality. It provides a paradigm from which one can fashion a morality not only fit for humankind, but worthy of God himself. How could it be otherwise against a background of Christianity's consistent affirmation of the truth of Scripture (sometimes reduced to the more limited and negative concept of inerrancy) and its divine origins? Nevertheless, as we have seen, history witnesses to interpretations of the Bible which have been baneful in their effects. Let us review the character, provenance and authority of the Bible.

All 39 books of the Hebrew *Tanakh* are recognized as Sacred Scriptures by the Christian Church and also by the Jewish community. The Roman Catholic Church and some Eastern Orthodox Churches accept an additional 7 books. A *canonical book* is one that the Christian Church regards as inspired by God and as having a function in regulating morals. The collection of canonical books has an unique status in the community of the Church. Within Judaism, the *Torah* has a special significance (see Schürer 1979: 314). However, the listing of books within the canon covers over a range of difficulties about how and why such and such a book was canonized and another was not. There is a strong link between the Canon, the authority of the Scriptures, their truth, their provenance and the divine element in their composition. These are interrelated in a complex way which makes comment on individual elements somewhat problematic.[6] Let us review first the divine origin of Scripture.

6.   There is no pretence here to give a comprehensive discussion of these immensely complex issues. Summaries of the arguments may be found in several places, for example, Brown, Fitzmyer and Murphy (1990) and Coggins and Houlden (1990) and more extensive treatments in the bibliographies provided. Thiselton (1992) is a major contribution to the ongoing discussion of hermeneutics, and Watson (1994) discusses some of the same ground, with a particular interest in the theological import of the questions. The Pontifical Biblical Commission's 1993 overview of the interpretation of the Bible in the Church is a masterly and judicious summary of the discussion.

The Bible as Divinely Inspired

In addition to the problems of ordinary interpretation, when it comes to the Bible we encounter the difficulty of the adequacy of human language for the task of expressing God's 'mind', 'will' or 'person'. Vatican II's *Dei Verbum* recapitulates the teaching of the Catholic Church on Revelation:

> [The] divinely revealed realities which are contained and presented in sacred Scripture have been committed to writing under the inspiration of the Holy Spirit. Holy Mother Church, relying on the belief of the apostles, holds that the books of both Old Testament and New Testament in their entirety, with all their parts, are sacred and canonical because, having been written under the inspiration of the Holy Spirit they have God as their author and have been handed on as such to the Church herself (par. 11).

With the document's equal affirmation of human authorship, the divine comes down to earth.

> In composing the sacred books, God chose men and while employed by him they made use of their powers and abilities, so with him acting in them and through them, they, as true authors, consigned to writing everything and only those things which He wanted. Therefore, since everything asserted by the inspired authors or sacred writers must be held to be asserted by the Holy Spirit, it follows that the books of Scripture must be acknowledged as teaching firmly, faithfully, and without error that truth which God wanted put into the sacred writings for the sake of our salvation (par. 11).

Par. 12 notes that the Word of God is a word to people, that Jesus is fully human and that the Word of God is also fully human language. Par. 16 insists that God is the inspirer and author of the books of both Testaments. The divine origin of the Bible is affirmed in several other paragraphs (9, 14, 16, 18, 20, 21, 24). The Old Testament (14), the New Testament (16), the Gospels (18), Paul's epistles and other writings (20) are all inspired. Some paragraphs ascribe inspiration to the biblical texts (8, 21, 24), while others affirm that they were written under the inspiration of the Holy Spirit (9, 14, 20).

The Hebrew Scriptures, however, while affirming the inspiration of prophets (2 Sam. 23.2; Hos. 1.1; Joel 3.1-2), nowhere assert explicitly that the writings which contain their words were inspired. For its part, the New Testament affirms that David was inspired by the Holy Spirit (Mt. 22.43; Mk 12.36; see also Acts 1.16; 28.25). The divine provenance of the content of the Jewish Bible is affirmed in a multitude of ways in the New Testament (see Prior 1995a: 128-29). The two major New Testament texts which affirm inspiration are 2 Tim. 3.16-17 and 2 Pet. 1.19-21. The early Christian Fathers viewed the inspiration of the Scriptures as self-evident, and various explanations were given for the phenomenon. The affirmation of God as author, of course, does not require the ascription of literary authorship to him—the Latin *auctor*, being much broader than the English *author*, designates a source or producer of something, and is close to the English *originator, beginner*, and so forth.

The Talmud also affirms the divine provenance of the *Torah*— *Torah min haShamayim*: 'Whoever says that the whole *Torah* is from heaven except this verse, for God did not utter it, but Moses from his own mouth, he is one (of whom it is written) "For he has despised the word of God" (Num. 15.31)' (*b. Sanh.* 99a), and that all Israelites have a share in the world to come except those who assert that the *Torah* is not from heaven (*m. Sanh.* 10.1). This affirmation is a touchstone of Jewish Orthodoxy to this day.[7]

Nevertheless, all authors, even those to whom one ascribes divine inspiration, write from within their own world view. The language and thought patterns they use are circumscribed by their cosmological, anthropological and theological perspectives, and very often reflect a quite specific social and political context. This must be kept in mind at all times as one considers the breadth of views within the Old Testament on land occupation and war (see Niditch 1993, *passim*). Nevertheless, there remains the major question of the portrayal of God as one who does not conform to even the minimal morality which nation states commit themselves to today. Is it sufficient to attempt to account for the existence within divinely inspired texts of traditions which portray God as a militaristic and xenophobic ethnicist by balancing them with the portrayal of an omnipotent, merciful and universal God which is known through some other traditions of the

7. At the heart of the differences in contemporary British Jewry between the United Synagogue and the Masorti movement is the appropriate understanding of the Hebrew Bible, especially the Pentateuch. In an article in the Orthodox *Jewish Tribune* (January, 1995), Chief Rabbi Jonathan Sacks claims, 'An individual who does not believe in *Torah min haShamayim* (i.e., that the Torah is from heaven) has severed his links with the faith of his ancestors.' The text was reproduced in the *Jewish Chronicle*, 20 January 1995, and was followed by a string of colourful letters and articles over the subsequent weeks.

Old Testament and Christian revelation? Does not the fact that God is portrayed as not living up to even the minimum moral ideals of the UN Declarations on Human Rights or the prescriptions of the Fourth Geneva Convention pose serious questions for a naive understanding of the nature of divine inspiration?

The Authority of the Scriptures and Challenges to that Authority
The doctrine of the divine inspiration of the Scriptures confers on them an especial authority. In addition to being included in the canon of the Church, the liturgy and theology confer upon the biblical writings a further authority. However, to speak of the Bible as the *Word of God* is polyvalent: the Word of God connotes at one and the same time the events of salvation, the spoken messages of God's emissaries (prophets *et al.*), the person of Jesus (the Logos of God—Jn 1.1), Christian preaching, God's general message to human beings and, finally, the Bible itself. The term *Word of God* is itself a product of human language, and *Word* can be used of God only analogously. The wisdom of God (another analogous term) is beyond the capacity of human expression. It would, therefore, be more apposite to speak of the Bible witnessing to the Wisdom of God, and doing so in a human way, and sometimes in an embarrassingly human way.

The authority of the Bible was bound to be contested. The impact of Higher Criticism, with its insistence on sources behind the finished Scriptures, was formidable and drove some believers further into a belief in verbal inspiration, and led some liberal scholars to the virtual abandonment of the idea of divine inspiration. Problems began to infiltrate the churches in a relentless fashion: if the Bible was historically inaccurate, how could it be theologically dependable? There is no simple solution to the obvious tension between biblical criticism and the authority which tradition confers on the Scriptures. When the Bible reached the final stage of canonization in the fourth century AD, it assumed a new status in authority for Christian belief. Brown describes the relationship between the divine provenance of the Bible and its authority in the following way: 'God as author of Scripture may be understood in terms of the authority who gives rise to the biblical books rather than in the sense of *writing* author' (1990: 1148; see further Brown and Schneiders 1990: 1146-65).

However, this, and the other conventional answers to the problem posed by the land traditions of the Bible do not remove the difficulty.

The Truth of the Bible

The concept of the truth of the Bible is no less complex than that of its authority. The inerrancy of Scripture is a major platform of evangelical and fundamentalist Christians, and the claim to it follows from the insistence on the divine authority of the Bible. Since it is the Word of God it must be without error, irrespective of the contribution of the human author. In such a view, a single error in any part of the Bible would undermine the inerrancy of the whole. However, there is a variety of literary forms in the Bible for which the designation *true* means different things. A major limitation of a 'fundamentalist' reading of the biblical text is the tendency to ignore its literary genre. In particular, such readings tend to conclude that all narratives which appear to deal with the past are in fact history and ignore the legendary nature of some stories and the paraenetic intent of their authors.

A more timid way of confronting the competing claims of tradition and modernity is to affirm that the statement that the Bible is true is to assert that it witnesses to the truth (*emeth*) or fidelity of God. However, it is clear that the whole doctrine of the inspiration and truth of Scripture needs to be rethought at its foundations in the light of the ongoing discovery of the nature of language and the complexity of God's creation and his redeeming intentions.

Christians and the Old Testament

To say that the Churches and the Synagogue have the Bible in common is ambiguous, until the question of the authority of the Bible and the authority of the Church and Synagogue have been clarified. Moreover, Christians did not write commentaries on the Old Testament texts, as did the Qumran community, but rather discussed Jesus in the light of the Old Testament. Jesus was a key to the Old Testament, rather than the Old Testament being a key to understanding Jesus. In Augustine's dictum, 'The New Testament lies hidden in the Old, and the Old becomes clear in the New' ('Novum Testamentum in Vetere latet, et in Novo Vetus patet' [see e.g. Evans and Stegner 1994]).

Palestinian Christians have a particular perspective. Both the Latin Patriarch of Jerusalem, Monsignor Michel Sabbah, and the Anglican Palestinian theologian, Canon Naim Ateek, both victims of Zionist colonialism, search for a hermeneutic of the Bible that will be valid both biblically and theologically. They find it in the person of Jesus Christ (Sabbah 1993: 25-31). Ateek insists that if a passage fits in with what one knows of God through Christ, it is valid and authoritative, and, if not, it is invalid (1989: 80-82). He sketches the biblical tension between the portrayal of God as nationalist and universalist, and traces the development of the nationalistic/exclusivist perspective which one finds in the early prophets (Joshua, Judges, 1 and 2 Samuel and 1 and 2 Kings), in the *Torah* and later in the tradition of the Pharisees. He detects in the later Prophets, and more especially in Jonah, greater emphasis on the universalism of God. He sees this third strand raised to a new intensity in the universalism of Jesus and the New Testament. He judges that

> The emergence of the Zionist movement in the twentieth century is a ret-rogression of the Jewish community into the history of its very distant past, with its most elementary and primitive forms of the concept of God. Zionism has succeeded in reanimating the nationalist tradition within Judaism. Its inspiration has been drawn not from the profound thoughts of the Hebrew Scriptures but from those portions that betray a narrow and exclusive concept of a tribal god (Ateek 1989: 101).

He regards the finely worded Declaration of Independence of the State of Israel to be no more than a mask behind which these retrogressive ideas hide: '[The State of Israel] will be based on the principles of liberty, justice and peace as conceived the Prophets of Israel; will uphold the full social and political equality of all its citizens, without distinction of religion, race, or sex.' He judges that ethical Judaism, with its universalist outlook, has been swamped by the resurgence of a racially exclusive concept of a people and their god (Ateek 1989: 102).

In his Pastoral Letter, written only a couple of months after the White House Rabin–Arafat handshake in 1993, Monsignor Sabbah discusses the problems raised by Palestinian Christians for whom the Bible is an integral part of faith and religious heritage:

> a) What is the relationship between the Old and the New Testament?
> b) How is violence that is attributed to God in the Bible to be understood?
> c) What influence do the promises, the gift of land, the election and covenant have for relations between Palestinians and Israelis? Is it possible for a just and merciful God to impose injustice or oppression on another people in order to favour the people He has chosen? (par. 8).

He confronts the problem of violence in the Bible (pars. 37-46). The Letter tackles head-on some of the most difficult aspects of the Bible for a Christian for whom the biblical text appears to warrant her or his oppression. For Palestinian Christians, biblical hermeneutics and questions about the relation between the testaments are not mere matters of interesting speculation. In general he allows those passages in the Bible which abhor violence to correct those which promote it, and rejects the notion of a 'holy war' and of any kind of violence which seeks justification in the biblical text (pars. 44-46).

Christians are accustomed to reading the Old Testament in the light of the Christian faith which derives from the paschal mystery of Christ. Under the influence of the Holy Spirit, they recognize in the New Testament the fulfilment of the Scriptures. While this modality of reading the Old Testament—seeking its 'spiritual sense'—reduces the impact of the more embarrassing traditions of the Old Testament with regard to occupation and war, it is not altogether satisfactory.

There are fundamental differences between the world view reflected in the writings of the New Testament and that within the forms of first-century Judaism about which we know something, and especially that perpetuated within Rabbinic Judaism, about which we know a great deal. In fundamental ways, the Christian vision cut itself adrift from Judaism. Paul and the author of the Letter to the Hebrews were in no doubt that the *Torah* had reached its end as a salvific legal system (cf. Gal. 2.15-5.1; Rom. 3.20-21; 6.14; Heb. 7.11-19; 10.8-9). Pagans admitted to the Christian Way were not to be required to observe all the requirements of the *Torah*, but were to find their salvation through faith in Jesus Christ. This is seen at its sharpest in the Christian redefinition of the fundamental biblical concepts of election and covenant (see Prior 1995a: 48-60, 141-48).

Although the allegorical method employed by the Fathers of the Church is very much out of vogue today, it represented one way of confronting texts which were scandalous. Another mode of dealing with the unacceptable elements in the biblical tradition is to assert that 'the Bible reflects a considerable moral development, which finds its completion in the New Testament'. The writings of the Old Testament contain certain 'imperfect and provisional' elements (*Dei Verbum* 15), which the divine pedagogy could not eliminate right away (Pontifical Biblical Commission 1993: 113-14). Predictably, the Church supplies another means of dealing with scandalous biblical texts. Let us examine how one liturgical tradition deals with the morally problematic land traditions of its Sacred Scriptures.

Liturgical 'Censoring' of the Word of God

Rather than confronting the issue of the moral unacceptability of some of the values reflected in some portions of the biblical narrative, there are more subtle ways of dealing with the problem. The preferred option in the Roman Catholic liturgy is to insist that the Bible is the Word of God in its entirety and in all its parts, while, at the same time, exercising a degree of ascesis in its liturgical use, the most solemn forum for the use of the Sacred Scriptures. This process can be seen in each of the main liturgies, the Mass (Eucharist) and the Liturgy of the Hours (*The Divine Office*).

The Liturgy of the Word at Mass
The New Roman Missal was promulgated by Pope Paul VI in 1970. The divine provenance of the Bible is reaffirmed:

> When the scriptures are read in the Church, God himself speaks to his people, and it is Christ, present in his word, who proclaims the Gospel (*The General Instruction of the Roman Missal*, par. 9)... In the readings, explained by the homily, God speaks to his people of redemption and salvation and nourishes their spirit; Christ is present among the faithful through his word (par. 33).

The guiding principles in the construction of the Lectionary are the 'harmony' between the Testaments and the centrality of Christ in salvation history. The new missal gives pride of place to the Gospel, with the readings for the Sunday Mass arranged in a triennial cycle, with a different synoptic gospel assigned to each year. The Old Testament reading is generally chosen to reflect the gospel reading, so that the Old Testament is presented as a *type*, whose promise is fulfilled in the New. The readings of the weekday Mass are in a biennial cycle, in which there is a semi-continuous reading from the books of the Old Testament, without respect to any theme suggested by the Gospel pericope of the day, or from a non-gospel text of the New Testament, followed by a semi-continuous reading from the gospels.

The amount of the Old Testament covered is modest. One notes the omission of great portions of the more problematic Old Testament narratives. In particular, when it comes to the land traditions of the Bible, 'the table of God's word' is rather bare. For example, although there are fourteen selections of readings from Genesis over the triennial Sunday cycle, the land traditions discussed in Chapter 1 are not used.

One sees a different device in operation in other texts, in the manner of selecting verses for use within the liturgy. For example, on the Third Sunday in Lent, Year C, the first reading is from Exodus 3, with the selected verses being 1-8 and 13-15. What will probably escape the worshipper, however, is that only the first half of v. 8 is used. The scene is that of Yahweh speaking to Moses on Mount Horeb:

> Then Yahweh said, '...I have come down to deliver them from the Egyptians, and to bring them up out of that land to a good and broad land, a land flowing with milk and honey, *to the country of the Canaanites, the Hittites, the Amorites, the Perizzites, the Hivites, and the Jebusites'* (Exod. 3.7-8).

However, v. 8b (italicized) is not read in the liturgical assembly, thereby eliminating any possibility that the readers might be perplexed by Yahweh's ethnocentrism.

It is surprising that the first reading of Mass on the 29th Sunday of Year C is from Exod. 17.8-13, which gives details of Israel's fight with Amalek at Rephidim. It includes,

> Whenever Moses held up his hand, Israel prevailed; and whenever he lowered his hand, Amalek prevailed...And Joshua defeated Amalek and his people with the sword (Exod. 17.11-13).

The Gospel reading of the day (Lk. 18.1-8), exhorting to persistence in prayer, is not enough to assuage one's chagrin. One might have hoped that the compilers of the lectionary would have found a less offensive choice of efficacious prayer from the Old Testament. Even the ever-resourceful Reginald Fuller is at a loss:

> It is puzzling to find this reading appointed for today...[it] does not appear to be particularly edifying. Despite the assurance of the second reading that 'all scripture is inspired by God and profitable for teaching'...It could be given a typological interpretation...If the preacher's exegetical conscience will permit him...he could expound the text typologically of Christ the heavenly priest interceding for his church militant on earth. Otherwise, he had better leave it alone (Fuller 1974: 77).[8]

The liturgical assembly is spared the most embarrassing readings by simply omitting them (e.g. Exod. 23.28-30). The Roman Lectionary has only six selections from Leviticus, and none includes the texts to

8.   Indeed Pseudo-Barnabas interpreted Moses' prayer with extended hands as a 'typos' of the Cross and the Crucified (12.2-3) (Simonetti 1994: 12).

which I drew attention in Chapter 1. There are only nine selections from the book of Numbers, and although the story of the returning spies, with its list of the inhabitants of the land, is read, the references to expelling them are not. The reading on Tuesday, Week 5 is from Num. 21.4-9. The preceding verses, 1-3, are not used. These record Israel's vow to Yahweh: '"If you will indeed give this people into our hands, then we will utterly destroy their towns"' (v. 2), which is followed by, 'Yahweh listened to the voice of Israel, and handed over the Canaanites; and they utterly destroyed them and their towns; so the place was called Hormah' (v. 3).

There are 18 selections from Deuteronomy. While Deut. 7.6-11, 'For you are a people holy to Yahweh...', is read on the Feast of the Sacred Heart, the preceding vv. 1-5 are not. These demand that the Israelites utterly destroy the seven nations which Yahweh will give over to them. Neither are the belligerent sections, Deut. 9, 12.29-30, 20.16-18, all of which promote ethnic cleansing as an act of piety, used in the liturgy.

There are only five selections from Joshua. The first, Josh. 3.7-11, 13-17 is used on Thursday of Week 19. Although it does record Joshua's message for the Israelites, promising that Yahweh will drive out the indigenous inhabitants, only one of the seven nations, the Canaanites, is named (v. 10). Moreover, the most striking accounts of the conquest, that of Jericho, and the campaigns in the south and the north, and the accounts of the fulfilment of the rules of the Holy War are not used in the Mass. In fact, the liturgical choice skips over the book from 5.12 to ch. 24, from which chapter there are three selections. In practice, then, church-going Catholics encounter virtually none of the land traditions which are offensive.

On an autobiographical note, some days after I had returned to Jerusalem from Amman, where I delivered a lecture on the land traditions of the Bible, I celebrated the Sunday Vigil Mass (28 Year A, on 12 October 1996) at Bethlehem University. Having traversed the Israeli checkpoint at Gilo, I joined the community. The first reading was from Isa. 25.6-10, which speaks so comfortingly of the eschatological banquet on the mountain of Yahweh. However, the liturgical reading stopped short at v. 10a, omitting, 'The Moabites shall be trodden down in their place as straw is trodden down in a dung-pit' (10b). However, the liturgical scalpel is not always so accommodating. Only some days earlier, after refusals at two different checkpoints, I arrived late at the university by a most circuitous route for the Mass of the Feast of Guardian Angels (2 October), which had already begun without my presidency. The first reading was from Exod. 23.20-23: 'I am going to send an angel in front of you, to guard you on the way and to bring you to the place that I have prepared, etc.' The Palestinian reader continued to the end of the liturgical pericope: 'I will be an enemy to your enemies and a foe to your foes. When my angel goes in front of you, and brings you to the Amorites, the Hittites, the Perizzites, the Canaanites, the Hivites, and the Jebusites, and I blot them out' (vv. 22b-23).[9]

The Liturgy of the Hours (the Divine Office)
In the Roman Catholic Church, all clerics are obliged to recite the *Liturgy of the Hours*, of which Morning Prayer and Evening Prayer are 'the two hinges'. Choosing one example at random, the following is the biblical diet for Morning Prayer of Saturday, Week 1. Imagine the scene in the chapel of a monastery. After the hymn, 'It were my soul's desire to see the face of God', the psalmody begins with Ps. 119.145-52, which is a plea of an individual for help. The particular fear of the psalmist is alluded to in the phrase, 'Those who harm me unjustly draw near.' Presumably to assure the petitioner that Yahweh is one who can deliver, an abridged version of the 'Hymn of Moses' after crossing the Sea of Reeds is sung next (Exod 15.1-27):

> Then Moses and the Israelites sang this song to Yahweh: 'I will sing to Yahweh, for he has triumphed gloriously; horse and rider he has thrown into the sea…Yahweh is a warrior; Yahweh is his name. Pharaoh's chariots and his army he cast into the sea…The floods covered them; they went down into the depths like a stone' (Exod. 15.1-5).

Perhaps to avoid upsetting sensitive stomachs before the monastic breakfast, vv. 6-8 are omitted. Perchance in the next verses, the monk can see a solution to his problem with 'those who harm me unjustly' drawing near:

> The enemy said, 'I will pursue, I will overtake, I will divide the spoil, my desire shall have its fill of them. I will draw my sword, my hand shall

9.   Somewhat intriguingly, the *Order of Prayer* for the Mass of the Feast of Guardian Angels of the Archdiocese of New York, used in Tantur, substitutes Job 9.1-12, 14-16 for the first reading from Exodus, and simply notes 'see Exod 23.20-23'.

destroy them.'...You stretched out your right hand, the earth swallowed them. In your steadfast love you led the people whom you redeemed; you guided them by your strength to your holy abode (Exod. 15.9-13).

Lest the monk be inclined to take pity on the enemy, the full implications of 'his deliverance' are hidden from him, with the omission of vv. 14-16:

The peoples heard, they trembled; pangs seized the inhabitants of Philistia. Then the chiefs of Edom were dismayed; trembling seized the leaders of Moab; all the inhabitants of Canaan melted away. Terror and dread fell upon them; by the might of your arm, they became still as a stone until your people, Yahweh, passed by, until the people whom you acquired passed by.

The canticle concludes with vv. 17-18, which would resonate with a monk champing at the bit to tend his flowerbed, or to plant trees on a mountain-side:

You brought them in and planted them on the mountain of your own possession, the place, Yahweh, that you made your abode, the sanctuary, Yahweh, that your hands have established. Yahweh will reign forever and ever.

Rather than follow on with the Song of Miriam and the account of the wandering in the wilderness of Shur for three days without water (Exod. 15.19-27), the canticle, like all psalms in the Catholic psalter, ends with, 'Glory be to the Father, and to the Son, and to the Holy Spirit.' Quickly, the celebration moves on to the final psalm of the Morning Prayer (Ps. 117). The remainder of the Morning Prayer consists of a short reading from the New Testament (2 Pet. 1.10-11), the singing of the Canticle of Zechariah (the *Benedictus*, Lk. 1.68-79), the intercessions and the concluding prayer. And then follows breakfast, undisturbed, one hopes, by thoughts of revenge against enemies.[10]

The *Liturgy of the Hours* uses the entire psalter, almost, but feels obliged to censor from the official prayer of the Church some 'offending' portions of the Word of God. This is the case with the three psalms, and those verses of other psalms which affront sensitive souls:

10. I recall reading a newspaper report some years ago that a monk had decapitated his religious superior while at the monastic table. The report, however, made no suggestion that the action was an example of applied hermeneutics.

> The psalms are distributed over a four-week cycle. In this cycle, a very
> small number of psalms are omitted...Three psalms are omitted from the
> current psalter because of their imprecatory character. These are Ps
> 57(58), Ps 82(83) and Ps 108(9). For similar reasons verses from several
> psalms are passed over...Such omissions are made because of certain
> psychological difficulties, even though the imprecatory psalms themselves
> may be found quoted in the New Testament, e.g., Rev 6.10, and in no
> way are intended as curses (*General Instruction on the Liturgy of the
> Hours*, pars. 126, 131).

When it comes to the land traditions of the Bible, then, one observes
that the liturgy deals with the problematic of divinely mandated ethnic
cleansing by a combination of omission of unsuitable narratives, or by
excision of offending verses. It insists that the Christian hermeneutical
key to the Old Testament lies in the estimation that the books of the
Old Testament pertain to and show forth their full meaning in the
New Testament, and that they shed light on it and explain it.[11] It
appears, then, that the worshipping community recognizes in practice
the difficulties which the land traditions of the Bible pose for faith and
Christian living. Since the Church's purpose in selecting readings
from the Scriptures is to enlighten and stimulate the faith of the community and invigorate its practice, one readily appreciates its prudence in overlooking those traditions which have provided theological
underpinning for various forms of colonialism, and which scandalize
most people today. One notes a corresponding ascesis in the use of the
Exodus paradigm among liberation theologians.

The Problem of the Exodus Paradigm

'Popular Bible reading' is the most profound and important work
done by the ecclesial base communities in Latin America (Richard
1990a: 211). Liberation theologians look on the Exodus story as a
paradigm for the liberation of their own people, and while their theology is criticized for stressing political aspects of the biblical witness,
its adoption of the Exodus paradigm is universally accepted.[12] As we

---

11. 'At the risk of oversimplifying somewhat, it may be broadly stated the sort of
prediction-fulfilment schema involved in the liturgical use of the OT texts does not
differ appreciably from much of the NT use of the OT...Obviously the NT profoundly transforms the literal understanding of the OT texts in using them' (Jensen
1988: 649).

12. Dupertuis is somewhat at a loss. While acknowledging the preferential position

shall see, its use of the narrative is selective and naive. In Berryman's archetype, after a sharing of responses to, 'What is God like?' 'Sister Elena' reads from Exod. 3.7-8:

> Then Yahweh said, 'I have observed the misery of my people who are in Egypt; I have heard their cry on account of their taskmasters. Indeed, I know their sufferings, and I have come down to deliver them from the Egyptians, and to bring them up out of that land to a good and broad land.'

After 'Sister Elena' has outlined the Exodus narrative, the people discuss what it means to say, 'God hears the cry of the oppressed people' and whether the message is still valid today. Significantly, in Berryman's account (1987: 39), the second half of v. 8 (italicized here) is omitted:

> a land flowing with milk and honey, *to the country of the Canaanites, the Hittites, the Amorites, the Perizzites, the Hivites, and the Jebusites.*

It appears that the villagers are encouraged to assume the fortunes of the liberated slaves, without being burdened with the guilt of dispossessing others. Berryman too omits the reference to 'the country of the Canaanites, etc.' in his reading from Exod. 3.7-8 (1987: 49).

Similarly, in his foundational work on liberation theology, Gutiérrez excludes the reference to the original inhabitants in his summary of Exod. 3.7-10. The Exodus event was,

> The breaking away from a situation of despoliation and misery and the beginning of the construction of a just and comradely society. It is the suppression of disorder and the creation of a new order (Gutiérrez 1988: 88).

Following a summary of a literalist reading of the Exodus narrative, clearly understanding it to be a record of what actually happened, Gutiérrez shifts to Isa. 42.5-7, as though the act of liberation from Egypt ended with such an idyllic scene:

> The God who makes the cosmos from chaos is the same God who leads Israel from alienation to liberation (Gutiérrez 1988: 89).

of the Exodus as a model for liberation, he shies away from any form of violence, even against the oppressor. 'The abiding symbol that comes to us from the Exodus is not a clenched fist, inviting to struggle and revolt, but rather a lamb that was slain, and blood "on the two doorposts"' (1982: 311). Indeed, Dupertuis himself seems to prefer the advice of Jeremiah to the exiles to pray for the welfare of Babylon etc.

Gutiérrez makes no reference to the plight of the indigenous inhabitants, whom, in the biblical legend, God reduces from order to chaos. Instead he invokes the support of André Neher who judges that,

> With the Exodus a new age has struck for humanity: redemption from misery. If the Exodus had not taken place, marked as it was by the twofold sign of the overriding will of God and the free and conscious assent of men, the historical destiny of humanity would have followed another course (in Gutiérrez 1988: 89-90).

The indigenous population of the narrative might well have hoped that another course had been followed.[13]

Berryman concludes that 'Exodus' is not simply an event, but a pattern of deliverance that provides a key for interpreting both the Scriptures and present experience (1987: 49). While traditionally the Bible is as a window through which one peeks out with curiosity, in the 'hermeneutic circle' of liberation biblical exegesis (from experience, to text, to experience) the base communities 'look at the Bible as in a mirror to see their own reality' (Frei Betto, in Berryman 1987: 60). In gazing into such a mirror they see their situation portrayed particularly in the Exodus legend, again read as history:

> Before it was an image or symbol that might be used like any other theological representation, the Exodus was an historical fact...It must be considered in terms of its historical reality before one attempts to speculate on its symbolic import (Fierro 1984: 476-77).

In this biblical paradigm they see the saving God of history at work both in the past and in the present, indicating the way to achieve full liberation, including political (Assmann 1976: 35).

Even James Cone, the father of Black Theology, falls into the trap of a partial reading of the Exodus motif. Although Cone is particularly sensitive to a reading of the Bible which sees it as a document giving preference to the poor, he never alludes to the destruction of

---

13. Pixley's liberation perspective on the Exodus (1983) also evades the problem of the violence associated with the Eisodus. He does not comment on the moral problem of the necessity of wiping out the indigenes in Exod. 3.8, and is silent on it in his comments on Exod. 33.1-3. The purity of the revolution seems to excuse the extermination of the natives in Exod. 34.11-15. Although he devotes a page to 'You shall not kill' (Exod. 20.13), he passes over the barbarous plunder of Exod. 23, and seems to excuse the slaughter of the 3000 kinspeople by the sons of Levi (Exod. 32.26-30) as the price of fidelity.

the people who pay the price for the liberation and settlement of the Israelites. His overview of the Old Testament is typical of that of Biblical Liberation Theology: the 'unanimous testimony [of the Old Testament is] to Yahweh's commitment to justice for the poor and the weak' (Cone 1974: 429). The God of the Bible, Cone continues, is deeply immersed in the affairs of the people of Israel, leading them from bondage in Egypt, and ending with his raising of Jesus from the dead. He is an active political God. God as liberator of the enslaved Israelites is at the heart of the confession of faith (Exod. 15.1-2; 19.4-5).

However, the real poor of the Exodus narrative, surely, are the ones forgotten in the victory, the Canaanites and others, who are pushed aside or exterminated by the religious zeal of the invading Israelites with God on their side. Cone's hermeneutical principle of reading the Bible in the light of the experience of black people cannot deliver him from the problem posed by the biblical legend (Cone 1975: 8). The Bible itself is not value-free, and in the Exodus narrative is disdainful of the rights of the indigenous people. One should not be satisfied, then, with interpreting black experience in the light of the Bible. Rather, one must allow black experience to interrogate the Bible, and expose those traditions which are fundamentally oppressive.

In the Palestinian context, Ateek protests against the use of the Exodus account as a paradigm for the establishment of the State of Israel. He regards the story of Naboth's vineyard (1 Kgs 21) as more promising and relevant to his people's concerns, in that it demonstrates God's unwavering concern for justice.[14] However, Ateek does not wish on the Israelis a retribution similar to that meted out to Ahab and Jezebel. Should the victims of oppression, such as Amerindians, black South Africans and Palestinians, not find themselves more naturally on the side of the Canaanites and others than on that of the

14. Ateek sees four Exodus paradigms: the first Exodus from Egypt; the second, the return from Babylon; the third, Luke's Transfiguration scene and the death-resurrection of Christ; and fourth, the picture in Revelation of the people of God coming out redeemed. If the Exodus paradigm is to be used, he pleads, one should move beyond the first Exodus. He points to four New Testament texts which 'de-Zionize' the Old Testament: Rom. 4.13 ('the promise that he would inherit the *kosmos* did not come to Abraham…'); Lk. 4.18-20's omission of Isa. 61.2's 'the day of vengeance'; the *Magnificat* (Lk. 1.46-55), and Jn 4.21's worship, neither on Gerizim nor Zion (Ateek Lecture and discussion, in Tantur Ecumenical Institute, 1996).

Chosen People, mandated to cleanse the land of its indigenes, a fate to which their own experience corresponds?

If people were not deprived of engagement with the second half of the Exodus paradigm, they would not escape morally unscathed from their communal encounter with the whole biblical paradigm. They would also see for themselves that the biblical text cannot be dealt with in such a partial fashion as is common among liberation theologians. *Pace* Gutiérrez and others, it is not the case that 'The entire Bible…mirrors God's predilection for the weak and abused of human history' (1988: xxvii). Combining the Exodus from Egypt with the Eisodus into the land of the Canaanites and others as the narrative requires, the biblical paradigm would more appropriately justify the behaviour of the *conquistadores*.

Many Puritan preachers in North America referred to Native Americans as Amalekites and Canaanites, who, if they refused to be converted were worthy of annihilation (see Cherry 1971). A Native American comments, 'As long as people believe in the Yahweh of deliverance, the world will not be safe from Yahweh the conqueror' (Warrior 1991: 294).

Without the spur of entering into the land of promise, the Israelites of the narrative would have languished in the desert, and would certainly have preferred reverting to the more tolerable life in Egypt. It is the entrance (Eisodus) into the land of milk and honey which is presented as keeping their hope alive: man does not live on manna and quails alone.[15]

Somewhat naively, if inadvertently accurately, the special Preface to the Eucharistic Prayer for the Catholic dioceses in the USA for Thanksgiving Day draws a parallel between the Israelite and European conquests:

> Once you chose a people and gave them a destiny and, when you brought them out of bondage to freedom, they carried with them the promise that

---

15. Michael Walzer's exegetical appetite also is exhausted simply by his comments on 'the land of milk and honey'. His mellifluous prose obscures the problem raised by the presence of the indigenes and the requirement of exterminating them in order to be a kingdom of priests and a holy nation (1985: 101-30). As the first description of revolutionary politics (p. 134), the book of Exodus provides the paradigm for political Zionism, with the Canaanites explicitly excluded from the world of moral concern (p. 142). Their extermination, gratefully, was effectively rescinded by talmudic and mediaeval commentators (pp. 143-44). See Said 1988.

all men would be blessed and all men could be free. What the prophets
pledged was fulfilled in Jesus Christ…It has come to pass in every generation…It happened to our fathers, who came to this land as if out of the
desert into a place of promise and hope…

It remains to be seen what long-term impact the reading of the expur-
gated Exodus paradigm will have on oppressed people, and how the
prevailing liberation hermeneutic faces up to the fact that some of the
major themes of the Bible are themselves exploitative. Indeed, the
Exodus–Eisodus motif is not a paradigm for liberation, but for colonial plunder. That is the plain sense of the biblical narrative, and the
way the text has been used.

Rehabilitating the Exodus
The problem has not gone unnoticed. A celebrated rabbinic tradition
presents a humane reaction to the problem of the destruction of the
Egyptian pursuers. God's ministering angels sought to rejoice after
the Israelites crossed the Sea of Reeds. But Yahweh asked, 'The work
of my hands has drowned in the sea and shall you chant songs?' and
says that he does not 'rejoice in the downfall of the wicked' (*b. Meg.*
10b; *b. Sanh.* 39b). Susan Niditch recounts how her grandfather
would participate in a sort of ritual wailing for the Egyptians in the
course of the ritual spilling of a drop of wine for each of the plagues
in the Passover seder. She attributes such sentiments to his

> …reaching out beyond the community of Israel to the community of
> humankind, bonded by Job-like experiences and the rocky relationships
> all of us share with the powerful forces of authority, familial, political and
> divine…The joy experienced in the liberation of one's own people, a vic-
> tory made possible by God's war against an oppressive tyrant, is tem-
> pered by sorrow for the enemy (Niditch 1993: 150).

Sentiment comes cheap. While it is understandable that the descendants
of the liberated slaves might even rejoice at the destruction of their
enemies, and take ghoulish pleasure in the sufferings of the
Egyptians—even to the extent of suggesting that the frogs castrated
them (*Exod. R.* 9.10)—to rejoice in the destruction of the innocent
indigenes is less condonable—even if, in the narrative, they were sin-
ning defilers. Nevertheless, when faced with suffering, senselessness,
absurdity and death, the notion of the promised land can function as a
very powerful symbol which sustains one in hope and inspires one to
action (Kwok 1995: 99-100). The promised land, however, must be

new, with a new Exodus and a new covenant, such as that spoken of by Second Isaiah (Isa. 55.2-13). Or, perhaps, one may add, that spoken of by Jesus.

From Jerusalem to Rome

As we have seen, the applied exegesis of some biblical narratives raises the question of the traditional role of the Bible as a source of moral inspiration. The ideals of divine revelation, read within the context of conventional colonial enterprises, do not come up to the standards required by human rights and acceptable international behaviour. The humiliation and destruction of indigenes is not morally acceptable, and surely is not in accordance with the divine will.

Every effort must be made to extricate interpretative communities from a literalist rendering of the biblical land traditions and the consequences to which such understandings of the text have led. The Christian Church reads the Old Testament in the light of the death and resurrection of Jesus Christ. The ministry of Jesus is considered to have been 'foreshadowed', 'adumbrated' or even 'foretold' in the Old Testament (Lk. 24.44). A christological and messianic interpretation of the Old Testament allows these books to show forth their full meaning in the New Testament (*Dei Verbum*, pars. 15-16).

The Promised Land

Several elements in the New Testament indicate a reaction to the territorialization of God's promise, and there is a tendency to eschatologize the theme of land. Paul, the diaspora Jewish Christian writes, 'our citizenship is in heaven' (Phil. 3.20). The gift of land is not explicitly mentioned among the attributes of his 'kindred according to the flesh' (Rom. 9.4). The anonymous author of the Letter to the Hebrews speaks of a new heaven and a new earth and of a rest not yet attained (11.13-15). The lack of interest in territoriality is reflected also in the notion of the new, heavenly, rather than the familiar, terrestrial Jerusalem. The Letter to the Hebrews contrasts the traditional modes of access to God provided by recurring Jewish ritual with the once-for-all atoning act of the death of Jesus. Just as the ritual of the Old Testament was superseded by the salvific death of Jesus, so the earthly Jerusalem yielded to the new, heavenly city (Heb. 12.22). Moreover, it is only the heavenly city which features in the book of

Revelation (Rev. 3.12; 21.2, 10). The contrast between the earthly and heavenly cities is reflected also in Paul's Letter to the Galatians (4.25-26).

In the Christian dispensation, the promise of *the new earth* extends, supersedes, completes or brings to its fruition the earlier promise of a bounded land. God's promises now involve the whole earth, indeed a *new heaven and a new earth*, which is available to all without distinction of race, nation or language. This vision, according to Christian claims, is the promised inheritance of those who are disciples of Jesus the Messiah, and especially those who are poor, exploited, etc. For those imbued with Christian hope, reversion to the initial promise as outlined in the Pentateuch does not mark an advance in the teleology of salvation and human destiny.

The promise of a *new creation* lifts up the eyes of believers from the earth. The early Church was attracted by the landlessness reflected in Noah's ark. In the Christian dispensation, Jesus Christ, who himself did not have the whereupon even to lay his head (Mt. 8.20), does not promise salvation in terms of possession of a particular territory, but invites the creation of a community of faith, hope and love engaged in the worship of God, 'neither on this mountain, nor in Jerusalem' (Jn 4.21). For the people of the New Covenant, salvation does not lie in any earthly security, not even that provided by Jerusalem itself (Acts 1.8).

Election and Covenant
There are fundamental differences between the world view reflected in the writings of the New Testament and that perpetuated within Rabbinic Judaism. This distinction is seen at its sharpest in the Christian redefinition of the fundamental biblical concepts of election and covenant. In the Christian dispensation, the Good News of God's care for his Chosen Ones is expanded beyond the categories established by racial, ethnic or national distinctions (Rev. 7.9). According to the Acts of the Apostles, Peter had a vision in prayer, through which he learned that the distinction between unclean and clean animals was void, which discovery he carried over to annul distinctions made on ethnic categories (Acts 10.28-35).

The universal appeal of the Christian vision can be comprehended from a number of New Testament texts. While for Christians, Jerusalem is the city in which the Church was born, the Christian dynamic demands movement away from it to *the ends of the earth*. This is seen nowhere more clearly than in Luke–Acts.[16] The climactic account of the resurrection appearance in Lk. 24.44-49 and its echo in Acts 1.3-8 synthesizes Luke's account of the ministry of Jesus and propels his readers forward into the continuation of that mission in the Church, a mission beginning in Jerusalem, but destined for the ends of the earth: 'Stay in the city, until you are clothed with power from on high' (Lk. 24.49); 'You shall receive power when the Holy Spirit has come upon you; and you shall be my witnesses in Jerusalem and in all Judea and Samaria and to the end of the earth' (Acts 1.8). In both Lk. 24.49 and Acts 1.8 the witness to Jesus will begin in Jerusalem and be carried forward into all Judea and Samaria, and finally to the end of the earth (see Prior 1995a: 24-25; 52-60). Christianity in Luke's view, then, is not tied to any specific land—its mission is to *the ends of the earth*.

From the perspective of the author of Luke–Acts, the New Order ushered in by Jesus expands the perceived horizons of God's care by moving beyond ethnic and religious categories, *from Jerusalem to the ends of the earth*. The Lukan Jesus' challenge to the prevailing view of election and covenant is seen in the programmatic text outlining the visit of Jesus to the synagogue in Nazareth, in which he gives a revolutionary interpretation of Isaiah 61 and the doctrine of election. The good news of Isaiah 61, originally directed at the consolation of the returned exiles from Babylon, is transposed into good news for all who are oppressed. The Isaiah 61 text as recorded by Luke is free of its references to that exclusiveness which is a feature of ethnicity and 'nationalism'. The Lukan Jesus' radical critique of the notion of God's choice of one people is intensified by his appeal to the Gentile overtures of Elijah and Elisha (see Prior 1995a: 141, 147-48). The New Order of Election (see Prior 1995a: 48-60) is brought about by the power of God which is for everyone who has faith—for the Jew first, but also for the Greek (Rom. 1.16—see Prior 1989: 125-39). This new revelation required Paul to reinterpret his Jewish heritage: his kinsfolk, previously exclusively by natural descent (Rom. 9.4-5) is expanded to include both Jew and Greek (Rom. 10.12; see Rom. 10.1; 11.25-26).

16. See also the scene on the Galilee mountain in Mt. 28.16-20, where as the climax of his Gospel, Matthew has the injunction of the Risen Jesus to make disciples of *all* nations.

As we have seen, the biblical claim of the divine promise of land is integrally linked with the claim of divine approval for the extermination of the indigenous people. It is assumed widely that its literary genre is history, even though this view runs in the face of all serious scholarly comment. These land traditions pose fundamental moral questions, relating to one's understanding of the nature of God, of his dealings with humankind and of human behaviour. They have been deployed in support of barbaric behaviour in a wide variety of contexts, for close on 2000 years. The communities which have preserved and promulgated those biblical traditions, then, must shoulder some of the responsibility for what has been done in alleged conformity with the values contained within them (Chapter 1).

The behaviour of communities and nation states is complex, and is rarely the result of one element of motivation. Colonialist and imperialist enterprises derive from a matrix of interactive determinants. The colonization of Latin America in the mediaeval period had a devastating effect on the indigenous population, the consequences of which perdure to this day. Although it was fuelled by a concurrence of motivations, mediaeval Christian theocratic imperialism was a major element of its ideological justification. Its ideological underpinning was traced back to biblical paradigms of 'ethnic cleansing' and 'belligerent settler colonialism', the legitimization of which had the authority of Sacred Scripture (Chapter 2).

Although the primary motivation of the Dutch colonizers who trekked from the Cape was economic and social, subsequent ideologues of a fabricated Afrikaner nationalism erected an ideological structure of Christian nationalism which had the biblical paradigm of settler colonialism at its foundation. The pattern of 'separation' and 'separate development' was justified by the prevailing Christian theologians, who traced its moral justification to the alleged behaviour of the Israelites in the pre-conquest and settlement periods. Although *apartheid* became a term that evoked virtually universal opprobrium, it was deployed within an ideological framework which derived from a particular form of Christian nationalism which looked to the biblical paradigm as its ultimate, Godly-assured justification. Although its durability proved to be very limited, *apartheid* wreaked havoc on the indigenous people, leaving South Africa with the greatest recorded inequality of any country of the world.

Political Zionism appealed to a range of factors to warrant its form of settler colonialism. Although it was resisted by most religious Jews from the beginning, it was able to exploit, somewhat cynically given the non- and anti-religious dispositions of its proponents, an appeal to God's gift of the land, as narrated in the *Torah-from-Heaven*: Zionism could rest its case on the source of all authority. As we have seen, the realization of the 'Zionist dream' has been an unmitigated nightmare for the indigenous population of Palestine (Chapter 4).

Although each enactment of the colonial enterprise has its own distinctive qualities, there are common elements by which virtually all colonial endeavours struggle to justify themselves. Invariably these include assertions of superiority over the natives and the pretence of endowing them with the fruits of a superior order—being 'outposts of progress' in 'the heart of darkness'. In the colonial ventures that emanated out of Europe, the motivation customarily had a strong religious element, and looked to the biblical paradigm for irreproachable authorization. South African Calvinists have repudiated and repented for their use of the biblical legend to justify their treatment of the blacks and coloureds. The descendants of mediaeval Spanish and Portuguese colonialists and their victims struggle to repair some of the devastation whose effects perdure.

The situation with respect to Israel–Palestine is unique. The application of a literalist reading of the biblical mandate appears to be more apposite for Jews than for others who appeal to it to justify land occupation. The predicament is particularly poignant in virtue of the Nazi determination to annihilate Jews and Judaism. However, the victims of Auschwitz would hardly approve of a previously oppressed people now oppressing an innocent third party and exacting as the price of its own liberation the permanent dispossession and servitude of the other: 'The victims of Auschwitz would never have bombed Beirut' (Timerman 1984: 7). There is little indication that Zionism will reverse the spoliation it has caused, or will be checked in its exploitative intentions.

Uniquely in the discourse of colonialist enterprises, Zionists not only protest their innocence, but, even while perpetrating the comprehensive oppression of another people, they retain the psychology of victims, and even blame the victims. No less uniquely, Zionism has managed to retain the support of much of the West, at least until recently. Instead of engaging in an ongoing critique of Zionism's reduction of the ideals of Judaism to those portions of its tradition that betray a narrow and exclusivist concept of a tribal god, some Christians, especially those involved in the Jewish–Christian dialogue, accept as a compulsory part of the dialogue the obligation to support unconditionally an unrestrained and militant Zionism, as if it were the sole authentic expression of Judaism. Meanwhile, without the critical solidarity of the Western 'Christian' world, whose conscience has been crippled in the wake of the Holocaust, the behaviour of the State of Israel towards the Palestinians has earned widespread international criticism, and is a cause of great distress among many people, including of course many Jews, albeit virtually entirely from the secular camp. *Torah*-driven zealotry is at the forefront of the oppression of the indigenous Palestinians (Chapter 5).

Recent scholarship on Israel's origins challenges profoundly many of the 'givens' of previous discourse. Literary and historical investigation has convinced virtually all scholars that the genre of the patriarchal, pentateuchal and conquest–settlement narratives is not history, but is part of the fabricated myth of origins in the process of 'nation'-building in the wake of the Babylonian exile, and perhaps later in the Persian period. In that light, it is injudicious to conclude that God made the promise of progeny and land to Abraham after the fashion indicated in Genesis 15, and that the occupation took place as described in Joshua 1–12. No critical biblical scholar regards the account in Joshua as reflecting what actually happened prior to the establishment of the Israelites as a 'national' group. The archaeological evidence suggests a sequence of periods marked by a gradual and peaceful coalescence of disparate peoples into a group whose achievement of a new sense of unity culminated only with the entry of the Assyrian administration. The biblical narratives are literary compositions which refract the unknown details of an unrecoverable historical past and serve them up in a series of legends, epics and myths of 'national' origins, which are deployed in a new social, political, and particularly religious context. The authors of these compositions, which, at a minimum, come from a period of not less than 500 years after the 'events' had no intention of using them as justification for the extermination of 'Others'.

Moreover, notions of a strictly linear ethnic descent from (a legendary) Abraham to today's Ukrainian Jewish emigrants to Israel are illusory. Historical sources do not allow us to differentiate between 'Israelites' and 'Canaanites', and they point to Israelite origins within the land rather than outside it as the biblical narrative insists. Moreover, the variety of people in Palestine at the time of the so-called Israelite settlement, and later included within the 'people of Israel' during the creation of the regional kingdoms of Israel and Judah, coupled with the effects of the population transfer and replacement by the Assyrian, Babylonian and Persian empires preclude the common assumption that one is dealing with a homogeneous 'people of Israel', ethnically, culturally and religiously one at all periods (Chapter 6).

The presumption that the biblical paradigm of land possession portrayed at one period has an automatic currency for quite a different one, whether in mediaeval Latin America, or nineteenth–twentieth-century Afrikaner and Zionist nationalism is not sustainable. Moreover, it is not without irony that the Bible, and its use as a legitimating document for the colonial ventures we have discussed, is applied against the interests of peoples for whom the biblical text had no corresponding authority. The very application by outsiders, Christian and Jewish, of the world view of the Bible to a people for whom it had no authoritative standing is a striking example of religious and political imperialism.[1]

Against the background of even some knowledge of the consequences of colonization for indigenous populations, biblical scholarship has been modest in its concern for the moral dimension of the

---

1. The pre-colonial inhabitants of southern Africa were not literate, and the peoples of Latin America had their own highly sophisticated systems of religion. In 1914 Palestine, three years before the British conquest, the population of the area was 757,182, with 590,890 (78 per cent) Muslim, 83,794 (11 per cent) Jewish and 73,024 (9.6 per cent) Christian (Abu-Lughod 1987: 142). Today, 98 per cent of the Palestinian population within the areas controlled by Israel are Muslims, for whom the biblical text, in the strict sense, is outside their religious and cultural framework.

problematic. Since virtually all of the scholarship has been done since the establishment of the State of Israel in 1948, and most of it since 1967, the achievement of biblical scholarship, when judged by its concern for the indigenous people and the values enshrined in international law and conventions on human rights is not impressive. The support that these colonizing activities have acquired from theological and exegetical assertions from within academic and religious circles, Jewish and Christian, is not a legacy I am proud to bequeath to the next generation of exegetes and religious. Such support in my generation will elicit condemnation and repudiation from future generations, in a manner corresponding to the way other forms of theocratic colonialisms have been rejected. Ultimately, and probably soon, other traditions within Judaism and Christianity will achieve enough support to ensure that Judaism will not be condemned forever to those forms of theocratic imperialism which receive support from only the more disreputable traditions of the Bible, and from those forms of Jewish and Christian eschatology that are scandalous to even secular humankind.

The ongoing identification in subsequent history with the warring scenes of the Hebrew Bible is a burden the biblical tradition must bear. The fact that the particular violence of the Hebrew Scriptures has inspired violence, and has served as a model of, and for persecution, subjugation and extermination for millennia beyond its own reality makes investigation of these biblical traditions a critical and important task (cf. Niditch 1993: 4). Nevertheless, the ethnocentric, xenophobic and militaristic character of the biblical fabricated myths of origins is treated in conventional biblical scholarship as if it were above any questioning on moral grounds, even by criteria derived from other parts of the Bible. Most commentators are uninfluenced by considerations of human rights, when these conflict with a naive reading of the sacred text, and appear to be unperturbed by its advocacy of plunder, murder and the exploitation of indigenous peoples, all under the guise of fidelity to the eternal validity of the Sinaitic covenant. Meanwhile, a God who insists on the destruction of people as an act of devotion to him is one from whom most decent people should recoil. The biblical doctrines of God's Chosen People and Promised Land assume a problematic character when viewed against the colonialist exploitation of them leading to the exspoliation of the indigenous peoples of Latin America, the humiliation of non-whites in

South Africa and, in our own day, to militaristic and xenophobic Zionism, which undermines the integrity of Judaism, embarrasses and shocks most moral people and wreaks havoc on an innocent third party. Christians have long abandoned circumcision, the killing of adulterers and other details of the *Torah* as essential expressions of fidelity to the progressive revelation of God.

'There is no document of civilization which is not at the same time a document of barbarism' (Benjamin 1973: 258). Biblical scholars have the most serious obligation to prevent outrages being perpetrated in the name of fidelity to the biblical covenant. The application of the Bible in defence of the Crusades, Spanish and Portuguese colonialism, South African apartheid and political Zionism has been a calamity, leading to the suffering and humiliation of millions of people, and to the loss of respect for the Bible as having something significant to contribute to humanity. Christians caught up in an uncritical approach to the Old Testament may seek refuge in the claim that the problem lies with the predispositions of the modern reader, rather than with the text itself. *Pace* Deist (1994: 28-29) and others, one cannot escape so easily. One must acknowledge that much of the *Torah*, and the book of Deuteronomy in particular, contains menacing ideologies and racist, xenophobic and militaristic tendencies, and is dangerous when read without respect for its literary genre and the circumstances of its composition.[2] The moral problem stems from the nature of some of the material of the Bible itself. As Niditch has shown, there is a variety of war traditions in the Bible—she discusses seven—which involve overlap and self-contradiction (1993: 154). The implications of the existence of dubious moral dispositions, presented as mandated by the divinity within a book that is canonized as Sacred Scripture invites the most serious investigation (Chapter 7).

However, a solution to the historical problem of Israelite origins does not eliminate the problem posed by the literary narrative. It is

2. *Pace* President Clinton, on the night before the White House signing of the Declaration of Principles (13 September 1993), the book of Joshua is not the best distraction for a person transfixed between wakefulness and sleep. Neither, *pace* Baruch Goldstein, should the book of Esther be accorded a favoured place in the search for moral exhortation. Hotel managers may need to censor their Gideon Bibles, lest their clients be driven to appalling behaviour in the wake of sleepless nights spent reading some of the more racist, xenophobic and militaristic traditions within the biblical text.

the narrative itself, rather than the sophisticated exegesis of it, that has fuelled colonial adventures. While early Israelite history belongs to the unrecoverable past, the biblical narrative perdures as an instrument of oppression. In the narrative, the entry into a land already occupied by others, followed by not only the warrant to violate the rights of the indigenes, but by the divine mandate to do so, becomes the climax of the liberation to be celebrated. What the narrative requires would be designated war-crimes and crimes against humanity according to modern secular standards of human and political rights. While the results of literary and archaeological investigation of the biblical narrative of Israelite origins, even at this stage, might be very welcome to the Amerindians, the southern African blacks and the Palestinians, they would be judged to have come rather too late on the scene.

However, while the investigation of the nature and period of composition of the biblical narrative is illuminating in its own right, it is the finished composition that has been accorded canonical status, reflecting its divine provenance. The biblical text has been accorded a position of foundational significance, whether in the Synagogue or the Church, and even, by extension, in the lecture-hall and the 'marketplace'. The Bible has enjoyed and retains a level of authority in much of the globe which is matched only by the Sacred Scriptures of other traditions. The divine provenance accorded it in all its parts, whether by the claim that it comes from heaven (*Torah min-haShamayim*), or as the Word of God (*Dei Verbum*), raises significant moral problems, which I have addressed here (Chapter 7). In confronting those traditions that appear to conflict with either one's own humane values, or that appear to contradict a whole range of other traditions, including many within the biblical text itself, one is engaged in a hermeneutical activity of considerable sophistication.

For much of the period of Christendom, Christian Theology—of which the study of the Bible is the soul—has enjoyed the status of 'queen of the sciences'. Increasingly since the Enlightenment and the scientific revolution, it has had to settle for a somewhat eccentric position on the periphery of Western culture, and now aspires to acquire a more modest position within the complex of human discourse. Precisely because of the tragedies that have shocked civilization in this century (two great wars, a list of partially completed genocides, wide availability of weaponry of awesome powers of destruction, etc.), there is wide agreement on questions of human rights, and a sensitivity to the need to curtail the excesses of belliger- ence. Although many of the conventions are respected more convinc- ingly at the level of rhetoric rather than in practice, they serve as benchmarks against which to measure moral behaviour. By such stan- dards, the biblical traditions we have examined here fall embarrass- ingly short.

While the scholastic community has provided 'rich and suggestive studies on the "land theme" in the Bible...they characteristically stop before they get to the hard part, contemporary issues of land in the Holy Land' (Brueggemann, in March 1994: vii). The preferred mode for dealing with the embarrassing traditions of the Bible in one major Christian tradition is by a combination of evasion of the offending traditions (that is, excluding them altogether from the lectionary and the *Divine Office*), and, where such texts contain edifying elements, of excising from the public liturgy those portions of the Word of God that would perplex worshippers sensitive to the ideals of human rights and international legality. Christian Theology and the Christian Church should confront the moral questions which I have considered here. The problem is no less acute for Jewish Theology and Judaism. I deem the present work to be an exploration into terrain virtually devoid of enquirers, and an attempt to map out some of the contours of that terrain. It does not pretend to have all the answers, but it does reflect the author's dissatisfaction with the prevailing scholastic assess- ments of the matter, especially the most common ones, which prefer the security of silence to risking the opprobrium of speaking out.

This study has moved beyond the conventional exegetical approaches, and attempted to subject the biblical narrative to a *moral- literary analysis*. Rather than provide an exegesis that removes itself from the social, political and moral context, it responds to Erich Auerbach's appeal to reunify the secular and the religious critical tradition, a task he undertook so tellingly in his *Mimesis* (1946, ET 1953). This study on the link between the Bible and colonialism is a work of applied biblical exegesis which is distinctive in its concern for morality and acceptable human behaviour. It is not simply a protest at the neglect of the moral question in Euro-American biblical herme- neutics, but is also an attempt to rescue the Bible from being a blunt instrument in the oppression of people. I trust that my conscientious probings into a web of immensely complicated issues, within and between conventionally disparate discourses, will encourage others to attempt to deal with the substantial issues I raise. I hope that my work contributes to a rise of moral indignation at what has been perpetrated on indigenous peoples by colonizers, with the support of the biblical paradigm of alleged settler colonization at the behest of the divinity. It is my hope that my enterprise will promote a discourse that questions present assumptions. It invites comment on the 'value of our values', and in particular on the problematic of the bloodshed that was justified by the piety of the 'good'. My study has a diagnostic function. It uncovers layers below the surface and names them. The intent is not only diagnostic, however, but aspires also to being recuperative, since I contend that the biblical texts have a specific value, and should not be deployed in ways that offend the basic, decent values of a culture most of us hope to create. I have indicated the lines along which the future discussion may run (Chapter 7). It will need to provide a more credible notion of the Bible as the Word of God, of Divine Inspiration, and of the Authority of Sacred Scripture. For no other reason, then, a scholar of the Bible must not be satisfied with an unearthing of the past, but must enquire into its significance and place in contemporary society.

> They were conquerors, and for that you want only brute force—nothing to boast of, when you have it, since your strength is just an accident arising from the weakness of others. They grabbed what they could get for the sake of what was to be got. It was just robbery with violence, aggravated murder on a great scale, and men going at it blind—as is very proper for those who tackle a darkness. The conquest of the earth, which mostly means the taking it away from those who have a different complexion or slightly flatter noses than ourselves, is not a pretty thing when you look into it too much. What redeems it is the idea only. An idea at the back of it; not a sentimental pretence but an idea; and an unselfish belief in the idea—something you can set up, and bow down before, and offer a sacrifice to (Marlow, in Joseph Conrad's *Heart of Darkness*).

Biblical scholarship must set its own house in order by articulating ethical criteria by which dispositions unworthy of a civilized person may not be accorded a privileged place as part of a sacred text. When the sacred pages are manipulated by forces of oppression, biblical scholars cannot continue to seek refuge by expending virtually all their intellectual energies on an unrecoverable past, thereby releasing themselves from the obligation of engaging in contemporary discourse. Nor are they justified in maintaining an academic detachment from significant engagement in real, contemporary issues. While it may be conceded by some that 'social and political action is not the direct task of the exegete' (Pontifical Biblical Commission 1993: 68), I can think of no circumstance in which such activity is not incumbent on a Christian exegete, *qua* Christian.

I wouldn't quite express it in these terms.

BIBLIOGRAPHY

Abu Lughod, Ibrahim (ed.)
   1982   *Palestine Rights: Affirmation and Denial* (Milwette, IL: Medina).
   1987   *The Transformation of Palestine: Essays on the Origin and Development of the Arab-Israeli Conflict* (Evanston: Northwestern University Press, 2nd edn).

Abu Lughod, Janet
   1987   'The Demographic Transformation of Palestine', in I. Abu Lughod 1987: 139-63.

Adams, Michael, and Christopher Mayhew
   1975   *Publish it not...: The Middle East Cover-Up* (repr.; London: Longman).

Adler, Marcus N.
   1894   'Jewish Pilgrims to Palestine', in *Palestine Exploration Fund Quarterly Statement*, October: 288-300.

Aharoni, Yohanan
   1979   *The Land of the Bible: A Historical Geography* (Philadelphia: Westminster Press, rev. edn).

Ahlström, Goesta W.
   1986   *Who Were the Israelites?* (Winona Lake: Eisenbrauns).
   1993   *The History of Ancient Palestine from the Palaeolithic Period to Alexander's Conquest* (JSOTSup, 146; Sheffield: Sheffield Academic Press).

Al-Haq
   1983   *In their Own Words: Human Rights Violations in the West Bank* (Geneva: World Council of Churches).

Albright, William F.
   1935   'Archaeology and the Date of the Hebrew Conquest of Palestine', *Bulletin of the American Schools of Oriental Research* 58: 10-18.
   1939   'The Israelite Conquest of Canaan in the Light of Archaeology', *Bulletin of the American Schools of Oriental Research* 74: 11-23.
   1942   'Why the Near East needs the Jews', *New Palestine* 32 (9): 12-13.
   1957   *From the Stone Age to Christianity: Monotheism and the Historical Process* (New York: Doubleday).
   1973   'From the Patriarchs to Moses. 1. From Abraham to Joseph', *Biblical Archaeologist* 36: 5-33.

Aldeeb, Sami.
   1992   *Discriminations contre les non-juifs tant chrétien que musulmans en Israël* (Lausanne: Pax Christi).

Alfaro, J. I.
1978   'The Land—Stewardship', *Biblical Theology Bulletin*, 8: 51-61.
Alt, Albrecht
1953a   'Josua', in *Kleine Schriften zur Geschichte des Volkes Israel* (Munich:
          Beck [1936]), I: 176-92.
1953b   'Erwägungen über die Landnahme der Israeliten in Palästina', in
          Kleine Schriften zur Geschichte des Volkes Israel (Munich: Beck
          [1939]), I: 126-75.
1966   'The Settlement of the Israelites in Palestine', in *Essays on Old
          Testament History and Religion* (Oxford: Basil Blackwell [1925]):
          135-69.
1989   'The God of the Fathers', in *Essays on Old Testament History and
          Religion* (The Biblical Seminar; Sheffield: JSOT Press [ET of orig.
          German of 1929]): 1-77.
Alter, Robert, and Frank Kermode
1987   *The Literary Guide to the Bible* (London: Collins, Fontana Press).
Amnesty International.
1979   *Report and Recommendation of an Amnesty International Mission to
          the Government of the State of Israel, 3–7 June 1979* (London:
          Amnesty International).
1988   *Israel and the Occupied Territories—Excessive Force: Beatings to
          Maintain Law and Order* (London: Amnesty International).
Anderson, Benedict
1991   *Imagined Communities: Reflections on the Origin and Spread of
          Nationalism* (London/New York: Verso).
Are, Thomas L.
1994   *Israeli Peace/Palestinian Justice: Liberation Theology and the Peace
          Process* (Regina, SK: Clarity).
Arendt, Hannah (ed.)
1973   *Illuminations* (London: Collins).
Ariel, Yaakov
1992   'In the Shadow of the Millennium: American Fundamentalists and the
          Jewish People', in *Christianity and Judaism: Studies in Church History*
          (ed. Diana Wood; Oxford: Blackwell), XXIX: 435-50.
Arizpe, Lourdes
1988   'Anthropology in Latin America: Old Boundaries, New Contexts', in
          Mitchell 1988: 143-61.
Aronoff, Myron J.
1985   'The Institutionalisation and Cooptation of a Charismatic, Messianic,
          Religious-Political Revitalisation Movement', in Newman 1985: 46-69.
Aronson, Gaza
1987   *Creating Facts: Israel, Palestinians and the West Bank* (Washington:
          Institute for Palestine Studies).
Assmann, Hugo
1976   *Theology for a Nomad Church* (Maryknoll, NY: Orbis Books).
Ateek, Naim Stifan
1989   *Justice and Only Justice: A Palestinian Theology of Liberation*
          (Maryknoll, NY: Orbis Books).

1991   'A Palestinian Perspective: The Bible and Liberation', in Sugirtharajah
              1991: 280-86.
Ateek, Naim Stifan, M.H. Ellis and R.R. Ruether (eds.)
1992   *Faith and the Intifada: Palestinian Christian Voice* (Maryknoll, NY:
              Orbis Books).
Auerbach, Erich
1957   *Mimesis: The Representation of Reality in Western Literature* (New
              York: Doubleday).
Avineri, Schlomo
1981   *The Making of Modern Zionism: The Intellectual Origins of the Jewish
              State* (New York: Basic Books).
Bainton, Roland H.
1960   *Christian Attitudes toward War and Peace* (Nashville: Abingdon
              Press).
Barr, James
1993   *Biblical Faith and Natural Theology: The Gifford Lectures for 1991*
              (Oxford: Clarendon Press).
Barraclough, Geoffrey, and Michael Burns
1979   *Main Trends in History* (New York: Holmes & Meier).
Bartlett, John R.
1989   *Edom and the Edomites* (JSOTSup, 24; Sheffield: Sheffield Academic
              Press).
1990   *The Bible: Faith and Evidence: A Critical Enquiry into the Nature of
              Biblical History* (London: British Museum Publications).
Bastide, Roger
1972   *African Civilisation in the New World* (New York: Harper & Row).
Baum, Gregory
1988   'The Church, Israel and the Palestinians', *The Ecumenist,* November–
              December: 1-6.
Bax, Douglas
1983   'The Bible and Apartheid 2', in De Gruchy and Villa-Vicencio 1983:
              112-43.
Beasley-Murray, G.R.
1986   *Jesus and the Kingdom of God* (Exeter: Paternoster; Grand Rapids:
              Eerdmans).
Beck, Mordechai
1994   'Inconsistent Prophet of the High Ground', *Jewish Chronicle*, August
              26: 23.
Bein, Alex
1961   'Von der Zionsehnsucht', in *Robert Weltsch zum Geburtstag* (Tel
              Aviv: Irgun Olej Merkas Europa).
Beit-Hallahmi, Benjamin
1987   *The Israel Connection: Who Israel Arms and Why* (New York:
              Pantheon Books).
Ben-Gurion, David
1971–72   *Zichronot* (Memoirs), vol. III (Tel Aviv: 'Am 'Oved).
1971   *A Personal History of Israel* (New York: Funk & Wagnalls; Tel Aviv:
              Sabra Books).

1972   *Ben-Gurion Looks at the Bible* (trans. Jonathan Kolatch; London: W.H. Allen).

Benjamin, Walter
1973   'Theses on the Philosophy of History', in Arendt 1973: 253-64.

Bennett, C.-M.
1983   'Excavations at Buseirah (Biblical Bozrah)', in Sawyer and Clines 1983: 9-17.

Benvenisti, Meron
1984   *The West Bank Data Project: A Survey of Israel's Policies* (Washington, DC: American Enterprise Institute of Public Policy Research).
1986   *The West Bank Handbook: A Political Lexicon* (Jerusalem: Jerusalem Post).

Benvenisti, Meron, and Shlomo Khayat
1988   *The West Bank and Gaza Atlas* (Jerusalem: The West Bank Data Base Project).

Ben-Yehuda, Nachman.
1995   *The Masada Myth: Collective Memory and Mythmaking in Israel* (Wisconsin: University of Wisconsin Press).

Beozzo, José Oscar
1990   'Humiliated and Exploited Natives', in Boff and Elizondo 1990: 78-89.

Bermant, Chaim
1994   'Rabbi's Blinkers and Professor's Vision', *Jewish Chronicle*, 26 August: 21.

Berryman, Philip
1987   *Liberation Theology: Essential Facts about the Revolutionary Movement in Latin America and Beyond* (London: Tauris).

Bezuidenhout, C.P.
1883   *De geschiedenis van het afrikaansch geslacht van 1688 tot 1882* (Bloemfontein).

Bickerman, E.J.
1984   'The Babylonian Captivity', in W.D. Davies and L. Finkelstein (eds.), *The Cambridge History of Judaism* (Cambridge: Cambridge University Press), I: 342-58.

Bimson, John, and David Livingston
1987   'Redating the Exodus', *Biblical Archaeology Review* 13: 40-53, 66-68.

Blackstone, William E.
1908   *Jesus Is Coming* (New York: Fleming Revel, 3rd edn [1978]).

Bloomberg, Charles
1990   *Christian-Nationalism and the Rise of the Afrikaner Broederbond in South Africa, 1918–48* (London: Macmillan).

Blum, Erhard
1990   *Studien zur Komposition des Pentateuchs* (Beihefte zur Zeitschrift für die altestamentliche Wissenschaft, 189; Berlin/New York: de Gruyter).

Boesak, Allan
1976   *Farewell to Innocence: A Socio-Ethical Study on Black Theology*
            (Kampen: Kok).
1979   *The Finger of God: Sermons on Faith and Socio-Political
            Responsibility* (Maryknoll, NY: Orbis Books).
1984   *Black and Reformed: Apartheid, Liberation and the Calvinist
            Tradition* (Maryknoll, NY: Orbis Books).
Boff, Leonardo
1974   'Salvation in Jesus Christ and the Process of Liberation', in Geffré and
            Gutiérrez 1974: 81-88.
Boff, Leonardo, and Clodivus Boff
1987   *Introducing Liberation Theology* (Tunbridge Wells: Burns & Oates).
Boff, Leonardo, and Virgil Elizondo
1990   'The Voices of the Victims: Who Will Listen to Them?', Editorial in
            Boff and Elizondo 1990: vii-x.
Boff, Leonardo, and Virgil Elizondo (eds.)
1990   *1492–1992: The Voice of the Victims* (Concilium, 1990, 6; London:
            SCM Press; Philadelphia: Trinity Press International).
Bonino, José Míguez
1975   *Revolutionary Theology Comes of Age* (London: SPCK).
1976   *Christians and Marxists: The Mutual Challenge of Oppression*
            (Maryknoll, NY: Orbis Books).
Boorer, Suzanne
1992   *The Promise of the Land as Oath: A Key to the Formation of the
            Pentateuch* (BZAW, 205; Berlin: de Gruyter).
Borah, Woodrow W.
1983   *Justice by Insurance: The General Indian Court of Colonial Mexico
            and the Legal Aides of the Half-Real* (Berkeley: University of
            California Press).
Boyd, Stephen M.
1971   'The Applicability of International Law to the Occupied Territories',
            in *Israel Yearbook on Human Rights* 1: 258-61.
Braaten, K.
1982   'The Kingdom of God and Life Everlasting', in P. Hodgson and
            R. King (eds.), *Christian Theology: Introduction to its Traditions and
            Tasks* (Philadelphia: Fortress Press).
Bream, H.N., R.D. Heim and C.A. Moore (eds.)
1974   *A Light unto my Path* (Philadelphia: Temple University Press).
Brenner, Lenni
1984   *The Iron Wall-Zionist Revisionism from Jabotinsky to Shamir*
            (London: Zed Books).
Brettler, Marc Zvi
1995   *The Creation of History in Ancient Israel* (London: Routledge).
Briend, Jacques
1992   'Lecture du pentateuque et hypothèse documentaire', in Haudebert
            1992: 9-32.

Bright, John
1956   *Early Israel in Recent History Writing: A Study in Method* (London: SCM Press).
1981   *A History of Israel* (London: SCM Press, 3rd edn [1960]).
Brody, H. (ed.)
1924   *Selected Poems of Jehudah Halevi* (trans. N. Salaman; Philadelphia: Jewish Publications of America).
Brooks, Roger, and John J. Collins (eds.)
1990   *Hebrew Bible or Old Testament: Studying the Bible in Judaism and Christianity* (Notre Dame, Indiana: University of Notre Dame Press).
Brown, Dee
1981   *Bury my Heart at Wounded Knee* (New York: Pocket Books, 2nd edn).
Brown, R.E., and S.M. Schneiders
1990   'Hermeneutics', in Brown, Fitzmyer and Murphy 1990: 1146-65.
Brown, R.E., J.A. Fitzmyer and R.E. Murphy (eds.)
1990   *The New Jerome Biblical Commentary* (London: Geoffrey Chapman).
Brown, Robert McAfee
1983   *Elie Wiesel: Messenger to All Humanity* (Notre Dame: University of Notre Dame Press).
1991   'Christians in the West Must Confront the Middle East', in Ruether and Ellis 1991: 138-54.
Brown, Robert McAfee (ed.)
1990   *Kairos: Three Prophetic Challenges to the Church* (Grand Rapids: Eerdmans).
Brueggemann, Walter
1977   *The Land: Place as Gift, Promise, and Challenge in Biblical Faith* (Overtures to Biblical Theology; Philadelphia: Fortress Press).
Buber, Martin
1952   *Eclipse of God: Studies in the Relation between Religion and Philosophy* (New York: Harper).
1973   *On Zion: The History of an Idea* (New York: Schocken Books).
Bultmann, Rudolf
1953   *Kerygma and Myth* (London: SPCK).
Burge, Gary M.
1993   *Who Are God's People in the Middle East?* (Grand Rapids: Zondervan).
Burkholder, Mark A., and Lyman L. Johnson
1994   *Colonial Latin America* (Oxford: Oxford University Press, 2nd edn).
Burrell, David, and Y. Landau
1992   *Voices from Jerusalem: Jews and Christians Reflect on the Holy Land* (New York: Paulist Press).
Cahill, Michael
1996   'Reader-Response Criticism and the Allegorizing Reader', *Theological Studies* 57: 89-96.
Callaway, Joseph
1984   'Village Subsistence at Ai and Raddana in Iron Age I', in *The Answers Lie Below: Essays in Honor of Lawrence Edmund Toombs* (ed. Henry Thompson; Lanham: University Press of America); 51-66.

Caradon, Hugh Foot, Baron
  1981   *United Nations Security Council Resolution 242: A Case in Diplomatic Ambiguity* (Washington, DC: Georgetown University).
Carmi, T.
  1981   *The Penguin Book of Hebrew Verse* (ed. and trans. T. Carmi; Harmondsworth: Penguin).
Carroll, Robert
  1991   *Wolf in the Sheepfold: The Bible as a Problem for Christianity* (London: SPCK).
  1992   'The Myth of the Empty Land', *Semeia* 59: 79-93.
Cassirer, Ernst
  1946   *Language and Myth* (New York: Dover Publications).
Chacour, Elias
  1985   *Blood Brothers: A Palestinian's Struggle for Reconciliation in the Middle East* (Eastbourne: Kingsway Publications).
  1992   *We Belong to the Land* (San Francisco: Harper).
Chapman, Colin
  1983   *Whose Promised Land?* (Tring: Lion).
Cherry, Conrad (ed.)
  1971   *God's New Israel: Religious Interpretations of American Destiny* (Englewood Cliffs, NJ: Prentice-Hall).
Childers, Erskine B.
  1987   'The Wordless Wish: From Citizens to Refugees', in I. Abu-Lughod 1987: 165-202.
Childs, Brevard S.
  1976   *Introduction to the Old Testament as Scripture* (London: SCM Press).
Chomsky, Noam
  1983   *The Fateful Triangle: The United States, Israel and the Palestinians* (Boston: South End Press).
Clements R.E. (ed.)
  1989   *The World of Ancient Israel: Sociological, Anthropological and Political Perspectives* (Cambridge: Cambridge University Press).
Cobb, Peter G.
  1980   'The Liturgy of the Word in the Early Church', in *The Study of Liturgy* (ed. Cheslyn Jones, G. Wainwright and E. Yarnold; London: SPCK): 179-88.
Coggins, Richard J., and J.L. Houlden (eds.)
  1990   *A Dictionary of Biblical Interpretation* (London: SCM Press).
Cohen, Arthur A., and Paul Mendes-Flohr (eds.)
  1987   *Contemporary Jewish Religious Thought: Original Essays on Critical Concepts, Movements and Beliefs* (New York: The Free Press; London: Collier Macmillan).
Cohen, S.J.D.
  1983   'From the Bible to Talmud: The Prohibition of Intermarriage', *Hebrew Annual Review* 7: 23-39
Collins, R.F.
  1990   'Inspiration,' in Brown, Fitzmyer and Murphy 1990: 1023-33.

Comaroff, Jean, and John Comaroff
    1991   *Of Revelation and Revolution: Christianity, Colonialism and Consciousness in South Africa,* I (Chicago: University of Chicago Press).
Cone, James H.
    1974   'Biblical Revelation and Social Existence', *Interpretation* 28: 422-40.
    1975   *God of the Oppressed* (New York: Seabury Press).
Coogan, Michael D.
    1989   'Joshua', in Brown, Fitzmyer and Murphy 1990: 110-31.
Coote, Robert B.
    1990   *Early Israel: A New Horizon* (Minneapolis: Fortress Press).
Coote, Robert B., and Keith W. Whitelam
    1987   *The Emergence of Early Israel in Historical Perspective* (Social World of Biblical Antiquity Series, 5; Sheffield: Almond Press).
Cossali, Paul, and Clive Robson
    1986   *Stateless in Gaza* (London: Zed Books).
Croatto, J. Severino
    1977   *Biblical Hermeneutics: Toward a Theory of Reading as the Production of Meaning* (Maryknoll, NY: Orbis Books).
Cross, Frank M. (ed.)
    1979   *Symposia Celebrating the Seventh-Fifth Anniversary of the Founding of the American Schools of Oriental Research (1900–1975).* (Cambridge MA: American Schools of Oriental Research).
Curtin, Philip D.
    1969   *The Atlantic Slave Trade: A Census* (Madison: University of Wisconsin Press).
Davies, E.W.
    1989   'Land: Its Rights and Privileges', in Clements 1989: 349-69.
Davies, Philip R.
    1995   *In Search of 'Ancient Israel'* (JSOTSup, 148; Sheffield: Sheffield Academic Press).
Davies, W.D.
    1974   *The Gospel and the Land: Early Christianity and Jewish Territorial Doctrine* (Berkeley: University of California Press).
    1981   'The Territorial Dimensions of Judaism', in *Intergerini Parietis Septum (Eph. 2:14): Essays Presented to Markus Barth on his Sixty-fifth Birthday* (ed. Dikran Y. Hadidian; Pittsburgh: Pickwick Press): 61-96.
    1982   *The Territorial Dimensions of Judaism* (Berkeley: University of California Press).
    1985   'The "Land" in the Pre-Exilic and Early Post-Exilic Prophets', in J.T. Butler, E.W. Conrad and B.C. Ollenburger (eds.), *Understanding the Word* (JSOTSup, 37; Sheffield: JSOT Press): 247-62.
    1991   *The Territorial Dimensions of Judaism: With a Symposium and Further Reflections* (Minneapolis: Fortress Press).
Davis, Moshe (ed.)
    1977   *World Jewry and the State of Israel* (New York: Arno Press).
Davis, Uri.
    1987   *Israel: An Apartheid State* (London: Zed Books).

Dayan, Moshe
    1978   *Living with the Bible* (Philadelphia: Jewish Publication Society; New
            York: William Morrow).
Degenaar, J.
    1992   'Deconstruction—the Celebration of Language,' in *The Reader and
            Beyond: Theory and Practice in South African Reception Studies*
            (ed. B.C. Lategan; Pretoria: Human Sciences Research Council).
De Geus, C.H.J.
    1976   *The Tribes of Israel: An Investigation into Some of the Presuppositions
            of Martin Noth's Amphictyony Hypothesis* (Amsterdam: Van Gorcum).
De Gruchy, John W.
    1979   *The Church Struggle in South Africa* (Grand Rapids: Eerdsman;
            London: SPCK).
    1991   *Liberating Reformed Theology: A South African Contribution to an
            Ecumenical Debate* (Grand Rapids: Eerdmans).
De Gruchy, John W., and Charles Villa-Vicencio (eds.)
    1983   *Apartheid Is a Heresy* (Grand Rapids: Eerdmans).
Deist, F.E.
    1987   *Revolution and Reinterpretation: Chapters from the History of Israel*
            (ed. F.E. Deist and J.H. le Roux; Cape Town: Tafelberg): 91-97.
    1986   'Aufstieg und Niedergang der Apartheid', *Politische Studien*
            (Sonderheft 2): 19-30.
    1994   'The Dangers of Deuteronomy: A Page from the Reception History of
            the Book', in Martínez *et al.* 1994: 13-29.
De Klerk, W.A.
    1975   *The Puritans in Africa: A History of Afrikanerdom* (Harmondsworth:
            Penguin).
Denzinger, H., and A. Schönmetzer
            *Enchiridion symbolorum, definitionum et declarationum de rebus fidei
            et morum* (Barcelona: Herder, 1973).
De Vaux, Roland
    1961   *Ancient Israel: Its Life and Institutions* (London: Darton, Longman &
            Todd).
    1965   'Les Patriarches hébreux et l'histoire', *Revue Biblique* 72: 5-28.
    1978   *The Early History of Israel* (2 vols.; London: Darton, Longman &
            Todd).
Deurleo, K.A.
    1994   'The One God and All Israel in its Generations', in Martínez *et al.*
            1994: 31-46.
Diepold, P.
    1972   *Israel's Land* (BWANT, 95; Stuttgart: Kohlhammer).
Dinstein, Yoram.
    1978   'The International Law of Belligerent Occupation and Human Rights',
            Israel Yearbook on Human Rights 8: 104-43.
Dion, P.E.
    1985   'Deuteronomy and the Gentile World: A Study in Biblical Theology',
            Toronto Journal of Theology 1: 200-21.

Don-Yehiya, Eliezer
    1987   'Jewish Messianism, Religious Zionism and Israeli Politics: The Impact and Origins of the Gush Emunim', *Middle Eastern Studies* 23: 215-34.

Dugard, John
    1992   'Enforcement of Human Rights in the West Bank and the Gaza Strip', in Playfair 1992: 461-87.

Dupertuis, Atilio R.
    1982   *Liberation Theology: A Study in its Soteriology* (Berrien Springs: Andrews University Press).

Du Plessis, J.S.
    n.d.   *President Kruger aan die woord* (Bloemfontein: Sacum).

Dussel, Enrique
    1979   *El episcopado latinoamericano y la liberación de los pobres 1504–1620* (Mexico City: Centro de Reflexión Teológica).
    1990   'The Real Motives for the Conquest', in Boff and Elizondo 1990: 30-46.

Du Toit, André
    1983   'No Chosen People: The Myth of the Calvinist Origins of Afrikaner Nationalism and Racial Ideology', *American Historical Review* 88: 920-52.
    1984   'Captive to the Nationalist Paradigm: Prof. F.A. van Jaarsveld and the Historical Evidence for the Afrikaner's Ideas on His Calling and Mission', *South African Historical Journal* 16: 49-80.

Du Toit, S.J.
    1877   *Die Geskiedenis van ons land in die taal van ons volk* (Capetown: Patriot-Vereniging).

Dyer, Charles H.
    1991   *The Rise of Babylon: Signs of the End Times* (Wheaton, IL: Tyndale House).
    1993   *World News and Biblical Prophecy* (Wheaton, IL: Tyndale House).

Eckardt, Alice, and Roy Eckardt
    1970   *Encounter with Israel: A Challenge to Conscience* (New York: Association Press).

Eckert, W.P., N.P. Levenson and M. Stöhr (eds.)
    1970   *Judaisches Volk-gelobtes Land* (Munich: Kaiser).

Eilberg-Schwartz, H.
    1986–87   'Creation and Classification in Judaism: From Priestly to Rabbinic Conceptions', *History of Religions* 26: 357-81.

Eiselen, W.W.M.
    1948   'The Meaning of Apartheid', *Race Relations* 15: 69-86.

Eisenstadt, S.N.
    1963   *The Political Systems of Empires: The Rise and Fall of Historical Bureaucratic Societies* (New York: Free Press).

El-Assal, Riah Abu
    1994   'The Birth and Experience of the Christian Church: The Protestant/Anglican Perspective. Anglican Identity in the Middle East', in Prior and Taylor 1994: 131-40.

Elath, Eliahu
   1957   *Israel and her Neighbors: Lectures delivered at Brandeis University,
             Waltham, Mass. in April–May 1956* (Cleveland: World Publishing
             Company).
Eliade, Mircea
   1958   *Patterns in Comparative Religion* (London: Sheed & Ward).
Ellacuría, Ignacio
   1976   *Freedom Made Flesh* (Maryknoll, NY: Orbis Books).
   1989   'El pueblo crucificado: Ensayo de soterología histórico', *Revista
             Latinoamerica de Teología* 18: 305-33.
Ellis, Marc
   1987   *Toward a Jewish Theology of Liberation* (Maryknoll, NY: Orbis
             Books).
   1990   *Beyond Innocence and Redemption: Confronting the Holocaust and
             Israeli Power. Creating a Moral Future for the Jewish People* (San
             Francisco: Harper & Row).
   1994   *Ending Auschwitz: The Future of Jewish and Christian Life* (Louisville:
             Westminster/John Knox).
Ellis, Marc, and Otto Maduro (eds.)
   1990   *Expanding the View: Gustavo Gutiérrez and the Future of Liberation
             Theology* (Maryknoll, NY: Orbis Books).
Elphick, Richard
   1977   *Kraal and Castle: Khoikoi and the Founding of White South Africa*
             (New Haven: Yale Historical Publications).
Esquivel, Julia
   1990   'Conquered and Violated Women', in Boff and Elizondo 1990: 68-
             77.
Evans, Christopher
   1971   *Is 'Holy Scripture' Christian? and Other Questions* (London: SCM
             Press).
Evans, Craig A., and W. Richard Stegner (eds.)
   1994   *The Gospels and the Scriptures of Israel* (JSNTSup, 104; Sheffield:
             Sheffield Academic Press).
Evron, Boas
   1981   'The Holocaust: Learning the Wrong Lessons', *Journal of Palestine
             Studies* 10 (spring): 16-26.
Exum, J. Cheryl, and David J.A. Clines
   1993   *The New Literary Criticism and the Hebrew Bible* (JSOTSup, 143;
             Sheffield: JSOT Press).
Fackenheim, Emil
   1970   *God's Presence in History: Jewish Affirmation and Philosophical
             Reflections* (New York: New York University Press).
   1975   *From Bergen-Belsen to Jerusalem: Contemporary Implications of the
             Holocaust* (Jerusalem: Institute of Contemporary Judaism).
   1977   'Post-Holocaust anti-Jewishness, Jewish Identity, and the Centrality of
             Israel: An Essay in the Philosophy of History', in Davis 1977: 11-31.
   1978   *The Jewish Return into History: Reflections in the Age of Auschwitz
             and a New Jerusalem* (New York: Schocken Books).

1982   *To Mend the World: Foundations of Future Jewish Thought* (New York: Schocken Books).

1987   'Holocaust', in Cohen and Mendes-Flohr 1987: 399-408.

Fackenheim, Emil, G. Steiner, R.H. Popkin and E. Wiesel
1967   'Jewish Values in the Post-Holocaust Future: A Symposium', *Judaism* 16: 266-99.

Fierro, Alfreido
1984   'Exodus Event and Interpretation in Political Theologies', in Gottwald 1984: 473-81.

Finkelstein, Israel
1988a   *The Archaeology of the Israelite Settlement* (Jerusalem: Israel Exploration Society).

1988b   'Searching for Israelite Origins', *Biblical Archaeology Review* 14: 5, 34-35, 58.

1990   *Archaeological Discoveries and Biblical Research* (Seattle: University of Washington).

1991   'The Emergence of Israel in Canaan: Consensus, Mainstream and Dispute', *Scandinavian Journal of the Old Testament* 2: 47-59.

Finkelstein, Norman G.
1995   *Image and Reality of the Israel–Palestine Conflict* (London/New York: Verso).

Fiorenza, E. Schüssler
1988   'The Ethics of Biblical Interpretation: Decentering Biblical Scholarship', *Journal of Biblical Literature* 107: 3-17.

Flanagan, James
1988   *David's Social Drama: A Hologram of Israel's Early Iron Age* (Sheffield: Almond Press).

Flapan, Simha
1979   *Zionism and the Palestinians, 1917–1947* (London: Croom Helm).

1987   *The Birth of Israel: Myths and Realities* (London: Croom Helm).

Fokkema, Douwe (and E. Ibsch)
1979   *Theories of Literature in the Twentieth Century: Structuralism, Marxism, Aesthetics of Reception* (London: Hurst).

Fowl, S.E.
1990   'The Ethics of Interpretation, or What's Left after the Elimination of Meaning', in *The Bible in Three Dimensions* (ed. D.J.A. Clines; JSOTSup, 87; Sheffield: JSOT Press): 379-98.

Fowler, R.M.
1989   'Postmodern Biblical Criticism', *Forum* 5: 3-30.

Fowler, Robert
1991   *Let the Reader Understand: Reader-Response Criticism and the Gospel of Mark* (Minneapolis: Fortress Press).

Fox, Richard Wrightman
1987   *Reinhold Niebuhr: A Biography* (New York: Harper & Row).

Freidman, T.
1990   *From Beirut to Jerusalem* (London: Fontana).

Frick, Frank
    1985   *The Formation of the State in Ancient Israel* (Sheffield: Almond Press).
Friedman, Robert I.
    1990   *The False Prophet: Rabbi Meir Kahane—From FBI Informant to Knesset Member* (London: Faber & Faber).
    1992   *Zealots for Zion: Inside Israel's West Bank Settlement Movement* (New York: Random House).
Fritz, Volkmar
    1981   'The Israelite "Conquest" in Light of Recent Excavations at Khirbet el-Mishnah', *Bulletin of the American Schools of Oriental Research* 241: 61-73.
    1987   'Conquest or Settlement? The Early Iron Age in Palestine', *Biblical Archaeologist* 50: 84-100.
Fuller, Reginald H.
    1974   *Preaching the New Lectionary: The Word of God for the Church Today* (Collegeville, MN: Liturgical Press).
Garbini, Giovanni.
    1988   *History and Ideology in Ancient Israel* (London: SCM Press).
Garrone, D., and F. Israel (eds.)
    1991   *Storia e tradizioni di Israele: Scritti in onore di J. Alberto Soggin* (Brescia: Paideia).
Geertz, Clifford
    1971   *Islam Observed: Religious Developments in Morocco and Indonesia* (Chicago: University of Chicago Press).
Geffré, Claude, and Gustavo Gutiérrez (eds.)
    1974   *The Mystical and Political Dimension of the Christian Faith* (Concilium, 96; New York: Herder/Seabury).
Geraisy, Sami
    1994   'Socio-Demographic Characteristics: Reality, Problems and Aspirations within Israel', in Prior and Taylor 1994: 45-55.
Gerhard, Dietrich
    1959   'The Frontier in Comparative View', *Comparative Studies in History and Society* 1: 34-51.
Gilbert, Martin
    1975   *Winston S. Churchill*. IV. *1916–1933* (London: Heinemann).
    1982   *Atlas of the Holocaust* (London: Michael Joseph in association with the Board of Deputies of British Jews).
Gnuse, Robert
    1985   *You Shall Not Steal: Community and Property in the Biblical Tradition* (Maryknoll, NY: Orbis Books).
    1991   'Israelite Settlement of Canaan: A Peaceful Internal Process—Part 1', *Biblical Theology Bulletin* 21: 56-66; Part 2, *Biblical Theology Bulletin* 21: 109-17.
Goguel, Anne-Marie, and Pierre Buis
    n.d.   *Chrétiens d'afrique du sud face a l'apartheid: Récits et textes présentés par Anne-Marie Goguel et Pierre Buis* (Paris: Editions l'Harmattan).

Goldingay, J.
1983   'The Patriarchs in Scripture and Tradition', in Millard and Wiseman 1983: 1-34.
Gordon, David G.
1966   *The Passing of French Algeria* (London: Oxford University Press).
Gorny, Yosef
1987   *Zionism and the Arabs, 1882–1948: A Study of Ideology* (Oxford: Clarendon Press).
Gottwald, Norman K.
1979   *The Tribes of Yahweh: A Sociology of the Religion of Liberated Israel, 1250–1050 BCE* (London: SCM Press).
Gottwald, Norman K. (ed.)
1984   *The Bible and Liberation: Political and Social Hermeneutics* (Maryknoll, NY: Orbis Books).
Gould, Stephen Jay
1981   *The Mismeasure of Man* (Harmondsworth: Penguin).
Green, Stephen
1988   *Living by the Sword: America and Israel in the Middle East, 1968–87* (London: Faber & Faber).
Gresh, A., and D. Vidal
1988   *The Middle East: War without End?* (London: Lawrence & Wishart).
Grillmeier, Alois
1969   'The Divine Inspiration and the Interpretation of Sacred Scripture', in *Commentary on the Documents of Vatican II*, III (ed. H. Vorgrimler; ET William Glen-Doepel; New York: Herder & Herder; London: Burns & Oates).
Gudorf, Christine E.
1987   'Liberation Theology's Use of Scripture: A Response to First World Critics', *Interpretation* 41: 5-18.
Guidi, Michelangelo
1951   *Storia e cultura degli Arabi fino alla morte di Maometto* (Florence: Sansoni).
Gutiérrez, Gustavo
1988   *A Theology of Liberation: History, Politics, and Salvation* (London: SCM Press, revised with a new Introduction).
1993   *Las Casas: In Search of the Poor of Jesus Christ* (Maryknoll, NY: Orbis Books).
Habermas, Jurgen
1979   *Communication and the Evolution of Society* (London: Beacon).
Hadawi, Sami
1988   *Palestinian Rights and Losses in 1948: A Comprehensive Study* (with Part V, 'An Economic Assessment of Total Palestinian Losses' written by Dr Atef Kubursi) (London: Saqi Books).
Hagenmeyer, H.
1901   *Die Kreuzzugsbriefe aus den Jahren 1088–1100* (Innsbruck: Wagner).
Halabi, Usamah
1985   *Land Alienation in the West Bank: A Legal and Spatial Analysis.* (Jerusalem: West Bank Data Base Project).

Halpern, Ben
    1969   *The Idea of the Jewish State* (Cambridge, MA: Harvard University Press, 2nd edn).

Halpern-Amaru, Betsy
    1981   'Land Theology in Josephus' *Jewish Antiquities*', *Jewish Quarterly Review* 71: 201-20.
    1994   *Rewriting the Bible: Land and Covenant in Post-Biblical Jewish Literature* (Valley Forge: Trinity Press).

Hanson, A.T., and R.P.C. Hanson
    1980   *Reasonable Belief: A Survey of the Christian Faith* (Oxford: Oxford University Press).

Harkabi, Y.
    1972   *Arab Attitudes to Israel* (Jerusalem: Keter Publishing House).

Harris, Marvin
    1980   *Cultural Materialism: The Struggle for a Science of Culture* (New York: Vintage Books).

Harris, William W.
    1980   *Taking Root: Israeli Settlement in the West Bank, the Golan and Gaza–Sinai, 1967–1980* (Chichester: Research Studies Press).

Harrison, Paul
    1993   *Inside the Third World* (London: Penguin).

Hartz, Louis (ed.)
    1964   *The Founding of New Societies: Studies in the History of the United States, Latin America, South Africa, Canada and Australia* (New York: Harcourt, Brace & World).

Haudebert, Pierre
    1992   *La pentateuque: Débats et recherches XIVe congrès de L'ACFEB, Angers (1991), publié sous la direction de Pierre Haudebert* (Lectio Divina, 151; Paris: Édition du Cerf).

Hayes, John H. and J. Maxwell Miller (eds.)
    1977   *Israelite and Judaean History* (London: SCM Press).

Hemelsoet, Ben
    1995   'Nächstes Jahr in Jerusalem', in Prudký 1995: 187-97.

Hennelly, Alfred T.
    1995   *Liberation Theologies: The Global Pursuit of Justice* (Mystic, CT: Twenty-third Publications).

Hennessy, Alistair
    1978   *The Frontiers in Latin American History* (Albuquerque: University of New Mexico Press).

Hertzberg, Arthur
    1990   'An Open Letter to Elie Wiesel', in Ruether and Marc Ellis 1990: 125-31.
    1996   'The End of the Dream of the Undivided Land of Israel', *Journal of Palestine Studies* 25 (2): 35-45.

Hertzberg, Arthur (ed.)
    1959   *The Zionist Idea: A Historical Analysis and Reader* (New York: Doubleday and Herzl Press).

Herzl, Theodor
    1896   *Der Judenstaat: Versuch einer modernen Lösung der Judenfrage* (Leipzig: M. Breitenstein's Verlags-Buchhandlung, 1896). Translated into English by Sylvie d'Avigdor as *A Jewish State*, and in 1946 as *The Jewish State*, published by the American Zionist Emergency Council. The version used here is *The Jewish State* (New York: Dover, 1988).
    1960   *The Complete Diaries of Theodore Herzl* (ed. Raphael Patai; 5 vols.; trans. Harry Zohn; New York: Herzl Press).
    1983–96   Vol. I: *Briefe und Autobiographische Notizen 1886–1895* (1983). Vol. II: *Zionistiches Tagebuch 1895–1899* (1983). Vol. III: *Zionistiches Tagebuch 1899–1904* (1985). (Vols. I–III ed. Johannes Wachten *et al.*) Vol. IV: *Briefe 1895–1898* (1900). Vol V: *Briefe 1898–1900* (1993). Vol VI: *Briefe Ende August 1900—Ende Dezember 1902* (1993). Vol VII: *Briefe 1903–1904* (1996) (Vols. IV–VII ed. Barbara Schäfer *et al.*) (Berlin: Propylaen Verlag.)
Heschel, Abraham
    1969   *Israel: An Echo of Eternity* (New York: Farrar, Straus & Ginoux).
Hitchens, Christopher
    1988   'Broadcasts', in Said and Hitchens 1988: 73-83.
Hitler, Adolf
    1961   *Hitler's Secret Book* (New York: Grove Press [1928]).
    1969   *Mein Kampf (My Struggle)* (ET; New York: Houghton Mifflin; London: Hutchinson).
Hobbs, T.R.
    1989   *A Time for War: A Study of Warfare in the Old Testament* (Wilmingtom, DE: Michael Glazier).
Hope, Marjorie, and James Young
    1981   *The South African Churches in a Revolutionary Situation* (Maryknoll, NY: Orbis Books).
Hopkins, David
    1985   *The Highlands of Canaan: Agricultural Life in the Early Iron Age* (Sheffield: Almond Press).
    1987   'Life on the Land: The Subsistence Struggle of Early Israel', *Biblical Archaeologist* 50: 178-91.
Huddleston, Trevor
    1956   *Naught for your Comfort* (London: Collins).
Hurbon, Laënnec
    1990   'The Slave Trade and Black Slavery in America', in Boff and Elizondo 1990: 90-100.
Hurwitz, Deena (ed.)
    1992   *Walking the Red Line: Israelis in Search of Justice for Palestine* (Philadelphia: New Society Publishers).
Ingrams, Doreen
    1972   *Palestine Papers, 1917–1922: Seeds of Conflict* (London: John Murray).

International Centre for Peace in the Middle East
    1985   *Research on Human Rights in the Occupied Territories, 1979–1983*
              (Tel Aviv: International Centre for Peace in the Middle East).

Jennings, Francis
    1976   *The Invasion of America: Indians, Colonialism and the Cant of*
              Conquest (New York: Norton).

Jensen, Joseph
    1988   'Prediction-Fulfilment in Bible and Liturgy', *Catholic Biblical*
              Quarterly 50: 646-62.

Kadir, Djelal
    1992   *Columbus and the Ends of the Earth: Europe's Prophetic Rhetoric as*
              Conquering Ideology (Berkeley: University of California Press).
    1986   *The Kairos Document: Challenge to the Church. A Theological*
              Comment on the Political Crisis in South Africa (Grand Rapids:
              Eerdmans, rev. 2nd edn).

Kalley, Jacqueline A.
    1987   *South Africa under Apartheid: A Select and Annotated Bibliography*
              (Pietermaritzburg: Shuter & Shooter).

Kamen, Henry
    1991   *Spain 1469–1714: A Society of Conflict* (London: Longman, 2nd
              edn).

Kayyali, Abdul Wahhab Al
    1979   'The Historical Roots of the Imperialist-Zionist Alliance', in Al
              Kayyali 1979: 9-26.

Kayyali, Abdul Wahhab Al (ed.)
    1979   *Zionism, Imperialism and Racism* (London: Croom Helm).

Keel, Othmar
    1994   *The Song of Songs: A Continental Commentary* (Minneapolis: Fortress
              Press).

Kelly, J.N.D.
  1958–60   *Early Christian Doctrines* (London: A. & C. Black).

Kennedy, Paul
    1988   *The Rise and Fall of the Great Powers: Economic Change and*
              Military Conflict from 1500 to 2000 (London: Fontana).

Kenyon, Kathleen
    1966   *Amorites and Canaanites* (Oxford: Clarendon Press).

Khalidi, Rashid
    1988   'Palestinian Peasant Resistance to Zionism before World War I', in
              Said and Hitchens 1988: 207-33.

Khalidi, Walid
 1984, 1991 *Before their Diaspora: A Photographic History of the Palestinians,*
              1876–1948 (Washington, DC: Institute for Palestinian Studies).
    1992   *Palestine Reborn* (London/New York: Tauris).

Khalidi, Walid (ed.)
    1970   *From Haven to Conquest* (Beirut: Institute for Palestine Studies).
    1992   *All that Remains: The Palestinian Villages Occupied and Depopulated*
              by Israel in 1948 (Washington, DC: Institute for Palestine Studies).

Khoury, F.J.
1985   *The Arab–Israeli Dilemma* (Syracuse: Syracuse University Press, 3rd edn).

Kidron, Peretz
1988   'Truth whereby Nations Live', in Said and Hitchens 1988: 85-96.

Kimmerling, Baruch
1983   *Zionism and Territory: The Socio-Territorial Dimensions of Zionist Politics* (Research Series, 51; Berkeley: University of California, Institute of International Studies).

Kochavi, Moshe
1985   'The Settlement of Canaan in the Light of Archaeological Surveys', in *Biblical Archaeology Today: Proceedings of the International Congress on Biblical Archaeology, Jerusalem, April 1984* (Jerusalem: Israel Exploration Society): 54-60.

Koestler, Arthur
1949   *Promise and Fulfilment: Palestine, 1917–1949* (London: Macmillan).

Kook, Abraham Isaac
1979   *The Lights of Penitence, the Moral Principles, Lights of Holiness, Essays, Letters, and Poems* (trans. and Introduction by Ben Zion Bokser; London: SPCK).

Kook, Zvi Yehuda
1991   *Torat Eretz Israel: The Teaching of HaRav Tzvi Yehuda HaCohen Kook.* Commentary by HaRav David Samson, based on the Hebrew *Sichot of HaRav Tzvi Yehuda* (trans. Tzvi Fishman; Jerusalem: Torat Eretz Yisrael Publications).

Kotzé, C.R.
1955   *Bie bybel en ons volkstryd* (Bloemfontein: Saccum).

Kreutz, Andrej
1990   *Vatican Policy on the Palestinian–Israeli Conflict: The Struggle for the Holy Land* (Contributions in Political Science, No. 246; New York: Westport; London: Greenwood Press).

Kulka, Otto Dov, and Paul R. Mendes-Flohr (eds.)
1987   *Judaism and Christianity under the Impact of National Socialism.* Jerusalem: Historical Society of Israel and the Zalman Shazar Center for Jewish History).

Kuttab, Jonathan
1992   'Avenues Open for Defence of Human Rights in the Israeli-Occupied Territories', in Playfair 1992: 489-504.

Kwok Pui-lan
1995   *Discovering the Bible in the Non-Biblical World* (Maryknoll, NY: Orbis Books).

Lamadrid, A.G.
1981   'Canaán y América: La Biblia y la teologia medieval ante la conquista de la tierra', in *Escritos de Biblia y Oriente* (Bibliotheca Salmanticensis Estudios, 38; Salamanca-Jerusalén: Universidad Pontificia): 329-46.

Landau, David
1993   *Piety and Power: The World of Jewish Fundamentalism* (London: Secker & Warburg).

1994   Obituary on Rabbi Schlomo, *The Guardian*, 22 November.

Lang, James
1975   *Conquest and Commerce: Spain and England in the Americas* (New York: Academic Press).

Laqueur, Walter
1972   *History of Zionism* (New York: Holt, Rinehart & Winston).

Las Casas, Bartolomé de
1989–94   *Obras Completas: Edición de Paulino Castañeda Delgado y Antonio García del Moral, O.P.* (14 vols.; Madrid: Alianza Editorial).

Lehn, Walter (in association with Uri Davis)
1988   *The Jewish National Fund* (London: Kegan Paul International).

Leibowitz, Steve
1993   'Kach's New Pitcher', *Jerusalem Post*, 30 July.

Lemche, Niels Peter
1985   *Early Israel: Anthropological and Historical Studies on the Israelite Society before the Monarchy* (Vetus Testamentum Supplements, 38; Leiden: Brill).
1991   *The Canaanites and their Land: The Tradition of the Canaanites* (Sheffield: JSOT Press).
1995   *Ancient Israel: A New History of Israelite Society* (The Biblical Seminar, 5; Sheffield: Sheffield Academic Press [reprint of 1988 original]).

Lenski, Gerhard
1980   'Review of N.K. Gottwald, *The Tribes of Yahweh*', *Recherches de science religieuse* 6: 275-78.

Lerner, Michael
1988   'The Occupation: Immoral and Stupid', Editorial in *Tikkun* 3, March–April.

Lesch, Ann, and Mark Tessler (eds.)
1989   *Israel, Egypt, and the Palestinians: From Camp David to the Intifada* (Bloomington, IN: Indiana University Press).

Lester, Alan
1996   *From Colonisation to Democracy: A New Historical Geography of South Africa* (London: Tauris).

Levine, Daniel H.
1981   *Religion and Politics in Latin America: The Catholic Church in Venezuela and Columbia* (Princeton, NJ: Princeton University Press).

Levine, Daniel H. (ed.)
1979   *Churches and Politics in Latin America* (London: Sage Publications).

Levinson, Jon D.
1990   'Theological Consensus or Historicist Evasion? Jews and Christians in Biblical Studies', in Brooks and Collins 1990: 109-45.

Lifton, Robert Jay
1987   *The Future of Immortality and Other Essays for a Nuclear Age* (New York: Basic Books).

Lind, Millard C.
1980   *Yahweh Is a Warrior: A Theology of Warfare in Ancient Israel* (Scottdale, PA: Herald).

Lindsey, Hal
    1970   *The Late, Great Planet Earth* (London: Lakeland).
    1983   *Israel and the Last Days* (Eugene, OR: Harvest House).
Littell, Franklin H.
    1987   'Christian Antisemitism and the Holocaust', in Kulka and Mendes-
                Flohr 1987: 513-29.
Locke, Richard, and Antony Stewart
    1985   *Bantustan Gaza* (London: Zed Books).
Lockhart, James, and Enrique Otte (eds.)
    1976   *Letters and People of the Spanish Indies: Sixteenth Century*
                (Cambridge: Cambridge University Press).
Lohfink, Norbert
    1996   'The Laws of Deuteronomy: Project for a World without any Poor',
                Scripture Bulletin 26: 2-19.
Lonsdale, J.
    1981   'States and Social Processes in Africa: A Historiographical Survey',
                African Studies Review 24.
López, F.G.
    1994   'Deut 34, Dtr History and the Pentateuch', in Martínez *et al.* 1994: 47-
                61.
Loubser, J.A.
    1987   *The Apartheid Bible: A Critical Review of Racial Theology in South
                Africa* (Cape Town: Maskew Miller Longman).
Lustick, Ian S.
    1988   *For the Land and the Lord* (New York: Council on Foreign Relations
                Press).
Lustick, Ian S. (ed.)
    1994   *Arab–Israeli Relations: Historical Background and Origins of the
                Conflict* (New York: Garland Publishing).
Maalouf, Amin
    1985   *The Crusades through Arab Eyes* (New York: Schocken Press).
MacBride, Seán (Chairman)
    1983   *Israel in Lebanon: The Report of the International Commission to
                Enquire into Reported Violations of International Law by Israel
                During its Invasion of the Lebanon* (London: Ithaca Press).
MacKnight, Edgar V.
    1988   *Postmodern Use of the Bible: The Emergence of Reader-Oriented
                Criticism* (Nashville: Abingdon Press).
Mahoney, John F.
    1992   'About this Issue', *The Link* (Americans for Middle East
                Understanding) 25.4: 2
Mair, Juan
    1510   *Libro II de las Sentencia*s (Paris).
Malamat, Abraham
    1979   'Israelite Conduct of War in the Conquest of Canaan', in Cross 1979:
                35-55.
    1982   'How Inferior Israelite Forces Conquered Fortified Canaanite Cities',
                Biblical Archaeology Review 8: 2, 25-35.

Mallison, Sally V.
    1982   'The Application of International Law to the Israeli Settlements in Occupied Territories', in I. Abu Lughod 1982. 55-66.

March, W. Eugene
    1994   *Israel and the Politics of Land: A Theological Cast Study* (Foreword by Walter Brueggemenn; Louisville: Westminster/John Knox Press).

Marks, Shula
    1980   'South Africa: The Myth of the Empty Land', *History Today* 30: 7-12.

Martínez, F. García, A. Hilhorst, J.T.A.G.M. van Ruiten, and A.S. van der Woude (eds.)
    1994   *Studies in Deuteronomy: In Honour of C.J. Labuschagne on the Occasion of his 65th Birthday* (Leiden: Brill).

Masalha, Nur
    1992   *Expulsion of the Palestinians: The Concept of 'Transfer' in Zionist Political Thought, 1882–1948* (Washington, DC: Institute for Palestinian Studies).

Masalha, Nur (trans. and ed.)
    1993   *The Palestinians in Israel: Is Israel the State of All its Citizens and 'Absentees'?* (Haifa: Galilee Centre for Social Research).

Matar, Ibrahim
    1981   'Israeli Settlements in the West Bank and Gaza Strip', *Journal of Palestine Studies* 41: 93-110.
    1983   'From Palestinian to Israeli: Jerusalem 1948-82', *Journal of Palestine Studies* 48: 57-63.
    1992   'Exploitation of Land and Water Resources for Jewish Colonies in the Occupied Territories', in Playfair 1992: 443-57.

Mayes, Andrew D.H.
    1981   *Deuteronomy* (NCBC; Grand Rapids: Eerdmans).
    1983   *The Story of Israel between Settlement and Exile: A Redactional Study of the Deuteronomistic History* (London: SCM Press).
    1989   *The Old Testament in Sociological Perspective* (London: Marshall Pickering).
    1994   'Deuteronomy 14 and the Deuteronomic World View', in Martínez *et al.* 1994: 163-81.

Mazar, Amihai
    1985   'The Israelite Settlement in Canaan in the Light of Archaeological Excavations, in *Biblical Archaeology Today: Proceedings of the International Congress on Biblical Archaeology, Jerusalem, April 1984* (Jerusalem: Israel Exploration Society): 61-70.
    1990   *Archaeology of the Land of the Bible, 10,000–586 BCE* (Garden City, NY: Doubleday).

McBride, S.D.
    1987   'Polity of the Covenant People: The Book of Deuteronomy', *Interpretation* 41: 229-44.

McCarthy, Justin
    1991   *The Population of Palestine: Population History and Statistics of the Late Ottoman Period and the Mandate* (New York: Columbia University Press).

McDowall, David
    1989   *Palestine and Israel: The Uprising and Beyond* (London: Tauris).
    1994   *The Palestinians: The Road to Nationhood* (London: Minority
              Rights).
McKenzie, John L.
    1990   'Aspects of Old Testament Thought', in Brown, Fitzmyer and Murphy
              1990: 1284-315.
McManners, John (ed.)
    1993   *The Oxford History of Christianity* (Oxford: Oxford University Press).
Mendenhall, George E.
    1962   'The Hebrew Conquest of Palestine', *Biblical Archaeologist* 25: 66-
              87.
    1983   'Ancient Israel's Hyphenated History', in *Palestine in Transition: The
              Emergence of Ancient Israel* (ed. D.N. Freedman and D.F. Graf;
              Sheffield: Almond Press): 91-103.
Menuhin, Moshe
    1969   *The Decadence of Judaism in our Time* (Beirut: Institute for
              Palestinian Studies).
Mergui, Raphael, and Philippe Simonnot
    1987   *Israel's Ayatollahs: Meir Kahane and the Far Right in Israel*
              (London: Saqi Books).
Metz, Johann Baptist
    1990   'With the Eyes of a European Theologian', in Boff and Elizondo
              1990: 113-19.
Meyers, Carol
    1988   *Discovering Eve: Ancient Israelite Women in Context* (New York:
              Oxford University Press).
Michener, James
    1982   *The Covenant* (London: Corgi).
Millard, A.R.
    1983   'Methods of Studying the Patriarchal Narratives as Ancient Texts', in
              Millard and Wiseman 1983: 35-51.
    1992   'Abraham', in *The Anchor Bible Dictionary*, I (A–C): 35-41.
Millard, A.R., and D.J. Wiseman (eds.)
    1983   *Essays on the Patriarchal Narratives* (Leicester: Inter-Varsity Press,
              2nd edn).
Miller, J.M.
    1977   'The Israelite Occupation of Canaan', in Hayes and Miller 1977: 213-
              84.
Miller, J. Maxwell, and John H. Hayes
    1986   *A History of Ancient Israel and Judah* (Philadelphia: Westminster;
              London: SCM Press).
Miller, Patrick D., Jr
    1969   'The Gift of God: The Deuteronomic Theology of the Land',
              Interpretation 23: 451-67.
Miranda, José
    1974   *Marx and the Bible: A Critique of the Philosophy of Oppression*
              (Maryknoll, NY: Orbis Books).

Mires, F.
  1986   *El hombre de la cruz: Discussiones teológicas y políticas frente al holocausto de los índios (periodo de conquista)* (San José: Dei).
Mitchell, Christopher
  1988   *Changing Perspectives in Latin American Studies: Insights from Six Disciplines* (Stanford: Stanford University Press).
Mo'az, Moshe
  1992   'The Jewish-Zionist and Arab-Palestinian National Communities: The Transposing Effect of a Century of Confrontation', in Spagnolo 1992: 151-68.
Mofokeng, Takatso A.
  1983   *The Crucified among the Crossbearers: Towards a Black Christology* (Kampen: Kok).
  1988   'Black Christians, the Bible and Liberation', *Journal of Black Theology* 2.
Moltmann, Jürgen
  1967   *The Theology of Hope: On the Ground and the Implications of a Christian Eschatology* (London: SCM Press).
Moodie, T. Dunbar
  1975   *The Rise of Afrikanerdom: Power, Apartheid, and the Afrikaner Civil Religion* (Berkeley: University of California Press).
Morris, Benny
  1987   *The Birth of the Palestinian Refugee Problem, 1947–1949* (Cambridge: Cambridge University Press).
  1990a   *1948 and After: Israel and the Palestinians* (Oxford: Oxford University Press).
  1990b   'The Eel and History', *Tikkun*, January–February: 20-21
  1993   *Israel's Border Wars* (Oxford: Oxford University Press).
  1995   'Falsifying the Record: A Fresh Look at Zionist Documentation of 1948', *Journal of Palestine Studies* 24.3: 44-62.
Murphy, Roland E.
  1990   'Introduction to the Pentateuch', in Brown, Fitzmyer and Murphy 1990: 3-7.
Neff, Donald
  1991   'The Differing Interpretation of Resolution 242', *Middle East International* 404 (*sic*, for 408, 13 September): 16-17.
  1993   'The Long Struggle for Recognition', *Middle East International* 459 (24 September): 13.
Neher, André
  1992   'The Land as Locus of the Sacred', in Burrell and Landau 1992: 18-29.
Nelson, Richard D.
  1981a   *The Double Redaction of the Deuteronomistic History* (JSOTSup, 18; Sheffield: JSOT Press).
  1981b   'Josiah in the Book of Joshua', *Journal of Biblical Literature* 100: 531-40.

Neusner, Jacob
    1990   'The Role of History in Judaism: The Initial Definition', in Neusner
                1990: 233-48.
Neusner, Jacob (ed.)
    1990   *The Christian and Judaic Invention of History* (Atlanta: Scholars
                Press).
Newman, David (ed.)
    1985   *The Impact of Gush Emunim: Political Settlement in the West Bank*
                (London: Croom Helm).
Nicholson, E.
    1991   'Deuteronomy's Vision of Israel', in Garrone and Israel 1991: 191-
                203
Niditch, Susan
    1993   *War in the Hebrew Bible: A Study of the Ethics of Violence* (Oxford:
                Oxford University Press).
Nixon, John
    1972   *The Complete Story of the Transvaal from the Great Trek to the
                Convention of London* (London: C. Struik, facsimile reprint [1885])
Nora, Pierre
    1961   *Les français d'Algérie* (Paris: Julliard).
Noth, Martin
    1960   *The History of Israel* (London: A. & C. Black).
O'Brien, M.A.
    1989   *The Deuteronomistic History Hypothesis: A Reassessment* (Orbis
                Biblicus et Orientalis, 92; Göttingen: Vandenhoeck & Ruprecht).
O'Connell, R.H.
    1992   'Deuteronomy vii, 1-26: Asymmetric Concentricity and the Rhetoric
                of the Conquest', *Vetus Testamentum* 42: 248-65.
Oded, Bustenay
    1979   *Mass Deportation and Deportees in the Neo-Assyrian Empire*
                (Wiesbaden: Ludwig Reichert Verlag).
Ohler, A.
    1979   *Israel, Volk und Land: Zur Geschichte der wechselseitigen
                Beziehungen zwischen Israel und seinem Land in alttestamentlicher
                Zeit* (Stuttgart: Kohlhammer).
O'Mahony, Anthony
    1994   'Church, State and the Christian Communities and the Holy Places of
                Palestine', in Prior and Taylor 1994: 11-27.
O'Neill, Dan, and Don Wagner
    1993   *Peace or Armageddon? The Unfolding Drama of the Middle East
                Peace Accord* (Grand Rapids: Zondervan Publishing House).
Orlinsky, Harry M.
    1985   'The Biblical Concept of the Land of Israel: Cornerstone of the
                Covenant between God and Israel', *Eretz-Israel* 18: 43-55.
Ott, David H.
    1980   *Palestine in Perspective: Politics, Human Rights and the West Bank*
                (London: Quartet Books).

Padrón, Francisco M.
1975   *Los conquistadores de América* (Madrid: Espasa-Calpe).
Palumbo, Michael
1987   *The Palestinian Catastrophe: The 1948 Expulsion of a People from
            their Homeland* (London: Faber & Faber).
1990   'What Happened to Palestine? The Revolution Revisited', *The Link* 23
            (September–October): 1-12.
Pappé, Ilan
1988   *Britain and the Arab–Israeli Conflict, 1948–1951* (London:
            Macmillan).
1992   *The Making of the Arab–Israeli Conflict, 1947–51* (New York:
            Macmillan/St Anthony's Press).
Parsons, M.C.
1992   'What's "Literary" about Literary Aspects of the Gospels and Acts?',
            SBL Seminar Papers 31: 14-39.
Peretz, Don, and Gideon Doron
1996   'Israel's 1996 Elections: A Second Political Earthquake', *Middle East
            Journal* 50: 529-46.
Peters, Joan
1984   *From Time Immemorial* (New York: Harper & Row).
Pickles, Dorothy
1963   *Algeria and France: From Colonialism to Cooperation* (New York:
            Praeger).
Pike, Fredrick B.
1993   'Latin America', in McManners 1993: 437-73.
Pikkert, Peter
1992   'Christian Zionism: Evangelical Schizophrenia', *Middle East
            International* 439: 19-20.
Pixley, George V.
1983   *On Exodus: A Liberation Perspective* (Maryknoll, NY: Orbis Books).
Playfair, Emma (ed.)
1992   *International Law and the Administration of Occupied Territories:
            Two Decades of Israeli Occupation of the West Bank and Gaza Strip*
            (Oxford: Clarendon Press).
Plöger, J.
1967   *Literarkritische, formgeschichtliche und stilkritische Untersuchungen
            zum Deuteronomium* (BBB, 26; Bonn: Peter Hanstein Verlag).
Pontifical Biblical Commission
1993   *The Interpretation of the Bible in the Church* (Boston: St Paul Books
            & Media).
Ponting, Clive
1994   *Churchill* (London: Sinclair-Stevenson).
Posel, Deborah
1991   *The Making of Apartheid, 1948–1961: Conflict and Compromise*
            (Oxford: Clarendon Press).
Preez, A.B. du
1953   'Die skrif en rasseverhoudinge', *Die Kerkbode*, 15 March, p. 502.

Preller, Gustav
    1909   *Piet Retief* (Pretoria: van Schaik, 9th edn [1906]).
Prior, Michael
    1989   *Paul the Letter-Writer and the Second Letter to Timothy* (JSNTSup, 23;
                Sheffield: JSOT Press).
    1990   'A Christian Perspective on the *Intifada*', *The Month* 23: 478-85.
    1993   'Palestinian Christians and the Liberation of Theology', *The Month*
                26: 482-90.
    1994a   'Isaiah and the Liberation of the Poor (Luke 4.16-30)', *Scripture
                Bulletin* 24: 36-46.
    1994b   'Pilgrimage to the Holy Land, Yesterday and Today', in Prior and
                Taylor 1994: 169-99.
    1994c   'Clinton's Bible, Goldstein's Hermeneutics', *Middle East
                International*, 16 December: 20-21.
    1995a   *Jesus the Liberator: Nazareth Liberation Theology (Luke 4.16-30)*
                (Sheffield: Sheffield Academic Press).
    1995b   'The Bible as Instrument of Oppression', *Scripture Bulletin* 25: 2-14.
    1996   'The Future of the Christian Community in the Holy Land', *The
                Month* 29: 140-45.
Prior, Michael, and William Taylor (eds.)
    1994   *Christians in the Holy Land* (London: WIFT/Scorpion).
Pritchard, James B. (ed.)
    1955   *Ancient Near Eastern Texts relating to the Old Testament* (Princeton,
                NJ: Princeton University Press, 2nd edn).
Prudký, Martin
    1995   *Landgabe: Festschrift für Jan Heller zum 70. Geburtstag* (Kampen:
                Kok Pharos).
    1995a   '"Geh hin in das Land, das ich dich sehen lassen werden."
                Beobachtungen zu den Motiven, die "Das Land" in der Einleitung
                des Abraham-Zyklus Bestimmen (Gen 11.27–12.5)', in Prudký 1995:
                44-63.
Quigley, John
    1990   *Palestine and Israel: A Challenge to Justice* (Durham, NC: Duke
                University Press).
Qupty, Mazen
    1992   'The Application of International Law in the Occupied Territories as
                Reflected in the Judgements of the High Court of Justice in Israel', in
                Playfair 1992: 87-124.
Ramsey, George
    1981   *The Quest for the Historical Israel* (Atlanta: John Knox Press).
Rantisi, Audeh
    1990   *Blessed Are the Peacemakers: The Story of a Palestinian Christian*
                (Guildford: Eagle).
Redford, Donald B.
    1992   *Egypt, Canaan, and Israel in Ancient Times* (Princeton, NJ: Princeton
                University Press).

Regehr, Ernie
    1979   *Perceptions of Apartheid: The Churches and Political Change in South Africa* (Scottdale, AZ: Herald Press; Kitchener, Ont.: Between the Lines).

Reitz, F.W.
    1900   *A Century of Wrong* (London: Review of Reviews).

Rendtorff, Rolf
    1970   'Das Land Israel im Wandel der alttestamentlichen Geschichte', in Eckert, Levenson and Stöhr 1970: 153-68.
    1977   *Das überlieferungsgeschichtliche Problem des Pentateuch* (BZAW, 147; Berlin: de Gruyter).
    1990   *The Problem of the Process of Transmission in the Pentateuch* (JSOTSup, 89; Sheffield: JSOT Press [German original 1977]).

Richard, Pablo
    1990a   '1492: The Violence of God and the Future of Christianity', in Boff and Elizondo 1990: 59-67.
    1990b   'Liberation Theology: A Difficult but Possible Future', in Ellis and Maduro 1990: 207-17.

Riley-Smith, Louise, and Jonathan, Riley-Smith
    1981   *The Crusades: Idea and Reality, 1095–1274* (London: Edward Arnold).

Rodinson, Maxime
    1982   *Israel and the Arabs* (Harmondsworth: Penguin, 2nd edn).

Rokach, Livia
    1980   *Israel's Sacred Terrorism: A Study Based on Moshe Sharett's Diaries* (Belmont, MA: Association of Arab-American University Graduates).

Rotenstreich, Nathan
    1980   *Essays on Zionism and the Contemporary Jewish Condition* (New York: Herzl Press).

Rowton, Michael
    1974   'Enclosed Nomadism', *Journal of the Economy and Social History of the Orient* 17: 1-30.

Roy, Jules
    1961   *The War in Algeria* (New York: Grove Press).

Ruether, Rosemary Radford
    1974   *Faith and Fratricide: The Theological Roots of Anti-Semitism* (New York: Seabury).
    1990   'The Occupation Must End', in Ruether and Ellis 1990: 183-97.

Ruether, Rosemary, and Marc Ellis (eds.)
    1990   *Beyond Occupation: American Jews, Christians and Palestinians Search for Peace* (Boston: Beacon Press).

Ruether, Rosemary, and Herman Ruether
    1989   *The Wrath of Jonah: The Crisis of Religious Nationalism in the Israeli–Palestinian Conflict* (New York: Harper & Row).

Sabbah, Michel
    1993   *Reading the Bible Today in the Land of the Bible* (Jerusalem: Latin Patriarchate).

Sabella, Bernard
 1996 'Demographic Trends in Jerusalem and the West Bank', in *Arab Regional Population Conference, 8–12 December 1996, Cairo* (Liège: International Union for the Study of Population): 177-96.

Said, Edward W.
 1988 'Michael Walzer's *Exodus and Revolution*: A Canaanite Reading', in Said and Hitchens 1988: 161-78.
 1994 *The Politics of Dispossession: The Struggle for Palestinian Self-Determination, 1969–1994* (New York: Pantheon Book).

Said, Edward W., and Christopher Hitchens (eds.)
 1988 *Blaming the Victims: Spurious Scholarship and the Palestinian Question* (London: Verso).

Salinas, Maximiliano
 1990 'The Voices of Those who Speak up for the Victims', in Boff and Elizondo 1990: 101-109.

Sandmel, Samuel
 1961 'The Haggada within Scripture', *Journal of Biblical Literature* 80: 105-22.

Sawyer, J.F.A., and D.J.A. Clines (eds.)
 1983 *Midian, Moab and Edom: The History and Archaeology of Late Bronze and Iron Age Jordan and North-West Arabia* (JSOTSup, 24; Sheffield: JSOT Press).

Schlink, Basilea
 1991 *Israel at the Heart of World Events* (Darmstadt-Eberstadt: Evangelical Sisterhood of Mary).

Schmid, H.H.
 1976 *Die sogennante Jahwist: Beobachtungen und Fragen zur Pentateuchforschung* (Zürich: Theologischer Verlag).

Schoenman, Ralph
 1988 *The Hidden History of Zionism* (Santa Barbara, CA: Veritas Press).

Schürer, E.
 1979 *The History of the Jewish People in the Age of Jesus Christ (175 BC–AD 135)*, II (rev. and ed. G. Vermes *et al.*; Edinburgh: T. & T. Clark).
 1986 *The History of the Jewish People in the Age of Jesus Christ (175 BC–AD 135)*, III.1 (rev. and ed. G. Vermes *et al.*; Edinburgh: T. & T. Clark).

Schweid, Eliezer
 1987 'Land of Israel', in Cohen and Mendes-Flohr 1987: 535-41.

Segev, Tom
 1986 *The First Israelis* (ed. Arlen N. Weinstein; New York: Free Press; London: Collier Macmillan).
 1993 *The Seventh Million. The Israelis and the Holocaust* (trans. Haim Watzan; New York: Hill & Wang).

Sepulvedae, Genessi
 1545 *Democrates alter sive de iustis belli causis apud indios* (ed. crítica con versión castellana por R. Losada; Madrid: 1951). A bi-lingual Latin-Spanish version is in *Tratado sobre las justas causas de la guerra contra los índios* (Mexico: Fondo de Cultura Económica, 1979).

Seward, Desmond
  1995   *The Monks of War: The Military Religious Orders* (London: Penguin
          Books).
Shahak, Israel
  1975   *Report: Arab Villages Destroyed in Israel* (Jerusalem: Shahak, 2nd
          edn).
  1994   'New Revelations on the 1982 Invasion of Lebanon', *Middle East
          International* 485 (7 October): 18-19.
Shapira, Anita
  1992   *Land and Power: The Zionist Resort to Force* (Oxford: Oxford
          University Press).
Shehadeh, Raja
  1988   *Occupier's Law: Israel and the West Bank* (Washington, DC: Institute
          for Palestine Studies, rev. edn).
Shiblak, Abbas
  1986   *The Lure of Zion: The Case of Iraqi Jews* (London: Al Saqi Books).
Shlaim, Avi
  1988   *Collusion across the Jordan: King Abdullah, the Zionist Movement,
          and the Partition of Palestine* (New York: Columbia University Press).
Siker, J.S.
  1992   '"First to the Gentiles": A Literary Analysis of Luke 4.16-30',
          Journal of Biblical Literature 111: 73-90.
Simon, Leon
  1962   *Selected Essays of Ahad Ha-'Am: Translated from the Hebrew, edited,
          and with an introduction by Leon Simon* (New York: Atheneum,
          reprint [1912]).
Simonetti, Manlio
  1994   *Biblical Interpretation in the Early Church: An Historical Introduction
          to Patristic Exegesis* (Edinburgh: T. & T. Clark).
Singer, Joel
  1982   'The Establishment of a Civilian Administration in the Areas
          Administered by Israel', *Israel Yearbook on Human Rights* 12: 259-
          89.
Sizer, Stephen R.
  1994   'Visiting the Living Stones' (MTh Thesis, University of Oxford).
Skocpal, Theda, and Margaret Somers
  1980   'The Uses of Comparative History in Macrosocial Inquiry',
          Comparative Studies in Society and History 23: 174-97.
Smelik, Klaas A.D.
  1992   *Converting the Past: Studies in Ancient Israelite and Moabite
          Historiography* (OTS, 28; Leiden: Brill).
  1995   'The Territory of Eretz Israel in the Hebrew Bible: The Case of the
          Transjordan Tribes', in Prudký 1995: 76-85.
Smick, E.B.
  1989   'Old Testament Cross-culturation: Paradigmatic or Enigmatic?',
          Journal of the Evangelical Theological Society 32: 3-16.
Sobrino, Jon
  1978   *Christology at the Crossroads* (Maryknoll, NY: Orbis Books).

1990   'The Crucified Peoples: Yahweh's Suffering Servant Today', in Boff
            and Elizondo 1990: 120-29.
Soggin, J. Alberto
1972   *Joshua* (Philadelphia: Westminster Press).
1984   *A History of Israel: From the Beginnings to the Bar Kochba Revolt,
            AD 135* (London: SCM Press).
Somerville, Robert
1972   *The Councils of Urban II.1: Decreta Claromontensia (Annuarium
            Historiae Conciliorum. Supplementum I)* (Amsterdam: Hakkert).
Spagnolo, John P. (ed.)
1992   *Problems of the Modern Middle East in Historical Perspective: Essays
            in Honour of Albert Hourani* (Reading: Ithaca).
Sprinzak, Ehud
1985   'The Iceberg Model of Political Extremism', in Newman 1985: 27-45.
1991   *The Ascendance of Israel's Radical Right* (Oxford: Oxford University
            Press).
Stager, Lawrence
1981   'Highland Village Life in Palestine Three Thousand Years Ago', in
            The Oriental Institute Notes and News 60: 1-3.
1985a   'Respondents', in *Biblical Archaeology Today: Proceedings of the
            International Congress on Biblical Archaeology, Jerusalem, April
            1984* (Jerusalem: Israel Exploration Society): 83-87.
1985b   'The Archaeology of the Family in Ancient Israel', *Bulletin of the
            American Schools of Oriental Research* 260: 1-35.
Stein, Leonard
1961   *The Balfour Declaration* (London: Vallentine Mitchell).
Stevens, Richard P.
1977   'South Africa, Zionism and Israel', in Stevens and Elmessiri 1977: 34-
            56.
Stevens, Richard P., and Abdelwahab M. Elmessiri (eds.)
1977   *Israel and South Africa: The Progression of a Relationship* (New
            Brunswick: North American, rev. edn).
Stiebing, William
1989   *Out of the Desert? Archaeology and the Conquest Narratives* (Buffalo:
            Prometheus).
Strecker, G. (ed.)
1983   *Das Land Israel in biblischer Zeit Jerusalem: Symposium 1981 der
            Hebräischen Universität und der Georg-August-Universität* (Göttingen:
            Vandenhoeck & Rupprecht).
Stuhlman, L.
1990   'Encroachment in Deuteronomy: An Analysis of the Social World of
            the D Code', *Journal of Biblical Literature* 109: 613-32.
Sugirtharajah, R.S. (ed.)
1991   *Voices from the Margin: Interpreting the Bible in the Third World*
            (London: SPCK).
Sykes, Christopher
1953a   'The Prosperity of his Servant: A Study of the Origins of the Balfour
            Declaration', in Sykes 1953b: 107-235.

1953b   *Two Studies in Virtue* (New York: Knopf).

1965   *Crossroads to Israel: Palestine from Balfour to Bevin* (London: Collins).

Tamarin, Georges R.

1973a   'The Influence of Ethnic and Religious Prejudice on Moral Judgement', in Tamarin 1973b [1963]: 183-90.

1973b   *The Israeli Dilemma: Essays on a Warfare State* (ed. Johan Niezing; Rotterdam: Rotterdam University Press).

Tessler, Mark

1989   'The Camp David Accords and the Palestinian Problem', in Lesch and Tessler 1989: 3-22.

Teveth, Shabtai

1985   *Ben-Gurion and the Palestinian Arabs* (Oxford: Oxford University Press).

Theal, George McCall

1891–1900   *History of South Africa* (3 vols.; London: Swan Sonnenschein).

Thiselton, Anthony C.

1992   *New Horizons in Hermeneutics: The Theory and Practice of Transforming Biblical Reading* (London: HarperCollins).

Thompson, Leonard

1985   *The Political Mythology of Apartheid* (New Haven: Yale University Press).

1995   *A History of South Africa* (New Haven: Yale University Press).

Thompson, Thomas L.

1974   *The Historicity of the Pentateuchal Narratives: The Quest for the Historical Abraham* (Berlin: de Gruyter).

1987   *The Origin Tradition of Ancient Israel. I. The Literary Formation of Genesis and Exodus 1–23* (JSOTSup, 55; Sheffield: JSOT Press).

1992   *Early History of the Israelite People from the Written and Archaeological Sources* (Studies in the History of the Ancient Near East, 4; Leiden: Brill).

1995   'A Neo-Albrightean School in History and Biblical Scholarship', *Journal of Biblical Literature* 114: 685-98.

Timerman, Jacobo

1984   *The Longest War: Israel in Lebanon* (New York: Simon & Schuster).

Todorov, Tzvetan

1984   *The Conquest of America: The Question of the Other* (New York: Harper & Row).

Toynbee, Arnold

1954   *A Study of History*, VIII (London: Oxford University Press).

Turner, Frederick Jackson

1920   *The Frontier in American History* (New York: Henry Holt).

Ukpong, Justin S.

1984   'Current Theology: The Emergency of African Theologies', *Theological Studies* 45: 501-36.

Vaage, L.E.
    1991   'Text, Context, Conquest, Quest: The Bible and Social Struggle in
              Latin America', *Society of Biblical Literature Seminar Papers* 30:
              357-65.
Van Buren, Paul
    1980   *Discerning the Way: A Theology of Jewish Christian Reality* (New
              York: Seabury).
Van Seters, John
    1972   'The Terms "Amorite" and "Hittite" in the Old Testament', *Vetus
              Testamentum* 22: 64-81.
    1975   *Abraham in History and Tradition* (New Haven: Yale University Press).
    1992   *Prologue to History: The Yahwist as Historian in Genesis* (Louisville:
              Westminster/John Knox).
Vervenne, Marc
    1994   'The Question of "Deuteronomic" Elements in Genesis to Numbers',
              in Martinez *et al.* 1994: 243-68.
Veyne, Paul
    1984   *Writing History* (ET; Middletown, CT: Wesleyan University Press).
Villet, Barbara
    1982   *Blood River: The Passionate Saga of South Africa's Afrikaners and of
              Life in their Embattled Land* (New York: Dodd).
Vital, David
    1975   *The Origins of Zionism* (Oxford: Clarendon Press).
    1990   *The Future of the Jews: A People at the Crossroads* (Cambridge:
              Harvard University Press).
Vitoria, Francisco de
    1960   *De indis recenter inventis relectio prior (1538–39)* (ed. crítica con
              traducción castellana por T. Urdánoz; Obras de Francisco de Vitoria.
              Relecciones Teológicas; Madrid): 541-726.
Voigt, J.C.
    1899   *Fifty Years of the History of the Republic of South Africa (1795–1845)*
              (2 vols.; London: Fisher Unwin).
Von Rad, Gerhard
    1966   'The Promised Land and Yahweh's Land in the Hexateuch', in *The
              Problem of the Hexateuch and Other Essays* (London: SCM Press;
              Philadelphia: Fortress Press, repr. 1984): 79-93.
Von Waldow, Hans Eberhard
    1974   'Israel and her Land: Some Theological Considerations', in Bream,
              Heim and Moore 1974: 493-508.
Vorster, Willem
    1983   'The Bible and Apartheid I', in De Gruchy and Villa-Vicencio 1983:
              94-111.
Wagner, Don
    1992   'Beyond Armageddon', *The Link* (Americans for Middle East
              Understanding) 25.4: 1-13.
    1995   *Anxious for Armageddon: A Call to Partnership for Middle Eastern
              and Western Christians* (Waterloo, Ont.: Herald Press).

Wagua, Aiban
    1990   'Present Consequences of the European Invasion of America', in Boff
                and Elizondo 1990: 47-56.
Walzer, Michael
    1985   *Exodus and Revolution* (New York: Basic Books).
Ward, Miriam
    1990   'The Theological and Ethical Context for Palestinian-Israeli Peace', in
                Ruether and Ellis 1990: 171-82.
Warrior, Robert Allen
    1991   'A North American Perspective: Canaanites, Cowboys, and Indians', in
                Sugirtharajah 1991: 287-95.
Watson, Francis
    1994   *Text, Church and World: Biblical Interpretation in Theological
                Perspective* (Grand Rapids: Eerdmans).
Weinfeld, Moshe
    1983   'The Extent of the Promised Land—the Status of Transjordan', in
                Strecker 1983: 59-75.
    1993   *The Promise of the Land. The Inheritance of the Land of Canaan by
                the Israelites* (Berkeley: University of California Press).
Weippert, Manfred
    1971   *The Settlement of the Israelite Tribes in Palestine: A Critical Survey of
                Recent Scholarly Debate* (London: SCM Press).
    1979   'The Israelite "Conquest" and the Evidence from Transjordan', in
                Cross 1979: 15-34.
Weitz, Yosef
    1965   *Yomani Ve'igrotai Labanim* (*My Diary and Letters to the Children*)
                (4 vols.; Tel Aviv: Massada).
Weizmann, Chaim
    1949   *Trial and Error: The Autobiography of Chaim Weizmann* (New York:
                Harper & Row).
Wellhausen, Julius
    1885   *Prolegomena to the History of Ancient Israel* (ET; Edinburgh: A. & C.
                Black).
West, G., and J. Draper
    1991   'The Bible and Social Transformation in South Africa: A Work-in-
                Progress Report on the Institute for the Study of the Bible', *Society of
                Biblical Literature Seminar Papers* 30: 366-82.
White, Hayden
    1978   *Tropics of Discourse: Essays in Cultural Criticism* (Baltimore: John
                Hopkins University Press).
Whitelam, Keith W.
    1989   'Israel's Traditions of Origin: Reclaiming the Land', *Journal for the
                Study of the Old Testament* 44: 19-42.
    1996   *The Invention of Ancient Israel: The Silencing of Palestinian History*
                (London: Routledge).
Whybray, R. Norman
    1987   *The Making of the Pentateuch: A Methodological Study* (Sheffield:
                JSOT Press).

1995   *Introduction to the Pentateuch* (Grand Rapids: Eerdmans).
Wildberger, H.
1956   'Israel und sein Land', *Evangelische Theologie* 16: 404-22.
Williams, Geoffrey
1962   *Portrait of World History* (London: Edward Arnold).
Wilson, H.
1981   *The Chariot of Israel* (London: W.W. Norton).
Wilson, Mary C.
1988   *King Abdullah: Britain and the Making of Jordan* (Cambridge:
              Cambridge University Press).
World Council of Churches, Programme to Combat Racism
1986   *Breaking Down the Walls: World Council of Churches' Statements and
              Actions on Racism* (Geneva: WCC).
Wright, Christopher J.H.
1983   *Living as the People of God* (Leicester: Inter-Varsity Press).
1990   *God's People in God's Land: Family, Land, and Property in the Old
              Testament* (Grand Rapids: Eerdmans; Exeter: Paternoster).
Wright, George E.
1960   'The Old Testament', in Wright and Fuller 1960: 32-37.
1962   *Biblical Archaeology* (Philadelphia: Westminster Press, 2nd edn).
Wright G.E., and R.H. Fuller (eds.)
1960   *The Book of the Acts of God: Christian Scholarship Interprets the
              Bible* (London: Duckworth).
Yadin, Yigael
1979   'The Transition from a Semi-Nomadic to a Sedentary Society in the
              Twelfth Century BCE', in Cross 1979: 57-68.
1982   'Is the Biblical Conquest of Canaan Historically Reliable?', *Biblical
              Archaeology Review* 8.2: 16-23.
Yapp, M.E.
1987   *The Making of the Modern Near East, 1792–1923* (London: Longman).
Yaron, Zvi
1991   *The Philosophy of Rabbi Kook* (Jerusalem: Eliner Library).
Younger, K.L., Jr
1990   *Ancient Conquest Accounts: A Study in Near Eastern and Biblical
              History Writing* (JSOTSup, 98; Sheffield: JSOT Press).
Zangwill, Israel
1920   *The Voice of Jerusalem* (London: Heinemann).
1937   *Speeches, Articles and Letters of Israel Zangwill, Selected and Edited
              by Maurice Simon* (London: Soncino Press).
Zimmerlei, W.
1976   'Land and Possession', in *The Old Testament and the World* (London:
              SCM Press): 67-79.
Zuckerman, William
1962   *Voice of Dissent: Jewish Problems, 1948–1961* (New York: Bookman
              Associates).
Zureik, Elia
1994   'Palestinian Refugees and Peace', *Journal of Palestine Studies* 24: 5-
              17.

INDEXES

INDEX OF REFERENCES

OLD TESTAMENT

20.13	280	19.34	124	21.3	275
21–23	21	20.2	23	21.4-9	275
22.21	21	20.9-21	23	21.21-24	24
22.28	229	20.22-27	23	21.34-35	24
23	280	20.22-24	261	22–24	25
23.9	21	21–22	22	22.1–36.13	24
23.14-17	205	23	22	25.1-3	25
23.20-23	276	23.10	204	25.12	25
23.22-23	276	23.22	204	25.16-17	25
23.23-24	21	23.28	22	25.34	224
23.27-33	21	25	22, 110	26.55	229
23.28-30	274	25.2-3	23	27	25
24.13	241	25.2	204	29–34	224
25–40	22	26	22, 23	31	25
32.17	241	26.3-13	23	31.8-16	25
32.19-21	21	26.11-39	23	31.18	25
32.26-30	21, 280	26.32-39	23	31.19-20	25
33.1-3	21, 280	26.40-42	23	32	25
33.1	218	26.42	218	32.6-23	25
34.1-5	21	26.44-46	23	32.11	218
34.8-9	21	26.44-45	207	33.50-56	25
34.11-15	22, 280	27	22, 23	33.50-52	229
34.16-23	22			34–35	26
34.24	22	*Numbers*		35.9-10	204
34.27-28	22	1–10	224	36.13	26
34.32	22	1.1–10.10	24		
35–40	22	1.45-46	24	*Deuteronomy*	
		4.48	24	1.1–33.29	223
Leviticus		5–6	24	1.1–4.49	26
1–7	22	6.24-26	151	1.6-8	26
8–10	22	7.1–10.10	24	1.8	218
10.8-11	22	10–36	224	1.30-31	26
11–16	22	10.10	19, 223	1.36	227
14.34	23	10.11–36.13	223	1.39	227
17–26	224	10.11–21.35	24	2.4-7	222
17–20	22	10.11–12.16	24	2.33-34	26
18	23	13.1–15.41	24	3.3	26
18.1-5	23	13.18	241	3.18	227
18.21	23	13.27-29	24	3.22	26
18.22	23	14.7-9	24	3.27-29	26
18.23	23	14.24	241	4.1-8	26
18.24-30	23, 224	14.25	24	4.25-31	224, 228
18.24-25	68, 261	14.30	241	4.26-27	26
18.24	229	15.31	268	4.35	227
19.23	203	20.12	24	4.37-38	92
19.29	224	20.22-29	24	4.39	227
19.33-34	23	21.1-3	24, 275	4.40	224
19.33	124	21.2	275	4.41-42	204